FOSTER BIBLICAL SCHOLARSHIP

Society of Biblical Literature

Biblical Scholarship in North America

Number 24

FOSTER BIBLICAL SCHOLARSHIP
Essays in Honor of Kent Harold Richards

FOSTER BIBLICAL SCHOLARSHIP

ESSAYS IN HONOR OF KENT HAROLD RICHARDS

Edited by

Frank Ritchel Ames and Charles William Miller

Society of Biblical Literature
Atlanta

FOSTER BIBLICAL SCHOLARSHIP
Essays in Honor of Kent Harold Richards

Copyright © 2010 by the Society of Biblical Literature

All rights reserved. No part of this work may be reproduced or transmitted in any form or by any means, electronic or mechanical, including photocopying and recording, or by means of any information storage or retrieval system, except as may be expressly permitted by the 1976 Copyright Act or in writing from the publisher. Requests for permission should be addressed in writing to the Rights and Permissions Office, Society of Biblical Literature, 825 Houston Mill Road, Atlanta, GA 30329 USA.

Library of Congress Cataloging-in-Publication Data

Foster biblical scholarship : essays in honor of Kent Harold Richards / edited by Frank Ritchel Ames and Charles William Miller.
    p. cm. — (Society of Biblical Literature biblical scholarship in North America ; no. 24)
Includes bibliographical references.
ISBN 978-1-58983-533-7 (paper binding : alk. paper) -- ISBN 978-1-58983-534-4 (electronic format)
1. Bible—Study and teaching. I. Ames, Frank Ritchel. II. Miller, Charles William.
BS600.3.F67 2010
220.071'1—dc22
                                                                                          2010043651

18 17 16 15 14 13 12 11 10   5 4 3 2 1
Printed in the United States of America on acid-free, recycled paper conforming to ANSI/NISO Z39.48-1992 (R1997) and ISO 9706:1994 standards for paper permanence.

Contents

Abbreviations   vii

Preface   xi

Part 1: Fostering Biblical Scholarship

Fostering Biblical Scholarship: The Contributions of Kent Harold Richards
Gail R. O'Day   3

Conditions That Foster Biblical Scholarship
Frank Ritchel Ames   11

The Modern (and Postmodern?) Society of Biblical Literature: Institutions and Scholarship
Gene M. Tucker   31

Study of the New Testament in the Pluralistic Context of the Twenty-First Century
Harold W. Attridge   53

Faith, Scholarship, and the Society of Biblical Literature
John J. Collins   65

Politics and Biblical Scholarship in the United States
Douglas A. Knight   83

Ex-Centric Reading: A Case for Critical Reorientation
Vincent L. Wimbush   101

The Bible in Public View
David L. Petersen   117

Part 2: New Pedagogies and the Biblical Studies Curriculum

A Republic of Many Voices: Biblical Studies in the Twenty-First Century
Elisabeth Schüssler Fiorenza   137

Teaching the Biblical Languages: Time for a Rethink?
  David J. A. Clines ... 161

The SBL in the Undergraduate Classroom: Pedagogical Reflections
  Elizabeth Struthers Malbon ... 169

"Psalms Are Not Interesting": Learner-Centered Approaches to Teaching Biblical Poetry and the Psalms
  Charles William Miller ... 189

Part 3: Studies in Methods and Contexts

Revisiting the Composition of Ezra-Nehemah: A Prolegomenon
  Tamara Cohn Eskenazi ... 215

Rome and the Early Church: Background of the Persecution of Christians in the First and Early Second Centuries
  Paul J. Achtemeier ... 235

Do You Feel Comforted? M. Night Shyamalan's *Signs* and the Book of Job
  J. Cheryl Exum ... 251

Canaan, Land of Promise: An Ecological Reading of Genesis 10:15–20 in Context
  Norman Habel ... 269

Revising the Myth of the "Biblical Family": Reflections on Issues of Methodologies and Interpretive Ideologies
  Athalya Brenner ... 279

Clandestine Relationship: An Approach to the Song of Songs
  Pablo R. Andiñach ... 295

God's *Anthropos* Project
  James Luther Mays ... 313

Liberating Readings of the Bible: Contexts and Conditions
  Erhard S. Gerstenberger ... 337

Contributors ... 353

Abbreviations

AAR	American Academy of Religion
AB	Anchor Bible
ABD	*The Anchor Bible Dictionary.* Edited by David Noel Freedman. 6 vols. New York: Doubleday, 1992.
ACLS	American Council of Learned Societies
AEL	*Ancient Egyptian Literature.* Miriam Lichtheim. 3 vols. Berkley and Los Angeles: University of California Press, 1971–1980.
ANET	*Ancient Near Eastern Texts Relating to the Old Testament.* Edited by James B. Pritchard. 3d ed. Princeton: Princeton University Press, 1969.
Ann.	Tacitus, *Annales*
Ant. rom.	Dionysius of Halicarnassus, *Antiquitates romanae*
AOAT	Alter Orient und Altes Testament
Apol.	Tertullian, *Apologeticus*
AT	Alpha Text of Esther
BA	*Biblical Archaeologist*
BAR	*Biblical Archaeology Review*
BASOR	*Bulletin of the American Schools of Oriental Research*
BibInt	*Biblical Interpretation*
BZAW	Beihefte zur Zeitschrift für die alttestamentliche Wissenschaft
CBQ	*Catholic Biblical Quarterly*
CC	Continental Commentaries
ChrCent	*Christian Century*
COS	*The Context of Scripture.* Edited by William W. Hallo. 3 vols. Leiden: Brill, 1997–2002.
CSSR Bulletin	*Council of Societies for the Study of Religion Bulletin*
De vita	Suetonius, *De vita Caesarum*
Ep.	Pliny the Younger, *Epistulae*
Epigr.	Martial, *Epigrammata*
ETS	Erfurter theologische Studien
ExuZ	Exegese in unserer Zeit

FCB	Feminist Companion to the Bible
FOTL	Forms of the Old Testament Literature
GBS	Guides to Biblical Scholarship
HB	Hebrew Bible
HBD	*HarperCollins Bible Dictionary*. Edited by Paul J. Achtemeier et al. 2nd ed. San Francisco: HarperSanFrancisco, 1996.
HBR	*Harvard Business Review*
Hist.	Tacitus, *Historiae*
Hist. eccl.	Eusebius, *Historia ecclesiastica*
Hist. rom.	Dio Cassius, *Historia romana*
HSM	Harvard Semitic Monographs
HUCA	*Hebrew Union College Annual*
IDB	*The Interpreter's Dictionary of the Bible*. Edited by G. A. Buttrick. 4 vols. Nashville: Abingdon, 1962.
Inst.	Quinilian, *Institutio oratoria*
JAAR	*Journal of the American Academy of Religion*
JBL	*Journal of Biblical Literature*
JNES	*Journal of Near Eastern Studies*
JPS	Jewish Publication Society
JR	*Journal of Religion*
JSNT	*Journal for the Study of the New Testament*
JSOT	*Journal for the Study of the Old Testament*
JSOTSup	Journal for the Study of the Old Testament Supplement Series
JTS	*Journal of Theological Studies*
KTU	*Die Keilalphabetischen Texte aus Ugarit*. Edited by M. Dietrich, O. Loretz, and J. Sanmartin. AOAT 24/1. Neukirchen-Vluyn: Neukirchener, 1976.
LAE	*The Literature of Ancient Egypt*. Edited by W. K. Simpson, R. K. Ritner, V. A. Tobin, and E. F. Wente Jr. 3rd ed. New Haven: Yale University Press, 2003.
LCL	Loeb Classical Library
LXX	Septuagint
Metam.	Apuleius, *Metamorphoses*
MT	Massoretic Text
NCC	National Council of Churches
NEH	United States National Endowment for the Humanities
NGO	Non-Governmental Organization
NIB	*The New Interpreter's Bible*. Edited by Leander E. Keck. 12 vols. Nashville: Abingdon, 1994–1998.
NRSV	New Revised Standard Version

NT	New Testament
OBT	Overtures to Biblical Theology
Oct.	Minucius Felix, *Octavius*
Or.	Dio Chrysostom, *Oratio*
OT	Old Testament
OTG	Old Testament Guides
OTL	Old Testament Library
Pan.	Pliny the Younger, *Panegyricus*
PMLA	Publications of the Modern Language Association of America
PW	*Paulys Real-Encyklopädie der classischen Altertumswissenschaft*. New edition by Georg Wissowa and Wilhelm Kroll. 50 vols. in 84 parts. Stuttgart: Metzler and Druckenmüller, 1894–1980.
RAC	*Reallexikon für Antike und Christentum: Sachwörterbuch zur Auseinandersetzung des Christentums mit der antiken Welt*. Edited by Theodor Kluser et al. Stuttgart: Hiersemann, 1950–.
RBL	*Review of Biblical Literature*
Sat.	Juvenal, *Satirae*
SBL	Society of Biblical Literature
SBLAcBib	Society of Biblical Literature Academia Biblica
SBLBMI	Society of Biblical Literature The Bible and Its Modern Interpreters
SBLBSNA	Society of Biblical Literature Biblical Scholarship in North America
SBLCP	Society of Biblical Literature Centennial Publications
SBLDS	Society of Biblical Literature Dissertation Series
SBLHS	*The SBL Handbook of Style for Ancient Near Eastern, Biblical, and Early Christian Studies*. Edited by P. H. Alexander et al. Peabody, Mass.: Hendrickson, 1999.
SBLMS	Society of Biblical Literature Monograph Series
SBLRBS	Society of Biblical Literature Resources for Biblical Study
SBLSCS	Society of Biblical Literature Septuagint and Cognate Studies
SBLSymS	Society of Biblical Literature Symposium Series
SBLWAW	Society of Biblical Literature Writings from the Ancient World
SBT	Studies in Biblical Theology
SemeiaSt	Semeia Studies
SJOT	*Scandinavian Journal of the Old Testament*
Sound	*Soundings*

TB	*Teaching the Bible*
ThTo	*Theology Today*
TLOT	*Theological Lexicon of the Old Testament.* Edited by Ernst Jenni and Claus Westermann. Translated by Mark E. Biddle. 3 vols. Peabody, Mass.: Hendrickson, 1997.
TThRel	*Teaching Theology and Religion*
TZ	*Theologische Zeitschrift*
UND	University of North Dakota
USQR	*Union Seminary Quarterly Review*
VT	*Vetus Testamentum*
WBC	Word Biblical Commentary
WCC	World Council of Churches
WMANT	Wissenschaftliche Monographien zum Alten und Neuen Testament
WUNT	Wissenschaftliche Untersuchungen zum Neuen Testament
WW	*Word and World*
ZAW	*Zeitschrift für die alttestamentliche Wissenschaft*

Preface

Frank Ritchel Ames and Charles William Miller

Critical is an apt term for contemporary biblical scholarship, for the academic study of the Bible entails rigorous analysis and evaluation;[1] is of vital importance to the humanities, social sciences, and theological studies;[2] and the discipline, in the opinion of more than a few observers, is at risk. "The notion that biblical studies have entered a period of crisis," writes Legaspi, "has become a commonplace among biblical critics."[3] Biblical scholarship, however, is not in a period of crisis but of profound change.

Foster Biblical Scholarship: Essays in Honor of Kent Harold Richards describes the far-reaching changes that have taken place in twentieth-century biblical scholarship and discusses the discipline's prospects for the twenty-first century. The essays identify trajectories within a vibrant, evolving discipline and suggest new directions. The title of the volume reiterates the mission of the Society of Biblical Literature—foster biblical scholarship—and invites the reader to pursue the task and to share in its

---

1. On the importance of method, see the essays in Joel M. LeMon and Kent Harold Richards, eds., *Method Matters: Essays on the Interpretation of the Hebrew Bible in Honor of David L. Petersen* (SBLRBS 56; Atlanta: Society of Biblical Literature, 2009).

2. See the chapter entitled "Biblical Studies as the Meeting Point of the Humanities" in Bernard M. Levinson, *Legal Revision and Religious Renewal in Ancient Israel* (New York: Cambridge University Press, 2008), 1–11.

3. Michael C. Legaspi, *The Death of Scripture and the Rise of Biblical Studies* (Oxford Studies in Historical Theology; New York: Oxford University Press, 2010), 7. For Hector Avalos, the trajectory of the discipline is not uncertain; rather, it is fundamentally wrong, and he calls for the dissolution of biblical scholarship in its present configuration, writing, "the only mission of Biblical Studies should be to end Biblical Studies as we know it" (Hector Avalos, *The End of Biblical Studies* [Amherst: Prometheus, 2007], 342).

definition and realization. The volume is part of the SBL's Biblical Scholarship in North America series, which focuses on "the scholars, movements, and organizations that have shaped and continue to shape North American biblical scholarship." The authors and editors of the essays are members of the Society, which is a microcosm of academic biblical studies. Their perspectives are emic but not uniform, reflecting the very nature of the Society and the discipline, and their experience and expertise are formidable. In the volume, particular attention is given to the mission of the Society, its role and contributions, and the leadership of Kent Harold Richards, who served as a member, volunteer, officer, and, finally, as the Society's longest-serving Executive Director. The essays honor Richards on the occasion of his retirement and are published at a time of transition in the 130-year history of the Society—a year that may prove to be pivotal. The collection is not a history of the organization per se, nor is it a systematic review of developments in the field; rather, the collection portrays the state of biblical scholarship after a century of intensive change.[4]

PART 1: FOSTERING BIBLICAL SCHOLARSHIP

Part 1 describes the contributions of Richards, identifies conditions that advance biblical scholarship, traces developments in Hebrew Bible and New Testament scholarship in the twentieth and twenty-first centuries, and discusses the complex interactions of biblical scholarship and faith, politics, and social location, and the use of the Bible in public arenas.

The first essay, Gail R. O'Day's "Fostering Biblical Scholarship: The Contributions of Kent Harold Richards," discusses the "values of public scholarship that have shaped his career" and characterizes the career as "unmatched in its commitment to the SBL and its mission." The values that Richards embraced in his own scholarship and that he fostered in the Society include collaboration, accessibility, accountability, and inclusiveness.

---

4. For the history of the Society, see Ernest W. Saunders, *Searching the Scriptures: A History of the Society of Biblical Literature, 1880–1980* (SBLBSNA 8; Chico, Calif.: Scholars Press, 1982). For systematic but now dated reviews of the literature, see Eldon Jay Epp and George W. MacRae, eds., *The New Testament and Its Modern Interpreters* (SBLBMI 3; Decatur, Ga.: Scholars Press, 1989); Douglas A. Knight and Gene M. Tucker, eds., *The Hebrew Bible and Its Modern Interpreters* (SBLBMI 1; Decatur, Ga.: Scholars Press, 1985); Robert A. Kraft and George W. E. Nickelsburg Jr., eds., *Early Judaism and Its Modern Interpreters* (SBLBMI 2; Decatur, Ga.: Scholars Press, 1986).

In "Conditions That Foster Biblical Scholarship," Frank Ritchel Ames observes that an increasing awareness of complexity propels contemporary biblical scholarship. He correlates formulations of the SBL mission with modern and postmodern developments in biblical studies, which "have led to a methodological impasse and to confusion about the Society's mission." His analysis underscores the tension between historical and ideological approaches, strategies that either describe perspectives or advocate ideals. Innocence in biblical scholarship has ended, he argues, for exegesis has presuppositions, and interpreters must acknowledge and own their interests. To explain the changing dynamics, Ames applies complexity theory and concludes that conditions that foster biblical scholarship are an evolving mission and processes that alert scholars to new findings, particularly the discovery of artifacts, recognition of neglected variables, application of new methods, and appropriation of emerging technologies.

Gene M. Tucker's "The Modern (and Postmodern?) Society of Biblical Literature: Institutions and Scholarship" identifies institutional developments and trends in scholarship and characterizes the Society's revision of its constitution and bylaws as the most significant change in the past fifty years—a revolutionary development "reshaping the form and substance of biblical scholarship." These revisions seem minor but have had far-reaching outcomes. Term limits for officers made participation in the guild more democratic and inclusive. Developing a publication program enhanced the skills and stature of SBL members, helped some achieve tenure, made research readily available, and created a need for advanced information technologies. Diversifying the program of the Annual Meeting increased the scope of exploration and the communication of findings. Biblical scholarship, however, is now "far more complicated." Categories have changed, methods have proliferated, and historical criticism is but one of several broad types of investigation—namely, historical, literary, and social-scientific—and each is multifaceted, interdisciplinary, and "more self-consciously political."

Harold W. Attridge's "Study of the New Testament in the Pluralistic Context of the Twenty-First Century" surveys changes in approach to New Testament studies during the past fifty years and concludes that twenty-first-century scholars must "develop a facility for engaging in conversation about scripture that addresses the concerns of a religiously plural world." Noting the growing awareness of the "complexity of Judaism at the end of the Second Temple period," his essay highlights the impacts of Nag Hammadi texts, existentialist hermeneutics, new modes of literary analysis, postmodern theory, and perspectival approaches, which, like feminist criticism, have "pursued the enterprise of reading the New Testament from particular, defined points of view, ethnic/racial, global, sexual." Attridge also recognizes progress and impediments in interfaith dialogue and understanding and calls "biblical scholars and their theological colleagues" to routine collaboration.

In "Faith, Scholarship, and the Society of Biblical Literature," John J. Collins responds to a recent charge that "the SBL has changed its position on the relationship between faith and reason."[5] The charge—elicited in part by omission of *critical* from the SBL's mission and vision statement and by *RBL*'s publication of a book review in which a reviewer's religious assumptions displaced the judgments of higher criticism—raises issues that are basic and divisive: What constitutes critical biblical scholarship? What role should the Society play in its regulation? Collins assumes that competent and incompetent readings can be distinguished but acknowledges that it would be difficult to muster a consensus regarding criteria for validating interpretations. He does, however, argue that Troeltsch's principle of criticism is fundamental: critics assert probability, not truth, so conclusions must remain open to revision. "Historical criticism," Collins argues, "is incompatible with dogmatic certainty." Collins likens the evolution of biblical criticism to a sustained conversation that welcomes new participants and perspectives, even contrary perspectives, for "no position is exempt from challenge, if evidence and argument warrant it." This, he avers is "the essence of critical scholarship."

Douglas A. Knight examines "Politics and Biblical Scholarship in the United States." Building on statistical data from the Pew Research Center, he characterizes Americans as religious but religiously diverse, noting the significant role that religious diversity plays in political alignment. Knight underscores the "intimate connection between the Bible and American culture and politics" and finds examples in conflicts over the display of the Ten Commandments, controversies about evolution and creation, and politics of sexuality and reproduction, recognizing also biblical appeals for civil rights, environmental responsibility, charitable activities, and

---

5. Ronald S. Hendel, "Farewell to SBL: Faith and Reason in Biblical Studies," *BAR* 36 (July-August 2010): 28, 74, online: http://www.bib-arch.org/bar/article.asp?PubID=BSBA&Volume=36&Issue=4&ArticleID=9.

establishing colleges. Knight also points out that "American biblical scholarship has been directly affected by American social and political issues" in its treatment of history, methodology, and social issues.

"Ex-Centric Reading: A Case for Critical Reorientation," by Vincent L. Wimbush, explores the power and difficulties of reading from the margins. The point of departure is the "mimetic excess" of Frederick Douglass's account of slave songs, the meaning of which varied with the social location of those who heard the singing. Wimbush writes, "From the positions off-center, things look different and require different sensibilities and practices, including sensibilities and apprehensions about centers and peripheries themselves." Words are meaningless to outsiders and meaningful to insiders. Ex-centric peoples—"Natives and Africans and the other Others"—have not been silent, invisible, or "un-knowing" but have written their own "texts." Ex-centric knowing "means reading America reading itself scripturally, all the while … 'per-forming' texts."

In "The Bible in Public View," David L. Petersen describes the functions of the Bible in civic ritual, artistic interpretation, and public secondary education. In civic ritual—at the coronation of a monarch, for example, or at the administration of a presidential oath—the Bible is an icon that can symbolize the presence and power of God or bestow "some routinized charisma." Artists, on the other hand, interpret the Bible and transform the selected media—whether, painting, film, or comic book—into commentary. Secondary schools, with varying degrees of success, are attempting to teach the Bible from a nonconfessional perspective. Policies and curriculum pose challenges, as do the religious commitments and education of teachers, but the SBL provides resources to support the endeavor.

Part 2: New Pedagogies and the Biblical Studies Curriculum

Part 2 brings together four essays on biblical scholarship and education, an interest that Richards championed at the graduate, undergraduate, and secondary levels. Two essays are primarily theoretical and attend to graduate education; two address undergraduate education and offer examples of course design and learning activities. Each proposes fundamental changes in the way that the Bible is taught.

In "A Republic of Many Voices: Biblical Studies in the Twenty-First Century," Elisabeth Schüssler Fiorenza describes a model of graduate biblical education that displaces the competitive dualism of academic study and the privatized individualism of spiritual reading. Schüssler Fiorenza envisions a forum in which "the radical democratic assembly of biblical scholars, students, and general readers can debate and adjudicate the public and personal meanings of the scriptures in their sociopolitical contexts and ours." The goal of such an educational experience would be to "explore the democratizing potential of the Bible, become methodologically aware of its social location in a democratic society, and reflect on its democratic sociopolitical context." In this way, biblical studies, as well as biblical education, may hope "to flourish in the twenty-first century."

David J. A. Clines encourages M.Div. instructors to consider alternative approaches in "Teaching the Biblical Languages: Time for a Rethink."[6] He describes four relevant transformations in educational theory and practice, including the shift from teacher-centered to student-centered pedagogies, the changing emphasis from acquisition of facts to development of skills, the recognition of different learning styles that should be complemented by a variety of teaching methods, and the acknowledgement that clearly defined outcomes should inform courses and curricula. Clines questions the allocation of too much time to teaching a subject that may be of little use to students who will not become biblical language teachers themselves and concludes with ten recommendations that challenge readers to "rethink" language instruction.

Elizabeth Struthers Malbon, in "The SBL in the Undergraduate Classroom: Pedagogical Reflections," describes the contextual shift that religious students experience when they study the Bible in the academic classroom and how SBL publications can serve as resources that enrich the educational experience. Malbon explains the use of the study Bible and Bible dictionary instead of conventional textbooks and the organization of a biblical studies course around five concepts: presuppositions; context; the relationship of author, text, and audience; interdisciplinarity; and hermeneutics. Malbon concludes by describing how SBL members can indirectly and directly contribute to student learning in courses.

The student is central in Charles William Miller's "'Psalms Are Not Interesting': Learner-Centered Approaches to Teaching Biblical Poetry and the Psalms." Students, Miller observes, usually bring to biblical studies courses previously formed ideas about the meaning of texts. Their

---

6. For broader treatment of the topic, see David J. A. Clines, "Learning, Teaching, and Researching Biblical Studies, Today and Tomorrow," *JBL* 129 (2010): 5–29.

religious communities, friends, and families have taught and conditioned them to read in ways that are at odds with academic reading. Approaches to teaching that rely solely on knowledge acquisition cannot address this problem as effectively as learner-centered activities that focus on critical reading skills and build on the prior learning experiences, which can be transferred to new reading contexts. To illustrate the claim, Miller describes learner-centered activities that have been used to introduce students to classical Hebrew poetry and literary genres in the book of Psalms.

Part 3: Studies in Methods and Contexts

Part 3 gathers eight studies in method and context. Each makes a contribution in its own right, but together the studies illustrate the methodological and contextual complexity that affects biblical interpretation and yields readings that span the historical, literary, social, and theological. Reading strategies and interpretive conclusions change as the focus shifts from the contexts and concerns of the past to those of the present, from the social world of the ancient author to that of the contemporary reader. The discipline remains uncomfortably wed to both. Theological and other ideological readings are provocative because the reader's beliefs and values are neither bracketed nor suppressed. Several of the essays are provocative, but they are included to illustrate contextual complexities and reading strategies that are not uncommon. The cross-section is illustrative and is neither comprehensive nor fully representative of the breadth of the discipline, which is inclusive. Some topics overlap Richards's own scholarly interests and activities, and the scholarship is international in scope.

Tamara Cohn Eskenazi, in "Revisiting the Composition of Ezra-Nehemiah: A Prolegomenon," returns to the issue of the compositional history of Ezra-Nehemiah and evaluates theories set forth by Williamson, Blenkinsopp, Dor, and Wright, each of which is judged "cogent and plausible." To further adjudicate the theories, Eskenazi compares compositional processes evident in the Gilgamesh Epic and Greek historiography. Evidence from the former "confirms the realistic nature of the compositional histories," but the latter "complicates, rather than clarifies," the evaluation, which serves as a prolegomenon for future studies.

In "Rome and the Early Church: Background of the Persecution of Christians in the First and Second Centuries," Paul J. Achtemeier reviews

Roman attitudes toward non-Roman religions, *collegia*, and social nonconformity and demonstrates that the persecution of Christians that is reported in the New Testament was "the result of outbreaks of local and regional hatred rather than due to some sort of continuous official Roman policy to persecute Christians in all parts of the empire at all times."

"Do You Feel Comforted? M. Night Shyamalan's *Signs* and the Book of Job," by J. Cheryl Exum, compares the science-fiction film and the biblical book. The analysis advances from superficial elements to deep perspectives that film and book have in common. Both explore the responses of protagonists who have lost family members and confidence in divine intervention; both create worlds in which God directs the course of events and tests the faithful. According to Exum, "They both raise the question, the possibility, of an inhospitable, unaccommodating universe, and the plot resolutions they provide beg the question."

In "Canaan, Land of Promise: An Ecological Reading of Genesis 10:15–20 in Context," Norman C. Habel asks, "What was God doing in Canaan before the Israelites, the 'people of God,' arrived?" Habel applies ecological hermeneutics and explores the habitat of Canaan, "where the material, social, natural, and spiritual interact creatively." Habel concludes that an ecological reading of Gen 10:15–20 leads to the conclusion that Canaan was a land of promise for more than one people group.

Athalya Brenner challenges the current conceptualization of the family unit in biblical studies in "Revising the Myth of the 'Biblical Family': Reflections on Issues of Methodologies and Interpretive Ideologies." The essay begins with a survey of biblical uses of *bêt 'āb*, "house of the father," then investigates alternative terminology, such as *bêt 'ēm*, "house of the mother," and alternatives such as "sons of the prophets." After consideration of additional evidence, Brenner concludes that present notions about the ancient Near Eastern family "are at best inadequate and at worst confessionally, emotionally, or academically biased."

"God's *Anthropos* Project," by James Luther Mays, illustrates a theological approach to biblical interpretation. Biblical texts are read as Scripture, and it is assumed that they cohere in content and speak about God and the human condition. These assumptions allow the theologian, in this case a Protestant theologian, to consolidate expressions of human identity from lament psalms, selected hymns, creation narratives, Gospels, and epistles and to draw theological conclusions. One conclusion that Mays draws is that lament discloses "the essential neediness of the human condition."

In "Clandestine Relationship: An Approach to the Song of Songs," Pablo R. Andiñach reads theologically from the margins, from the perspective of the oppressed. "The Song of Songs," Andiñach argues, "invites the reader to be freed from the hypocrisy wrapped around sexuality, and it does this through the voice of a woman who does not accept the norms and stereotypes that male society has assigned her." Andiñach reads with suspicion and introspection, finding interpretive clues in oppositions within the text (personal/depersonalized love; giving/withholding), the criticism of the dominant (Solomonic model of sexuality); a valuing of the body rather than its adornment; and the woman's point of view that is embedded in the linguistic structure. Andiñach emphasizes the book's criticism of the Solomonic model and its denunciation of the notion that love and sexuality are controlled by power and money.

Though rejecting dogmatism, Erhard S. Gerstenberger assumes the role of pastor as well as theologian in "Liberating Readings of the Bible: Contexts and Conditions," for Gerstenberger advocates readings that promote justice for the oppressed and underprivileged. To build the case, Gerstenberger describes the function of Scriptures in liberation movements in Latin America, Africa, Asia, Europe, and elsewhere; they functioned as "a revolutionary, antiestablishment force." Reflecting on human need and interpretive method, Gerstenberger concludes that interpretation must attend to "present-day calamities and hopes, values, and institutions." Aware of the implications and risks of the conclusion, he writes, "Do we concede it as an improper, if not warranted, influence on exegesis to employ modern life-conditions? I do not think so. On the contrary, in my opinion we must interpret Scripture always within the tense relationship of ancient and present-day conditions and viewpoints."

Though provocative, Gerstenberger's confessional treatment of liberation theology does raise a central issue in contemporary biblical scholarship. The realization that experience and location affects interpretation and that interpretation, in turn, affects experience and location—a notion that interpreters cannot deny but embrace and resist in varying degrees—is evident and acknowledged throughout the essays in the collection. Exegesis has presuppositions and impact. It is this realization that, in significant measure, accounts for a present unease in biblical scholarship, and for its remarkable vitality and potential.

Acknowledgments

The editors thank the authors for their essays. Special recognition belongs to Tamara Cohn Eskenazi and Charles William Miller, former students of Richards, for first proposing the Festschrift. The editors thank Bob Buller, Editorial Director of the Society of Biblical Literature, also a former student of Richards, for accepting the project and guiding it to a timely completion. The editors also thank SBL publication staff members Leigh Andersen, Kathie Klein, and Lindsay Lingo, who assisted with the preparation and publication of the manuscript. A word of appreciation is due to SBL Development Officer, Sandra Stewart Kruger; to Drew University Dean of Libraries and SBL Archivist, Andrew Scrimgeour, who helped provide access to archival information; and, finally, to Benita Roberts and Liz Neuhalfen, staff members at the Rocky Vista University Health Sciences Library.

Bibliography

Avalos, Hector. *The End of Biblical Studies*. Amherst: Prometheus, 2007.
Clines, David J. A. "Learning, Teaching, and Researching Biblical Studies, Today and Tomorrow." *JBL* 129 (2010): 5–29.
Epp, Eldon Jay, and George W. MacRae, eds. *The New Testament and Its Modern Interpreters*. SBLBMI 3. Decatur, Ga.: Scholars Press, 1989.
Knight, Douglas A., and Gene M. Tucker, eds. *The Hebrew Bible and Its Modern Interpreters*. SBLBMI 1. Decatur, Ga.: Scholars Press, 1985.
Kraft, Robert A., and George W. E. Nickelsburg, Jr., eds. *Early Judaism and Its Modern Interpreters*. SBLBMI 2. Decatur, Ga.: Scholars Press, 1986.
Legaspi, Michael C. *The Death of Scripture and the Rise of Biblical Studies*. Oxford Studies in Historical Theology. New York: Oxford University Press, 2010.
LeMon, Joel M., and Kent Harold Richards, eds. *Method Matters: Essays on the Interpretation of the Hebrew Bible in Honor of David L. Petersen*. SBLRBS 56. Atlanta: Society of Biblical Literature, 2009.
Levinson, Bernard M. *Legal Revision and Religious Renewal in Ancient Israel*. New York: Cambridge University Press, 2008.
Saunders, Ernest W. *Searching the Scriptures: A History of the Society of Biblical Literature, 1880–1980*. SBLBSNA 8. Chico, Calif.: Scholars Press, 1982.

Part 1
Fostering Biblical Scholarship

Fostering Biblical Scholarship: The Contributions of Kent Harold Richards

Gail R. O'Day

In 2003 the Society of Biblical Literature Council engaged in major strategic planning for the ongoing and future work of the Society, assessing and reformulating the Society's mission statement, its core institutional values, and its strategic visions. The results of this strategic planning were published in the 2003 *Society Report*, so that all SBL members could share in the newly articulated vision of the Society.[1] This new plan put the Society's work in language appropriate for the late twentieth century, with an eye toward the place of the SBL as a learned society in the twenty-first century.

The strategic plan's articulation of the mission of the SBL to "foster biblical scholarship" is more than fitting as the title for this volume of essays in Kent Richards's honor, as the Council undertook this important strategic planning process under Kent's executive leadership. The phrase "foster biblical scholarship" as a mission statement seems redundant at first glance—what else would a learned society dedicated to biblical literature do other than foster biblical scholarship—yet this simplicity is the key to the mission statement's effectiveness. The verb "foster" is an active verb, indicating that the Society's mission is not simply that its members undertake individual research but that the Society as a society has an active role in biblical scholarship. "Biblical scholarship" indicates the primary (but not exclusive) body of literature with which the Society is concerned, but more importantly, also names the primary activity of the Society—scholarship, the critical production and promotion of new knowledge.

---

1. Kent Harold Richards, "Leadership with New Vision," *SBL Society Report* (2003): 3. See also idem, "New Strategic Vision," *SBL Society Report* (2004): 10.

The Society's mission statement is also a fitting title for this volume of essays because Kent's entire career is an embodiment of this simple sentence. Most scholars on the occasion of their retirement can reflect back on a career of teaching and scholarship as their contributions to their disciplines, and Kent's career has those traditional markers: the volume is edited by two of Kent's former students and contains many essays by Hebrew Bible scholars that reflect Kent's long-standing research interests. Kent's contributions to fostering biblical scholarship are marked not only by these traditional scholarly pursuits, but also by his career-long commitments to public scholarship. The values of public scholarship that have shaped his career include a commitment to scholarly collaboration and conversation, accessibility, accountability, and inclusiveness. His commitment to these focal values of public scholarship has led Kent to a career that is unmatched in its commitment to the SBL and its mission.

Scholarly Conversation and Collaboration

In 1970, as an assistant professor in his first full-time teaching job at the University of Dayton, Kent Richards was a founding member of the Eastern Great Lakes Section (now Region) of the SBL. The regions are autonomous groups of SBL members who gather locally for scholarly meetings, and Kent's early engagement with forming a regional group demonstrated his commitment to scholarly conversation and collaboration. It is a striking and distinctive mark of his career commitments that Kent understood the value of engagement with the learned society of one's academic discipline at such an early point in his own career.

The SBL remained the central venue for Kent's expression of his commitments to scholarly conversation and collaboration. Kent's curriculum vitae records the time and energy he gave to the SBL as a volunteer, even before assuming the professional full-time job of its executive director in 1995. He served on the program committee of the Rocky Mountain Great Plains Region, as a member or chair of program groups at the SBL annual meeting (Form Criticism, Process Hermeneutic and Biblical Theology), and was a member of the development committee (1991–1995). In addition to these committee roles, Kent exercised key leadership in several other volunteer capacities. In an earlier governance model, the SBL did not have a professional executive director, and society leadership rested with the Society's officers. From 1976 to 1987, Kent served as an officer of the Society, first as treasurer (1976–1980) and then as executive secretary (1981–1987), the office in the earlier model most similar to Executive Director.

I rehearse these details of Kent's CV not primarily to call attention to Kent's unparalleled career of volunteer service to the SBL, but because this career of volunteer service embodies the value of conversation and collaboration to public scholarship. Kent himself regularly gives explicit expression to the role of volunteers in fostering these key scholarly values. In one annual report, for example, Kent wrote that the success of the Society was

> measured largely by the ability to engage many colleagues in the diverse program areas of the Society. The Society would never have grown to its current level of activity and size were it not for the volunteers who guide annual meeting program units, write and edit for our publications, and provide innovative leadership on committees.… The expanded circle of members strengthens the voice of each of us because it demonstrates the depth and breadth of our activities.… The "spiral of benefits" for all of us starts with each volunteer.[2]

Kent's legacy in fostering biblical scholarship through scholarly conversation and collaboration is apparent in what most members of the Society now take for granted as business as usual. For example, one of Kent's most innovative contributions as a volunteer derived from his service as chair of the International Meeting program (1982–1992). Kent's commitments to public scholarship enabled him to recognize early on the importance of opening up the SBL to international partners. The international profile of the SBL is now a significant part of its identity—through the international meeting, international memberships, and partnerships with international publishers, to name but a few.

As executive director, Kent also advanced the public scholarship value of conversation and collaboration by bringing the SBL into active participation with the American Council of Learned Societies (ACLS). The ACLS is comprised of seventy member societies in the humanities and related social sciences that represent the highest scholarly standards in their respective disciplines, and its mission is to advance the humanities. By participating actively in ACLS, the SBL aligns itself with scholarly

---

2. Kent Harold Richards, "The 'Spiral of Benefits,'" *SBL Society Report* (1998–1999): 3.

societies that are "involved in the promotion of research, scholarly publication, and education" (www.acls.org/mission). Engagement with ACLS enhances the public scholarly profile of the SBL and fosters biblical scholarship by underscoring its place in general humanities research and education.

Accessibility

Kent was also an active volunteer for Scholars Press, enabling him to enhance the value of accessibility to public scholarship. He was a volunteer member of its Board of Trustees (1976–1987), its Executive Committee (1978–1987), and its Board of Directors (1980–1985). As a volunteer he also served as chair of the Press's Board of Directors, Building Committee, and Nominating Committee. As a volunteer member of the Scholars Press leadership team, Kent participated in negotiations to bring Scholars Press to the Emory University campus, and was instrumental in securing grant money to help build the original Scholars Press building. This building allowed Scholars Press to increase its presence and production, serving the goal of increasing the availability and accessibility of peer-reviewed scholarship.

Such service continued when Kent became SBL Executive Director. As Scholars Press grew, and the AAR and SBL also outgrew their offices in Atlanta, Kent, in his capacity as SBL Executive Director, was again one of the leaders in securing additional funding, negotiating land contracts with Emory University, and shaping the design for the Luce Center, a beautiful building constructed adjacent to the original Scholars Press building. This new building continued to foster the scholarly value of accessibility, because it enabled the two largest U.S.-based learned societies for the study of religion, as well as Scholars Press, to share physical space.

When Scholars Press ceased publication in 2000, the SBL Council, in consultation with the professional SBL staff, decided to become a publisher in its own right. This was a bold decision on the SBL's part, because it meant taking on the financial costs of running a press, as well as the intellectual and scholarly benefits. This decision has proven wise over time. SBL Publications is now a member of the Association of American University Presses, operates in the black, and is a leader in many electronic publishing innovations (e.g., downloadable fonts for biblical languages). Yet it is the core value behind the decision—the Society's commitment to ensuring that the best of biblical scholarship is accessible and available—that reflects the ethos of the Society and the ways in which Kent's leadership enabled the society to claim its mission of fostering biblical scholarship.

The value of accessibility can also be seen in the Society's ventures in electronic publication. The *Review of Biblical Literature* (*RBL*) was launched during Kent's tenure as executive director, and the *Journal of Biblical Literature* (*JBL*) also added an electronic version to its print publication. *RBL* has not been without its critics, but even its critics cannot but notice that it has revolutionized the way that biblical scholars have access to book reviews. The launch and success of *RBL* have contributed to important conversations about the nature of a book review, the place of reviews in the scholarly life, and, indeed, how scholars read and respond to one another's work. *RBL* is international in scope and accessibility in a way that would not be possible in a print medium, and the *RBL* review notification system for members makes the most recent literature immediately available to scholars. Through the innovation of a book review system that puts a premium on the public scholarship value of accessibility, the SBL, under Kent's leadership, fostered a new dimension of biblical scholarship.

Perhaps nothing more clearly represents how attention to accessibility can foster biblical scholarship than the SBL website. The SBL staff, under Kent's leadership, was very quick to recognize the contributions that electronic technologies could make to the work of the Society. The SBL website also shows how the different values of public scholarship intersect with one another, because the accessibility of the website, and the information and resources that it makes available to Society members and the general public, enhance conversation and collaboration.

Accountability

Accountability is a key value of public scholarship, because the integrity of the scholarly enterprise demands mutual accountability and transparency about the forms of accountability on all fronts. For a learned society, accountability can take many forms, from the mutual accountability of its members to adhere to the standards of scholarly integrity to the leadership's accountability to the membership to advance the mission of the society and safeguard the society's values.

The infrastructure of any organization is key to its success in accomplishing its mission, and for a learned society it is the responsibility of the administrative officer to ensure that the organization meets the accountability demands of its members. The mission to foster biblical scholarship cannot be accomplished without the society itself meeting the highest professional and operational standards. Under Kent's leadership, the SBL Executive Office has assembled a staff that is second to none at any learned society and who are indispensable partners with the volunteers who guide the Society's many projects. The quality and professionalism of the staff ensure that the work of the SBL Executive Office enacts the mission and values of the Society's members. Given the size of its publication program, as well as its robust set of congresses and meetings, the SBL sets a heavy agenda for itself and the professional staff holds itself accountable to advance that agenda and so foster biblical scholarship.

Of equal importance, during his tenure as executive director, Kent led Council through a major governance restructuring and revision of the constitution and by-laws. The current governance structure now more closely resembles that of other non-profits and learned societies, as the Council increasingly took on the responsibilities of a governing board, ensuring sustained accountability to the membership through its volunteer leaders. This attention to questions of organizational integrity is essential to fully formed public scholarship, because it ensures that each member has the same access as any other member to the proceedings of the Society. Each year's Society report contains the audit of the Society's finances, another enactment of accountability. Governance accountability does not ensure that all members agree with each decision that their governing body makes, but it does ensure that all members know that their governing body is constituted with public accountability for mission-related decisions in view.

These two contributions of Kent's leadership of the SBL—the development of a high-quality professional staff and the restructuring of the Society's governance—are the work of a seasoned administrator, who not only is able to imagine a vision for his organization, but also to lead others into participating in the hard work to bring that vision to fruition. While most members think of papers, articles, and books as the most obvious fruits of biblical scholarship, Kent's commitment to governance accountability created the professional context where those more obvious fruits may flourish.

The value of accountability was in evidence in other activities of the Society during Kent's tenure. Increased attention to professional development of members issued in a variety of new or enhanced programs—the regional scholars program, partnerships with the Fund for Theological Education, the Louisville Institute, the American Academy of Religion (AAR), and United States National Endowment for the Humanities (NEH). Accountability also shaped the SBL's decision to participate in the annual Humanities Advocacy Day in Washington, D.C., as well as the increased presence on the website of resources that addressed the place of biblical literature in public life.

Under Kent's leadership—first as a volunteer on the Development Committee and then as Executive Director—the SBL communicated to its members their accountability for the financial future of the Society. Each Society Report now includes the list of members who have donated to the Society Fund, and Kent spearheaded the fundraising related to the SBL's 125th anniversary. The emphasis on member donations marks a shift in ethos from a dues-only approach, and this shift reflects the value of accountability. As the learned society must be accountable to its members, the members also are accountable for the helping their society move into the future.

Inclusiveness

Kent's commitment to the value of inclusiveness is of a piece with his commitments to scholarly conversation and collaboration, accessibility, and accountability. Each of these values alone ensures the public role and voice of biblical scholarship, but all of them together create an inclusive scholarly community. For Kent Richards, biblical scholarship cannot be fostered exclusively, but can only be fostered inclusively. This commitment to the value of inclusiveness can be seen in the SBL's increased involvement with ACLS under Kent's leadership, as he has acted on his understanding of the vocation of the biblical scholar to be linked to that of broader intellectual citizenship. During Kent's tenure, student members were given a larger role in the Society, and sessions on teaching and publishing, as well as how to become involved in the SBL, became regular features of annual meeting programs. Kent's determination that the SBL would have an international meeting also grew out of the value of inclusiveness and wanting to expand the publics that the SBL served.

The understanding that public scholarship is inclusive shapes the expanding number of partner scholarly societies who meet concurrently or consecutively with the SBL meeting—new knowledge is produced and promoted by having more voices in the scholarly conversation not fewer.

The recent joint announcement by the executive directors of AAR and SBL to return to holding their annual meetings concurrently grows out of the same commitment.

The central place of inclusiveness in Kent's career is given powerful voice by the array of scholars who have contributed essays to this volume. This list of contributors is an accurate reflection of the shape and direction of the SBL during Kent's tenure as executive director. The contributors mark the international breadth that has been so important to Kent, as well as disciplinary range. The contributors demonstrate gender, religious, and ethnic inclusiveness that reflect the demographics of the Society. Many of the contributors are former students and friends of Kent, but perhaps most notably, the contributors all have distinguished volunteer service records with the SBL. This volume thus pays tribute to Kent by reflecting the values of public scholarship that have shaped his own career.

Bibliography

Richards, Kent Harold. "Leadership with New Vision." *SBL Society Report* (2003): 3.

———. "New Strategic Vision." *SBL Society Report* (2004): 10.

———. "The 'Spiral of Benefits.'" *SBL Society Report* (1998–1999): 3.

Conditions That Foster Biblical Scholarship

Frank Ritchel Ames

The Society of Biblical Literature's mission statement—foster biblical scholarship—is a masterpiece of the genre and of the *Realpolitik* of academic biblical studies. Brevity aids the memory, and generality provides guidance without micromanaging the scholarly enterprise. The delineation of the task is deceptively simple, though with no intent to deceive, and the direct, intelligible wording reflects the genius of its author.[1] The statement is simple, but the mission is not, and the challenging nature of the task invites a practical question: What fosters biblical scholarship? This essay proposes an answer that begins with the mission itself.

A Mission That Advances with the Discipline

The inaugural constitution and by-laws of the Society did not include a mission statement, an omission that Society historian Ernest W. Saunders deemed "curious."[2] It might have been a simple matter of oversight on the part of the eighteen scholars who attended the first meeting of the Society on 4 June 1880, but the odd exclusion may be considered an artifact of presumption and incidental evidence of a tacit agreement concerning the trajectory of biblical studies. Members of the newly formed organization might not have sensed any pressing need to delineate the Society's mis-

---

1. Kent Harold Richards was instrumental in the formulation of the Society's mission statement, which captures in miniature his passion and the scholarly, organizational, and political achievement of a life devoted to fostering biblical scholarship. His knowledge of the discipline is encyclopedic, his leadership formidable yet generous and self-effacing, and his contribution remarkable and enduring.
2. Ernest W. Saunders, *Searching the Scriptures: A History of the Society of Biblical Literature, 1880–1980* (SBLBSNA 8; Chico, Calif.: Scholars Press, 1982), 4.

sion because the task seemed obvious to them. At the turn of the century, many members equated biblical scholarship with exegesis and increasingly equated exegesis with the historical-critical method. It is, of course, equally possible that the omission of the statement might have been a passive attempt to put off the conflict of crossed purposes, the struggle that inevitably ensues after full disclosure or recognition of conflicting historical interests and theological agendas. One can only speculate about the actual reasons for the oversight, but the juxtaposition of the terms *biblical* and *criticism* often stir debate and divide organizations. In the nineteenth-century ascendency of German scholarship, biblical criticism had bested religious confession in higher education, though more than a few Society members endeavored to serve two masters—the church and the academy—and some suffered the indignities of heresy trials and dismissals. Infamous but not unique are the trials of Hebrew Bible/Old Testament scholars Charles Augustus Briggs and Henry Preserved Smith, who espoused critical methods and were ousted from church-related appointments. Briggs and Smith pursued the mission and met resistance, learning firsthand the social and professional consequences of advocating critical methods within the sphere of influence of a staunch, confessing community.[3]

In 1884, the Society formally articulated its mission: "The purpose of the Society shall be to stimulate the *critical* study of the Scriptures by presenting, discussing, and publishing original papers on Biblical topics."[4] The Society announced its corporate intentions, and the mission statement acknowledged and embraced the scientific impulse of the era, with its deference to fact rather than faith. The *fin de siècle* was an era of sight, and the efforts of the Society were to be critical and scientific. The guild valorized the scientific model, and historical analysis trumped religious dogma, even though many pursued, often indirectly but at times overtly, critical scholarship out of religious devotion and in support of sacred institutions.[5] Biblical criticism remained a suspect ally and a troublesome

---

3. Lefferts A. Loetscher, "C. A. Briggs in the Retrospect of Half a Century," *ThTo* 12 (1955): 27–42; Thomas P. Slavens, "The Librarianship of Charles Augustus Briggs," *USQR* 24 (1969): 357–63.

4. Emphasis added. The draft of the constitution and by-laws was commissioned and prepared by Frederic Gardiner, Francis Brown, and H. G. Mitchel on 12 June 1884 and was approved by the membership on the morning of the following day. See H. G. Mitchel, "Proceedings," *JBL* 4 (1884): 150–60.

5. See James A. Montgomery, "Present Tasks of American Biblical Scholarship,"

antagonist within confessional circles that studied the Bible for theological perspective and spiritual formation.[6] Nonetheless, the Society's betrothal to historical-critical methodology would define biblical scholarship for much of the twentieth century for better or worse.

In 1962, the Society of Biblical Literature and Exegesis shortened its name to the Society of Biblical Literature and revised its mission statement to "promote the creation and dissemination of scholarly knowledge pertaining to biblical literature and ancillary fields."[7] The revision of the mission statement did not redirect scholarly praxis; rather, it codified the prevalent understanding of the related literary corpus:

> The object of the Society is to stimulate the critical investigation of the classical biblical literatures, together with other related literature, by the exchange of scholarly research both in published form and in public forum. The Society endeavors to support those disciplines and subdisciplines pertinent to the illumination of the literatures and religions of the ancient Near Eastern and Mediterranean regions, such as the study of ancient languages, textual criticism, history, and archaeology.[8]

Between the 1880s and 1980s, the SBL's public declarations of purpose redefined both the object of analysis and the analytical approach. *Scriptures* were dubbed *classical biblical literatures*, and the literary corpus was transformed from sacred to secular. Methodology drifted with the same current, and *investigation* replaced *study*, perhaps because the latter term connoted a confessional interest in what was known as *personal Bible study*.[9] The task was reconceptualized in its wording, as well as in its prac-

---

JBL 38 (1991): 1–14. Montgomery declared, "The mere measurements of the Bible must not deter us from the appreciation of it as that which it claims to be, a book of religion. And none can fully interpret it who is not possessed by that prepossession. Not the childish fear of the appearance of faith or confessionalism should keep us from this full approach to the Bible. It is after all, on the whole, those who have believed in it who have been its greatest interpreters. And the duty lies upon us Biblical scholars to show the world that we believe in its worth and assert its value with an enthusiasm that is tinged by emotion as well as moderated by reason" (7).

6. Mark A. Noll, *Between Faith and Criticism* (2nd ed.; Grand Rapids: Baker, 1991).

7. Saunders, *Searching the Scriptures*, 98.

8. Ibid., xi.

9. E.g., Larry Richards, *Creative Bible Study: A Handbook for Small Group, Family, and Personal Bible Study* (Grand Rapids: Zondervan, 1971).

tice. As the Society's change of name implied, the endeavor encompassed more than exegesis, which would now be only one method among many. A historical reading strategy was no longer privileged within the Society as its former name indicated, even though the pertinent disciplines and subdisciplines largely remained historical in nature, and the incongruity of a detached engagement of an engaging religious text was felt. The watershed question that the Society could not comfortably ask, answer, or ignore in the decade before its centennial was "the question of Scripture."[10] Robert W. Funk gave this explanation of the problem: "Because the question of Scripture is just below the surface in American liberal scholarship, it is systematically suppressed in discussion."[11] The guild found it difficult to talk about what the guild wanted to talk about, namely, Scripture and hermeneutics. Ironically, interpreters were confounded by meaning and by the significance of the biblical text. For this reason, Brevard S. Childs's introduction to the Old Testament *as Scripture* proved revolutionary.[12] Nonetheless, the mission at the end of the twentieth century delineated ancient contexts ("ancient Near Eastern and Mediterranean") and historical methods ("ancient languages, textual criticism, history, and archaeology"), expressed a desire for insight ("illumination of literatures and religions"), and did so without readily acknowledging the afterlife of texts or contemporary theological interests in them. Contextual study joined classical philology on the dais, but the enterprise largely remained antiquarian, oriented to minutiae, and ostensibly objective. The interests of the Society's membership, however, were evolving and were outpacing the mission.

In 2003, the leadership of the Society wrote the current mission statement—foster biblical scholarship—and appended six vision statements,

---

10. Robert W. Funk, "The Watershed of the American Biblical Tradition: The Chicago School, First Phase, 1892–1920," *JBL* 95 (1976): 4–22.

11. Ibid., 21.

12. Brevard S. Childs, *Introduction to the Old Testament as Scripture* (Philadelphia: Fortress, 1979). See the three reviews in Ralph W. Klein, Gary Stansell, and Walter Brueggemann, "The Childs Proposal: A Symposium," *WW* 1 (1981): 105–15. Stansell writes, "The historical-critical method … is both praised and damned by Childs. On the one hand, he recounts its definite gains over the past generations and makes use of its results; on the other, he attempts to show its great limitations for the task of understanding the Hebrew Bible's canonical authority and theological significance. In my judgment, there is little to quarrel with here" (109–10). Brueggemann adds, "Childs has not gone nearly far enough" (115).

with minor phrases; a seventh vision statement was added in 2004.[13] The leadership also listed twelve core values: accountability, collaboration, collegiality, commitment, communication, efficiency, inclusiveness, leadership in biblical scholarship, productivity, responsiveness to change, scholarly integrity, and tolerance. Interests beyond the antiquarian are evident in the Society's most recent vision and values, which interpret and focus its concise mission. To foster biblical scholarship today, the Society seeks to

> advance the academic study of biblical literature and its cultural contexts; collaborate with educational institutions and other appropriate organizations to support biblical scholarship and teaching; develop resources for diverse audiences, including students, religious communities, and the general public; facilitate broad and open discussion from a variety of perspectives; offer members opportunities for mutual support, intellectual growth, and professional development as teachers and scholars; organize congresses for scholarly exchange; [and] publish biblical scholarship.[14]

The current mission, vision, and values of the Society are altruistic, as well as ambitious. Unlike any forerunners, the present vision is explicitly populated with stakeholders: scholars, teachers, students, general public, educational institutions, and others. The ivory tower has been renovated, and its doors and windows are now open to the public square and town hall. The vision is extensive and inclusive, inviting broader participation in the scholarly dialogue and offering the findings of critical scholarship to those outside of the guild. Public needs are to be addressed, and resources are to be developed for various communities, including religious communities. To some, developing resources for religious communities is inconsistent with the critical agenda of the Society, but the wording of the vision statement neither invites nor institutes a parochial agenda. The academy has not been transformed into a synagogue or church, because resources are to be developed *for*, not *by*, religious communities. The choice of the preposition used on this point in the vision statement is sig-

---

13. Kent Harold Richards, "Leadership with New Vision," *SBL Society Report* (2003): 3. The following statement was added in 2004: "develop resources for diverse audiences, including students, religious communities, and the general public" (Kent Harold Richards, "New Strategic Vision," *SBL Society Report* [2004]: 10).

14. "About SBL," http://www.sbl-site.org/aboutus.aspx.

nificant. The impulse to serve other communities, of course, is not new within the Society, but now it is embedded in the defining documents of the organization.

Not insignificant is the breadth of exploration expressed in the phrase "biblical literature and its cultural contexts." Ancient Near Eastern and Mediterranean contexts are no longer specified; the new wording recognizes that the contexts that legitimately frame a scholarly understanding of biblical literature are modern as well as ancient, encompassing both the imagined provenance of the text and the social location of the reader. The literary corpus is no longer canonical or even classical. Strictly speaking, it is not exclusively literary. The corpus encompasses Judeo-Christian scriptures, comparative literatures in cognate languages, commentaries and translations, and creative works such as novels, paintings, sculptures, and films affected by biblical motifs and expressions.[15] Historical criticism has not been abandoned, but it is now effective in the sense of *Wirkungsgeschichte*, with a realization that "the traditions one criticizes are already integral to one's own position."[16] Rudolf Bultmann's famous question has been answered, and the answer informs the enterprise: exegetes presuppose, and when they read texts they read and reveal themselves.[17]

The Society's mission and biblical scholarship have evolved together, and a significant shift is now evident. It is palpable in the recharacterization of *Scripture* as *biblical literature*, which entails both a conscious rejection of special pleading for the text and a fuller recognition of human processes.[18] Historical criticism, from nascent forms in the sev-

---

15. The mission statement is a response to movement within the field. See J. Cheryl Exum, *Plotted, Shot, and Painted: Cultural Representations of Biblical Women* (JSOTSup 215; Sheffield: Sheffield Academic Press, 1996).

16. John McCole, *Walter Benjamin and the Antinomies of Tradition* (Ithaca, N.Y.: Cornell University Press, 1993), 27.

17. Rudolf Bultmann, "Ist voraussetzungslose Exegese müglich?" *TZ* 13 (1957): 409–17.

18. Capitalization is an arbitrary orthographic convention that expresses grammatical function but at times accrues cultural value, and two capitalization rules in *The SBL Handbook of Style for Ancient Near Eastern, Biblical, and Early Christian Studies* (ed. Patrick H. Alexander et al.; Peabody, Mass.: Hendrickson, 1999) routinely confound devout college and seminary students who have enrolled in biblical studies courses: the use of lowercase for pronouns referring to God (§4.4.8) and for adjectives derived from proper names, especially the ubiquitous term *biblical* (§4.4.5). Modern usage increasingly demonstrates a preference for lowercase wherever possible, but the

enteenth century through its maturation in the twentieth, has enabled biblical scholars to confess that *the* Bible is *a* book—with all that such a fundamental observation implies—and they have done so while appreciating the ubiquitous and enduring influence of Bibles and resisting the imposition of religious dogmas. Early in the twentieth century, the guild embraced the notion that provenance matters, and biblical scholars have increasingly recognized other aspects of the social and material worlds behind texts: the informing contexts of authors, redactors, scribes, and translators. Historical criticism taught us to open our eyes to mundane processes.[19] By the end of the twentieth century, however, we learned that mundane processes include our own predispositions and perceptions. The reader matters. The current mission statement, whether intentionally or not, accommodates this postmodern insight. The statement shuns the arrogant myopia of positivism and values multiple intelligences and viewpoints. Movement within biblical scholarship, therefore, is also manifest in both a growing awareness of the politics of reading and a more rigorous criticism of criticism. Scholars have not only redefined *biblical*; they have reevaluated *scholarship*. The once-assured results are no longer assured, and suspicion infuses hermeneutics. We realize, in every reading, that the past is varnished by the present and is not essential for an

---

SBLHS editorializes that "the days of using capitalization as a sign of reverence are past" (19). Of the many details of writing style that I have been asked to explain and to justify to college and seminary students and even to professional colleagues, the most common are the *SBLHS* rules prescribing the noncapitalization of divine pronouns and derived adjectives. These prescriptions are often resisted, at times zealously so. My observation about the shift in terminology from *Scripture* to *biblical literature* is not about style; it is about symbolism, for historical criticism had reconstructed the concept of the Bible.

19. John J. Collins, *The Bible after Babel: Historical Criticism in a Postmodern Age* (Grand Rapids: Eerdmans, 2005), 1–26. Historical criticism encompasses a range of methods. Collins observes, "What these methods have in common is a general agreement that texts should be interpreted in their historical contexts, in light of the literary and cultural conventions of their time. There is also a general assumption that the meaning of a text can be established in an objective manner, but this assumption is more complicated than it may seem. The meaning intended by an ancient author can, at best, only be reconstructed tentatively, and few historical critics would deny that a text may take on new meanings in changing circumstances. (This is in fact the *raison d'être* of redaction criticism.) But historical critics usually assume a hierarchy of meanings and regard the historical context as basic or primary" (4).

appreciation of the text, for a composition has its architecture and can assume significance in multiple contexts. The shift of which I speak is evident in valuing the context of the author and the artistry of the text in new ways and in acknowledging the reader's role, which is undeniably profound: there is an author and a text, but the reader also writes the text and is written by the text.[20] Attachment of the reader to the text, as opposed to the imagined clinical detachment of the critical historian, has localized conclusions and politicized readings in undeniable and sometimes subversive and discomfiting ways. Objectivity, we now admit, is not so objective, but it remains alluring and perhaps attainable, albeit in a qualified or redefined form.[21] Arguments about the locus of meaning, popularized in the writings of E. D. Hirsch and Stanley E. Fish, still reverberate in the halls of academe, but final arguments on subjects such as these have not been heard.[22] For some, contrary positivistic and postpositivistic sensibilities have led to a methodological impasse and to confusion about the Society's mission and the trajectory of a conflicted discipline.[23] Yet the evolution of the mission, which parallels developments in biblical scholarship, is itself an evidence and a condition of its achievement. A mission that advances with the discipline fosters biblical scholarship. It is not, however, the only condition.

A Recognition of Promising Developments

During the 130-year history of the Society, biblical scholarship has shifted

---

20. See examples throughout Bob Ekblad, *Reading the Bible with the Damned* (Louisville: Westminster John Knox, 2005).

21. So Jürgen Habermas, "Modernity versus Postmodernity," *New German Critique* 22 (1981): 3–14. Habermas writes, "I think that instead of giving up modernity and its project as a lost cause, we should learn from the mistakes of those extravagant programs which have tried to negate modernity" (11).

22. Stanley E. Fish, *Is There a Text in This Class? The Authority of Interpretive Communities* (Cambridge: Harvard University Press, 1980); E. D. Hirsch, *Validity in Interpretation* (New Haven: Yale University Press, 1967); and idem, *The Aims of Interpretation* (Chicago: University of Chicago Press, 1976).

23. Hector Avalos, "Whither Biblical Studies?" *CSSR Bulletin* 38 (2009): 13–15. See the extended arguments in Jacques Berlinerblau, *The Secular Bible* (Cambridge: Cambridge University Press, 2005); and Hector Avalos, *The End of Biblical Studies* (Amherst: Prometheus, 2007).

from theological prescription to historical criticism[24] and from historical criticism to literary analysis, ideological criticism (such as feminist, racial-ethnic, postcolonial, and disability), and postmodernist deconstruction.[25] Modern and postmodern sensibilities have given rise to a panoply of reading strategies, which in turn have accelerated the processes of discovery.[26] The discipline has burgeoned, but new findings and methods have not made a simple endeavor more complicated nor a complicated one more complex, though at times it may seem so. Funk rightly characterized North American biblical scholarship of the 1970s as "extremely complex."[27] Biblical scholarship, however, has always been complex. Complexity has not increased, but awareness of complexity has.

For this reason, complexity theory affords a framework for making sense of the Society's evolving mission and the conditions that foster biblical scholarship.[28] In a complex system, agents interact and patterns emerge, but specific actions and nontrivial outcomes cannot be predicted. In complexity theory, *complex* is neither a synonym of *complicated* nor an antonym for *simple*; it denotes multidimensional nonlinear interaction.[29] In simple and complicated systems, interactivity is linear, and cause-and-effect relationships are either known or knowable; patterns of behavior repeat, and outcomes can be anticipated. In complex systems, however, emerging patterns do not necessarily repeat, and interdependencies only cohere in retrospect. Discrete, nontrivial outcomes cannot be predicted, but complex systems are not chaotic; they are self-organizing and exhibit emergent properties.[30]

The Society of Biblical Literature is a complex social system, and the dynamics of complexity have implications for decision making

---

24. Krister Stendahl, "Biblical Theology, Contemporary," *IDB* 1:418–32.

25. Elisabeth Schüssler Fiorenza, *Rhetoric and Ethics: The Politics of Biblical Studies* (Minneapolis: Fortress, 1999).

26. See, e.g., Steven L. McKenzie and Stephen R. Haynes, eds., *To Each Its Own Meaning: An Introduction to Biblical Criticisms and Their Applications* (rev. ed.; Louisville: Westminster John Knox, 1999).

27. Funk, "Watershed," 5.

28. Cynthia F. Kurtz and David J. Snowden, "The New Dynamics of Strategy: Sense-Making in a Complex and Complicated World," *IBM Systems Journal* 42 (2003): 462–83.

29. Paul Cilliers, *Complexity and Postmodernism: Understanding Complex Systems* (London: Routledge, 1998), 12–35.

30. Kurtz and Snowden, "New Dynamics of Strategy," 467–469.

and organizational leadership, though the implications are sometimes counterintuitive and typically contrary to established administrative practices.[31] First, long-range planning becomes moot in a complex enterprise because nontrivial outcomes cannot be predicted or staged. Second, consensus can be counterproductive because the feedback that guides adaptation and stimulates innovation diminishes as consensus grows. In organizations that achieve consensus, ideas are merely reiterated, and a think tank becomes a mere echo chamber. Echoes can locate objects but are not new information.[32] Consensus, therefore, aids refinement and implementation, rather than the development of concepts. Paradoxically, though a complex social system is self-organizing, leadership plays a crucial role.[33]

> It [leadership] is, first, to promote and protect order and stability in the day-to-day conduct of the existing business and in the existing strategic direction. But it is also to create an atmosphere of questioning and contention, disorder and chaos, that threatens the bureaucracy, and then manage the boundaries around the instability that has been generated. This second task is what opens up the possibility of innovation.[34]

Leadership in a complex social system, then, both facilitates cooperation and safeguards dissent. It maintains civil discourse but does not silence the contrary voice in the wilderness. Hard questions destabilize consensus yet prompt innovation. New ideas often emerge from the margins and the conflicts. To borrow a phrase made popular by the theorists, a complex enterprise thrives on "the edge of chaos."[35] This does not imply that

---

31. David J. Snowden and Mary E. Boone, "A Leader's Framework for Decision Making," *HBR* (November 2007): 69–76.

32. Joan E. Ricart and Adrian A. Caldart, "Complexity Theory," *International Encyclopedia of Organizational Studies* (ed. Stewart R. Clegg and James R. Bailey; Thousand Oaks, Calif.: Sage), 233.

33. Leadership itself is an emergent property of a self-organizing system.

34. Ricart and Caldart, "Complexity Theory," 233.

35. For a popular discussion of the concept, see M. M. Waldrop, *Complexity: The Emerging Science at the Edge of Order and Chaos* (New York: Simon & Schuster, 1992), 12, 198–240. For fuller development and application to social systems, see John H. Miller and Scott E. Page, *Complex Adaptive Systems: An Introduction to Computational Models of Social Life* (Princeton Studies in Complexity; Princeton: Princeton University Press, 2007), 129–40.

a thriving organization should be disorganized or that chaos advances an institutional agenda. Equilibrium and anarchy are the boundaries of vital interactivity, not its center field. Planning and consensus building have their place, and the edginess of complexity does not "negate the need for strategy. Rather, it means that organizational strategy should evolve based on feedback and change as it occurs."[36] Leadership in a complex enterprise emerges to articulate vision and values, facilitate engagement and communication, and contextualize patterns of experience. Effective leadership in the midst of complexity "concentrates on collective sense-making as a consequence of discourse."[37] Effective leadership in a complex social system also recognizes emergence. Recognition is a strategic process of discovery and communication, that is, the iterative finding and conveying of information about new ideas, resources, and opportunities. Leaders in complex enterprises observe promising initiatives and alert stakeholders, and they repeat this process early and often. In this way, achievement of mission and adaptation to environment are encouraged through feedback, and emergence is guided by its effects.[38]

---

36. Wendy H. Mason and Hal P. Kirkwood Jr, "Complexity Theory," *Encyclopedia of Management* (ed. Marilyn M. Helms; Farmington Hills, Mich.: Gale, 2005), 97.

37. Kurtz and Snowden, "New Dynamics of Strategy," 471. In the schema described by Kurtz and Snowden (467–71), the complex enterprise occupies one of four sense-making domains, and effective leadership changes from one domain to the next. In the simple domain, cause and effect are known, so effective leadership entails the adoption of best practice. In the complicated domain, cause and effect are unknown but knowable. Effective leadership, therefore, starts with analysis of the system and then progresses to strategic planning and implementation. When chaos breaks out, leaders must act without the benefit of a thorough analysis, for causes and effects are unknown and unknowable. Managing complexity, however, requires recognition of emergent properties. See immediately below.

38. The leadership that emerges within a social group directs the activities of the group through the dissemination of information, which can be reported, suppressed, distorted, or censored. Discovery and communication have ethical components, and the misuse of information is ill-advised for idealistic and pragmatic reasons. Reallocations through incomplete or inaccurate information will be short-lived and will have negative consequences, for alternative feedback mechanisms will emerge to inform and redirect the system, albeit slowly and only after damage becomes evident. Complex social systems can be manipulated for a time but tend to have redundant capacities that make them robust and resistant to artificial feedback. Nonetheless, if disinformation significantly disrupts adaptation to the environment, a complex enterprise will drift into stasis or plunge into chaos.

Such recognition is essential in fostering biblical scholarship. In fact, recognizing emergence has enabled the Society to accomplish much. Leadership and membership—working together and in concert with likeminded organizations, universities, and publishers—have advanced biblical scholarship in proportions and directions that could not have been forecast at the time of the Society's founding. Additionally, congresses and publications have proved to be effective feedback mechanisms for the profession. The task is not, however, diminished by the achievements. Kent Harold Richards reminded leadership and membership in his 2005 annual report that the mission, vision, and values of the Society must be assessed periodically and always translated into tangible programs and initiatives: "Our vision is clear, as evidenced by our seven strategic visions. We must continually evaluate them, but more importantly, at this time we must secure these strategic visions with concrete operational strategies and tactics."[39] Accordingly, areas that promise new developments and routinely create, refine, and redirect understandings of the Bible merit early and sustained recognition. Four areas stand out in the history of biblical interpretation.

The first is the discovery of evidentiary material artifacts. In the world of biblical scholarship, a discovery of material evidence elicits numerous publications and presentations that examine and reexamine the authenticity, provenance, classification, and implications of the artifact—whether textual, monumental, or ordinary household items, day-to-day apparel, and other "small things forgotten."[40] A relatively minor find generates broad public attention and extensive scholarly debate, and it does so for two reasons: the potential ramifications for religious perspectives and stakeholders and the paucity of the current available evidence undergirding historical reconstructions.[41] One is reminded of the lively exchanges

---

39. Kent Harold Richards, "[Director's Letter]," *SBL Society Report* (2005): 2.

40. Philip J. King and Lawrence E. Stager, *Life in Biblical Israel* (Library of Ancient Israel; Louisville: Westminster John Knox, 2001), 1. King and Stager draw the phrase from James Deetz, *In Small Things Forgotten: An Archaeology of Early American Life* (New York: Doubleday, 1996).

41. Walter E. Aufrecht quips, "It has been remarked that archaeologists in North America developed archaeological theory out of necessity because they have so few artifacts to talk about. And while this statement has a grain of truth to it, it must also be remarked that because archaeologists of the ancient Near East have so many artifacts, they often devote little reflection to what an artifact is or how they deter-

between minimalist and maximalist historians regarding the Tel Dan inscription and its apparent reference to the "House of David." It is fair to say that these two words, *byt dwd*, provoked two monographs, dozens of articles, countless references, and an ongoing debate.[42] Major and minor finds abound, but the discovery of the Dead Sea Scrolls, which could prompt then sustain publication of a focused journal, *Dead Sea Discoveries: A Journal of Current Research on the Scrolls and Related Literature* (Brill, 1994–), four decades after the fact and in the aftermath of a divisive controversy regarding access to the documents, demonstrates the impact of a major find.[43] A discovery need not be sensational to be profound. The pioneering work of Sir William Matthew Flinders Petrie at Tell el-Ḥesi, though less sensational than his discovery of the Merneptah Stela, has had a profound impact on archaeology by demonstrating that the mound was composed of debris layers that afforded a relative chronology of settlements, which he correlated with styles of pottery.[44]

A second is the foregrounding of unattended variables. A variable is an abstraction of factors, which are characteristics or circumstances that influence other variables and outcomes. For example, *sex* is an abstraction of the factors *male, female,* and *intersex*.[45] Though drawn from the vocabulary of quantitative research, the term *variable* is certainly applicable to biblical interpretation, which considers not only texts but also authors and

---

mine what they think it is" ("What Does the Tel Dan Inscription Say and How Do We Know It?" *BASOR* 345 [2007]: 63).

42. George Athas, *The Tel Dan Inscription: A Reappraisal and a New Interpretation* (JSOTSup 360; Sheffield: Sheffield Academic Press, 2003); and Hallvard Hagelia, *The Tel Dan Inscription: A Critical Investigation of Recent Research on Its Palaeography and Philology* (Studia Semitica Upsaliensia 22; Uppsala: Uppsala University, 2006). Recent articles include Matthew Suriano, "The Apology of Hazael: A Literary and Historical Analysis of the Tel Dan Inscription," *JNES* 66 (2007):163–76; and Lisa Fosdal, "Was the Tel Dan Inscription Referring to '*BYTDWD*' as a Fundamentalistic Faction?" *SJOT* 23 (2009): 85–102. See also the analysis in Lawrence J. Mykytiuk, *Identifying Biblical Persons in Northwest Semitic Inscriptions of 1200–539 B.C.E.* (SBLAcBib 12; Atlanta: Society of Biblical Literature, 2004), 114–32.

43. James H. Charlesworth, "Sense or Sensationalism: The Dead Sea Scrolls Controversy," *ChrCent* 109 (29 January 1992): 92–98.

44. W. F. Stinespring, "Flinders Petrie—1853–1942," *BA* 5 (September 1942): 35. See also Margaret S. Drower, *Flinders Petrie: A Life in Archaeology* (London: Gollancz, 1985).

45. I. A. Hughes, "Intersex," *BJU International* 90 (2002): 769–76.

readers, who are "conditioned by a range of variables—social, economical, political, ecclesiastical, doctrinal, methodological, and philosophical."[46] Biblical scholarship progresses when previously unrecognized variables are identified and explored. For instance, the foregrounding of gender, through the political initiatives of first-, second-, and third-wave feminisms and in feminist, womanist, *muejerista*, and related theoretical reflections and readings of biblical texts, has transformed mainline biblical scholarship, and biblical feminist studies may yet emerge as an autonomous academic discipline.[47]

A third area to monitor is the application of new reading strategies. Critical methods abound in biblical interpretation, but the introduction of a new strategy invites experimentation that can lead to broad recognition and adoption of the method.[48] For instance, the early stages of the process are evident in Brill's publication of the ten-year-old Pericope series, which applies delimitation criticism to unit demarcations in biblical manuscripts. New reading strategies address perceived shortcomings in established methods, and delimitation criticism considers textual evidence that has been neglected by exegetes.[49] Similarly, rhetorical criticism, the first concern of which "is to define the limits or scope of the literary unit, to recognize precisely where and how it begins and where and how it ends," addressed limitations in form criticism, which, in turn, had compensated for excesses in source and literary criticism.[50] Nevertheless, as the title and the concluding paragraph of James Muilenburg's seminal article emphasize, the new does not displace the old: "We affirm the

---

46. W. Randolph Tate, *Biblical Interpretation: An Integrated Approach* (3rd ed.; Peabody, Mass.: Hendrickson, 2008), 103.

47. Esther Fuchs, "Biblical Feminisms: Knowledge, Theory and Politics in the Study of Women in the Hebrew Bible," *BibInt* 16 (2008): 205–26.

48. On newer methods, see Janice Capel Anderson and Stephen D. Moore, eds., *Mark and Method: New Approaches in Biblical Studies* (2nd ed.; Minneapolis: Fortress, 2008); Gail A. Yee, ed., *Judges and Method: New Approaches in Biblical Studies* (2nd ed.; Minneapolis: Fortress, 2007); and Richard N. Soulen and R. K. Soulen, *Handbook of Biblical Criticism* (3rd ed.; Louisville: Westminster John Knox, 2001).

49. The most recent volume in the series is Raymond de Hoop, Marjo C. A. Korpel, and Stanley E. Porter, eds., *The Impact of Unit Delimitation on Exegesis* (Pericope 7; Leiden: Brill, 2008).

50. James Muilenburg, "Form Criticism and Beyond," *JBL* 88 (1969): 1–18; quotation from 8–9.

necessity of form criticism, but we also lay claim to the legitimacy of what we have called rhetorical criticism. Form criticism and beyond."[51]

A fourth area is the appropriation of emerging technologies. Biblical scholarship entails close reading, and reading is "shaped by the technologies of the scroll, the codex, the [printed] book, and the screen."[52] The activity is enhanced and constrained by the design of the medium, and each technology affects the intertextuality of reading. The scroll encourages linear reading and limits comparison within the document to neighboring columns of text. The codex, on the other hand, facilitates direct and rapid movement between noncontiguous pages. Mass production makes it possible to own and simultaneously compare the contents of printed books. Computer technology allows the reader to connect and compare related passages from large digital collections. The technology of the codex undergirded christological readings of Old Testament texts, the printed book personalized the study of the Bible, and affordable digital technology is democratizing biblical scholarship in both significant and superficial ways. Wireless access, handheld devices, and high-speed networks are making popular-level scholarship ubiquitous and university-class scholarship more collaborative. The technological future of biblical scholarship cannot be predicted, but software packages such as Accordance, BibleWorks, and Logos and manuscript digitizations such as the Sinai Codex Project afford glimpses.[53]

Conclusion

Conditions that foster biblical scholarship include (1) a mission that advances with the discipline and (2) processes that recognize promising developments, especially the discovery and interpretation of material evidence, the identification and foregrounding of variables that have been neglected, the development and application of new methods, and the appropriation of emerging information technologies.

Practical concerns also abound, and those who dare to foster biblical

---

51. Ibid., 18.
52. Jeffrey Masten, Peter Stallybrass, and Nancy Vickers, "Introduction: Language Machines," in *Language Machines: Technologies of Literary and Cultural Production* (ed. Jeffrey Masten, Peter Stallybrass, and Nancy Vickers; Essays from the English Institute; London: Routledge, 1997), 2.
53. "Codex Sinaiticus," http://codexsinaiticus.org/en/.

scholarship will face, to a greater and lesser degree, the antagonisms of ignorance and power, both of which are born of fear. Innovation generates dissonance and can unleash resistance. The neglected variable may have been neglected for a reason, and exposure makes vulnerable the mechanisms of power. Knowledge is power, and biblical scholarship can be interpreted as an assault on sacred and social bastions, even when no attack is intended. Biblical scholars themselves must expose their own interests and inclinations, and institutions of higher learning must safeguard academic freedoms and courageous acts of scholarship. Ultimately, the conditions that foster biblical scholarship—a mission that advances with the discipline and the recognition of promising new developments—are the products of an environment that is truly academic.

Bibliography

Alexander, Patrick H., John F. Kutsko, James D. Ernest, Shirley Decker-Lucke, and David L. Petersen, eds. *The SBL Handbook of Style for Ancient Near Eastern, Biblical, and Early Christian Studies*. Peabody, Mass.: Hendrickson, 1999.

Anderson, Janice C., and Stephen D. Moore, eds. *Mark and Method: New Approaches in Biblical Studies*. 2nd ed. Minneapolis: Fortress, 2008.

Athas, George. *The Tel Dan Inscription: A Reappraisal and a New Interpretation*. JSOTSup 360. Sheffield: Sheffield Academic Press, 2003.

Aufrecht, Walter E. "What Does the Tel Dan Inscription Say and How Do We Know It?" *BASOR* 345 (2007): 63–70.

Avalos, Hector. *The End of Biblical Studies*. Amherst: Prometheus, 2007.

———. "Whither Biblical Studies?" *CSSR Bulletin* 38 (2009): 13–15.

Berlinerblau, Jacques. *The Secular Bible*. New York: Cambridge University Press, 2005.

Bultmann, Rudolf. "Ist voraussetzungslose Exegese müglich?" *TZ* 13 (1957): 409–17.

Charlesworth, James H. "Sense or Sensationalism: The Dead Sea Scrolls Controversy." *ChrCent* 109 (January 29, 1992): 92–98.

Childs, Brevard S. *Introduction to the Old Testament as Scripture*. Philadelphia: Fortress, 1979.

Cilliers, Paul. *Complexity and Postmodernism: Understanding Complex Systems*. London: Routledge, 1998.

Collins, John J. *The Bible after Babel: Historical Criticism in a Postmodern Age*. Grand Rapids: Eerdmans, 2005.

De Hoop, Raymond, Marjo C. A. Korpel, and Stanley E. Porter, eds. *The Impact of Unit Delimitation on Exegesis*. Pericope 7. Leiden: Brill, 2008.
Deetz, James. *In Small Things Forgotten: An Archaeology of Early American Life*. New York: Doubleday, 1996.
Drower, Margaret S. *Flinders Petrie: A Life in Archaeology*. London: Gollancz, 1985.
Ekblad, Bob. *Reading the Bible with the Damned*. Louisville: Westminster John Knox, 2005.
Exum, J. Cheryl. *Plotted, Shot, and Painted: Cultural Representations of Biblical Women*. JSOTSup 215. Sheffield: Sheffield Academic Press, 1996.
Fish, Stanley E. *Is There a Text in This Class? The Authority of Interpretive Communities*. Cambridge: Harvard University Press, 1980.
Fosdal, Lisa. "Was the Tel Dan Inscription Referring to '*BYTDWD*' as a Fundamentalistic Faction?" *SJOT* 23 (2009): 85–102.
Fuchs, Esther. "Biblical Feminisms: Knowledge, Theory and Politics in the Study of Women in the Hebrew Bible." *BibInt* 16 (2008): 205–26.
Funk, Robert W. "The Watershed of the American Biblical Tradition: The Chicago School, First Phase, 1892–1920." *JBL* 95 (1976): 4–22.
Habermas, Jürgen. "Modernity versus Postmodernity." *New German Critique* 22 (1981): 3–14.
Habermas, Jürgen. *Knowledge and Human Interests*. Boston: Beacon, 1971.
Hagelia, Hallvard. *The Tel Dan Inscription: A Critical Investigation of Recent Research on Its Palaeography and Philology*. Studia Semitica Upsaliensia 22. Uppsala: Uppsala University, 2006.
Hirsch, E. D. *The Aims of Interpretation*. Chicago: University of Chicago Press, 1976.
———. *Validity in Interpretation*. New Haven: Yale University Press, 1967.
Hughes, I. A. "Intersex." *BJU International* 90 (2002): 769–76.
King, Philip J., and Lawrence E. Stager. *Life in Biblical Israel*. Library of Ancient Israel. Louisville: Westminster John Knox, 2001.
Klein, Ralph W., Gary Stansell, and Walter Brueggemann. "The Childs Proposal: A Symposium." *WW* 1 (1981): 105–15.
Kurtz, Cynthia F., and David J. Snowden. "The New Dynamics of Strategy: Sense-Making in a Complex and Complicated World." *IBM Systems Journal* 42 (2003): 462–83.
Loetscher, Lefferts Augustine. "C. A. Briggs in the Retrospect of Half a Century." *ThTo* 12 (1955): 27–42.

Mason, Wendy H., and Hal P. Kirkwood Jr. "Complexity Theory." Pages 95–98 in *Encyclopedia of Management*. Edited by Marilyn M. Helms. 5th ed. Farmington Hills, Mich.: Gale Group, 2005.

Masten, Jeffrey, Peter Stallybrass, and Nancy Vickers. "Introduction: Language Machines." Pages 1–16 in *Language Machines: Technologies of Literary and Cultural Production*. Edited by Jeffrey Masten, Peter Stallybrass, and Nancy Vickers. Essays from the English Institute. London: Routledge, 1997.

McCole, John. *Walter Benjamin and the Antinomies of Tradition*. Ithaca, N.Y.: Cornell University Press, 1993.

McKenzie, Steven L., and Stephen R. Haynes, eds. *To Each Its Own Meaning: An Introduction to Biblical Criticisms and Their Applications*. Rev. ed. Louisville: Westminster John Knox, 1999.

Miller, John H., and Scott E. Page. *Complex Adaptive Systems: An Introduction to Computational Models of Social Life*. Princeton Studies in Complexity. Princeton: Princeton University Press, 2007.

Mitchel, H. G. "Proceedings." *JBL* 4 (1884): 150–60.

Montgomery, James A. "Present Tasks of American Biblical Scholarship." *JBL* 38 (1991): 1–14.

Muilenburg, James. "Form Criticism and Beyond." *JBL* 88 (1969): 1–18.

Mykytiuk, Lawrence J. *Identifying Biblical Persons in Northwest Semitic Inscriptions of 1200–539 B.C.E.*. SBLAcBib 12. Atlanta: Society of Biblical Literature, 2004.

Noll, Mark A. *Between Faith and Criticism*. 2nd ed. Grand Rapids: Baker, 1991.

Ricart, Joan Enric, and Adrian A. Caldart. "Complexity Theory." Pages 229–34 in *International Encyclopedia of Organizational Studies*. Edited by Stewart R. Clegg and James R. Bailey. Thousand Oaks, Calif.: Sage, 2008.

Richards, Larry. *Creative Bible Study: A Handbook for Small Group, Family, and Personal Bible Study*. Grand Rapids: Zondervan, 1971.

Richards, Kent Harold. "[Director's Letter]." *SBL Society Report* (2005): 2.

———. "Future Directions." *SBL Society Report* (2007): 16.

———. "Leadership with New Vision." *SBL Society Report* (2003): 3.

———. "New Strategic Vision." *SBL Society Report* (2004): 10.

Saunders, Ernest W. *Searching the Scriptures: A History of the Society of Biblical Literature, 1880—1980*. SBLBSNA 8. Chico, Calif.: Scholars Press, 1982.

Schüssler Fiorenza, Elisabeth. *Rhetoric and Ethics: The Politics of Biblical Studies*. Minneapolis: Fortress, 1999.
Slavens, Thomas P. "The Librarianship of Charles Augustus Briggs." *USQR* 24 (1969): 357–63.
Smith, Henry Preserved. "Old Testament Ideals: Presidential Address, 1909." *JBL* 29 (1910): 1–20.
Snowden, David J., and Mary E. Boone. "A Leader's Framework for Decision Making." *HBR* (November 2007): 69–76.
Soulen, Richard N., and R. K. Soulen. *Handbook of Biblical Criticism*. 3rd ed. Louisville: Westminster John Knox, 2001.
Stendahl, Krister. "Biblical Theology, Contemporary." *IDB* 1:418–32.
Stinespring, W. F. "Flinders Petrie—1853–1942." *BA* 5 (September 1942): 33–36.
Suriano, Matthew. "The Apology of Hazael: A Literary and Historical Analysis of the Tel Dan Inscription." *JNES* 66 (2007): 163–76.
Tate, W. Randolph. *Biblical Interpretation: An Integrated Approach*. 3rd ed. Peabody, Mass.: Hendrickson, 2008.
Waldrop, M. Mitchel. *Complexity: The Emerging Science at the Edge of Order and Chaos*. New York: Simon & Schuster, 1992.
Yee, Gale A., ed. *Judges and Method: New Approaches in Biblical Studies*. 2nd ed. Minneapolis: Fortress, 2007.

The Modern (and Postmodern?) Society of Biblical Literature: Institutions and Scholarship

Gene M. Tucker

At the one hundredth meeting of the Society of Biblical Literature, held in New York in 1964, I was standing outside the auditorium where a distinguished scholar was delivering an address. Before the presentation was finished, Theodore Gaster, the noted historian of religion, came storming out of the hall muttering: "Well, just as I expected. Nothing new is happening in biblical studies."

There are legitimate criticisms of the discipline today and of its major organization, the Society of Biblical Literature, but Gaster's accusation is not among them. One only has to observe the breadth and diversity of the SBL Annual Meeting program, the programs of regional meetings, and the long list of publications by the Society to conclude that we have an embarrassment of riches. At the Annual Meeting held in New Orleans in 2009, the President of the Society reported a conversation with several senior scholars outside the publishers' book displays. Those members of my generation were complaining that far too many books were being published these days. The President asked them if they were willing to address that problem by agreeing to stop their own writing and publishing.

Scholarship may shape institutions, but institutions certainly shape scholarship. My goal here is threefold: to give an account of some of the transformations of the institutions that have supported biblical studies over the last forty years, especially the Society of Biblical Literature; to sketch the major currents in contemporary biblical interpretation, particularly the appropriation and development of a range of alternatives to historical-critical scholarship; and to reflect on some of the problems and possibilities of our present institutional and methodological situation.

As the two anecdotes above already indicate, this essay will combine oral history and analysis, both of which are suspect, and for good reason.

Oral history (even if written down) consists of the recollections of a single individual. One does not need to be a critical historian, only a participant in any conversations about the past, to know that recollections can be flawed for various reasons. Beyond the loss from the biological deterioration of brain cells, memories are shaped by individual perspective, including ideology. Although juries may tend to trust it, attorneys will confirm that eyewitness evidence is among the least reliable testimony.[1] As for analysis, all of us are in the business of analyzing and of calling into question and disagreeing with analysis.

Institutions

I begin by drawing upon my own experience to compare the present state of affairs in North American biblical scholarship with what it was more than fifty years ago when I entered the Society of Biblical Literature as a college student. It is obvious that in North America, and around the world as well, there have been major transformations of the institutions that surround and support scholarship. My point of departure is the change in the Society of Biblical Literature over the past fifty years, but such changes are representative of, and in large measure the result of, other social and economic forces of the period.

I became a member of the Society in 1957 and, until quite recently, participated in every Annual Meeting since 1959. The meetings of the Society of Biblical Literature in the late 1950s and early 1960s were small gatherings of perhaps two hundred members at Union Theological Seminary in New York. Virtually all who attended were white males. Ernest W. Saunders described the Society as

> essentially an east coast establishment based in New York City consisting of a small staff of officers and a regional attendance at the meetings.... In substance it was an amplified faculty club, benevolently presided over by a cadre of senior and highly respected scholars who enjoyed proprietary rights among awed but ambitious junior colleagues.[2]

---

1. Jennifer L. Overbeck, "Beyond Admissibility: A Practical Look at the Use of Eyewitness Expert Testimony in the Federal Courts," *New York University Law Review* 80 (2005): 1898.

2. Ernest W. Saunders, *Searching the Scriptures: A History of the Society of Biblical Literature, 1880–1980* (SBLBSNA 8; Chico, Calif.: Scholars Press, 1982), 41.

I remember well that junior members were to be seen and not heard. Typically, the meetings had all of two or three sessions going on at the same time, one Old Testament and one New Testament. There was, of course, a plenary meeting for the presidential address.

But in the mid-1960s the winds of change were blowing, even in the staid bastions of scholarship. First, there was the creation of the American Academy of Religion out of the old National Association of Biblical Instructors that had for decades met with the Society. This development, of course, was part and parcel of major changes in higher education in North America, with the growth of departments of religion in colleges and universities, including state universities.

The most significant change in the Society of Biblical Literature since the initial meeting of eighteen scholars in 1880 was the approval of a revised constitution and by-laws at the Annual Meeting in Toronto in 1969. A number of members, both young and old, were involved in the transformation of the Society, but the architect and visionary was Robert W. Funk, to whom we owe a great debt of gratitude for what we have become. One hardly thinks of the orderly revision of a constitution as a revolution, but this one was—perhaps because the members of the biblical guild take written texts so seriously. The effects of those changes, and the others that came in their train, have been far-reaching, reshaping both the form and substance of biblical scholarship. The action in 1969 included the following:

First, it included the establishment of term limits for the officers and the introduction of a structure to encourage wide participation in leadership, including by younger scholars. This meant that many who had ruled the organization and the discipline would have to step aside. What those who opposed the changes feared has come to pass: the old elite organization quickly become more democratic, open, and inclusive. By the turn of the millennium, there were several hundred active participants in the Society at the national level, even more in the regions. These include chairs and members of committees, participants in the program, editors, members of editorial boards, and authors of books published by the Society. Far more persons are in active leadership positions today than actually attended the meetings before 1969.

Second, it established a publications program, which began with the creation of the SBL's Research and Publications Committee. The scholarly guild intended to take the initiative for the publication of scholarship. This step was quickly followed by the invention of Scholars Press, again under the leadership of Funk, and in collaboration with the AAR and other societies. Scholars Press, which also provided the professional management of the Annual Meetings, was initially located at the University of Montana. (Not so incidentally, that location only symbolized another significant change: by the 1970s the geographical center of biblical as well as other scholarship had moved west and south of New York and New England.)

Peer review and a volunteer editorial process were at the heart of the publications program. I recall reviewing an early submission and found it worthy of publication, but I reported to Funk that the typescript was sloppy and, in fact, ugly, and therefore I recommended it be retyped. He replied, "No. Let it go as it is. It will be embarrassing and will encourage future authors to improve." It did.

Why did the Society go to all the trouble of becoming a publisher? There were vigorous debates about that very question in the years immediately following the constitutional revolution. In the context of expanding higher education and departments of religion, Funk argued that our tribe of biblical scholars would not survive unless its members could be tenured, and that could not happen without publications. So a Darwinian metaphor is apt: to survive and grow, our species needed to adapt, to take charge of the publication of its own work.

We continue to bear the fruits of the vision that scholars would initiate, edit, publish, and distribute their work at relatively low cost to students and teachers. Fifty years ago, there was one North American series that published scholarly monographs in biblical studies (the SBL Monograph Series), and it published a book every three or four years. Today the publications program of the SBL alone includes two journals, the traditional *Journal of Biblical Literature* and the *Review of Biblical Literature*, mainly online but also in print. Soon after the publications program began there was a third journal, *Semeia*, explicitly experimental and dialogical, which, after 2002, became a book series. For decades, the Society has published more than twenty-five books each year. In 2008 the Society published some thirty-three new titles, not counting reprints. It is worth emphasizing that the publisher of these works from the beginning was not its partner, Scholars Press, but the Society, whose editors, editorial boards, and Research and Publications Committee continue to make the all-important decisions concerning what is to be printed and distributed by the press. It is a peer process from beginning to end. Now the publications program is an explicit wing of the Society.

Furthermore, the Society has taken seriously the need to interpret biblical scholarship to audiences beyond itself, initially through a program with HarperCollins but with others as well. Edited and written by members of the Society are *The HarperCollins Bible Dictionary, The Harper's Bible Commentary,* and *The HarperCollins Study Bible*.[3] Income generated from the sale of these volumes helps support the technical research and publications program.

As a result of these efforts, as well as those by organizations such as JSOT Press, with its monograph series and *Journal for the Study of the Old Testament*, commercial houses are publishing many more serious works, some in collaboration with professional societies. In short, the sheer amount of research being circulated has taken a quantum leap forward.

The third change set into motion in 1969 concerned the program of the Society's Annual Meeting. The goal was to invite wider participation as well as diverse forms of scholarly communication, from seminars with specific research agendas to groups to sections. It is a lively and often productive affair, and it has become essential not only for scholarly communication but also for the business of the discipline at many levels, including job placement. The early hope for genuinely collaborative research has met with only limited success.

If the number of participants is the measure—and not everyone agrees that it is—then the Annual Meeting program is a rousing success. More than half of the membership (approaching 9,000) attends the meeting. Registration has grown steadily to the point that the meeting often involves approximately 5,000 participants. In the middle of an economic crisis, the 2009 meeting registered approximately 4,500. Even more significant are the number and diversity of program units. To be sure, these developments are not without problems, and many, if not most, of them are closely related to the scholarly issues that we face and to the methods that we now employ, problems to which we will turn later.

The vision for the meeting of the Society was dramatically expanded under the leadership of Kent Harold Richards—the last of the volunteer Executive Secretaries—with the initiation of an additional gathering, an

---

3. Paul J. Achtemeier et al., eds., *The HarperCollins Bible Dictionary* (rev. ed.; San Francisco: HarperSanFrancisco, 1996), and the abridged version, Mark Allan Powell, ed., *HarperCollins Bible Dictionary* (New York: HarperOne, 2009); James Luther Mays et al., eds., *The Harper's Bible Commentary* (rev. ed.; San Francisco, HarperSanFrancisco, 2000); and Harold W. Attridge, ed., *The HarperCollins Study Bible: Revised Edition* (San Francisco: HarperSanFrancisco, 2006).

International Meeting. Those meetings now register far more participants than did the Annual Meetings that were held before 1969. Meeting initially in Europe, but then in other parts of the globe, the International Meetings expanded the democratizing policies of that constitutional revision.

As indicated above, the changes in the Society did not occur in a vacuum but were shaped by demographic factors and developments in higher education. As the first wave of the baby boomers began college in the early 1960s, colleges and universities were growing rapidly, as were departments of religion. Because of court rulings concerning the study of religion, new positions or departments were created in state universities.

Now, because of demographic as well as economic forces, some of those gains are being lost, but by no means all of them. The scholarly study of the Bible and of religion is here to stay in North American higher education. The pattern of expansion and contraction applies as well to theological education. Seminaries were expanding and some new ones were established in the 1960s, but they were contracting or even closing as early as the 1980s and 1990s. Now the future of some theological schools appears to be in doubt.

In the era of the 1960s and 1970s there was a significant increase in the number of universities offering Ph.D. degrees in biblical studies and other areas in religion. There is ebb and flow here as well. Remarkably, some of the strongest programs today (judged by recent reports as well as more "objective" factors such as money, numbers, and placement of graduates) did not exist fifty years ago or were just being established.

One other significant cultural if not institutional force must be mentioned. To say that technological change has been dramatic in the last fifty years is an understatement. Three or four decades ago, most scholars composed work on the manual typewriter, a once revolutionary technological innovation that now makes headlines only in news about criminal cases, such as the case of Theodore Kaczynski, the Unabomber.[4] Those days—before there was a computer on every desk and in every briefcase, before there were SBL fonts for biblical languages, and before digital biblical texts and reference works became readily accessible not only on desktops and laptops but even in handheld electronic devices—now seem like the Dark

---

4. See Delphine Gardey, "Mechanizing Writing and Photographing the Word: Utopias, Office Work, and Histories of Gender and Technology," *History and Technology* 17 (2001): 319–52.

Ages. In the mid-1960s and even into the early 1980s, the most advanced technology that was readily available for the preparation of technical manuscripts was the IBM Selectric typewriter, because it used interchangeable font elements (balls) that allowed the biblical scholar to switch between English, Hebrew, and Greek character sets.

The present use of the computer for composition and the laser printer to prepare camera-ready copy for publication is only the tip of the technological iceberg. Reference works and bibliographical databases are readily accessible, both to libraries and individuals. Highly sophisticated means for both the storage and analysis of ancient texts are available. Within just the last two decades we have seen a virtual explosion of access to and use of the Internet and e-mail communication.

Various forms of electronic communication and publication are, quite literally, at our fingertips. Although electronic journals have begun to appear, biblical studies, like most of the humanities, are far behind the sciences in this respect. But the Society is making progress. It is safe to say that members now read book reviews online in *The Review of Biblical Literature*, and the *Journal of Biblical Literature* is available on the Society's website before it ever appears in print. Other online, peer-reviewed publications have appeared, including *The Journal of Hebrew Scriptures*. Early fears that electronic publications would not be taken as seriously as the printed page seem not to have been realized. To be sure, such rapid change in the form of scholarly communication brings questions and problems that are economic, cultural, and intellectual, including concerns about the exclusion of some. Early on, many expressed concern that these technological developments would leave behind scholars who do not have electronic resources. One hears such concerns less frequently now, and it seems safe to predict that electronic forms of communication and publication will continue to advance, and rapidly.

Trends in Biblical Scholarship

Fifty years ago, the issues facing North American biblical scholarship—and I focus primarily on the study of the Hebrew Bible—seemed relatively clear. The main choices for students were whether they would focus on historical and archaeological research, on the one hand, or upon historical exegesis, on the other. Most work in North America was historical and archaeological, and there were two main camps: the American Albright camp and the German Noth and Alt camp. John Bright's *Early Israel and*

Recent History Writing summarized the status of the most important debate: Could more (the American) or less (the German) be said about the history of early Israel?[5] The main American contribution was biblical archaeology and a theory of history. Those who followed Alt and Noth, as well as those of us who turned our attention to exegesis, constantly looked over our shoulders to Germany. British scholarship was moribund; Israel produced some archaeological work, but little more, and a student could safely navigate graduate school without reading any new works in French. But the center of gravity did not remain in Europe. By the celebration of the centennial of the SBL in 1980, one could legitimately claim that North American biblical scholarship had come of age.

More significantly, the issues are now far more complicated than they were fifty, or even ten, years ago. In the 1960s, one could review H. H. Rowley's *The Old Testament and Modern Study* and find a solid consensus on most major issues, from the source criticism of the Pentateuch to the question of the Bible in the modern world. Successors to that volume by the British Society for Old Testament Study, *The Hebrew Bible and Its Modern Interpreters* and, more recently, *Old Testament Interpretation: Past, Present, and Future*, have analyzed the main lines of development according to both the bodies of biblical literature and methods of interpretation.[6]

The categories of fifty years ago were relatively simple and seemed straightforward to us, even self-evident: typically, history, literature, languages, theology, and religion. This is the way that doctoral exams were ordered—and still are in many cases—and this is the way that most of us organized our libraries and bibliographies. Within categories, topics were developed historically: (1) History focused on the history of Israel, archaeology, and ancient Near Eastern backgrounds. (2) Literature, or introduction in the technical sense, considered the shape and contents of the biblical books. Included in this category were the methodologies

---

5. John Bright, *Early Israel in Recent History Writing: A Study in Method* (SBT 19; London: SCM, 1956).

6. H. H. Rowley, ed., *The Old Testament and Modern Study* (Oxford: Clarendon, 1951); Douglas A. Knight and Gene M. Tucker, eds., *The Hebrew Bible and Its Modern Interpreters* (SBLBMI 1; Philadelphia: Fortress; Decatur, Ga.: Scholars Press, 1985); James Luther Mays, David L. Petersen, and Kent Harold Richards, eds., *Old Testament Interpretation: Past, Present, and Future: Essays in Honor of Gene M. Tucker* (Nashville: Abingdon, 1995).

of source, form, tradition, redaction, and textual criticism, and, with the exception of the analysis of the shape and contents of the literature, all of these entailed historical inquiry, both into the history of the development of the literature and of its historical context. (3) Languages involved the study of the grammar, philology, and lexicography of biblical and other ancient Near Eastern texts. These were—and still are—pursued in fundamentally historical terms, although it is increasingly recognized that definition and translation are established more by context than by etymology. (4) Theology of the Old Testament was pursued, and the dominant perspectives related to the history of Israel (following G. Ernest Wright and John Bright) or to Israel's historical credo (following Gerhard von Rad).[7] Both approaches were understood in terms of historical development. In the 1960s and 1970s, Krister Stendahl's distinction between descriptive and normative biblical theology became commonplace.[8] (5) The religion of Israel and its neighbors was pursued but commanded relatively little attention and could be subsumed under the category of history, since religion was examined almost entirely in terms of its historical development. In terms of methodology, this situation has not changed significantly, although there are some moves to examine religion in more phenomenological terms.

Thirty years ago some were announcing the end of the historical-critical method or, only somewhat more modestly, a paradigm shift from historical to literary categories. Whether or not we have experienced such a paradigm shift—and there is some evidence that we have—the terrain of biblical scholarship has changed dramatically so that it can be mapped only with difficulty.

Many of the changes and new developments can be seen by comparing two volumes addressing the current state of the discipline, then and now. The first, *The Hebrew Bible and Its Modern Interpreters*, was published among the works commemorating the one-hundredth anniversary of the Society of Biblical Literature in 1980. Seven of the fifteen chapters looked at the discipline thematically (e.g., Israelite history, Israelite reli-

---

7. G. Ernest Wright, *God Who Acts: Biblical Theology as Recital* (SBT 8; London: SCM, 1952); John Bright, *The Kingdom of God: The Biblical Concept and Its Meaning for the Church* (New York: Abingdon-Cokesbury, 1953); Gerhard von Rad, *Old Testament Theology* (trans. D. M. G. Stalker; 2 vols.; New York: Harper, 1962), 1:121–39.

8. Krister Stendahl, "Biblical Theology, Contemporary," *IDB* 1:418–32.

gion, and ancient Near Eastern environment).⁹ All but two of the chapters focused almost exclusively on historical-critical issues: one, "Exploring New Directions," considered new developments in literary and sociological methods, and the other considered the theology of the Hebrew Bible. Another seven chapters considered developments in the study of the different parts of the canon, and a final chapter dealt with the Hebrew Bible and modern culture. Although new impulses were recognized, it seems clear that the energy of the first decade and a half since the SBL revolution was devoted mainly to historical-critical inquiry.

The second volume, published just last year, is *Method Matters: Essays on the Interpretation of the Hebrew Bible in Honor of David L. Petersen,* also published by the SBL.¹⁰ Explicitly focused on methods and approaches, the book is not organized according to parts of the canon, and a review of the table of contents demonstrates how methods have proliferated in the last three decades. Historical-critical methods are alive and well, for chapters address form, source, redaction, textual, and traditio-historical criticism, and it is clear from the remaining chapters that a great many ways of investigating and interpreting the Hebrew Bible have gained sufficient followings and clarity that they deserve to be called *methods,* both modern and postmodern. Beyond that are distinctive approaches, which could be identified as ideological or hermeneutical visions, such as feminist criticism, ecological approaches, and liberationist readings, among others.

Today the categories by which one might organize methods and approaches are neither simple, self-evident, nor straightforward. It is clear, however, that those older divisions of the discipline do not begin to include all that biblical scholars are doing. Caricatures and oversimplifications abound in this discussion of the "older methods" and of the new, and from those who identify themselves with one camp or the other, but caricatures and oversimplifications are not helpful.

In terms of a broad framework for understanding current methods as such, the major recent trends alongside of and beyond historical forms of inquiry are two: literary-critical and social-scientific approaches. In most instances, literary critics disengage from the questions of the author-

---

9. Knight and Tucker, *The Hebrew Bible*, v–ix.
10. Joel M. LeMon and Kent Harold Richards, eds., *Method Matters: Essays on the Interpretation of the Hebrew Bible in Honor of David L. Petersen* (SBLRBS 56; Atlanta: Society of Biblical Literature, 2009), vii–ix.

ship, date, and development of the book or text in question, analyzing and interpreting it as it stands, in the so-called "final form." However, it was not so long ago in the study of the Hebrew Bible that "literary criticism" was synonymous with source criticism. The second trend, the application of methods from the social sciences, is not entirely new, although the form, substance, and the results are significantly different.

A somewhat different and popular way of organizing current methods is in terms of the three foci of study: the first, concern with the world *behind* the text, is author-centered and encompasses most of the well-established historical-critical methods as well as many of the social-scientific approaches; the second, concern with the world *within* the text, would include many but not all of the literary approaches, particularly those derived from new criticism, rhetorical criticism, various incarnations of formalism, and poetics; the third, concern with the world in *front* of the text, includes the reader-centered or reader-response approaches.

But even these broad categories are problematic. On the one hand, the situation is unstable, with many critics refusing—legitimately—to be confined to a single pigeonhole. Moreover, some argue that the very effort to make sense of the situation in terms of such categories is a misguided and distinctly "modern" interest in a postmodern world. But most prefer to enter strange new lands with maps in hand, even if those maps must be revised at each crossroad. On the other hand, a listing of methods and of the subject of inquiry does not yet include all the important new dimensions of biblical study today. Our map must take account of a range of ideological interests that at points intersect with and at points conflict with the diverse approaches.

We turn now to a somewhat more detailed consideration of the three broad methodological trends: historical-critical, literary-critical, and social-scientific.

Although it has been under fire from many quarters for some time, historical-critical scholarship still is the dominant point of view and continues to generate the most work. This includes the history and archaeology of ancient Israel and those forms of exegesis concerned with the background and development of the texts: issues of authorship, oral history, tradition and redaction criticism. The authors of *The Postmodern Bible*, an excellent analysis of current developments, agree: "while the terrain has changed significantly, historical criticism has not ended, nor has traditional biblical scholarship been widely discredited, displaced, or taken up into a new synthesis. Instead, certain uncomfortable questions have come back with insistence."[11] Indeed, John Bright's *The History of Israel* continued to command the market and was widely used as the major textbook in a great many seminary and even college courses until quite recently.[12] Even as many scholars want to move beyond them, historical questions refuse to die. A major factor must be the power of late nineteenth- and early twentieth-century culture with its pervasive concern with the importance of what actually happened in history. For decades I have tried, with only limited success, to persuade students that there is a difference between history, the disciplined reconstruction of past events, and exegesis, or the interpretation of texts. Truth, for many, is in events more than in words. In many quarters, knowing "what really happened" is considered to be both possible and essential.

So historical inquiry persists, although there is no longer a set of assured results on any of the important questions. The old debate about what counts for evidence and how much can be said about ancient Israel is no longer limited to the earliest periods but applies to every era. The question of when one can begin the history of Israel has shifted from the Late Bronze or early Iron Ages to the Persian period. There is a lively debate on the issue under the heading of "the new historicism," a debate that is beautifully analyzed by Iain W. Provan in *JBL*.[13] The question of the authorship of the Pentateuch, once thought settled and then considered dead, is another lively battleground. The same could be said for the sources and the historical reliability of the Gospels. Some are calling the work of the Jesus Seminar the third quest for the historical Jesus, while others are calling it misguided.[14] But there is no mistaking the intense interest in historical questions, both among scholars and in the culture

---

11. George Aichele et al., *The Postmodern Bible: The Bible and Culture Collective* (New Haven: Yale University Press, 1995), 12.

12. John Bright, *A History of Israel* (4th ed.; Louisville: Westminster John Knox, 2000). The perspective of the volume is signaled by the dedicatory note, "To the Memory of WILLIAM FOXWELL ALBRIGHT in recognition of a debt of gratitude that cannot be repaid" (v). The current edition includes an introduction and appendix by William P. Brown.

13. Iain W. Provan, "Ideologies, Literary and Critical: Reflections on Recent History Writing on the History of Israel," *JBL* 114 (1995): 586–606.

14. See, e.g., the subtitles of Luke Timothy Johnson, *The Real Jesus: The Misguided Quest for the Historical Jesus and the Truth of the Traditional Gospels* (San Francisco: HarperSanFrancisco, 1996), and Ben Witherington III, *The Jesus Quest: The Third Search for the Jew of Nazareth* (2nd ed.; Downers Grove, Ill.: InterVarsity Press, 1997).

generally. Recent furor over the content of American history courses in public schools provides an example. The names, dates, and events that all American students should learn stirs intense debate, and it does so because power and politics are deeply and directly engaged in the way that social groups remember or report who they are. One is not surprised that politicians enter the discussion, for the story that is told defines identity individually and collectively. Would the story be traditional or newer and more diverse and complicated?

In an article on the study of the prophets, Patrick D. Miller said, "the prophets and their message are only intelligible in the context of an understanding of the social, political, and religious conditions and circumstances of their prophecy."[15] Not so long ago it would have been difficult to find biblical scholars who would question that judgment, and, at a certain level, it is difficult to dispute. To understand the prophets and their messages requires competence in an ancient language, Hebrew, and even to translate that language demands knowledge of such matters as allusions to ancient times and places. On the other hand, the prophetic words have been "intelligible" to millions of readers who knew not a word of Hebrew. To be sure, those readers rested on the work of scholars who, at least, knew Hebrew.

More to the point, many scholars now believe that interpretation of the prophetic words in their social, political, and religious context—that is, historically—is one critical approach among others. Historical inquiry is an honorable and centrally important vocation, and it is an approach that still bears fruit. Such research locates the prophetic literature in the framework of events and circumstances, sometimes reveals the problems addressed by the messages, and almost without exception shows the individual books to be the work of more than one hand or voice. In short, such an approach can show the depth and complexity of the books and connect the words to the stories of individuals and societies.

But to engage in historical interpretation requires knowing what it is for and what its limits are. It is *for* human self-understanding. Thus, to the extent that it is "objective," it means to understand human life from a distance. But that also means it is political to the core: the one who defines who I am rules me. Particularly for that reason historical inquiry must

---

15. Patrick D. Miller Jr., "The World and Message of the Prophets," in Mays, Petersen, and Richards, *Old Testament Interpretation*, 97.

always be aware of its *limits*. It can never say what actually happened but proposes reconstructions that at best are beyond a reasonable doubt. But it is important—indeed, essential—to say that much. It is often a matter of life and death, and not just in the law courts.

The two most enduring legacies of historical-critical inquiry are in tension with one another. On the one hand, historical research from the nineteenth century to the present day relativizes all events and all texts. They are specific or individual points on a continuum. Thus the crisis of historical consciousness was the recognition that this text—the Bible—did not fall down from heaven, nor was it written in our time and for us. We know and can never forget that the Hebrew Bible is an ancient oriental document. On the other hand, historical-critical study of the texts was and is based on the conviction that meaning resides *in* those texts, that, while there may not be *a* meaning of the Bible, individual texts have meanings. Texts have voices that can be recovered by serious study.

It is fundamentally at these two points that literary-critical readings have raised questions and posed alternatives to historical-critical interpretation. First, most contemporary literary critics challenge the view that biblical texts must be understood in their context and that study of the production of the text is essential to understanding it. Prominent here are text-centered approaches, some of which are indebted to new criticism. One of the first North American "schools" of literary analysis is the rhetorical criticism of James Muilenberg and his successors. This approach pays careful attention to the literary dimensions of the text, especially the compositional and literary techniques, such as inclusio, chiasm, wordplay, and repetition.[16] In the words of its most prominent practitioner, Phyllis Trible, "The concept of organic unity (form-content) underlies all rhetorical critical readings,"[17] and "a proper articulation of form-content yields a proper articulation of meaning."[18] Other literary approaches are those of Robert Alter, Adele Berlin, David Gunn, and Danna Fewell. Formalism and narratology are represented by the Russians Bakhtin and Medvedev as well as Meir Sternberg, whose dense tome sets out a full biblical poetics.[19]

---

16. James Muilenburg, "Form Criticism and Beyond," *JBL* 88 (1969): 1–18.
17. Phyllis Trible, *Rhetorical Criticism: Context, Method, and the Book of Jonah* (GBS; Minneapolis: Augsburg, 1994), 92.
18. Ibid., 91.
19. Robert Alter, *The Art of Biblical Narrative* (New York: Basic Books, 1981);

It is the reader-response critics who question the location of meaning in the text itself. The theoretical work of Stanley Fish, Wolfgang Iser, Jane Tompkins, and Wayne Booth has influenced the thinking of many biblical scholars, including some of the literary critics already mentioned.[20] Although several different approaches legitimately claim to be reader-oriented, the main themes have been stated by Stanley Fish.[21] He argues that no "text" is a real entity apart from the reader, that finally text and reader cannot be distinguished from one another, and thus interpretation is the only game in town. However, interpretation is not the work of a solitary reader but takes place in interpretive communities.

The third broad area of current activity is the use of social-scientific research, primarily sociology and anthropology, in the service of biblical interpretation or the reconstruction of Israelite history and institutions. Certainly the most prominent figure in this discussion has been Norman K. Gottwald, with a series of works including *The Tribes of Yahweh* and *The Hebrew Bible: A Socio-literary Introduction*.[22] Considerable attention has been given to the social location of prophecy, including the mainly sociological work of Robert R. Wilson.[23] Thomas W. Overholt has investigated prophecy from an anthropological perspective. He considers data ranging from the Old Testament, to the ghost-dance traditions of native North Americans, to Shirley Maclaine to explain the relationships between prophetic figures and their audiences.[24] He shows how the mes-

---

Adele Berlin, *Poetics and Interpretation of Biblical Narrative* (Bible and Literature Series 9; Sheffield: Almond, 1983); David M. Gunn and Danna Nolan Fewell, *Narrative in the Hebrew Bible* (Oxford Bible Series; New York: Oxford University Press, 1993); Meir Sternberg, *The Poetics of Biblical Narrative: Ideological Literature and the Drama of Reading* (Indiana Studies in Biblical Literature; Bloomington: Indiana University Press, 1985).

20. Edgar V. McKnight, "Reader-Response Criticism," in *To Each Its Own Meaning: An Introduction to Biblical Criticisms and their Application* (rev. ed.; ed. Steven L. McKenzie and Stephen R. Haynes; Louisville: Westminster John Knox, 1999), 230–52.

21. Stanley E. Fish, *Is There a Text in This Class? The Authority of Interpretive Communities* (Cambridge: Harvard University Press, 1980).

22. Norman K. Gottwald, *The Tribes of Yahweh: A Sociology of the Religion of Liberated Israel, 1250–1050 BCE* (Maryknoll, N.Y.: Orbis, 1979); idem, *The Hebrew Bible: A Socio-literary Introduction* (Philadelphia: Fortress, 1985).

23. Robert R. Wilson, *Prophecy and Society in Ancient Israel* (Philadelphia: Fortress, 1980).

24. Thomas W. Overholt, "The Ghost Dance of 1890 and the Nature of the Pro-

sage is changed in the feedback that the prophets receive from those who hear them. One could also mention, among others, the use of folklore studies by Susan Niditch.[25] The use of both data and theories from these disciplines and others have been used to reconstruct aspects of the past as well as to interpret biblical documents. Robert Carroll, for example, has employed dissonance theory from social psychology to explain why prophecies from the past are interpreted and reinterpreted in particular ways.[26]

Even this catalogue of historical, literary, and social-scientific methods does not begin to complete the picture of biblical scholarship in the first decade of the new century. Equally important directions that have emerged in the last few decades are liberation hermeneutics, feminist criticism, womanist criticism, and forms of ideological criticism that both are and are not related to these others. And is deconstruction a method or an ideology? All these have explicit ethical and political concerns and are related variously to the changing methodological scene.

Ideological criticism, and specifically liberation and third-world readings, are closely tied to sociological interpretations through the work of Gottwald. Feminist interpretation has been most closely affiliated with some forms of literary criticism. But simple parallels of methods with ideologies would be caricatures. A great deal of significant feminist work has been done by historical critics such as Elisabeth Schüssler Fiorenza,[27] and Carol Meyers's work is both anthropological and archaeological.[28] Nevertheless, some of the most influential feminist work, such as that of Mieke

---

phetic Process," *Ethnohistory* 21 (1974): 37–63; idem, *Channels of Prophecy: The Social Dynamics of Prophetic Activity* (Philadelphia: Fortress, 1989); idem, *Cultural Anthropology and the Old Testament* (GBS; Minneapolis: Fortress, 1996).

25. Susan Niditch, *Underdogs and Tricksters: A Prelude to Biblical Folklore* (New Voices in Biblical Studies; New York: HarperCollins, 1987); idem, ed., *Text and Tradition: The Hebrew Bible and Folklore* (SemeiaSt 20; Atlanta: Society of Biblical Literature, 1990); idem, *Folklore and the Hebrew Bible* (GBS; Minneapolis: Fortress, 1993).

26. Robert P. Carroll, "Prophecy and Dissonance: A Theoretical Approach to the Prophetic Tradition," *ZAW* 92 (1980): 108–19.

27. Most recently, e.g., Elisabeth Schüssler Fiorenza, *Democratizing Biblical Studies: Toward an Emancipatory Educational Space* (Louisville: Westminster John Knox, 2009).

28. Carol Meyers, *Households and Holiness: The Religious Culture of Israelite Women* (Minneapolis: Augsburg Fortress, 2005).

Bal, is literary criticism that focuses on the reader and has strong affinities with deconstruction.

In the afterword to her radical and compelling treatment of biblical love stories, *Lethal Love*, Bal, like many other feminists, argues that historical-critical interpretation has been used in the service of particular ideologies—most fundamentally, the ideology of the academy even more than that of the church.[29] According to its canons of truth inherited since the Enlightenment, the "original meaning" was the test for all others. Moreover, that original meaning was recognized through the eyes of the dominant, male, institutions. But her proposal is more radical than giving one authoritative reading against others: "My readings present an alternative to other readings, not a 'correct,' let alone the 'only possible' interpretation of what the texts 'really say.' Texts trigger readings; that is what they are: the occasion of a reaction."[30] She began by asking about the point of literary analysis and concludes by saying, "I came up with the answer: The point is that there is none, at least not a single one; the point of literary analysis is that there is no truth, and that this contention can be reasonably argued."[31] Contrast that with Sternberg's foolproof narration and his "ideologically singular" Bible.[32]

Moreover, there are radicals and reactionaries—both political and theological—in all methodological camps, including the historical-critical camp. Witness the sharp exchange between Fewell and Gunn, on the one hand, and Sternberg, on the other.[33] Many literary critics seem genuinely postmodern while others seem premodern, seeming to suggest that a literary reading of the final form of the text is a way to avoid the crisis of historical consciousness.

Several themes run through the life of contemporary biblical studies. First, it is explicitly and vigorously interdisciplinary or multidisciplinary in ways unheard of in earlier generations. Some biblical scholars may be

---

29. Mieke Bal, *Lethal Love: Feminist Literary Readings of Biblical Love Stories* (Indiana Studies in Biblical Literature; Bloomington: Indiana University Press, 1987).
30. Ibid., 131.
31. Ibid., 132.
32. Sternberg, *Poetics of Biblical Narrative*, 37.
33. See Danna Nolan Fewell and David M. Gunn, "Tipping the Balance: Sternberg's Reader and the Rape of Dinah," *JBL* 110 (1991): 193–211, and response in Meir Sternberg, "Biblical Poetics and Sexual Politics: From Reading to Counter Reading," *JBL* 111 (1992): 463–88.

searching for authority or respectability down this road, but it is a distinctly two-way street. Other disciplines have as much to learn from biblical studies as the reverse. Max Weber constructed his sociological theories to a great extent on the foundations of late nineteenth-century biblical scholarship. Second, biblical criticism as a whole is more self-consciously political, by which I mean it attempts to exercise power toward what it is convinced is the common good. Issues of justice are always at stake in the interpretation of biblical texts even and especially when they are denied. Readers—if they talk or write about what they read, or even if they simply let their lives be shaped by that reading—are responsible for their readings.

Problems and Possibilities

In concluding I limit myself to reflection on two issues that seem to be critical in the present institutional and methodological environment. The first is evoked by the large and elaborate Annual Meeting program of the SBL in the light of the complex range of approaches to biblical interpretation. Is this chaotic or creative? The problem, in my view, is neither the size and diversity of our program nor the fact that it is difficult to make sense of all the alternative means of interpretation presently available. It is a vast and rich marketplace. The problem is rather the potential tribalism in the Society's meetings as well as in the discipline. It is possible, and in some instances actual, that instead of one large meeting we have a great many small ones in which members of individual groups speak only to one another. The danger is that the boundaries between the tribes might be reinforced to the point that it is difficult to learn from or to receive criticism from others. Is it possible, on the other hand, that diverse methods might complement one another? Moreover, there is no room in academic discourse for exchanges that are *ad hominem* or mean-spirited. Another way of putting this is to caution against making any one method or one theory of text and interpretation the banner under which all should be collected. Rather, there are various legitimate theories. That, I admit, is a distinctly postmodern observation. It acknowledges the difficulty if not the impossibility of a single theory or approach.

The second, and most pressing, concern is whether, in this diverse marketplace, there are, any longer, criteria for valid interpretations. Is one proposal just as good as any other? Is interpretive right determined by might? Is there such a thing as a competent reading of a text or an incompetent one? We may sharpen the issue by moving it beyond the academy and returning to the allusion with which we began: What, finally, is wrong with the interpretation of the Bible by racist and violent sects? I do not mean to compile a list of the "errors" of their readings. What is fundamentally wrong is that such interpretations are isolated, turned in upon themselves, and not subject to criticism by others. In short, those interpretations are not critical, not open to debate nor a part of public discourse. Communities—and that certainly includes interpretive communities—become invidious when they are closed to the wider community or to other communities—Waco, Jamestown, and Jordan, Montana, are examples.

The guild could learn from such examples. To be sure, there are no longer—if there ever were—universally accepted canons of truth in interpretation. But we operate every day on the assumption that it is possible to establish some practical limits of what can be claimed to be valid, even concerning the past and concerning our most formative documents.

So, let us make a virtue of necessity: Whatever our approach, we should seek to define our goals, whether historical, literary, or theological. We should make every effort to understand, if not always articulate, our point of departure, values, and social location. We should spell out, at least to ourselves, the methods we use, including an awareness of what counts for evidence and how a claim could be disputed and disproven. Any critical reading is self-aware and is, therefore, self-critical, and it is open to public scrutiny.

These proposals do not claim to be new: "In 1923 Max L. Margolis ... argued against an orthodoxy of criticism 'hardened into a tradition and woefully lacking in self-criticism,'"[34] and in 1936 Henry J. Cadbury said, "'The history of biblical scholarship is marred by the too fond clinging to the debris of exploded theories.' He concluded that responsible scholarship can never be divorced from the values, problems, and need of the hour."[35]

Bibliography

Achtemeier, Paul J., et al., eds. *The HarperCollins Bible Dictionary*. Rev. ed. San Francisco: HarperSanFrancisco, 1996.

---

34. Saunders, *Searching the Scriptures*, 37.
35. Ibid., 38.

Aichele, George, Fred W. Burnett, Elizabeth A. Castelli, Robert M. Fowler, David Jobling, Stephen D. Moore, Gary A. Phillips, and Tina Pippin. *The Postmodern Bible: The Bible and Culture Collective*. New Haven: Yale University Press, 1995.

Alter, Robert. *The Art of Biblical Narrative*. New York: Basic Books, 1981.

Attridge, Harold W., ed. *The HarperCollins Study Bible: Revised Edition*. San Francisco: HarperSanFrancisco, 2006.

Bal, Mieke. *Lethal Love: Feminist Literary Readings of Biblical Love Stories*. Indiana Studies in Biblical Literature. Bloomington: Indiana University Press, 1987.

Berlin, Adele. *Poetics and Interpretation of Biblical Narrative*. Bible and Literature Series 9. Sheffield: Almond, 1983.

Bright, John. *Early Israel in Recent History Writing: A Study in Method*. SBT 19. London: SCM, 1956.

———. *A History of Israel*. 4th ed. Louisville: Westminster John Knox, 2000.

Carroll, Robert P. "Prophecy and Dissonance: A Theoretical Approach to the Prophetic Tradition." *ZAW* 92 (1980): 108–19.

Fewell, Danna Nolan, and David M. Gunn. "Tipping the Balance: Sternberg's Reader and the Rape of Dinah." *JBL* 110 (1991): 193–211.

Fish, Stanley E. *Is There a Text in This Class? The Authority of Interpretive Communities*. Cambridge: Harvard University Press, 1980.

Gardey, Delphine. "Mechanizing Writing and Photographing the Word: Utopias, Office Work, and Histories of Gender and Technology." *History and Technology* 17 (2001): 319–52.

Gottwald, Norman K. *The Hebrew Bible: A Socio-literary Introduction*. Philadelphia: Fortress, 1985.

———. *The Tribes of Yahweh: A Sociology of the Religion of Liberated Israel, 1250–1050 BCE*. Maryknoll, N.Y.: Orbis, 1979.

Gunn, David M., and Danna Nolan Fewell. *Narrative in the Hebrew Bible*. Oxford Bible Series. New York: Oxford University Press, 1993.

Johnson, Luke Timothy. *The Real Jesus: The Misguided Quest for the Historical Jesus and the Truth of the Traditional Gospels*. San Francisco: HarperSanFrancisco, 1996.

Knight, Douglas A., and Gene M. Tucker, eds. *The Hebrew Bible and Its Modern Interpreters*. SBLBMI 1. Philadelphia: Fortress; Decatur, Ga.: Scholars Press, 1985.

Mays, James Luther, et al., eds. *The Harper's Bible Commentary*. Rev. ed. San Francisco, HarperSanFrancisco, 2000.

Mays, James Luther, David L. Petersen, and Kent Harold Richards, eds. *Old Testament Interpretation: Past, Present, and Future: Essays in Honor of Gene M. Tucker.* Nashville: Abingdon, 1995.

McKnight, Edgar V. "Reader-Response Criticism." Pages 230–52 in *To Each Its Own Meaning: An Introduction to Biblical Criticisms and Their Application.* Rev. ed. Edited by Steven L. McKenzie and Stephen R. Haynes. Louisville: Westminster John Knox, 1999.

Meyers, Carol. *Households and Holiness: The Religious Culture of Israelite Women.* Minneapolis: Augsburg Fortress, 2005.

Miller, Patrick D., Jr. "The World and Message of the Prophets." Pages 97–112 in *Old Testament Interpretation: Past, Present, and Future: Essays in Honor of Gene M. Tucker.* Edited by James Luther Mays, David L. Petersen, and Kent Harold Richards. Nashville: Abingdon, 1995.

Muilenburg, James. "Form Criticism and Beyond." *JBL* 88 (1969): 1–18.

Niditch, Susan. *Folklore and the Hebrew Bible.* GBS. Minneapolis: Fortress, 1993.

———. *Underdogs and Tricksters: A Prelude to Biblical Folklore.* New Voices in Biblical Studies. New York: HarperCollins, 1987.

———, ed. *Text and Tradition: The Hebrew Bible and Folklore.* SemeiaSt 20. Atlanta: Society of Biblical Literature, 1990.

Overbeck, Jennifer L. "Beyond Admissibility: A Practical Look at the Use of Eyewitness Expert Testimony in the Federal Courts." *New York University Law Review* 80 (2005): 1895–920.

Powell, Mark Allan, ed. *HarperCollins Bible Dictionary.* Abridged ed. New York: HarperOne, 2009.

Provan, Iain W. "Ideologies, Literary and Critical: Reflections on Recent History Writing on the History of Israel." *JBL* 114 (1995): 586–606.

Rowley, H. H., ed. *The Old Testament and Modern Study.* Oxford: Clarendon, 1951.

Saunders, Ernest W. *Searching the Scriptures: A History of the Society of Biblical Literature, 1880–1980.* SBLBSNA 8. Chico, Calif.: Scholars Press, 1982.

Schüssler Fiorenza, Elisabeth. *Democratizing Biblical Studies: Toward an Emancipatory Educational Space.* Louisville: Westminster John Knox, 2009.

Sternberg, Meir. "Biblical Poetics and Sexual Politics: From Reading to Counter Reading." *JBL* 111 (1992): 463–88.

———. *The Poetics of Biblical Narrative: Ideological Literature and the Drama of Reading.* Indiana Studies in Biblical Literature. Bloomington: Indiana University Press, 1985.

Stendahl, Krister. "Biblical Theology, Contemporary." *IDB* 1:418–32.

Trible, Phyllis. *Rhetorical Criticism: Context, Method, and the Book of Jonah.* GBS. Minneapolis: Augsburg, 1994.

Wilson, Robert R. *Prophecy and Society in Ancient Israel.* Philadelphia: Fortress, 1980.

Witherington, Ben, III. *The Jesus Quest: The Third Search for the Jew of Nazareth.* 2nd ed. Downers Grove, Ill.: InterVarsity Press, 1997.

Study of the New Testament in the Pluralistic Context of the Twenty-First Century

Harold W. Attridge

It is a pleasure to contribute to a collection of essays that honors one of the leaders in the field of biblical studies of the last thirty years. By his steady and visionary leadership of the Society of Biblical Literature during much of that time, he has been at the forefront of important developments in the field, bringing new awareness of the international connections among biblical scholars and of the potential for new forms of dissemination of the results of biblical scholarship. During his term at the helm of the Society, this professional organization of scholars and teachers has developed a more effective and responsive organizational structure and has systematically thought about the roles that it and its members can play in the next century. Given that thrust of Kent's leadership, it is particularly appropriate to reflect in his honor on the future of the discipline, or at least that part of it that I inhabit.

The last fifty years have witnessed remarkable changes in the approach to the study of the New Testament. When I began serious engagement with the field in the late 1960s, the shape of the discipline was complex but rather traditional. The overarching concern was the historical task of attempting to understand what the documents of early Christian history meant in their original context. "Introductory" questions still occupied considerable attention. So there was intense debate in some circles about alternative solutions to the Synoptic Problem. Others wrestled with the problems of the chronology of Paul's life and the discrepancies between Acts and the Pauline letters. "New" approaches, such as redaction criticism operated still within the larger historical paradigm. The most exciting challenges that confronted New Testament critics were occasioned by relatively recent discoveries. By that time the Dead Sea Scrolls had already made a significant impact on students of early Christianity, although there was much material from the caves of Qumran yet to be published. The complexity of Judaism at the end of the Second Temple period was becoming apparent and there seemed to be intriguing connections between a hitherto unknown Judean sect and elements of early Christianity.[1] At that time some texts from the Nag Hammadi find were in the public domain, and many more were being distributed to limited circles of collaborators on pale blue dittograph sheets, with strict injunctions on each page to preserve confidentiality.[2] There was a sense that these texts would produce seismic shifts equal to those being produced by the Scrolls. The old hypothesis of a pre-Christian Gnosticism that "explained" the origins of Christology for at least some adherents of the history of religions school was soon to be tested against new data and found wanting.[3] Yet in many ways the developments surrounding these discoveries followed traditional scholarly patterns. Challenging philological and linguistic work needed to be done to make the new documents accessible and to analyze their place in the history of ancient religion and culture.

Hints of some of the more paradigm shifting novelties to come might be detected among those interested in hermeneutical issues, when biblical scholars shifted their focus from what the texts meant in their original contexts to what they might mean for contemporary audiences, particularly audiences who encountered the texts in some ecclesiastical setting. The radical existentialist hermeneutical stance, of which Rudolf Bultmann was the paradigm, had long since challenged European students of the New Testament and by the 1970s was having its impact on North American scholarship, largely through the work of Americans who had studied with Bultmann and Ernst Käsemann in Germany. A key question

---

1. For a good overview of the impact of the scrolls, see Peter W. Flint and James C. VanderKam, eds., *The Dead Sea Scrolls after Fifty Years: A Comprehensive Assessment* (2 vols.; Leiden: Brill, 1998), and James H. Charlesworth, ed., *The Bible and the Dead Sea Scrolls: The Princeton Symposium on the Dead Sea Scrolls* (3 vols.; Waco, Tex.: Baylor University Press, 2006).

2. A milestone was the publication of the first comprehensive English translation by the "Claremont team" in James M. Robinson, *The Nag Hammadi Library in English* (San Francisco: HarperCollins, 1977; repr. 1988, 1996).

3. For a survey of the state of many of the questions raised by the Nag Hammadi collection, see Birger A. Pearson, *Ancient Gnosticism: Traditions and Literature* (Minneapolis: Fortress, 2007), and Einar Thomassen, *Spiritual Seed: The Church of the "Valentinians"* (Leiden: Brill, 2006).

in this whole hermeneutical enterprise, was whether, once one had come to understand in some sense or other what the texts of the first century meant, they had anything meaningful to say to a contemporary audience, whether one could in some sense or other "believe" them, given their time-conditioned and clearly outmoded presuppositions about the structure of time and space and the place of human beings in them.

If all of that was enough to keep young scholars occupied, new challenges soon arose that have presented a series of shifting models of what scholars of the New Testament might do with their time. Forms of literary analysis, involving various reading strategies and attending to varying dimensions of ancient texts, shifted the focus from how the biblical texts affected their presumed ancient audiences to their potential for being read meaningfully in different times and places. Some of this literary analysis was certainly compatible with, and supplemented, the more traditional forms of historical criticism. The analysis of ancient rhetorical patterns, for example, which burst onto the Pauline scene in the work of Hans Dieter Betz,[4] involved taking seriously what ancient theoreticians did and said and finding reflections of their organizational categories in the writings of the New Testament. Other literary analysis moved further from historical context to contemporary theory. These included the appeals to forms of narratology and theories of metaphor by parable critics such as John Dominic Crossan[5] and critics of the gospels such as John Donahue,[6] or to forms of structuralist analysis such as that practiced by Daniel Patte.[7] Experimentation, in any case, was in the air, and old patterns of scholarship no longer held sway in the field.

While there was considerable ferment in the closing decades of the twentieth century, there was still a sense among those who engaged in the

---

4. Hans Dieter Betz, *Galatians, A Commentary on Paul's Letter to the Churches in Galatia* (Hermeneia; Philadelphia: Fortress, 1979).

5. John Dominic Crossan, *In Parables: The Challenge of the Historical Jesus* (New York: Harper & Row, 1973), which was followed by more specialized studies such as *Finding Is the First Act: Trove Folktales and Jesus' Treasure Parable* (Philadelphia: Fortress, 1978) and *Cliffs of Fall: Paradox and Polyvalence in the Parables of Jesus* (New York: Seabury, 1980).

6. John Donahue, *Gospel in Parable: Metaphor, Narrative and Theology in the Synoptic Gospels* (Philadelphia: Fortress, 1988).

7. Daniel Patte, *What Is Structural Exegesis?* (GBS; Philadelphia: Fortress, 1976); and Daniel Patte and Aline Patte, *Structural Exegesis: From Theory to Practice* (Philadelphia: Fortress, 1978).

study of the New Testament out of a commitment to communities of faith that all of this methodological variety could be helpful in constructing and conveying a meaningful message through reading and interpreting these ancient texts.

Another dimension of the shifts of the late twentieth century posed even more of a challenge to such theologically minded folk. The "turn to the subject," a characteristic of "postmodern" interpretative strategies, was gaining prominence as a theoretical perspective in literary circles.[8] That perspective would soon come to be widely accepted as a premise of much contemporary biblical study. Meaning now was not assumed to reside within an ancient text, but emerged in the process of reading shaped by communities of readers who brought to the text their assumptions, hopes, and aspirations. Meaning emerged not by a process of scholarly unpacking, but by a critical engagement among readers with a text.

The theoretical stance of "postmodernism," with its critique of assumptions about a fixed meaning to be discovered within a text, provided a framework that readily incorporated and reinforced impulses from the social movements of the late twentieth century. Scholars engaged with those movements refused to leave their commitments and engagements in the locker when they came to wrestle with biblical texts. A model of objective scholarship prevailed half a century ago, a model that encouraged the critical reader to be aware of his or her own biases and not let them guide the quest for the meaning of the text.[9] The new models first recognized that all readers and interpreters do indeed come to their task with their own point of view, their own interests, and their own concerns. These should be acknowledged, identified, and then used to frame the questions addressed to the texts, as well as the strategies for answering them.

---

8. For surveys of the "postmodern," see Stephen Moore, *Literary Criticism and the Gospels: The Theoretical Challenge* (New Haven: Yale University Press, 1989); idem, *Mark and Luke in Poststructuralist Perspectives* (New Haven: Yale University Press, 1992); A. K. M. Adam, *Handbook of Postmodern Biblical Interpretation* (St. Louis: Chalice, 2000); and idem, ed., *Postmodern Interpretations of the Bible: A Reader* (St. Louis: Chalice, 2001).

9. The most famous example, widely used to introduce new exegetes to their task, was the essay by Rudolf Bultmann, "Is Exegesis without Presuppositions Possible" ("Ist voraussetzungslose Exegese müglich?" *TZ* 13 [1957]: 409–17).

Foremost among the "perspectival" approaches that have proliferated in the last forty years has been feminist criticism,[10] whose emergence in the biblical area was part of the larger movement to empower women that was affecting both Church and civil society. That movement has come a long way, even if there are inequalities yet to be addressed. Reading the New Testament from a woman's point of view led to various results, some reconstructing the lost stories of the women whose work founded the Christian movement, some emphasizing the kinds of patriarchal structures embedded in the New Testament that continue to support structures of repression and marginalization. The moves made by feminist critics have been pursued by others who have pursued the enterprise of reading the New Testament from particular, defined points of view, ethnic/racial, global, sexual.[11]

The field of New Testament has become complex—no, compound complex—and lively conversations about the meaning of these ancient texts abound. Amidst all of this complexity, an ancient and central concern associated with reading the Bible has resurfaced. Where once theological concerns were muted to a secondary hermeneutical level, or assigned to the tasks of practical theologians, they now have returned to the business of New Testament interpretation with new insistence.[12]

What next, then, for the study of the New Testament? New discoveries may well change the landscape in unexpected ways, but absent new data to analyze, scholars, particularly those who engage the text from the perspective of religious commitment, will continue to be concerned with

---

10. See Elisabeth Schüssler Fiorenza, *In Memory of Her: A Feminist Theological Reconstruction of Christian Origins* (New York: Crossroad, 1983). Resources for feminist criticism abound, including Carol Newsom and Sharon Ringe, eds., *The Women's Bible Commentary* (Louisville: Westminister John Knox, 1992), Elisabeth Schüssler Fiorenza, ed., with the assistance of Shelly Matthews, *Searching the Scriptures* (2 vols.; New York: Crossroad, 1993–1994).

11. For some examples of racial-ethnic interpretations, see Brian Blount, *Cultural Interpretation: Reorienting New Testament Criticism* (Minneapolis: Fortress, 1995), idem, *Go Preach! Mark's Kingdom Message and the Black Church Today* (Maryknoll, N.Y.: Orbis, 1998), idem, ed., *True to Our Native Land: An African American New Testament Commentary* (Minneapolis: Fortress, 2007). On gender issues, see Dale Martin, *Sex and the Single Savior: Gender and Sexuality in Biblical Interpretation* (Louisville: Westminster John Knox, 2006).

12. See Dale Martin, *Pedagogy of the Bible: An Analysis and Proposal* (Louisville: Westminster John Knox, 2008).

the ways in which the New Testament affects the lives of those who read it today. Some challenges to that kind of theologically committed reading will mirror those that have surfaced in the last several decades. Conservative and reactionary moves within some religious communities, such as the shift toward fundamentalism within the Southern Baptist Convention of the late twentieth century, or the general growth of evangelicalism that is a worldwide Christian phenomenon, will ensure that old issues of historical credibility and ethical relevance will continue to engage those who teach the New Testament in both religious and secular environments.

In addition to such traditional challenges, a major issue that will no doubt be on the agenda is the necessity to approach the New Testament within the context of a complex global reality. In the next generation not only the forces of secularism, but also the forces of committed people of other religious traditions will become an increasingly important fact of life. Alongside the need to address the threat to the global environment, finding ways of constructively collaborating with religiously committed people from a variety of traditions will be necessary for the survival and well-being of the planet. New Testament scholarship should be part of that process of constructive engagement.

We might learn how it can do so in part from a reflection on some of the interfaith issues that it has already addressed and in part by a reflection on the practices of contemporary interfaith engagement that are part of the larger context, but not at present a significant part of the preparation of New Testament scholars.

The historical memory of the discipline revolves around issues of the relationship between Christianity and Judaism that have been at the forefront of much scholarly activity since the Holocaust. The outlines of the story are well known and need only be briefly sketched here. While traditional analyses of the relationship of Christianity and Judaism[13] continued and intensified after the Second World War, new critical analysis of anti-Judaism in the New Testament came to the fore. This large body of scholarship resulted in two major accomplishments. On the one side, the intimate connections both historical and conceptual between the early followers of Jesus and their Jewish contemporaries have become more and more apparent. Thus in the so called "new perspective" on Paul, scholars

---

13. Such as James W. Parkes, *The Conflict of the Church and the Synagogue: A Study in the Origins of Antisemitism* (London: Soncino, 1934).

have emphasized the essential rootedness of the apostle to the Gentiles in the prophetic tradition of Israel.[14] Even so "anti-Jewish" a text as the Fourth Gospel has been increasingly recognized as the most Jewish of the Gospels,[15] its polemic a function of inner Jewish disputes over the identity and character of the Messiah. The most "supersessionist" text of the New Testament, the Epistle to the Hebrews, has also been seen to be firmly rooted in Jewish traditions. Whatever its author thinks of the sacrificial cult, the epistle's understanding of the significance of Christ is shaped by Jewish sapiential and apocalyptic thought.[16] Though the author of the book of Revelation can condemn a rival "synagogue of Satan," it does so from the perspective of fidelity to traditional observance and to its vision of a messianic future.[17]

Emphasis on the rootedness of the followers of Jesus in Jewish culture has led scholars increasingly to call into question what had come to be the conventional wisdom about the early "parting of the ways" between Jewish and Christian groups. It becomes increasingly clear that those groups remained in many ways and in many places intimately interconnected and permeable down to the fourth century.

While scholars have pursued a revised version of the relationship between Judaism and Christianity, they have been equally sensitive to the ways in which the polemical language of the early Christian movement works. Whatever the original referent of the Johannine "Jews" might have been, use of their condemnation as children of the devil (John 8:44) has been dangerous to the health and well being of generations of Jews. However much the cry of the crowds in Matthew that "his blood be upon our heads and the heads of our children" (Matt 27:25) might be a way of explaining, in good Deuteronomic terms, the disaster of the destruction of

---

14. See, e.g., N. T. Wright, *Climax of the Covenant: Christ and the Law in Pauline Theology* (Minneapolis: Fortress, 1992), or James D. G. Dunn, *New Perspectives on Paul: Collected Essays* (Tübingen: Mohr Siebeck, 2005).

15. For a general review of the interpretation of the Fourth Gospel, see John Ashton, *Understanding the Fourth Gospel* (Oxford: Oxford University Press, 1991, 2007).

16. The point is made by several of the essays in the conference volume, Richard Bauckham, Daniel Driver, Trevor A. Hart, and Nathan MacDonald, eds., *The Epistle to the Hebrews and Christian Theology* (Grand Rapids: Eerdmans, 2009).

17. See, e.g., John Marshall, *Parables of War: Reading John's Jewish Apocalypse* (Waterloo, Ont.: Wilfrid Laurier University Press, 2001).

the temple, repetition of that phrase grounded the persecution of Jews for centuries. Church bodies have recognized these deleterious consequences of the biblical heritage and have formally repudiated the implications of those passages.[18]

It would be unrealistic to expect that all tensions between Christians and Jews have been eliminated because of the scholarly developments of the last fifty years, but it is probably fair to say that there is a much greater degree of understanding and tolerance than was typical prior to World War II. One can hope that similar progress might be made in other forms of interfaith understanding and collaboration in the years ahead. Progress in that area will involve the work of many people of goodwill collaborating within the framework of many institutions, traditional and new.[19]

As part of that effort, biblical scholars in general, and students of the New Testament in particular, will need to address elements of the biblical tradition that impede interfaith understanding. Two sorts of texts will be particularly prominent in this effort, those that support exclusive claims for Christian revelation and those that present specific challenges to other religious traditions.

In some ways the first problem is the easier. Texts making exclusive claims include prominently the texts of the Fourth Gospel that insist that Jesus is the only way to the Father (John 14:6). How exactly to construe such claims has been a topic debated among theologians for generations, and the spectrum of opinion on the topic ranges broadly from those inter-

---

18. A major statement from the Roman Catholic Church was the Second Vatican Council's document, *Nostra aetate*.

19. E.g., Parliament of World Religions (http://www.parliamentofreligions.org/); the interfaith offices of churches, such as the Vatican's Pontifical Council for Interreligious Dialogue (http://www.vatican.va/roman_curia/pontifical_councils/interelg/documents/rc_pc_interelg_pro_20051996_en.html) and the Archbishop of Canterbury (http://www.archbishopofcanterbury.org/2869); organizations or church bodies, such as the NCC (http://www.ncccusa.org/interfaith), and the WCC (http://www.oikoumene.org/en/programmes/interreligiousdialogue.html), organizations weaker perhaps now than they were a generation ago, but still with the potential for effective work; academic programs stressing interfaith understanding, such as the Center for the Study of World Religions at Harvard (http://www.hds.harvard.edu/cswr/), Hartford Seminary (http://www.hartsem.edu), or the partnership between Andover Newton Theological Seminary and Hebrew College (http://www.hebrewcollege.edu/interfaith); and NGOs such as the Tony Blair Faith Foundation (http://www.tonyblairfaithfoundation.org).

preters who insist on their literal truth and universal validity to those who marginalize them or, in one way or another, subordinate them to some other principle. Liberal Protestants and Unitarians have long since marginalized them; Catholic theologians such as Karl Rahner, with his notion of "anonymous Christians," have found ways to live with them within a more encompassing framework.[20] Biblical scholars have not been particularly vocal in addressing these texts with the same sensitivity to contemporary concerns, although there have been efforts to understand the "sectarian" dynamics that originally produced those claims.[21] Collaboration between biblical scholars and their theological colleagues regarding such texts should be a regular feature of scriptural study.

Addressing the issues raised by exclusivist claims made by specific scriptural texts will be a constant task of scholars of the Bible in the years ahead, whether those scholars have a theological perspective on the biblical text or simply an interest in their cultural impact. Even more promising for the future engagement of biblical study and the global realities of the twenty-first century is the concrete practice of reading scripture in the presence of others who revere a sacred text. The practice of doing that kind of exercise, which has emerged under the banner of "scriptural reasoning," is predicated on an important assumption about the development of interfaith encounter. Understanding between different communities of belief and practice is, according to this premise, most likely to take place when people of goodwill actually share in the experience of a religiously committed "other" who is reading and wrestling with another "sacred" text.[22]

To conclude, those who engage in the professional study of scripture for the twenty-first century need, among all the other skills and knowledge

---

20. See, among other essays, Karl Rahner, S.J., "Christianity and Non-Christian Religions," in *Later Writings* (vol. 5 of *Theological Investigations*; trans. Karl-H. Kruger; London: Darton, Longman & Todd, 1966), 115–34; and "Anonymous Christians," in *Concerning Vatican Council II* (vol. 6 of *Theological Investigations*; trans. Karl-H. and Boniface Kruger; London: Darton, Longman & Todd, 1969), 390–439.

21. For the Fourth Gospel, see, for example, Wayne Meeks, "The Man from Heaven in Johannine Sectarianism," *JBL* 91 (1972): 44–72, repr. in John Ashton, ed., *Interpretation of the Fourth Gospel* (London: SPCK; Philadelphia: Fortress, 1986), 141–73.

22. The most prominent example of this process is the "scriptural reasoning" project, developed as a tool of interfaith encounter in Great Britain. See http://www.scripturalreasoning.org and http://etext.lib.virginia.edu/journals/jsrforum.

that they are called upon to master, to develop a facility for engaging in conversation about scripture that addresses the concerns of a religiously plural world. The traditional communities of belief from which such scholars generally come require that expertise, but, more importantly, a world in which religious divisions threaten the future well-being of a large segment of humankind demands this kind of expertise.

Bibliography

Adam, A. K. M. *Handbook of Postmodern Biblical Interpretation.* St. Louis: Chalice, 2000.

———, ed. *Postmodern Interpretations of the Bible: A Reader.* St. Louis: Chalice, 2001.

Ashton, John. *Understanding the Fourth Gospel.* Oxford: Oxford University Press, 1991, 2007.

Bauckham, Richard, Daniel Driver, Trevor A. Hart, and Nathan MacDonald, eds. *The Epistle to the Hebrews and Christian Theology.* Grand Rapids: Eerdmans, 2009.

Betz, Hans Dieter. *Galatians, A Commentary on Paul's Letter to the Churches in Galatia.* Hermeneia. Philadelphia: Fortress, 1979.

Blount, Brian. *Cultural Interpretation: Reorienting New Testament Criticism.* Minneapolis: Fortress, 1995.

———. *Preach! Mark's Kingdom Message and the Black Church Today.* Maryknoll, N.Y.: Orbis, 1998.

———, ed. *True to Our Native Land: An African American New Testament Commentary.* Minneapolis: Fortress, 2007.

Bultmann, Rudolf. "Ist voraussetzungslose Exegese müglich?" *TZ* 13 (1957): 409–17.

Charlesworth, James H., ed. *The Bible and the Dead Sea Scrolls: The Princeton Symposium on the Dead Sea Scrolls.* 3 vols. Waco, Tex.: Baylor University Press, 2006.

Crossan, John Dominic. *Cliffs of Fall: Paradox and Polyvalence in the Parables of Jesus.* New York: Seabury, 1980.

———. *Finding Is the First Act: Trove Folktales and Jesus' Treasure Parable.* Philadelphia: Fortress, 1978.

———. *In Parables: The Challenge of the Historical Jesus.* New York: Harper & Row, 1973.

Donahue, John. *Gospel in Parable: Metaphor, Narrative and Theology in the Synoptic Gospels.* Philadelphia: Fortress, 1988.

Dunn, James D. G. *New Perspectives on Paul: Collected Essays*. Tübingen: Mohr Siebeck, 2005.
Flint, Peter W., and James C. VanderKam, eds. *The Dead Sea Scrolls after Fifty Years: A Comprehensive Assessment*. 2 vols. Leiden: Brill, 1998.
Marshall, John. *Parables of War: Reading John's Jewish Apocalypse*. Waterloo, Ont.: Wilfrid Laurier University Press, 2001.
Martin, Dale. *Pedagogy of the Bible: An Analysis and Proposal*. Louisville: Westminster John Knox, 2008.
———. *Sex and the Single Savior: Gender and Sexuality in Biblical Interpretation*. Louisville: Westminster John Knox, 2006.
Meeks, Wayne. "The Man from Heaven in Johannine Sectarianism." *JBL* 91 (1972): 44–72. Repr. as pages 141–73 in *Interpretation of the Fourth Gospel*. Edited by John Ashton. London: SPCK; Philadelphia: Fortress, 1986.
Moore, Stephen. *Literary Criticism and the Gospels: The Theoretical Challenge*. New Haven: Yale University Press, 1989.
———. *Mark and Luke in Poststructuralist Perspectives*. New Haven: Yale University Press, 1992.
Newsom, Carol, and Sharon Ringe, eds. *The Women's Bible Commentary*. Louisville: Westminster John Knox, 1992.
Parkes, James W. *The Conflict of the Church and the Synagogue: A Study in the Origins of Antisemitism*. London: Soncino, 1934.
Patte, Daniel. *What Is Structural Exegesis?* GBS. Philadelphia: Fortress, 1976.
Patte, Daniel, and Aline Patte. *Structural Exegesis: From Theory to Practice*. Philadelphia: Fortress, 1978.
Pearson, Birger A. *Ancient Gnosticism: Traditions and Literature*. Minneapolis: Fortress, 2007.
Rahner, Karl. "Anonymous Christians." Pages 390–439 in *Concerning Vatican Council II*. Vol. 6 of *Theological Investigations*. London: Darton, Longman & Todd, 1969.
———. "Christianity and Non-Christian Religions." Pages 115–34 in *Later Writings*. Vol. 5 of *Theological Investigations*. London: Darton, Longman & Todd, 1966.
Robinson, James M. *The Nag Hammadi Library in English*. San Franisco: HarperCollins, 1977. Repr., 1988, 1996.
Schüssler Fiorenza, Elizabeth. *In Memory of Her: A Feminist Theological Reconstruction of Christian Origins*. New York: Crossroad, 1983.

———, ed., with the assistance of Shelly Matthews. *Searching the Scriptures*. 2 vols. New York: Crossroad, 1993–1994.

Thomassen, Einar. *Spiritual Seed: The Church of the "Valentinians."* Leiden: Brill, 2006.

Wright, N. T. *Climax of the Covenant: Christ and the Law in Pauline Theology*. Minneapolis: Fortress, 1992.

Faith, Scholarship, and the Society of Biblical Literature

John J. Collins

The July-August 2010 issue of *Biblical Archaeology Review* carries an item, under "Biblical Views," entitled "Farewell to SBL." The short piece does not mark the retirement of Kent Harold Richards after an extraordinary career in the service of the Society,[1] as might have been expected from the timing of the article, but rather announces the resignation of a prominent scholar from the Society on a matter of principle.[2] According to the author, Ron Hendel, "in recent years the SBL has changed its position on the relationship between faith and reason, falling into dissension and hypocrisy." Whereas the traditional mission statement said that "the object of the Society is to stimulate the critical investigation of the classical biblical literatures,"[3] the new mission, as revised in 2004, is simply to "foster biblical scholarship." So, Hendel infers, "critical inquiry—that is to say, reason—has been deliberately deleted as a criterion for the SBL. The views of creationists, snake-handlers and faith-healers now count among the kinds of Biblical scholarship that the society seeks to foster."

Some allowance must be made here for my good friend Ron's rhetorical flair, which serves the purposes of *BAR* but would probably not pass muster with *The New York Times*. If snake-handling or faith-healing

---

1. This career includes not only his fifteen years as Executive Director but also a decade as Treasurer, Executive Secretary, and then Executive Secretary–Treasurer from the mid-1970s to the mid-1980s.

2. Ronald S. Hendel, "Farewell to SBL: Faith and Reason in Biblical Studies," *BAR* (July-August 2010): 28, 74, http://www.bib-arch.org/bar/article.asp?PubID=BSBA&Volume=36&Issue=4&ArticleID=9.

3. Ernest W. Saunders, *Searching the Scriptures: A History of the Society of Biblical Literature, 1880-1980* (SBLBSNA 8; Chico, Calif.: Scholars Press, 1982), xi.

have been carried out under the auspices of the SBL, I have missed them. (Whether creationism has been defended at an SBL meeting or in an SBL publication, I am not so sure, but I do not believe that there has been any official endorsement of such a position). I participated in at least some of the discussion that led to the reformulation of the Society's mission statement. It never occurred to me that the point was to delete "critical inquiry" but rather to find a pithy expression that would express the Society's mission in an inclusive way. The change was not specifically designed to cater to religious conservatives but arose from the recognition that biblical scholarship now takes many and various forms (many of which are not especially religious at all).

But Hendel's piece raises a serious issue that was perhaps not adequately addressed in the revision of the Society's mission statement: Should the Society of Biblical Literature have a regulative function with regard to what passes for biblical scholarship? It has traditionally had such a function. The *Journal of Biblical Literature* is not a blog where anyone can post his or her opinion. Program units at the Annual Meeting still have to be approved by the Program Committee. To some degree, some such regulation is unavoidable. I do not recall any explicit change of policy in that matter. Yet it seems to many of us that the regulative function has been greatly relaxed in recent years. People are invited to volunteer to review books in the *Review of Biblical Literature*, and some of the reviews published lead to the suspicion that there is little editorial control.[4] Students who have not yet been admitted to Ph.D. programs and, in some cases, who do not even intend to go into biblical studies, increasingly have their papers accepted for presentation at the both the Annual and International Meetings. Of course, many fine reviews are published too, and there is plenty of excellent material at the Annual

---

4. The policy published on the *RBL* website reads, "The *Review of Biblical Literature* (*RBL*) editorial board has the final discretion in assigning *RBL* reviews. They seek the most qualified reviewers for works submitted, so in most cases the board first offers a review copy to one or more established scholars in the field. When we are unable to secure a reviewer, we rely on qualified volunteers. Thus we invite you to volunteer to review any available book. If you are declined, please understand that this is most likely due to one of two factors: an editor-chosen reviewer has accepted our offer to review the work; or some other qualified volunteer made an offer prior to yours" (http://bookreviews.org/volunteer.asp). It is my understanding that measures are being taken to tighten editorial control in *RBL*.

Meeting, but Hendel is not the only scholar who thinks that the meeting, and *RBL*, have been unduly diluted in recent years, quite apart from considerations of religious faith.

In formulating a critique such as this, I assume that there is a valid distinction between competence and incompetence. I am aware that some colleagues question the distinction. The "multidimensional exegesis" advocated by Daniel Patte in his 1995 book on *The Ethics of Biblical Interpretation* apparently regards all interpretations, scholarly and popular, as equally valid, so long as they are not absolutized.[5] This kind of inclusiveness is sometimes characterized as postmodern, but it is not justified by serious engagement with the theoretical writings of Derrida or Foucault. Rather, *The Postmodern Bible* warns that "deconstructive reading relies necessarily on traditional historical criticism as 'an indispensable guard-rail' or 'safeguard' for reading. If it were not so, Derrida cautions, 'one could say just anything at all.'"[6] But as Robert Morgan put it, "A Bible that can mean anything means nothing."[7]

More typically, however, scholars do not deny any requirement of competence but are suspicious of the grounds on which judgments of incompetence are made and suspect that these always reflect the interests of one group to the exclusion of others. Consequently, they are wary of universal standards. The implications of this situation are summed up lucidly by David Clines:

> If there are no "right" interpretations, and no validity in interpretation beyond the assent of various interest groups, biblical interpreters have to give up the goal of determinate and universally acceptable interpretations and devote themselves to producing interpretations they can sell—in whatever mode is called for by the communities they choose to serve. Those who pay the piper get to call the tune. And biblical inter-

---

5. Daniel Patte, *The Ethics of Biblical Interpretation: A Reevaluation* (Louisville: Westminster John Knox, 1995), 355–57. See the review by William Schweiker in *JR* 76 (1996): 355.

6. George Aichele et al., *The Postmodern Bible: The Bible and Culture Collective* (New Haven: Yale University Press, 1995), 64, with reference to Jacques Derrida, *Limited Inc.* (Evanston, Ill.: Northwestern University Press, 1988), 141. See further my comments in *The Bible after Babel: Historical Criticism in a Postmodern Age* (Grand Rapids: Eerdmans, 2005), 11–17.

7. Robert Morgan, with John Barton, *Biblical Interpretation* (Oxford: Oxford University Press, 1988), 13.

preters are … no more than pipers, playing their tunes in the service of some community or other that authorizes their work and signs their salary cheques.[8]

It is arguable that this is a fair description of how biblical scholarship works in practice. Whether it is a satisfactory model for a society such as the SBL is worthy of reflection.

The Formation of the Society

The formation of the Society of Biblical Literature in 1880 was inspired to a great degree by the rise of higher criticism, the critical approach to the Bible that was often at odds with traditional Christian and Jewish faith. It was not the case that all members endorsed the critical approach. Early articles in *JBL* defended the Mosaic origin of Deuteronomic legislation and the Pauline authorship of the Pastorals, and the famous conservative B. B. Warfield joined the Society in 1882.[9] From the beginning, an effort was made to draw conservative scholars into the discussion.[10] But some prominent early members of the Society found themselves in conflict with their churches. Charles A. Briggs and H. Preserved Smith were tried for heresy, as was their contemporary W. Robertson Smith in Scotland.[11] The tension between the findings of critical scholarship and traditional faith has remained a source of tension within the Society and within the discipline.

The Society of Biblical Literature was not the first association dedicated to the study of the Bible in North America, but it was the first group that was both interinstitutional and interdenominational. To be sure, it was dominated by white Protestant males for much of its first century, yet it is instructive to find that that there were some (few) female members already in the 1890s,[12] that the Society met on occa-

---

8. David J. A. Clines, "Possibilities and Priorities of Biblical Interpretation in an International Perspective," *BibInt* 1 (1993): 79–80.

9. Saunders, *Searching the Scriptures*, 6, 11. The Pauline authorship of the Pastorals is still defended by Luke Timothy Johnson, *The First and Second Letters to Timothy* (AB 33A; New York: Doubleday, 2001), 91–99.

10. Saunders, *Searching the Scriptures*, 3.

11. Ibid., 17.

12. Ibid., 8.

sion at the Jewish Theological Seminary, and that the Catholic scholar M.-J. Lagrange was offered honorary membership in 1913.[13] Not until the 1960s would the demographics of the Society, or of the field, begin to change significantly. Here again there is an abiding source of tension within the discipline between the commitment to open, unprejudiced discussion in principle and the inevitable prejudices of the actual membership at any given time.

HISTORICAL CRITICISM

The long-standing mission of the Society was "to stimulate the critical investigation of the classical biblical literatures."[14] Critical investigation was understood in the context of the regnant methodology of biblical scholarship, loosely called "historical criticism." James Barr has rightly insisted that it is misleading to speak of "the historical-critical method": "there are methods used by historical-criticism, but there is no such thing as the historical critical method."[15] Nonetheless, there is at least a family resemblance between the methods usually called historical-critical: they take account of the fact that the biblical texts were written long ago, in a cultural matrix very different from our own, and attempt to understand the texts first of all in the context of that ancient setting. Historical considerations are a necessary part of that discussion, since it requires at least an approximate idea of the time, place, and circumstances of composition. The goal of the inquiry, however, is not necessarily historical in a narrow sense. It might just as well be the theology or rhetoric of the text, seen in light of its historical context.

The classic formulation of the principles of historical criticism is that of Ernst Troeltsch, in 1898, summarized lucidly by Van Harvey in 1966:

> (1) the principle of criticism: our judgments about the past cannot simply be classified as true or false but must be seen as claiming only a greater or a lesser degree of probability, and as always open to revision;

---

13. Ibid., 23.

14. Ibid., xi. This formulation was revised in 2003 to read "foster biblical scholarship" (see Kent Harold Richards, "Leadership with New Vision," *SBL Society Report* [2003]: 3).

15. James Barr, *History and Ideology in the Old Testament: Biblical Studies at the End of a Millennium* (Oxford: Oxford University Press, 2000), 32.

(2) the principle of analogy: we are able to make such judgments of probability only if we presuppose that our present experience is not radically dissimilar to the experience of past persons; and

(3) the principle of correlation: the phenomena of historical life are so related and interdependent that no radical change can take place at any one point in the historical nexus without effecting a change in all that immediately surrounds it. Historical explanation, therefore, necessarily takes the form of understanding an event in terms of its antecedents and consequences, and no event can be isolated from its historically conditioned time and place.[16]

To these, Harvey would add the principle of autonomy, which is associated especially with Immanuel Kant and the Enlightenment.[17] On the one hand, the historian, or the biblical critic, must be free from constraint by authority, either clerical or secular. One cannot work with integrity if the conclusions one has to reach are prescribed in advance. On the other hand, this principle warns against undue influence from received opinion. In the words of the historian R. G. Collingwood, "so far from relying on an authority other than himself, to whose statements his thought must conform, the historian is his own authority."[18] As Harvey observed, the principle of autonomy represented a radical change in the morality of knowledge. Where medieval culture had celebrated belief as a virtue and regarded doubt as sin, the modern critical mentality regards doubt as a necessary step in the testing of knowledge and sees belief as an obstacle to rational thought.

Perhaps the most basic of these principles is Troeltsch's principle of criticism. The results of scholarship are never final. This, in fact, is simply the human condition, but it is perhaps especially true in historical scholarship, where today's assured results may be overturned by tomorrow's excavation. Therefore, in theory at least, historical criticism is incompatible with dogmatic certainty. Critics of historical criticism sometimes

---

16. Van A. Harvey, *The Historian and the Believer: The Morality of Historical Knowledge and Christian Belief* (New York: MacMillan, 1966), 14–15.

17. Ibid., 39.

18. R. G. Collingwood, *The Idea of History* (Oxford: Oxford University Press, 1946), 236.

accuse it of being a quest for "some kind of absolute truth."[19] At least insofar as Troeltsch's principles are representative of historical criticism, quite the opposite is the case.

Neither Troeltsch nor Harvey mentions objectivity as a principle of historical criticism. There is surely a general assumption in historical criticism that the meaning of a text can be established in an objective manner, but this assumption is more complicated than it may seem. The meaning intended by an ancient author can only be reconstructed tentatively, and texts can clearly take on new meanings in new circumstances. Contrary to what is often alleged, historical criticism does not necessarily reduce a text to a single meaning.

The principles set out above are not necessarily representative of all who would describe themselves as historical critics. Few if any scholars are autonomous in the sense that Harvey requires, and the field has never been free of dogmatism. But the shortcomings of practitioners do not invalidate the principles. We may take it that the principles represent an ideal to which most historical critics would subscribe, even if they do not always attain it in practice. They do not necessarily commit the practitioner to a historical mode of inquiry. They may be viewed rather as the presuppositions of public discourse in an academic setting. In principle, one can argue for anything if one can adduce evidence and make an argument, but the fact that the interpreter happens to believe something can carry no weight in the discussion.

For much of the twentieth century, historical criticism broadly defined provided a relatively unproblematic framework for biblical scholarship. On the one hand, the practitioners who attended the meetings of the Society of Biblical Literature at Union Seminary were generally homogeneous, with similar religious commitments and shared assumptions. On the other hand, the results of scholarship were not perceived as threatening traditional belief in any fundamental way. This was the heyday of the biblical theology movement, which looked to archaeology to confirm the basic historicity of the biblical account. Representative works of that era, such as those of William Foxwell Albright, John Bright, or Bernhard Anderson, were critical works of scholarship that tried to take full account of the latest archeological findings, but they proceeded on an assump-

---

19. So David M. Gunn and Danna Nolan Fewell, *Narrative in the Hebrew Bible* (Oxford: Oxford University Press, 1993), 7.

tion that the biblical account was basically reliable and that biblical values could, with occasional exceptions, be affirmed. As Robert Funk remarked, the SBL was "a fraternity of scientifically trained biblical scholars with the soul of a church."[20] Over the last forty years or so, however, this situation has changed.

Multiple Perspectives

The most basic reason for the change is surely the shift in the demography of the field. While the SBL from the beginning was open in principle to male and female and all religious persuasions, it was for long a very homogeneous society. It has been said that objectivity is the agreement of everybody in the room.[21] In recent decades there has been a lot more people, and different kinds of people, in the room, and they have brought a new range of sensitivities and concerns to the table.[22] Before the 1960s, scarcely anyone was sensitive to the patriarchal bias of biblical texts, despite the work of Elizabeth Cady Stanton and her "Women's Bible" colleagues in the late nineteenth century. Now it is axiomatic. The moral superiority of Israel in its ancient Near Eastern context was long taken for granted, and the supposed extermination of the Canaanites prescribed in Deuteronomy and Joshua did not seem problematic. We (or at least some of us) are now more sensitive to the "Canaanite perspective," from which the exodus does not appear to be a story of liberation at all.[23] Many of these new perspectives have come with vigorous ideological agendas. For example, Elisabeth Schüssler Fiorenza writes that the main task of a critical feminist hermeneutics is "to articulate the theological authority of women."[24] While she respects the canons of historical scholarship, she

---

20. Robert W. Funk, "The Watershed of the American Biblical Tradition: The Chicago School, First Phase, 1892–1920," *JBL* 95 (1976): 7.

21. Walter Brueggemann, *Texts under Negotiation: The Bible and Postmodern Imagination* (Minneapolis: Fortress, 1993), 8, citing Richard Rorty, *Philosophy and the Mirror of Nature* (Princeton: Princeton University Press, 1979), 335.

22. See, for example, Katharine Doob Sakenfeld, "Whose Text Is It?" *JBL* 127 (2008): 5–18.

23. Collins, *The Bible after Babel*, 64-69; Edward Said, "Michael Walzer's 'Exodus and Revolution,' A Canaanite Reading," *Grand Street* 5 (Winter 1986): 86–106; Keith Whitelam, *The Invention of Ancient Israel: The Silencing of Palestinian History* (London: Routledge, 1996).

24. Elisabeth Schüssler Fiorenza, "Feminist Hermeneutics," *ABD* 2:785.

calls for an "ethics of accountability"[25] and demands that the interpretations that support the feminist agenda be given the benefit of the doubt.[26] But while some of the new perspectives have tended to undermine the religious and moral authority of the biblical text, there has also been a resurgence of conservative believers who demand a "hermeneutic of assent" to counteract the dominant hermeneutic of suspicion in biblical studies. The upsurge of theologically conservative scholarship in the SBL must be seen in this wider context.

Traditional Faith and Historical Criticism

The multiplicity of perspectives characteristic of the modern academy may be described as a "postmodern situation," even if the perspectives in question are not especially indebted to postmodern theory.[27] This new postmodern situation has had the somewhat surprising effect of casting the old conflict between traditional faith and modern scholarship in a new light. Some faith-based interpreters welcome postmodern relativism:

> Postmodern readers come to Scripture with a plurality of interpretative interests, including (perhaps) the theological, though no one interest may claim more authority than any other. Biblical interpretation in postmodernity means that there are no independent standards or universal criteria for determining which of many rival interpretations is the "right" or "true" one.[28]

This argument is somewhat disingenuous, since most theological interpreters strongly believe that their way of interpreting the text is the right way. In fact, the argument is not entirely dependent on the postmodern situation. Already in 1966 Van Harvey wrote an incisive critique of "hard perspectivism" (or the view that all positions are perspectival) as a form of

---

25. Elisabeth Schüssler Fiorenza, "The Ethics of Biblical Interpretation: De-centering Biblical Scholarship," *JBL* 107 (1988): 15.

26. Elisabeth Schüssler Fiorenza, *Jesus and the Politics of Interpretation* (New York: Continuum, 2000), 50.

27. Cf. Walter Brueggemann, *Theology of the Old Testament: Testimony, Dispute, Advocacy* (Minneapolis: Fortress, 1997), 61–64.

28. Kevin J. Vanhoozer, "Introduction: What Is Theological Interpretation of the Bible?" in *The Dictionary for Theological Interpretation* (ed. Kevin J. Vanhoozer; Grand Rapids: Baker, 2005), 20–21.

Christian apologetics.[29] While there may not be universally valid criteria, this is hardly justification for exempting a preferred theological perspective from critique.

Troeltsch himself concluded that the principles of historical criticism were basically incompatible with traditional Christian faith, insofar as it is based on a supernaturalist metaphysics.[30] Many conservative theological interpreters would agree. The principle of analogy has been especially contentious. Troeltsch and Harvey are often accused of having a closed universe and of undue dogmatism in excluding the possibility of miracles or divine intervention. So Richard Niebuhr argued that historical thinking requires an openness to the uniqueness and novelty of past events and that a historian cannot rule out in advance the possibility of such events.[31] The recent *Biblical History of Israel* by Provan, Long, and Longman goes further. The authors find no reason to believe "that an account that describes the unique or unusual is for that reason to be suspected of unreliability."[32] They ask:

> Why should verification be a prerequisite for our acceptance of a tradition as valuable in respect of historical reality? Why should not ancient historical texts rather be given the benefit of the doubt in regard to their statements about the past unless good reasons exist to consider them unreliable in these statements? ... Why should we adopt a verification instead of a falsification principle?"[33]

But to give one's sources "the benefit of the doubt" is poor historical method by any measure. If unique and unusual events do not give the interpreter pause, one wonders what would.

Regardless of how Troeltsch may have understood the principle of analogy, there is no reason why historical criticism should deny the possibility of anything. It is not concerned to establish possibility, but probability. If someone wants to argue for the historicity of an exceptional or even unique event, which can only be explained by appeal to divine

---

29. Harvey, *The Historian and the Believer*, 204–42.
30. Ibid., 5.
31. Richard R. Niebuhr, *Resurrection and Historical Reason* (New York: Scribners, 1957).
32. Iain Provan, V. Phillips Long, and Tremper Longman III, *A Biblical History of Israel* (Louisville: Westminster John Knox, 2003), 70–72.
33. Ibid., 55.

intervention (say, the exodus or the resurrection), he or she must assume the burden of proof by establishing as far as possible what happened and providing arguments as to why the supernatural explanation is probable. That burden is not easily assumed. It is not the business of the historical critic to disprove the supernaturalist interpretation, only to explain the events as far as possible in historical terms. The principle of analogy, then, should not be conceived as a doctrine (or denial) of metaphysics. It simply reflects the limits of human understanding. If something were to happen for which there is no analogy in human experience, it would be incomprehensible. Appeals to divine intervention can carry no weight in discussion when they are not accepted by some of the participants.

Conservative scholars also object to the principle of autonomy. According to Provan, Long, and Longman, "what is commonly referred to as 'knowledge of the past' is more accurately described as 'faith in the testimony,' in the interpretations of the past offered by other people."[34] They acknowledge, briefly, that testimony may be unreliable, but they articulate no criteria for evaluating it. Rather, they insist that "autonomous thinking is entirely compatible with fundamental reliance on the word of others, as a path to knowledge."[35] In practice, they do not question the reliability of the biblical "testimony" at all. Such a "hermeneutic of belief" cannot be accepted as critical scholarship. Even though they do not appeal explicitly to considerations of faith and try to present their case as a rational argument, it is clear that this argument is determined by their prior belief in the historical reliability of the Bible.

There is, however, a serious issue to be raised with respect to the autonomy of the scholar. Jon Levenson acknowledges the importance of academic freedom but insists on the social character of knowledge:

> It is not at all the case, however, that the contemporary academy has found a way to dispense with all social processes for the validation of knowledge.... Instead of setting forth a sharp dichotomy between autonomy and submission to a collective body, therefore, we would be wiser to note the inevitable correlation between the character of a social body and the nature of the knowledge it validates.[36]

---

34. Ibid., 36. See further Collins, *The Bible after Babel*, 35–39.
35. Provan, Long, and Longman, *Biblical History*, 48.
36. Jon D. Levenson, *The Hebrew Bible, The Old Testament, and Historical Criticism* (Louisville: Westminster John Knox, 1993), 121.

The scholar, in short, does not work in a vacuum but depends on the standards, criteria, and conventions of the academic community. The academy is a community of interpretation, with its own presuppositions and traditions, just as are the synagogue and the church.

It is by now a commonplace of hermeneutics that there is no exegesis without presuppositions.[37] There is no such thing as pure reason, detached from all tradition, and so the critic can never be completely autonomous. Historical criticism, too, is a tradition. But then, asks Levenson, "why follow Troeltsch's three axioms, augmented by … [the] principle of autonomy, if they are not intrinsic to human rationality but themselves partake of historical and cultural particularity?"[38] Here Levenson allies himself, somewhat improbably, with the theological agenda of Brevard S. Childs, which is based on the status of canonicity as a statement of Christian belief.[39] Levenson does not share Childs's Christian postulates, but he welcomes his approach because it subordinates historical criticism to religious faith. Levenson's position here—Why one tradition rather than another?—is not especially new. It is broadly in line with "nonfoundationalism," an influential movement in twentieth-century philosophy that holds that there is no objective, universally valid way of grasping reality that is independent of specific historical-cultural traditions. Truth is not the correlation of mind and reality but a matter of coherence within a shared set of beliefs. Nonfoundationalism has often been adapted for apologetic ends in Christian theology, with the significant modification that there is no secure foundation except belief in Christ.[40]

The validity and value of historical criticism does not require that its principles be intrinsic to human rationality or that they do not arise from a particular cultural tradition. The question is whether it is able to give an adequate account of its subject matter, one that is satisfactory in our present time and circumstances. It is a matter of making an argument by appeal to assumptions and knowledge shared by the participants in a particular conversation, a quest for what might be called a "regional truth." One test of the adequacy of a tradition is the degree to which it can accommodate new insights and discoveries and adapt to changing

---

37. Hans-Georg Gadamer, *Truth and Method* (New York: Crossroad, 1975).
38. Levenson, *The Hebrew Bible*, 120.
39. Brevard. S. Childs, *Biblical Theology in Crisis* (Philadelphia: Westminster, 1970), 99.
40. See Collins, *The Bible after Babel*, 137–40.

circumstances. It makes a great difference here whether the tradition in which one stands is itself dogmatic or rather abides by Troeltsch's principle of criticism. Scholarship is, in effect, an ongoing conversation. Everyone enters the conversation with some presuppositions, and some positions are accepted as given around the table. What is essential to historical criticism, and indeed to critical thinking of any kind, is that everything in principle is open for discussion. Any position, no matter how venerable, can be challenged by new arguments and evidence. Of course, the challenger will usually have an uphill battle. Entrenched positions are not lightly abandoned, nor should they be. But the history of biblical scholarship over the last half century shows that challenges can indeed succeed. In the end, arguments are not settled by appeals to authority but by the quality of evidence and argument.

Hendel and the *RBL*

The immediate occasion of the *BAR* piece was a review by Bruce K. Waltke of Michael Fox's commentary on Proverbs 10–31, which was published in the *Review of Biblical Literature*. Waltke's review is written from an explicitly evangelical perspective. Evangelical scholars, we are told,

> by their faith in the God of Abraham, Isaac, and Jacob … hear God's voice in his "lisping" spokesmen as a sweet sound and hear the voice of higher biblical criticism, which replaces faith in God's revelation with faith in the sufficiency of human reason, as the grating of an old scratched record. It matters not whether the tune of higher biblical criticism be Troeltschian, Durkheimian, or Spinozistic.[41]

One of his main criticisms of Fox's commentary is that it dates Prov 10–29 to the eighth and seventh centuries rather than to the time of Solomon: "why not locate the author-editor in Solomon's court, as the biblical writers assert?" He holds that "the factual data validates Solomon's authorship of Prov 1:1–24:33" and contends that scholars rejected the biblical ascription of Solomon's authorship because they thought their created typologies of theology and of language pointed to a late date. Those argu-

---

41. Bruce K. Waltke, review of Michael V. Fox, *Proverbs 10–31: A New Translation with Introduction and Commentary*, *RBL*; online: http://bookreviews.org/pdf/7219_7855.pdf.

ments, however, have been discredited." Despite Waltke's undisputed competence in the ancient languages, it is difficult to accept this as a competent assessment. I cannot think of any scholar who is not constrained by religious presuppositions who thinks that a Solomonic date of any part of Proverbs is plausible. Given Waltke's derogatory remarks on higher criticism, I think it is clear that he has a prior commitment to accept the biblical ascription, even if he limits it to part of the book.[42]

Should the Society of Biblical Literature publish such a review? The question here is not whether evangelical scholars should be allowed to review books in an organ of the Society. Of course they should. The question is whether they should be held to the canons of public discourse when they write them. Here, I believe, the Society does have a regulative function, not only with regard to evangelical scholarship but with regard to any evident bias, regardless of its ideological character. In the case of Waltke, however, as in the case of Provan, Longman, and Long, the case is complicated by the fact that the evangelical scholars claim to be doing critical scholarship, even if their evangelical bias is evident to those who do not share it. (Presumably, they would say that "liberal" scholars are biased in the opposite direction. Bias is a negative characterization of views we do not find reasonable.) It should also be said that the intrusion of belief into historical scholarship is by no means a new development in recent years. The confidence of an earlier generation in the historicity of the exodus, or even the patriarchs, now seems to many to be a clear example of the distorting effect of the will to believe.

Waltke's comments on higher criticism seem inappropriate, but they are also revealing and clarify the positions he takes later in the review. The question, perhaps, is whether his views on Proverbs are so far outside the mainstream of scholarship as to cast doubt on the competence of the review. But in general it seems to me that the participation of evangelical scholars in the Society and its publications should be welcomed, as B. B. Warfield was welcomed into the Society in its early years. Also, the attempt to defend conservative positions by formulating arguments that do not appeal explicitly to faith is surely to be welcomed, even by those of

---

42. Waltke recognizes that Solomon cannot be the author of the whole book of Proverbs. He dates the final form of the book to the Achaemenid or Persian period. Similarly, he holds that Deuteronomy reached its final form in the exile. He has recently been forced to resign from Reformed Theological Seminary for allowing the possibility of evolution.

us who do not find these arguments convincing. The proper response to Waltke's remarks on the Solomonic origin of Proverbs is a review of the "typologies of theology and language" that he claims to have been discredited. For many scholars, this seems like a demand to reinvent the wheel, but we must recognize that many traditional positions long rejected by "mainstream" scholarship are still held tenaciously by a significant segment of the membership of SBL. If the LP of higher criticism is scratchy, this is not because of its trust in human reason but because it has been played for more than a century. But many still have not heard it.

Biblical criticism as it has developed during the lifetime of the SBL has had the character of a conversation. Over time, the participants and the kinds of participants in that conversation have changed. New participants bring new perspectives. It is of the essence of critical scholarship that no position is exempt from challenge, if evidence and argument warrant it (Troeltsch's principle of criticism). The task of the Society of Biblical Literature, in fostering biblical scholarship, is to facilitate that conversation. In the process, it should ensure that scholarship retains its critical focus and respects the presuppositions of public discourse. But it is also its mission to broaden the conversation, to bring new people to the table and to engage their concerns. This process may be uncomfortable, and it is not without danger to the coherence and collegiality of the Society, but it is necessary nonetheless. So when we bid farewell to Kent Harold Richards, who has been the most consistent face of the Society for a generation, we should not bid farewell to the SBL or abandon the task of ongoing dialogue.

Bibliography

Aichele, George, Fred W. Burnett, Elizabeth A. Castelli, Robert M. Fowler, David Jobling, Stephen D. Moore, Gary A. Phillips, and Tina Pippin. *The Postmodern Bible: The Bible and Culture Collective*. New Haven: Yale University Press, 1995.

Barr, James. *History and Ideology in the Old Testament: Biblical Studies at the End of a Millennium*. Oxford: Oxford University Press, 2000.

Brueggemann, Walter. *Texts under Negotiation: The Bible and Postmodern Imagination*. Minneapolis: Fortress, 1993.

———. *Theology of the Old Testament: Testimony, Dispute, Advocacy*. Minneapolis: Fortress, 1997.

Childs, Brevard S. *Biblical Theology in Crisis*. Philadelphia: Westminster, 1970.

Clines, David J. A. "Possibilities and Priorities of Biblical Interpretation in an International Perspective." *BibInt* 1 (1993): 67–87.

Collingwood, R. G. *The Idea of History*. Oxford: Oxford University Press, 1946.

Collins, John J. *The Bible after Babel: Historical Criticism in a Postmodern Age*. Grand Rapids: Eerdmans, 2005.

Derrida, Jacques. *Limited Inc*. Evanston, Ill.: Northwestern University Press, 1988.

Funk, Robert W. "The Watershed of the American Biblical Tradition: The Chicago School, First Phase, 1892–1920." *JBL* 95 (1976): 4–22.

Gunn, David M., and Danna Nolan Fewell. *Narrative in the Hebrew Bible*. Oxford Bible Series. Oxford: Oxford University Press, 1993.

Harvey, Van A. *The Historian and the Believer: The Morality of Historical Knowledge and Christian Belief*. New York: MacMillan, 1966.

Hendel, Ronald S. "Farewell to SBL: Faith and Reason in Biblical Studies." *BAR* 36 (July–August 2010): 28, 74, http://www.bib-arch.org/bar/article.asp?PubID=BSBA&Volume=36&Issue=4&ArticleID=9.

Gadamer, Hans-Georg. *Truth and Method*. New York: Crossroad, 1975.

Johnson, Luke Timothy. *The First and Second Letters to Timothy*. AB 33A. New York: Doubleday, 2001.

Levenson, Jon D. *The Hebrew Bible, The Old Testament, and Historical Criticism*. Louisville: Westminster John Knox, 1993.

Morgan, Robert, with John Barton. *Biblical Interpretation*. Oxford: Oxford University Press, 1988.

Niebuhr, Richard R. *Resurrection and Historical Reason*. New York: Scribners, 1957.

Patte, Daniel. *The Ethics of Biblical Interpretation: A Reevaluation*. Louisville: Westminster John Knox, 1995.

Provan, Iain, V. Phillips Long, and Tremper Longman III. *A Biblical History of Israel*. Louisville: Westminster John Knox, 2003.

Richards, Kent Harold. "Leadership with New Vision." *SBL Society Report* (2003): 3.

Rorty, Richard. *Philosophy and the Mirror of Nature*. Princeton: Princeton University Press, 1979.

Said, Edward. "Michael Walzer's 'Exodus and Revolution,' A Canaanite Reading." *Grand Street* 5 (Winter 1986): 86–106.

Sakenfeld, Katharine Doob. "Whose Text Is It?" *JBL* 127 (2008): 5–18.

Saunders, Ernest W. *Searching the Scriptures: A History of the Society of*

Biblical Literature, 1880–1980. SBLBSNA 8. Chico, Calif.: Scholars Press, 1982.

Schüssler Fiorenza, Elisabeth. "The Ethics of Biblical Interpretation: De-centering Biblical Scholarship." *JBL* 107 (1988): 3–17.

———. "Feminist Hermeneutics." *ABD* 2:783–91.

———. *Jesus and the Politics of Interpretation.* New York: Continuum, 2000.

Schweiker, William. Review of Daniel Patte, *Ethics of Biblical Interpretation,* and David Penchansky, *The Politics of Biblical Interpretation: A Postmodern Reading. JR* 76 (1996): 355–57.

Vanhoozer, Kevin J. "Introduction: What Is Theological Interpretation of the Bible?" Pages 19–25 in *The Dictionary for Theological Interpretation.* Edited by Kevin J. Vanhoozer. Grand Rapids: Baker, 2005.

Waltke. Bruce K. Review of Michael V. Fox, *Proverbs 10–31: A New Translation with Introduction and Commentary, RBL.* Online: http://bookreviews.org/pdf/7219_7855.pdf.

Whitelam, Keith. *The Invention of Ancient Israel: The Silencing of Palestinian History.* London: Routledge, 1996.

Politics and Biblical Scholarship in the United States*

Douglas A. Knight

Inside many churches in the United States, near the pulpit in the front, stand two flags, the American flag and the Christian flag. The presence of the American flag in a house of worship may appear odd to many from other countries, but it is not considered out of place to a large portion of the American population. Patriotism and piety go hand in hand, supporting each other and in fact even defining each other. A believer may be patriotic because it is God's will to work through the country, and a patriot may consider freedom to be a gift from God. We will return shortly to this relationship between religiosity and patriotism, but first more on the second flag, the Christian flag. A majority may not even know that it exists, and I doubt that it is present in other parts of the world except for those places, especially in South America and Africa, to which missionaries have taken it. In appearance it has a solid white field with a blue square in the upper inside corner and a red cross against the blue background, each of these colors symbolizing Christian attributes. It was reportedly developed in New York in 1897 in the wake of flag fervor evident in the pledge of allegiance to the American flag, which was composed only five years earlier:

---

* This essay is based on a lecture delivered at the Centre for Bible and Cultural Memory, Faculty of Theology, University of Copenhagen, on February 24, 2010. I want to express my gratitude especially to Dr. Pernille Carstens, the Centre's director, for the invitation. This revised version is presented to Kent Harold Richards in recognition of his many years of service as Executive Director of the Society of Biblical Literature, in which position he devoted considerable effort to enhancing the cultural and political significance of biblical scholarship, including its international scope.

> I pledge allegiance to the flag of the United States of America, and to the republic for which it stands, one nation under God, indivisible, with liberty and justice for all.

Designed to be concise and pointed and to take less than fifteen seconds to recite, this pledge to the American flag was written by a Baptist minister, Rev. Francis Bellamy. In 1954 the phrase "under God" was added by act of Congress, although various groups had used it earlier.

In 1907, soon after the creation of the Christian flag, a Methodist minister named Rev. Lynn Harold Hough wrote a so-called "pledge of allegiance" to the Christian flag, patterned in cadence and style after the oath to the American flag. The pledge to the Christian flag states:

> I pledge allegiance to the Christian Flag, and to the Savior for whose kingdom it stands, one Savior, crucified, risen and coming again, with life and liberty for all who believe.

An alternate pledge is sometimes used:

> I pledge allegiance to the Christian Flag and to the Savior for whose kingdom it stands, one brotherhood uniting all mankind in service and love.

The Christian flag is commonplace in mainline Protestant churches in the United States, although it normally receives little notice. Groups of children in church are sometimes taught to recite the pledge, with all standing and placing the right hand over the heart, as is done when pledging allegiance to the American flag. More striking, perhaps, is yet another pledge, this one to the Bible, which typically follows the Christian flag oath:

> I pledge allegiance to the Bible, God's Holy Word. I will make it a lamp unto my feet and a light unto my path and will hide its words in my heart that I might not sin against God.

To my knowledge, there is no Bible flag. The Christian flag and the pledges to it and to the Bible serve as an example of the intermingling of politics and religion for some Americans. I say "some Americans" because, while certain circles express these sentiments vigorously, many other citizens do not share them but consider them as expressions of the religious Right. It is one example of a phenomenon in American life: the remarkable diversity in the general populace, and even just among religious adherents, regarding religious beliefs and practices.

American Religiosity

Before we turn to politics and biblical scholarship, a sketch of American religiosity and then of politics and the Bible may help to make the impact of this culture on biblical scholarship more understandable. While much of this information will be familiar to those who study or observe carefully the practice of religion in the United States, others, whether residents of other countries or Americans who do not belong to a religious community, may not fully appreciate how deeply religious the United States is as a nation, both in terms of the numbers and in light of popular culture. In 2007 the Pew Forum on Religion and Public Life, one of the projects of the nonpartisan Pew Research Center, conducted a poll of more than 35,000 American adults, one of the most comprehensive assessments ever completed.[2] The results may or may not be surprising, depending on the extent of one's familiarity with American culture. Here is a sampling of the findings:

(1) When asked whether they believe in God or some type of universal spirit, 71 percent replied they were absolutely certain and 17 percent fairly certain of the existence of God or a universal spirit, for a total of 88 percent of the general population. Among those who self-identified as Christians, the percentages were 95 percent and above. Only 5 percent of the respondents stated they were atheists. Of the various religious traditions, the Jewish community accounted for the largest single group of atheists and agnostics, with 21 percent denying or doubting the existence of God.[3]

(2) The 35,000 respondents were also asked how often they attended religious services, not counting weddings and funerals; 39 percent said at least once a week, and another 15 percent reported once or twice a month.

---

2. For the results of the U.S. Religious Landscape Survey, see http://religions.pewforum.org.

3. *U.S. Religious Landscape Survey: Religious Beliefs and Practices: Diverse and Politically Relevant* (June 2008): 26. The Pew Forum on Religion and Public Life. Online: http://religions.pewforum.org/pdf/report2religious-landscape-study-chapter-1.pdf.

Thus 54 percent indicate they attend services relatively frequently. Only 11 percent never go to services.[4]

(3) But whether or not they attend religious services, how did the respondents view the role of religion in their lives? A total of 82 percent considered religion to be very important or somewhat important in their lives. Only 16 percent dismissed it as unimportant.[5]

(4) Another intriguing question in the survey focused on convictions. If respondents indicated they were connected to some religious group, they were asked to choose between two statements: "My religion is the one, true faith leading to eternal life, OR: many religions can lead to eternal life." The results are rather unexpected in light of the answers to the earlier questions in the survey. Only 24 percent said their religion is the one, true faith leading to eternal life, while 70 percent responded that many religions can lead to eternal life. Of course, some specific groups had a significantly higher percentage of true and exclusive believers, but the only ones above 50 percent were the Mormons and the Jehovah's Witnesses. At 33 percent the Muslims were not much higher than the national average. On the other hand, only 5 percent of the Jews believed that their religion is the one true faith.[6]

(5) One final result of the survey is worth mentioning because of our focus on the role of the Bible. The Pew Forum tried to determine how the various religious adherents viewed their Scriptures, and depending on each person's religion they asked about the Bible, the Torah, the Koran, or "the Holy Scripture" for other traditions. Then for each there were three options: first, the Scripture is the word of God, literally true word for word; second, the Scripture is the word of God, but not literally true word for word; and third, the Scripture is a book written by humans, not the word of God. For the United States average, a third of the answers went to each option, with slightly more for the first—that the Scripture is the word of God, literally true word for word. There were three groups that answered this way at 50 percent or above—historically black churches, evangelical churches, and Muslims, in that order. On the other hand, of the groups that registered above 50 percent in believing

---

4. Ibid, 36 and 117.
5. Ibid, 23.
6. Ibid, 58.

that their Scripture was written by humans and was not the word of God, there were only two, the highest being the Buddhists and then the Jews.[7]

The results of this extensive survey support the sense that American citizens are, by and large, a very religious people. By comparison, I suspect that in Europe, for example, the first numbers in each category would be considerably lower—regarding belief in God, attendance at religious services, sense of the personal importance of religion, view of the exclusive truth of one's religion, and belief in the divine or human origin of one's Scripture. Other countries will vary according to their own secular or religious character. The distinctiveness of the United States would be especially apparent if I were to say that it is highly unlikely—perhaps even impossible—for a person to be elected to the American presidency or other high office if he or she is not publicly religious, that is, does not publicly acknowledge adherence to some religious tradition and demonstrate it by attending religious services. Citizens in other countries would need to say whether the same applies in their homelands.

Another point is crucial for understanding American religiosity, namely the remarkable diversity of belief within the United States population. This diversity may, in fact, play an even greater role in the country than does secularism as the lines dividing religious groups from each other are at times formidable. Christians constitute by far the largest portion of the population, and of them Roman Catholicism claims the greatest single group, almost a fourth of the adult population, although this number has declined over the past several years. All of the Protestant groups taken together have long been in the majority, but they may be moving toward minority status if the trend holds: only 51 percent of the population identify themselves as Protestant currently, compared to more than 60 percent only thirty years ago.[8] While the mainline Protestant denominations—Lutherans, Anglicans, Presbyterians, Methodists, Baptists, and others—have also declined, so-called evangelical churches have increased dramatically. Most of the latter are not aligned with traditional denominations, and some mainline churches have also deliberately stopped advertising their own denominational identity in order to appeal to those individuals who may find it too confining to be connected to an

---

7. Ibid, 31.

8. *U.S. Religious Landscape Survey: Religious Affiliation: Diverse and Dynamic* (February 2008): 18. Pew Forum on Religion and Public Life. Online: http://religions.pewforum.org/pdf/report-religious-landscape-study-chapter-1.pdf.

explicit denomination. Some Christian groups try to proselytize among other Christian groups, not just among non-Christians. On the other hand, some fundamentalist groups, convinced that their faith alone is the true faith, avoid contact with other Christian congregations. Divisiveness also occurs within groups, and churches splinter over a controversial minister or a heated issue such as abortion or simply suspicion about the piety of others in the congregation.

Two other recent developments are worth noting. One is the rise of many so-called megachurches, defined as those with 2,000 or more persons attending worship services weekly and with an active program throughout the whole week. According to a recent study by The Hartford Institute, there are more than 1,200 such Protestant megachurches in the United States and another 3,000 large Roman Catholic churches. Many megachurches average 10,000–35,000 people in attendance every Sunday, meeting in what seems an arena. Most are conservative in theology, and more than a third have no connection with traditional denominations. To be sure, several churches in Korea are even larger than these in size.[9]

The other new development is sometimes referred to as "new-paradigm churches," a form of cultural response to the formality of traditional churches. With roots in the Jesus movement of the 1960s and 1970s, they are characterized by contemporary worship styles, evangelical theology, personal religious experiences, Christian rock music (usually 30–45 minutes of it during the worship service), informal dress, and lay leadership. They typically meet not in church buildings but in schools, warehouses, or other secular settings. These new-paradigm churches have sprung up everywhere, and studies of them have only recently begun to emerge.[10]

The extent of the Bible's influence on popular culture can scarcely be overemphasized. While any number of studies and examples demonstrate the extent of the Bible's reach in the culture, one recent publication makes the point in a visually dramatic manner: photographer Sam Fentress's *Bible Road: Signs of Faith in the American Landscape*.[11] It is the result of

---

9. "Megachurch Definition" (September 2008). Hartford Institute for Religious Research. Online: http://hirr.hartsem.edu/megachurch/definition.html.

10. For example, Donald E. Miller, *Reinventing American Protestantism: Christianity in the New Millennium* (Berkeley and Los Angeles: University of California Press, 1997).

11. Sam Fentress, *Bible Road: Signs of Faith in the American Landscape*, with a foreword by Paul Elie (Cincinnati: David & Charles Publishers, 2007).

twenty-five years of photographing chance sightings of signs throughout the United States. Especially noteworthy are the expressions of an absolutistic demand of faith ("Prepare to meet thy God"; "God's got an army all over this land"; "Go to Church or the Devil will get you!") as well as the images showing the intersection of religion and economics ("Jesus is Lord of this Company"; "Praise the Lord Burger & Fries"; "Jesus said ye must be born again John 3:7 – Area Size Rug Sale 20% off").

Finally, the diversity among non-Christian religions plays a significant role on the American scene as well. The United States is a heterogeneous nation of immigrants. In another thirty to forty years the white majority now will be in the minority; that is, all of the minority groups, taken together, will total more than the white population of European descent. Immigrants have continually brought new faiths from their lands of origin. About 5 percent of the population follows other world religions. Judaism, at about 2 percent, is the largest of them at present. Islam is among the faster growing religions in the country now, as it is in the world. Buddhism and Hinduism have many followers as well, and there is a long list of smaller groups, including Bahá'í, Taoist, and Wiccan. In addition, many individuals avoid structured religious institutions altogether in favor of some other context in which they can express their spirituality, a code word for a variety of nontraditional or non-Western forms of religious expression.

Politics and the Bible

What difference does this religiosity make on the political scene in the United States? Specifically, what role does the Bible play in it? The short answer is that the Bible figures prominently in collective life—socially, politically, and economically, as may only be expected in light of people's beliefs. According to the Pew survey, over 60 percent of the population believes that the Bible is the word of God, and more than half of them consider it to be literally true, word for word.[12] It would be surprising if people did not think that something so true and so divine should influence common life. To anyone who doubts the intimate connection between the Bible and American culture and politics I recommend perusal of a new edition of the Bible that appeared in 2009: *The Ameri-*

---

12. *U.S. Religious Landscape Survey: Religious Beliefs and Practices*, 31 and 126.

can *Patriot's Bible: The Word of God and the Shaping of America*, edited by Richard G. Lee.[13] Interspersed among the pages of the New King James Version are historical notes from American history, biographical comments on the Presidents, and observations that connect biblical themes with American patriotism.

A quick review of constitutional issues will set the stage for some specific instances showing the potential conflict between law and religion. Ratified in 1791, the First Amendment of the United States Constitution lays out the fundamental principle regarding the relationship between religion and government:

> Congress shall make no law respecting an establishment of religion, or prohibiting the free exercise thereof; or abridging the freedom of speech, or of the press; or the right of the people peaceably to assemble, and to petition the Government for a redress of grievances.

The first part—"no law respecting an establishment of religion"—is known as the Establishment Clause and explicitly prohibits Congress from any action that in effect establishes a national or state religion. The second part—"or prohibiting the free exercise thereof"—is referred to as the Free Exercise Clause and focuses more on practices than on beliefs or state sanctions. Neither clause is free of ambiguities, and for years the United States Supreme Court has made rulings to interpret the meaning and application of each.

The recurring issue in American politics of "states' rights" keeps before the public and the courts the problem of distinguishing between the laws individual states are allowed to make for themselves and the laws the federal government can pass to override any special interests the states may have. For example, can a given state allow prayers in school, or should the Supreme Court prohibit all such laws, disallowing prayers that are overtly confessional in nature and that seem to be sanctioned by the school administration? Or again, are schools permitted to plan Bible-study courses or assigned readings? There are limitless specific examples, but the general point is that it is contrary to the First Amendment for any level of government to allow any religious action or practice that in effect favors one religious view or one religious institution over others. Thomas Jeffer-

---

13. Richard G. Lee, *The American Patriot's Bible: The Word of God and the Shaping of America* (Nashville: Thomas Nelson, 2009).

son, the third president of the United States (1801–1809), expressed the general meaning of this Amendment with his famous metaphor—that the law was intended to erect "a wall of separation between church and State."

In 1971 the Supreme Court ruled in Lemon v. Kurtzman on a violation of the Establishment clause, and that ruling resulted in what has become known as the "Lemon Test," which involves three basic principles: (1) A statute must have a secular legislative purpose; (2) A statute must not have the primary or principal effect of either advancing or inhibiting religion; and (3) A statute must not foster an "excessive government entanglement with religion." These principles seem clear enough, and they have often been cited in recent decades, even though the present conservative leaning of the Supreme Court seems to be eroding their strength. The problem lies in the interpretation and application of the First Amendment. Three examples from areas with which scholars and educators in biblical fields have some familiarity can demonstrate the legal complexities. Each case involves a convergence of social conservatism and religion, in short: politics.

(1) The Ten Commandments are frequently on display in private and public settings, but a line was crossed in July 2001 when Roy Moore, Chief Justice of the Alabama state Supreme Court, installed a monument bearing the Decalogue in the rotunda of the state judicial building. It was a large granite block weighing 2,400 kg, and on the top was an image like an open book with an engraving of the Ten Commandments on it. Considerable national attention focused on this incident, with severe divisions among people as to whether or not it represented state support of a specific religion. Justice Moore had not been vague about his intents. At the installation of the monument he made the statement: "Today a cry has gone out across our land for the acknowledgment of that God upon whom this nation and our laws were founded.... May this day mark the restoration of the moral foundation of law to our people and the return to the knowledge of God in our land." I doubt he would have said the same if someone had erected a replica of Hammurabi's stele. Eventually a federal judge ruled that the Ten Commandments monument violated the Establishment Clause of the First Amendment, and he ordered that it be removed. Justice Moore refused, and a large crowd of supporters protested outside while it was taken away. Subsequently, Moore was removed from his Chief Justice position. He later ran for the office of governor of the state of Alabama but lost by a two-to-one margin.

(2) The theory of evolution has long been a target of people on the reli-

gious Right, and their alternative usually goes by the name "creationism." There is even a $27-million park in Kentucky devoted to it—the "Creation Museum," complete with images of Adam and Eve in the garden, a panoramic theater presentation showing God's creation of the earth in six days, a model of Noah's ark, and a special "Biblical Authority Room" to show "how God's Word has been attacked over and over, but has withstood every attack." The park opened in 2007 and has been popular with certain groups of Christians ever since. Although not specifically focusing on the issue of evolution, another effort to create a theme park, to be named Bible Park USA[14] and planned to cost $175 million, failed when it met with local opposition.

The early twentieth century witnessed several controversies over creation vs. evolution, probably the best known being the court case called the Scopes Monkey Trial, which brought national attention to the small town of Dayton, Tennessee. In 1925 John T. Scopes, a local school teacher, was charged with teaching human evolution to his young students. The Tennessee state law at the time (the Butler Act) prohibited the teaching of human evolution in public schools: public school teachers were forbidden "to teach any theory that denies the story of the Divine Creation of man as taught in the Bible, and to teach instead that man has descended from a lower order of animals." At points the trial took on a circus-like atmosphere as the courtroom packed with spectators, the lawyers sparred with each other, and many journalists reported on the drama and the local citizens, who were often depicted as uneducated buffoons. The trial has, in fact, been fictionalized in the well-known 1960 movie *Inherit the Wind*, directed by Stanley Kramer and starring Spencer Tracey and Frederic March.[15]

Much of the trial intrigue centered not so much on the defendant Scopes but on his lawyer Clarence Darrow and one of the lawyers for the prosecution, William Jennings Bryan, a well-known orator and politician who had previously run unsuccessfully for United States president. Darrow, the defense lawyer, managed to get Bryan on the stand as a witness. Darrow then asked Bryan about making calculations on the basis of the flood accounts in the Bible, and the following exchange occurred:

---

14. The website http://www.bibleparkusa.com was still posted on 23 June 2010.
15. The movie was based on the play by Jerome Lawrence and Robert E. Lee, *Inherit the Wind* (New York: Random House, 1955).

Bryan: I never made a calculation.
Darrow: What do you think?
Bryan: I do not think about things I don't think about.
Darrow: Do you think about things you do think about?
Bryan: Well, sometimes.[16]

The trial ended with Scopes being convicted and fined $100 (equal to over $1,000 now, adjusted to inflation). The Tennessee law was not repealed until 1967, and the United States Supreme Court in 1968 (Epperson v. Arkansas) ruled that such laws were unconstitutional. In 1981 another case, McLean v. Arkansas Board of Education, became well known in religious studies circles because of the book about it by theologian Langdon Gilkey, who testified as an "expert" witness.[17]

This issue of evolution vs. creationism has never died. A remarkable number of people still consider evolution to be contrary to biblical teachings, and many agree with the notion of a "young earth"—that the earth and all life in it were created less than ten thousand years ago, somewhat in line with the well-known calculations of Irish Archbishop James Ussher in the seventeenth century, who placed the date of creation in 4004 B.C.E. The most recent form of the controversy is the notion of "Intelligent Design"—an attempt to circumvent the law prohibiting confessional discussions of God in public schools. Advocates of this notion avoid explicit mention of "God," speaking instead of an intelligence or intelligent force that underlies all of reality and must have produced it. A recent court case (Dover in 2005) held that it is unconstitutional to mandate that "Intelligent Design" be taught in schools. While its proponents talk of "creation science" and bring forth scientists to support it, it is widely considered a pseudo-science that deserves no place in the classroom. As I have argued in several contexts, the notion of "Intelligent Design" is unclear, unhelp-

---

16. "Day 7: Darrow Examines Bryan," Famous Trials in American History: State v. Scopes: Trial Excerpts (February 2004). Online: http://www.law.umkc.edu/faculty/projects/ftrials/scopes/day7.htm. See also Martin Marty, "America's Iconic Book," in *Humanizing America's Iconic Book: Society of Biblical Literature Centennial Addresses 1980* (ed. Gene M. Tucker and Douglas A. Knight; SBLBSNA 6; Chico, Calif.: Scholars Press, 1982), 8–9.

17. Langdon Gilkey, *Creationism on Trial: Evolution and God at Little Rock* (Minneapolis: Winston, 1985; repr., Charlottesville: University Press of Virginia, 1998).

ful, uninformed, unbiblical, unscientific, and quite likely unconstitutional as a topic taught in public education.

(3) The final example of the intersection of politics and the Bible deals with human sexuality and reproduction, especially the separate issues of homosexuality and abortion. According to recent polls, the majority of the United States population supports certain gay rights and the rights of a woman to get an abortion. However, those who oppose both sets of rights are extremely vocal, active, and well financed. What is relevant for us in this context is that they look to the Bible to legitimate their positions.

While the Bible has almost nothing to say explicitly about homosexuality and abortion, those with a strict view of the Bible's authority look for even the slightest support and seize upon it as sufficient for dogma. Only two verses in the Hebrew Bible address male homosexuality, Lev 18:22 and 20:13, and nothing is present about lesbianism. The New Testament also has very little on the subject (Rom 1:26–27; 1 Cor 6:9–10; and 1 Tim 1:9-10). Abortion is not even treated in the Bible, but contemporary opponents have singled out certain verses and interpreted them in an anti-abortion manner. For example, Jer 1:5 states, "Before I formed you in the womb I knew you, and before you were born I consecrated you." Another is Ps 139:13, which states, "You fashioned me in my mother's womb." Neither says anything about abortion, but the idea that God is involved with fetal growth seems sufficient enough for many. Abortion opponents also try to show how the Bible affirms life, although they do not apply these texts to issues of wartime killing or capital punishment. They could have found more explicit grounds in the Middle Assyrian law (no. A53) that condemns a woman to death by impalement if she has had an abortion, but of course such a source does not carry the canonical authority of the Bible. One response to this proof-texting comes from a well-known evangelical Christian and activist, Jim Wallis, the founder and editor of *Sojourners Magazine*. He is more concerned with peace and social justice issues than with same-sex relationships and abortion, and he has often observed that the Bible contains more than 2,000 verses about poverty. To focus on the narrow base of only a few verses about homosexuality and nothing about abortion represents, he maintains, a gross misdirection away from dominant biblical themes.

Much more could be said about the reciprocity between the Bible and politics in the United States. Preachers, writers, politicians, and other citizens have seized upon biblical images and statements to legitimate their own causes: the pilgrims were escaping their Egyptian masters when they left Europe; crossing the Atlantic Ocean was like crossing the Red Sea; the settlers were a chosen people; it was their "manifest destiny" to take the land as their God-given inheritance; the Native American tribes were to be conquered just as Joshua attacked and annihilated the Canaanites (and to this day Native Americans are understandably offended by the story of Joshua's conquest); slavery and segregation were legitimate just as in biblical days; oppression of women and dominion over nature were grounded in the creation stories.

On the other hand, the Bible has also been used for the ends of justice. Just as one side pointed to the Bible to legitimate slavery, another side drew on it to condemn slavery. Martin Luther King Jr., and many others turned to the Bible for support of civil rights. More recently, environmentalists, many now among evangelicals, have found in the Bible warrants for taking care of the earth. The biblical heritage has also stimulated numerous acts of charity and intervention. And not to be overlooked is the role of religion, based on the Bible, in founding and maintaining hundreds of colleges and universities in the United States. William Rainey Harper, himself a scholar of the Hebrew Bible, was co-founder and first president of the University of Chicago, during which time he advocated life-long learning and even developed a course of study for the general public to learn Hebrew.

Politics and Biblical Scholarship in the United States

Religion in its many forms represents the general context for biblical scholarship in the United States. By no means are all Americans devout theists, but many are and many combine it with social and political activism. Biblical literacy is rather low, yet wide sectors of the population seem to have an interest in the Bible and often regard it as authoritative. For this reason those of us who are biblical scholars are frequently approached by the press to comment on some social or political issue—to make a statement for a newspaper, to appear on television, to participate in a radio talk show. We are not necessarily respected or believed by the audience or readership, but we are consulted for opinions and authoritative information.

The Society of Biblical Literature is itself an example of the role of the Bible in American life and education. The SBL has experienced remarkable growth since its founding—from thirty-five members in 1880 to approximately 8,500 at the present time; from eighteen at its first meeting in 1880 to almost five thousand now. It helped to organize the American Schools of Oriental Research in 1900 and the American Academy of Religion in 1909. It is now more of an international society than ever before: about 25 percent of its members come from outside the United States, and over fifty countries are usually represented at the Annual Meetings. Other professional societies, including the European Association of Biblical Studies, increase the presence of biblical studies in international contexts. Within the United States, the SBL has promoted diversity and in turn has been shaped by underrepresented minorities, a prime example of the reciprocal relationship between scholarship and culture, including politics. Until the 1960s it was largely a homogeneous group—male, white, and North American. Now 23 percent of its members are women, and a sizeable number are African American, Hispanic, and members of other nonwhite groups. Many group sessions and individual papers now focus on these minorities—their distinctive experiences, their unique perspectives, and their economic and political situations. Without the chance to meet regularly with others to pursue these discussions, we would not have reached our current stage of understanding and appreciating these differences. In fact, difference has itself become a topic of investigation, as have power, privilege, hegemony, and marginalization. Whereas the SBL and similar international organizations have not introduced these analyses, they have certainly fostered them and will continue to do so.

For much of its history until recent times, American biblical scholarship was a stepchild of European scholarship. Since the end of the nineteenth century many Americans went abroad for their academic training, or they studied with others who had done so. Publications from Germany, Britain, Scandinavia, and elsewhere set the agenda for biblical research, and it was a very rare book from North America that was translated into a European language and read there. Most academic lecturers traveling between Europe and North America went from east to west, not from west to east. American sabbaticants were more likely to spend their study-leaves in Europe than vice versa. When I did my doctoral studies in Göttingen during the tumultuous years from 1968 to 1972, I was in the last wave of students who went to Europe for training. Just as the student generation was throwing off the mantle of authoritative institutions, American students beginning in the 1970s embarked on a new scrutiny of the scholarly status quo and generally stayed at home for their advanced training because of the new intellectual movements emerging at the time.

As a nation of immigrants, the United States is multicultural, but nonetheless its residents—including academics—need to tutor themselves not to become parochial in outlook. To use a common expression, American biblical scholars have now found their own voice, which is actually a choir of voices representing a variety of cultures found in the United States. Yet at the same time, we also have to train students to be mindful of cultures and scholarship from elsewhere in the world. Many if not most graduate programs in biblical studies still require their students to use at least two modern research languages in addition to English, which is one productive way to keep an international focus.

I should also note that biblical scholarship has spread from seminaries, that is, from confessional contexts, to secular university settings. The 1960s introduced a distinction between theological studies and religious studies: theological studies were understood to be oriented toward the practice of religion and the theological affirmation of specific beliefs, whereas religious studies were conducted without any specific confessional community or belief in view. Thus if it does not advocate a specific Christian or Jewish point of view, biblical studies can be included in a state-owned university context without constitutional conflict, just as it has been offered in private secular universities. This distinction between religious and theological studies has more recently come under question as being vague and specious, but it still indicates the way in which the Bible can be taught in universities without violating concerns about religious advocacy.

I conclude by describing three general areas in which American biblical scholarship has been directly affected by American social and political issues. First, as is presumably the case in other countries also, the religious climate, especially in its more conservative form, has influenced many of the historiographical positions taken by American scholars. There is a long-standing intrigue with both history and archaeology among the American people, which takes on distinctive coloring when combined with religious beliefs. The two interrelated movements known as "biblical archaeology" and "biblical theology" in the 1950s and 1960s had a distinctive American form associated with such figures as William F. Albright, John Bright, and G. Ernest Wright. The German scholar Martin Noth, who engaged in a controversy with them about how to assess archaeological and historical evidence, reportedly suspected in private that Albright was theologically conservative, which was entirely likely of this son of Christian missionaries to Chile. Of Nelson Glueck it was said that he went to the southern Levant with a Bible in one hand and a spade in the other as he looked for material traces of biblical Israel. Bright's history of Israel tends to use the biblical narrative as a point of departure, much as both Albright and Wright approached history. For them, the Bible occupied a privileged position that matched the general religious sentiment of many Americans. It was a time rife with political significance as the Second World War came to a close and the opposition between democracy and communism sharpened. As part of the biblical theology movement Wright's notion of the "God who acts," together with von Rad's *Heilsgeschichte*, fit the times and gave biblical studies special weight.

A second area where culture and scholarship have intersected is the rise of new methods since the 1960s and 1970s. Driven more by cultural than religious motives, "*die Achtundsechziger*" relentlessly placed question marks by all manner of institutions, practices, and officials. Foucault and other advocates of critical theory had paved the way with their analyses of power, and social movements focusing on race, gender, class, politics, and colonialism emerged in due course. Biblical critics, in turn, vigorously adopted the methods of feminism, critical race theory, postcolonial criticism, ideological criticism, and postmodernism in general. The relation of these methods to religion is double-sided. On the one hand, religious institutions, authority, doctrines, and traditions have also been the object of these critical analyses. Thus the political and social movements have had the effect of reforming or attempting to reform religious practices or, in some cases, of putting religions on the defensive. On the other hand, moral principles stemming from religions have often reinforced the critique itself. Notions of liberation, accountability, and justice are very much at home in many religious traditions and have provided the motivation for many biblical critics to find in the Bible the warrants for reform. So the question may be: Is the Bible systemically and irredeemably sexist, or racist, or classist, or hegemonic? Or, can biblical scholarship find in the Bible a source for overcoming sexism, racism, classism, and hegemony? Scholars in America, as elsewhere, have taken positions on both sides of these questions.

Finally, social issues are prevalent in both political discussions and biblical scholarship. Whether coming from the Right or the Left, such issues as poverty, health care, immigration, abortion, homosexuality, education, scientific research, the natural environment, disabilities, crime, warfare, domestic violence, and drug use will continue to need attention. Religious groups did not introduce most of these issues, although one or the other religious group is likely to advance or oppose each. Biblical scholars often address these same issues, not necessarily because they are inclined on their own to do so but because they are often asked to clarify the Bible's stance on the issues. I think this attention to social issues also explains why so many biblical scholars, myself included, are interested in the social history of ancient Israel and the ancient Near East. The sociohistorical method, bolstered with a critique of society and culture, is now evident in many dissertations and monographs, and I expect it will only increase in coming years.

Biblical scholarship in the United States has frequently been influenced by the country's political and social environment, as is only to be expected. In turn, the Bible and biblical scholarship have affected societal discussions, political rhetoric, and partisan voting. The roots for the Bible's enormous role reach back to the early history of the country, but the forms of the Bible's impact have been anything but predictable or uniform. Biblical scholarship and culture have continuously shaped each other, and it will likely not abate in light of America's unique history with religion. At the same time, new impulses will only intensify as new immigrants bring their own histories to add to the mixture already present in the country, and changes to the status quo are inevitable. Biblical scholarship will need to keep responsive to these cultural developments—both to stay relevant and to remain intellectually alive.

BIBLIOGRAPHY

"Day 7: Darrow Examines Bryan." Famous Trials in American History: State v. Scopes: Trial Excerpts (February 2004). Online: http://www.law.umkc.edu/faculty/projects/ftrials/scopes/day7.htm.

Fentress, Sam. *Bible Road: Signs of Faith in the American Landscape*, with a foreword by Paul Elie. Cincinnati: David & Charles Publishers, 2007.

Gilkey, Langdon. *Creationism on Trial: Evolution and God at Little Rock*. Minneapolis: Winston Press, 1985. Repr., Charlottesville: University Press of Virginia, 1998.

Lawrence, Jerome, and Robert E. Lee. *Inherit the Wind*. New York: Random House, 1955.

Lee, Richard G. *The American Patriot's Bible: The Word of God and the Shaping of America*. Nashville: Thomas Nelson, 2009.

Marty, Martin. "America's Iconic Book." Pages 1-23 in *Humanizing America's Iconic Book: Society of Biblical Literature Centennial Addresses*

1980. Edited by Gene M. Tucker and Douglas A. Knight. SBLBSNA 6. Chico, Calif.: Scholars Press, 1982.
"Megachurch Definition" (September 2008). Hartford Institute for Religious Research. Online: http://hirr.hartsem.edu/megachurch/definition.html.
Miller, Donald E. *Reinventing American Protestantism: Christianity in the New Millennium.* Berkeley and Los Angeles: University of California Press, 1997.
U.S. Religious Landscape Survey: Religious Affiliation: Diverse and Dynamic (February 2008). Pew Forum on Religion and Public Life. Online: http://religions.pewforum.org/pdf/report-religious-landscape-study-chapter-1.pdf.
U.S. Religious Landscape Survey: Religious Beliefs and Practices: Diverse and Politically Relevant (June 2008). The Pew Forum on Religion and Public Life. Online: http://religions.pewforum.org/pdf/report2religious-landscape-study-chapter-1.pdf.

Ex-Centric Reading:
A Case for Critical Reorientation*

Vincent L. Wimbush

I should like to recall one of the famous passages from Frederick Douglass's famous *Narrative of the Life of Frederick Douglass, An American Slave, Written by Himself* (1845).[1] The slightly older, writerly Douglass makes the incident a singularly pointed one for narratological effect, but it may very well have been a recurring one. It is an incident that Douglass, still the relatively young but emerging lion-voiced abolitionist, remembers and recounts for the (assumed abolitionist-minded) reader, with the poignant glosses of one who has been a slave. What he touches upon and opens up are several issues that provide perspective and challenge for all moderns, especially those interested and invested in thinking about critical thinking and interpretation.

> The home plantation of Colonel Lloyd wore the appearance of a country village.... It was called by the slaves the *Great House Farm*.... The slaves selected to go to the Great House Farm, for the monthly allowance for themselves and their fellow-slaves, were peculiarly enthusiastic. While on their way, they would make the dense woods, for miles around, reverberate with their wild songs, revealing at once the highest joy and the deepest sadness. They would compose and sing as they went along, consulting neither time nor tune. The thought that came up, came out—if not in the word, in the sound; and—as frequently in the one as in

---

* This essay is a revision of an address delivered at a conference sponsored by the Institute for Signifying Scriptures on Communities of Color, Scriptural Interpretation and Readings of American Culture, Claremont Graduate University, October 2009.

1. Found in Frederick Douglass, *Narrative of the Life of Frederick Douglass, An American Slave, Written by Himself*, in *The Oxford Frederick Douglass Reader* (ed. William L. Andrews; Oxford: Oxford University Press, 1996 [1845]), 1–97.

the other. They would sometimes sing the most pathetic sentiment in the most rapturous tone, and the most rapturous sentiment in the most pathetic tone. Into all of their songs they would manage to weave something of the Great House Farm. Especially would they do this, when leaving home. They would then sing most exultingly…

"I am going away to the Great House Farm!
O, yea! O, yea! O!"

This they would sing, as a chorus, to words which to many would seem unmeaning jargon, but which, nevertheless, were full of meaning to themselves…. I did not, when a slave, understand the deep meaning of those rude and apparently incoherent songs. I was myself within the circle; so that I neither saw nor heard as those without might see and hear. They told a tale of woe which was then altogether beyond my feeble comprehension; they were tones loud, long and deep; they breathed the prayer and complaint of souls boiling over with the bitterest anguish. Every tone was a testimony against slavery, and a prayer to God for deliverance from chains. The hearing of those wild notes always depressed my spirit, and filled me with ineffable sadness. I have frequently found myself in tears while hearing them. The mere recurrence [of] those songs, even now, afflicts me; and while I am writing these lines, an expression of feeling has already found its way down my cheek. To those songs I trace my first glimmering conception of the dehumanizing character of slavery….[2]

In this recounting Douglass names many issues for consideration—subjectivity and consciousness, collective and individual; discourse and power; power and knowledge; knowledge and positionality, or situatedness within a circle; knowledge and the center, knowledge and centers. He names at least three different categories of knowers: slave singers, as those who through their songs provide evidence that they have knowledge (but are not necessarily invested in or skilled at translation work beyond themselves); those without or outside (that is, being outside both within and beyond the narrative), as those who hear the songs only as jargon and so are ignorant and cannot know; and Douglass himself, as the one in the middle, the one who although technically at first "within the circle," did not/could not know; but later, as reflected in his writerly self—ironi-

---

2. Ibid., 37–38.

cally outside the circle of slavery—comes to know. Douglass here makes the point, almost totally lost in the Western Enlightenment/post-Enlightenment world, that the subalterns, who were African slaves, were always knowers, always possessed knowledge that he could not fathom and that others—the outside white world, represented by the Great House Farm—could not fathom.

Douglass's recounting of the incident raises, among many other issues, the problematics of the center, in relationship to which, and long before Foucault, power is structured primarily through knowledge that is produced and apprehended and communicated in relationships. Obviously, the Great House Farm was the center around which the slaves' lives turned; it was a sign of dominance—of whiteness, of racialist and racist colonial slavocracy. Douglass made it clear that the slaves were necessarily oriented toward, and creatively wove into their singing some things about, the Great House Farm; there was simply no way not to reflect the Farm as center. But Douglass also seemed to recognize other different centers/circles—including that center/circle the slaves made among themselves for themselves, with its own discourses, gestures, performances, and epistemologies. This raised the question about the relationships between centers and of the phenomenon of the center itself.

Psychologist and theorist of art Rudolf Arnheim has taught us to think of the center most generally as "a focus of energy from which vectors radiate into the environment."[3] He has reminded us that across cultures the position of the center has been used to give perceivable expression to the divine or some exalted power—the gods, the saint, the monarch, and so forth. These symbols of the center were understood to "dwell above the pushes and pulls of the milling throng ... outside the dimension of time, immobile, unshakable"; they were thought of as the only elements "at rest," whereas everything else must "strain in some specific direction."[4] This squares with what historian of religion and culture Mircea Eliade advanced as an important theme in almost all his works: "Every microcosm, every inhabited region," he argued in *Images and Symbols*, has what may be called a "'Centre' ... a place that is sacred above all."[5]

---

3. Rudolf Arnheim, *The Power of the Center: A Study of Composition in the Visual Arts* (rev. ed.; Berkeley and Los Angeles: University of California Press, 1982), 13.

4. Ibid., 109.

5. Mircea Eliade, *Images and Symbols: Studies in Religious Symbolism* (trans. Philip Mairet; Princeton: Princeton University Press, 1991 [1952]), 39.

With a focus on modern-world social-political formation, but with attention actually paid mainly to Europe, comparative sociologist Shmuel Eisenstadt suggested that social-political centers were "the major foci and frameworks of charismatic orientations," through which the modern social and cultural orders, were defined, and identities were constructed. He also thought that, in the first (read: European) stages of the modern era, most movements of social protest revolved around "the broadening of the scope of participation [in] and channels of access to the centres," and were almost always a reflection of and response to social-class distinctions.[6]

Social scientists have argued that, in comparison to Europe, participation in and access to the center or centers in the United States did not revolve around class/status distinctions. Historical sociologist Adam Seligman sums up this view:

> As an immigrant society, of diverse religious faiths and with divergent cultural backgrounds[,] the American conception of membership and collective identity [was] based on its political ideals[,] not "primordial criteria." The result of this has been that "Americanism is to the American not a tradition, or a territory, not what France is to a Frenchman or England to an Englishman, but a doctrine—what socialism is to a socialist." Adherence to this doctrine and its codes of civil religion and to the political ideals articulated and instituted in the republic, set the parameters of American collective identity. Thus ... becoming an American has meant becoming a believer in this civil religion.[7]

Like every "religion," at least, since the invention of writing and printing, this American "civil religion" has its foundational texts, its scriptures—among which, in the earliest period, were the Declaration of Independence, the Constitution, and Washington's Farewell Address. These texts reflected roots in the English tradition of common law and

---

6. S. N. Eisenstadt, L. Roniger, and A. Seligman, eds., *Centre-Formation, Protest Movements, and Class Struggles in Europe and the United States* (New York: New York University Press, 1987), 19.

7. Adam Seligman, "The American System of Stratification: Some Notes towards Understanding Its Symbolic and Institutional Concomitants," in Eisenstadt, Roniger, and Seligman, *Centre Formation*, 171–72; quoting L. Samson, "America as Surrogate Socialism," in *Failure of a Dream? Essays in the History of American Socialism* (ed. J. H. M. Laslett and S. M. Lipset; Garden City, N.Y.: Anchor, 1974), 426–42.

natural rights, as well as in dissenting Puritanism. These civic texts, as canonical texts, reflected and helped to produce a nationalism that in turn promoted what Americanist François Furstenberg in his book *In the Name of the Father: Washington's Legacy, Slavery, and the Making of a Nation* called "consent ... and a sense of mutual obligation."[8] Furstenberg argued that the civic texts were made to help create, in what has become the U.S., "a powerful mythology" of the Founding Fathers, centered chiefly around George Washington as the "Father of the Nation," the "national patriarch." These civic texts thereby "bound Americans into members of a single nation."[9]

In Protestant Christian America, the civic texts were made to parallel the phenomenon of the reading of the Bible, not just in the scope (or universality) of its readership, but also in the types of practices by which they were engaged.[10] "Citizens" were told to read and interpret these civic texts as "sacred practice." They were taught to "'engrave' Washington's words on their hearts just as they had been taught to internalize passages from the bible ... to take Washington into their hearts just as they took Jesus into their hearts ... to read the Constitution as they read the Ten Commandments."[11] One cleric, in eulogizing Washington as he referenced Washington's Farewell Address, is recorded as having exhorted mourners to take a rather amazing psycho-cultural and hermeneutical step: "bind [the Address] in your Bible next to the Sermon on the Mount that the lessons of your two Saviors may be read together."[12] Juxtapositions of, and identifications between, the nation, the Constitution, the Bible, and the texts of the founders were strong to the point of being at fever pitch in some places. The force of the phenomenon is made clear in the frontispiece to a Bible, the first to be printed in New York, in 1792.[13] The center

---

8. François Furstenberg, *In the Name of the Father: Washington's Legacy, Slavery, and the Making of a Nation* (New York: Penguin, 2006), 10–11, 14, 16–17, 19–20, 220. That such a phenomenon is not unique to the U.S., and should be understood in terms of a comparative history of religions and culture, is reflected in several works, including the work of Buddhism scholar Alan Cole, *Text as Father: Paternal Seductions in Early Mahayana Buddhist Literature* (Berkeley and Los Angeles: University of California Press, 2005).
9. Furstenberg, *In the Name of the Father*, 21.
10. Ibid., 51.
11. Ibid., 52.
12. Ibid.
13. See *The Self-Interpreting Bible: Containing the Sacred Text of the Old and New*

of the image was an allegorical representation of "America" as a woman in a headdress, her elbow resting on a plinth with the names of Revolutionary "fathers" listed, Washington first. In one hand, she holds a scroll of the U.S. Constitution; her other hand reaches forward to accept the Bible from a kneeling woman. A third woman holds a pole atop, which is the liberty cap. Washington's life had become, in effect, a sacred text, needing to be read in order for citizenship to be secured, for American-ness to be confirmed.[14] The skill and practice of reading these civic texts were made the requirement for and registration of civic engagement. Like the situation in ancient Athens or Alexandria or India or China or Calvin's early modern Geneva, citizens in the society that was becoming the United States were understood to be scripture-readers who through their reading could continually affirm their consent to the fathers.

Such practices in the United States were also complexly intertwined with the problem of slavery. The reading of civic texts promoted a paternalist understanding of slavery supposedly grounded in "bonds of affection"; and slavery itself seemed to make more plausible the social-political myth of tacit consent. Insofar as the paternalist image of slavery—to some degree, for some—masked the brutal violence upon which it was established, it helped make easier the acceptance of the lesser forms of coercion involved in persuading "free" Americans to "consent" to their nation.[15] The notion that had obtained in the oratory and writings of Jefferson and Madison (to a lesser degree) that citizenship for "all" was a matter of consent of the living in ongoing dynamic relationship with the living was quite powerful.[16] But by making allegiance to the nation "in the name of the fathers," in connection with the use of civic texts, some forces had betrayed at least one vision of a nation grounded in the consent of the living. The exaltation of the Founding Fathers and the founding documents were turned into objects of uncritical veneration and genuflection. Furstenberg leaves us with a haunting question: "By persuading future generations to live by the will of dead fathers, and to do so *by their own choice*, had civic texts ultimately turned Americans—this people so

---

Testaments, edited by Scottish cleric-theologian the Rev. John Brown (New York: Hodge & Campbell, 1792 [1778]), http://www.electricscotland.com/bible/brown/index.htm. See also Furstenburg, *In the Name of the Father*, 60.

14. Ibid., 61.
15. Ibid., 103.
16. Ibid., 220.

proud of its individual achievements, so prepared to live free or die—into slaves?"[17]

To put the matter as plainly and as bluntly as does Furstenburg—but with respect to the irony of building a box into which one forces oneself to fit—it was, of course, it was white folks (those who first named themselves as such on the basis of their first contact with, including their eventual violent domination of, the Other who was red and black and brown)and then those (who, having been previously dominated and not considered white, but as a result of later social changes over the decades and centuries, including a coarsening of racialist ideologies and the ratcheting up of racial violence) were later grafted into whiteness; it was these folks who were identified with and participated in this center-ing formation that involved reading civic texts and scriptures, civic texts as scriptures.[18] As the late critic and theorist in whiteness studies Ruth Frankenberg helped us to understand, these were the folks who were and remain to this day, as a result of a remarkable trick of strategic discourses, "unmarked," referred to in categories not needing to be hyphenated, those whose very existence, their language use, style, looks, tastes, sentiments and feelings are assumed to be standard or conventional.[19] The new white formation that was to be called "America" was made so primarily on the basis of scripture-reading. And the "scriptures"—in consonance with the arguments made above and in conversation with Wilfred C. Smith and other theorists of the phenomenology of scriptures[20]—were (and still are) understood to be quite elastic and tensive, including both "sacred" and "civic" texts. All such texts, not-

---

17. Ibid., 230–31.
18. For general and broad historical perspective, see Martin E. Marty, *Religion and Republic: The American Circumstance* (Boston: Beacon, 1987); idem, *Righteous Empire: Protestant Experience in America* (New York: Scribner's, 1986); and Sydney Ahlstrom, *Religious History of the American People* (New Haven: Yale University Press, 1972).
19. See Ruth Frankenberg, "The Mirage of an Unmarked Whiteness," in *The Making and Unmaking of Whiteness* (ed. Birgit Brander Rasmussen et al.; Durham, N.C.: Duke University Press, 2001), 72–73.
20. See Wilfred C. Smith, *What Is Scripture? A Comparative Approach* (Minneapolis: Fortress, 1993); Miriam Levering, ed., *Rethinking Scripture: Essays from a Comparative Perspective* (Albany: State University of New York Press, 1989); and Vincent L. Wimbush, ed., *Theorizing Scriptures: New Critical Orientations to a Cultural Phenomenon* (Signifying [on] Scriptures Series; New Brunswick, N.J.: Rutgers University Press, 2008).

withstanding their tendencies to include rhapsodic paeans regarding the "all," regarding radical inclusivity, were (and still are) understood, according to the terms of Euro-American canonical-ideological construction and activation, not to have included any but white peoples. The "scriptures" were white—they were presumed to be written *by* white folk, written *about* white folk, written *for* white folk. But, by making the culturalist foundation texts into white scriptures, those who made themselves white ironically made themselves slaves—ideological-discursive slaves, slaves to white texted-ness and canonicity, to the Weberian "iron cage," of scripture-reading.[21] This is in my view the root and baseline of fundamentalisms—religious, social, legal, and so forth—in the United States.

But for this trick regarding whiteness in connection with scriptures to work at all, the Other, the nonwhite person, was supposed to be made invisible and rendered silent. Just as in Robert Penn Warren's famous poem "Pondy Woods" in which the black male character Big Jim, over-determined by the Buzzard (a figure of the American Philological Association/Modern Language Association/Society of Biblical Literature-like authority) was kept silent by the remark: "Nigger, your breed ain't hermeneutical"![22] Or like the astounding almost ex-officio pronouncement "That's not scriptural!" made during the last presidential year by conservative movement leader Tony Perkins on CNN in response to the Rev. Jeremiah Wright's jeremiads against the history of domination and exploitation in the United States.[23] Or like South Carolina congressman

---

21. See Max Weber, *Protestant Ethic and the "Spirit" of Capitalism*, in *The Protestant Ethic and the Spirit of Capitalism: And Other Writings* (ed. and trans. Peter Baehr and Gordon C. Wells; Penguin Twentieth-Century Classics; New York: Penguin, 2002 [1905]), 1–202; and, of course, the different arguments and controversies among his many interpreters, including the issue about how best to translate "stahlhartes Gehaeuse." See, e.g., Peter Baehr, "The 'Iron Cage' and the 'Shell as Hard as Steel': Parsons, Weber, and the Stahlhartes Gehäuse Metaphor in the Protestant Ethic and the Spirit of Capitalism," *History and Theory* 40 (2001): 153–69.

22. Robert Penn Warren, "Pondy Woods," *New and Selected Poems: 1923–1985* (New York: Random House, 1985), 319–21.

23. Tony Perkins (religious conservative and head of the Family Research Council), "Interview with Illinois Senator Barack Obama: Follow Up with Analysts," *Anderson Cooper 360 Degrees*, 14 March 2008, transcript online: http://archives.cnn.com/TRANSCRIPTS/0803/14/acd.01.html. Regarding the Rev. Jeremiah Wright's prophetic words against the United States, Perkins said more fully: "But, clearly, his message was unscriptural. I mean, as Christians, we're instructed in the New Testa-

Joe Wilson's recent unprecedented outburst at the first black president, which represented, according to Emory political scientist Andra Gillespie, an effort to keep Obama from holding forth in authoritative mode and was a refusal to see him (in my view) as the occupant of the office that is our symbol of the center.[24] Notwithstanding these efforts, which have a rather long history, nonwhite folks, who were from the beginning written out of all the scriptures and their mythic histories, and out of the very possibility of legitimate and authoritative interpretation of scriptures, have not kept silent and have not remained invisible.

But, of course, as Douglass's account makes clear, ex-centric peoples—Natives and Africans and the other Others, different still, those who have of their own freewill come to this place, from various places at various times, through various means—have not only not remained silent and invisible, they have not been un-knowing, have not been inept at reading and interpreting scriptures, have not gone without inventing and using their own scriptures. Their "unmeaning jargon" has always "been full of meaning." Not only have they created their own "texts," as writer Ishmael Reed helps us to see they must,[25] they have also "read," signified on, and thus decentered and destabilized—as W. E. B. Du Bois, Zora Neale Hurston, Henry Louis Gates, Jr., Houston Baker, and Toni Morrison and many other critics have helped us understand—the nationalist white scriptures and the white readings of white scriptures.[26]

---

ment to pray for the well-being of our government, so that we might live a peaceful and quiet life. It's — it's hard to imagine how praying for the damnation of one's own country could lead to tranquility, and clearly an un-American message." Given his worldview and assumptions, Perkins's almost apodictic assertion that Wright was "unscriptural" was supposed to discredit his words and essentially end the debate, end Wright's legitimacy as a public religious figure.

24. Regarding challenges to Obama's leadership and the attempt to silence him, see Andra Gillespie, "Obama Vulnerable on Leadership, says Emory's Gillespie." *Emory University News Release*, online: http://shared.web.emory.edu/emory/news/releases/2009/09/obama-vulnerable-leadership-gillespie.html.

25. See Ishmael Reed's fascinating work *Mumbo Jumbo* (New York: Scribner, 1996 [1972]).

26. These writers do not address these matters in direct terms regarding scriptures in the traditional or narrow terms, but their theorizing and argumentation do address scriptures in broad and expansive terms, as argued for in this essay. The work of making connections between such critics and scriptures and setting forth some implications of their projects for the critical study of scriptures remains to be done.

Scripturalizing and scripture readings from the peripheries may seem at first to represent only, as W. E. B. Du Bois first indicated in *Souls of Black Folk* and as later theorized by Houston Baker in *Afro-American Poetics: Revisions of Harlem and the Black Aesthetic*, "omissions and silences."[27] But with deeper excavation of what Baker calls the "frenzied, laconic, and fragmented discursive 'lowgrounds and inaudible valleys,'" we can hear the songs of the sort sung by the slaves Douglass knew.[28] On the peripheries, the silence is really code, like Zora Neale Hurston's "hidden meanin'" and its strategic off-stage double-voicing.[29]

From the positions off-center, things look different and require different sensibilities and practices, including sensibilities and apprehensions about centers and peripheries themselves. This may be what Krister Stendahl in his 1983 Society of Biblical Literature presidential address was getting at when he nervously acknowledged that the apparent scribal-guild penchant (as he perceived it in the 1980s) for story and language play, away from history, may reflect a social order's happiness index.

Could it be that preoccupation with history comes natural when one is part of a culture that feels happy and hopeful about the historical process? Hegel's pan-historic philosophy belongs, after all, to the ascendancy of Western imperialism—it was even said that other parts of the world were lifted "into history" when conquered, colonized, or converted by the West. Now the Western world is not so sure or so optimistic about where history—that is, "our" history—is going. So the glamour, the glory, the Shekinah, has moved away from history.[30]

---

27. W. E. B. Du Bois, *Souls of Black Folk* (New York: Bantam, 1989 [1903]); and Houston A. Baker, *Afro-American Poetics: Revisions of Harlem and the Black Aesthetic* (Madison: University of Wisconsin Press, 1988).

28. See Houston A. Baker, "Lowground and Inaudible Valleys: Reflections on Afro-American Spirit Work," in idem, *Afro-American Poetics: Revisions of Harlem and the Black Aesthetic* (Madison: University of Wisconsin Press, 1988), 88–110, esp. 106, 109.

29. See Zora Neale Hurston, *Mules and Men* (New York: Perennial Library, 1990 [1935]), 125. See also Grey Gundaker, *Signs of Diaspora, Diaspora of Signs: Literacies, Creolization and Vernacular Practice in African America* (Oxford: Oxford University Press, 1998); and James C. Scott, *Domination and the Arts of Resistance: Hidden Transcripts* (New Haven: Yale University Press, 1990), for social-scientific development of this theme.

30. See Krister Stendahl's 1983 presidential address: "The Bible as a Classic and

Ex-centric situations, where the oppressed and subaltern are concentrated, reflect, according to Walter Benjamin, the truth that "the 'state of emergency' in which we live is not the exception but the rule."[31] Physician-trained turned transgressive anthropologist and social critic Michael Taussig helps us to understand that Benjamin's unsettling statement was intended to provoke us into coming to "a radically different way" of knowing through the positionality of the outliers: "in a state of siege order is frozen, yet disorder boils beneath the surface. Like a giant spring slowly compressed and ready to burst at any moment, immense tension lies in strange repose ... we are required to rethink our notions of order, of center, and base."[32]

In a fascinating essay, written in 1991, entitled "Deforming Mirror of Truth: Slavery and the Master Narrative of American History" the late Americanist Nathan Huggins argued that the times—the state of emergency defined by a history of brutalization and marginalization of blacks and other nonwhites in the United States—call for a new "narrative" that would force us to face "the deforming mirror of truth,"[33] that is, how our narratives have been woven in relationship to, but at the high expense of, the enslaved. Toni Morrison has called for something similar in her book *Playing the Dark: Whiteness and the Literary Imagination*.[34] She challenged writers and critics, actually, all of us, to "avert the critical gaze from the racial object to the racial subject; from the described and imagined to the describers and imaginers; from the serving to the served."[35] Critical studies, she argued,

> should be investigations of the ways in which a nonwhite, Africanist presence and personae have been constructed—invented—in the United

---

the Bible as Holy Scripture," *JBL* 103 (1984): 209–15, http://www.sbl-site.org/assets/pdfs/PresidentialAddress_Stendahl.pdf.

31. The statement is from Walter B. S. Benjamin, "Theses on the Philosophy of History," in *Illuminations* (ed. Hannah Arendt; trans. Harry Zahn; New York: Schocken, 1969), 253–64. See Michael Taussig's engagement of it in *The Nervous System* (London: Routledge, 1992), 10.

32. Taussig, *The Nervous System*, 10.

33. Nathan Huggins, "Deforming Mirror of Truth: Slavery and the Master Narrative of American History," *Radical History Review* 49 (1991): 44.

34. Toni Morrison, *Playing the Dark: Whiteness and the Literary Imagination* (New York: Vintage Books, 1993).

35. Ibid., 90.

States, and of the literary uses this fabricated presence has served.... All of us, readers and writers are bereft when criticism remains too polite or too fearful to notice a disrupting darkness before its eyes.[36]

The averted critical gaze about which Morrison writes should mean more not less focus on the ex-centrics who have always addressed the "disrupting darkness" that they were.

In *Aircraft Stories: Decentering the Object in Technoscience*,[37] British scholar John Law addresses these same matters, but as sociologist of technology. He argues the need for a different epistemology that would reflect the truth about the multi-dimensionality and fractional nature of reality. Using the pinboard as metaphor for the "object" that was the British aircraft called TSR2 and the approach to studying it, Law offered a generalizable argument for an approach to knowledge of objects that goes beyond the "singularities and multiplicities of modernism and postmodernism."[38] The mere juxtaposition of images and the making of pastiches raises for him the notion that the world is "not a singular place," that objects in the world—an object like an aircraft—are both multiple and singular. This in turn suggests the importance of the "ordering logics of the fractionally coherent object," the prospect that there are different and valid knowledges that can be neither entirely reconciled nor dismissed, that knowing may be a process that is "decentered, distributed, but also partially connected."[39]

Then John Law makes a claim that is astounding: "it requires fractional subjects to know…fractional objects."[40] His "logic of the pinboard" is understood as epistemology and methodology, ways of knowing that escape the possibilities of a single narrative that performs "denial of the conditions of its possibility," that makes it possible to know about features of the world that deny themselves when everything is drawn together into a single story.[41] Law's logic of the pinboard salutes "noncoherence, the play of the fractional."[42]

---

36. Ibid., 90–91.
37. John Law, *Aircraft Stories: Decentering the Object in Technoscience* (Durham, N.C.: Duke University Press, 2002).
38. Ibid., 203.
39. Ibid., 193–94.
40. Ibid., 197.
41. Ibid., 197–98.
42. Ibid., 203.

But who are the "fractional objects"? Who or what might model such knowing for us? Law ends his book with a sigh, despairing of the world of which he is part to orient itself in the direction he thinks important. He seems oblivious to the knowledge-making experiences of others as possible historical refractions of the orientation for which he sighs.

In *Mimesis and Alterity: A Particular History of the Senses*,[43] Michael Taussig, ironicially, one of the theorists from whom Law draws some of his arguments, suggests a bridge that would take us, as a way forward, back to the haunting scene that Frederick Douglass paints for us. Taussig challenges readers to consider the mimetic faculty, especially that as performed by the "Third and Other worlds" as a result of their being forced into contact with the "First World." The mirroring that is mimetic excess—"mimetic self-awareness ... turned on itself, on its colonial endowment"[44]—ruptures and destabilizes all identities and all knowledges. In this situation "mastery," canonical knowledge, is no longer possible. In the ongoing fraught histories of contact, dominance is "mirrored in the eyes and handiwork of its Others."[45] This is, of course, an "unsettled" and "unsettling" situation, "a Nervous System—because the interpreting self is itself grafted into the object of study. The self enters into the alter against which the self is defined and sustained."[46]

Taussig here helps to explain the power of Douglass's account: the latter is an example of "mimetic excess"—Douglass the writer is as removed from the slave singers as he is removed from Great House Farm. He thinks about the singers and their mimetics and about the discourse of Great House Farm: he is our window, our way out, our way forward in knowing ex-centric peoples and in ex-centric knowing. And ex-centric knowing is nothing if not marked, that is, self-reflexive, fractional, and decentered.

So ex-centric knowing must now mean reading the center reading itself scripturally and singing all the while doing so. In the context we all share, it means reading America reading itself scripturally, all the while (as Imamu Baraka suggests) "per-forming"[47] texts.

---

43. Michael Taussig, *Mimesis and Alterity: A Particular History of the Senses* (London: Routledge, 1993).
44. Ibid., 252.
45. Ibid., xv, 236.
46. Ibid., 237.
47. Regarding Imamu Baraka, see Kimberly W. Benston, *Performing Blackness: Enactments of African-American Modernism* (Oxford: Routledge, 2000), 13.

But take caution here: not all ex-centrics know they can read or play in this way. Not all flip their reading back in mimetic excess. The lack of such flipping is mimetics of the fundamentalist sort. Not all know how to read themselves reading America.

The challenge remains to find those who may model for us ways out of the fog. We need more ex-centric readers and knowers, who may help us learn that we must always seek, as did Douglass, to know the self by positioning ourselves in complex relationship to—inside and outside—the circle and its center.

Bibliography

Ahlstrom, Sydney. *Religious History of the American People* (New Haven: Yale University Press, 1972).

Arnheim, Rudolf. *Power of the Center: A Study of Composition in the Visual Arts*. Rev. ed. Berkeley: University of California Press, 1982.

Baker, Houston A. *Afro-American Poetics: Revisions of Harlem and the Black Aesthetics*. Madison: University of Wisconsin Press, 1988.

———. "Lowground and Inaudible Valleys: Reflections on Afro-American Spirit Work." Pages 88–110 in idem, *Afro-American Poetics: Revisions of Harlem and the Black Aesthetics*. Madison: University of Wisconsin Press.

Baehr, Peter. "The 'Iron Cage' and the 'Shell as Hard as Steel': Parsons, Weber, and the Stahlhartes Gehäuse Metaphor in the Protestant Ethic and the Spirit of Capitalism." *History and Theory* 40 (2001): 153–69.

Benjamin, Walter B. S. "Theses on the Philosophy of History." Pages 253–64 in *Illuminations*. Edited by Hannah Arendt. Translated by Harry Zahn. New York: Schocken, 1969.

Benston, Kimberly. *Performing Blackness: Enactments of African-American Modernism*. London: Routledge, 2000.

Brown, John. *The Self-Interpreting Bible: Containing the Sacred Text of the Old and New Testaments*. New York: Hodge & Campbell, 1792 (1778). Online: http://www.electricscotland.com/bible/brown/index.htm.

Cole, Alan. *Text as Father: Paternal Seductions in Early Mahayana Buddhist Literature*. Berkeley and Los Angeles: University of California Press, 2005.

Douglass, Frederick. *Narrative of the Life of Frederick Douglass, An American Slave, Written by Himself*. Pages 1–97 in *The Oxford Frederick*

Douglass Reader. Edited by William L. Andrews. Oxford: Oxford University Press, 1996 (1845).
Du Bois, W. E. B. *Souls of Black Folk*. New York: Bantam, 1989 (1903).
Eisenstadt, S. N., L. Roniger, and A. Seligman, eds. *Centre-Formation, Protest Movements, and Class Struggles in Europe and the United States*. New York: New York University Press, 1987.
Eliade, Mircea. *Images and Symbols: Studies in Religious Symbolism*. Translated by Philip Mairet. Princeton: Princeton University Press, 1991 [1952].
Frankenberg, Ruth. "The Mirage of an Unmarked Whiteness." Pages 72–96 in *The Making and Unmaking of Whiteness*. Edited by Birgit Brander Rasmussen, Eric Klinenberg, Irene J. Nexica, and Matt Wray. Durham, N.C.: Duke University Press, 2001.
Furstenberg, François. *In the Name of the Father: Washington's Legacy, Slavery, and the Making of a Nation*. New York: Penguin, 2006.
Gillespie, Andra. "Obama Vulnerable on Leadership, says Emory's Gillespie." *Emory University News Release*. Online: http://shared.web.emory.edu/emory/news/releases/2009/09/obama-vulnerable-leadership-gillespie.html.
Gyndaker, Grey. *Signs of Diaspora, Diaspora of Signs: Literacies, Creolization, and Vernacular Practice in African America*. Oxford: Oxford University Press, 1998.
Huggins, Nathan. "Deforming Mirror of Truth: Slavery and the Master Narrative of American History." *Radical History Review* 49 (1991): 25–48.
Hurston, Zora Neale. *Mules and Men*. New York: Perennial Library, 1990 (1935).
Law, John. *Aircraft Stories: Decentering the Object in Technoscience*. Durham, N.C.: Duke University Press, 2002.
Levering, Miriam, ed. *Rethinking Scripture: Essays from a Comparative Perspective*. Albany: State University of New York Press, 1989.
Marty, Martin E. *Religion and Republic: the American Circumstance*. Boston: Beacon, 1987.
———. *Righteous Empire: Protestant Experience in America*. New York: Scribner's, 1986.
Morrison, Toni. *Playing in the Dark: Whiteness and the Literary Imagination*. New York: Vintage, 1993.
Perkins, Tony. "Interview With Illinois Senator Barack Obama: Follow Up with Analysts." *Anderson Cooper 360 Degrees*, 14 March 2008.

Transcript online: http://archives.cnn.com/TRANSCRIPTS/0803/14/acd.01.html.

Rasmussen, Birgit Brander, Eric Klinenberg, Irene J. Nexica, and Matt Wray, eds. *The Making and Unmaking of Whiteness*. Durham, N.C.: Duke University Press, 2001.

Reed, Ishmael. *Mumbo Jumbo*. New York: Scribner, 1996 (1972).

Samson, L. "America as Surrogate Socialism." Pages 426–42 in *Failure of a Dream? Essays in the History of American Socialism*. Edited by J. H. M. Laslett and S. M. Lipset. Garden City, N.Y.: Anchor, 1974.

Scott, James C. *Domination and the Arts of Resistance: Hidden Transcripts*. New Haven: Yale University Press, 1990.

Seligman, Adam. "The American System of Stratification: Some Notes towards Understanding Its Symbolic and Institutional Concomitants." Pages 161–79 in *Centre-Formation, Protest Movements, and Class Struggles in Europe and the United States*. Edited by S. N. Eisenstadt, L. Roniger, and A. Seligman. New York: New York University Press, 1987.

Smith, Wilfred C. *What Is Scripture? A Comparative Approach*. Minneapolis: Fortress, 1993.

Stendahl, Krister. "The Bible as a Classic and the Bible as Holy Scripture." *JBL* 103 (1984): 209–15. Online: http://www.sbl-site.org/assets/pdfs/PresidentialAddress_Stendahl.pdf.

Taussig, Michael. *Mimesis and Alterity: A Particular History of the Senses*. London: Routledge, 1993.

———. *The Nervous System*. London: Routledge, 1992.

Warren, Robert Penn. "Pondy Woods." Pages in 319–21 in idem, *New and Selected Poems: 1923–1985*. New York: Random House, 1985.

Weber, Max. *Protestant Ethic and the "Spirit" of Capitalism*. Pages 1–202 in *The Protestant Ethic and the Spirit of Capitalism: And Other Writings*. Edited and translated by Peter Baehr and Gordon C. Wells. Penguin Twentieth-Century Classics. New York: Penguin, 2002 (1905).

Wimbush, Vincent L., ed. *Theorizing Scriptures: New Critical Orientations to a Cultural Phenomenon*. Signifying [on] Scriptures Series. New Brunswick, N.J.: Rutgers University Press, 2008.

The Bible in Public View

David L. Petersen

The Christian Bible obviously plays a prominent role in religious communities.[1] It is read, sung, and interpreted. In some faith traditions, Bibles are present throughout the sanctuary in pews. In some faith traditions, the Bible is carried in a procession. In some faith traditions, it is put in a place of honor such as on a communion table, typically with the Bible opened and on a special stand. Whether the Christian Bible is of minimal (a pew Bible) or grandiose (a lectern Bible) size, the phrase "Holy Bible" is routinely printed on the spine. Many publishers and their consumers appear interested in demarcating their Bibles as belonging to the world of the sacred.

Study Bibles do not regularly appear with the phrase "Holy Bible" on their spines. This is true for the *New Oxford Annotated Bible, HarperCollins Study Bible, New Interpreter's Study Bible, and NIV Study Bible*. One might infer that some people distinguish between a "Holy Bible" and a study Bible, an interesting disjunction. Though it is difficult to generalize about the difference in function between a Holy Bible and a study Bible, I would hypothesize that a Holy Bible is likely to be present in a religious context (e.g., a sanctuary), whereas a study Bible may appear in a classroom (e.g., a college class) or in a public library. This distinction attests to the different contexts in which the Bible may be present and the uses to which it may be put.

The character of a study Bible is, more or less, straightforward. Whether in the margins, introductions or appendices, editors and publishers have included material that they think will help readers to understand better the ancient literature. Such supplements include maps,

---

1. I am indebted to Paige Ann Miller for assistance with this essay.

tables explaining ancient weights and measures, indices, timelines, and introductions to biblical books, offering information about when and where they were written as well as sketching the contents of that book. In contrast, a Holy Bible typically includes far less supplementary material. There may be a lectionary to help the owner read through the Bible in one year. Some such Bibles include indices (e.g., "Prayers of the Old and New Testaments" or "Events in Biblical Chronology"). In a "Holy Bible," particularly of the lectern variety, the biblical text is a more or less a stand-alone product.

These two material forms of the Christian Bible attest to the different contexts in which the Bible can appear: one religious; another public. In this essay, I propose to examine three ways in which the Bible functions in the public arena: in a civic ritual, in artistic interpretations, and in public secondary education. In all three venues, the Bible is in public view, beyond the walls of churches.

Civic Ritual

First, based on the distinction between a Holy Bible and a study Bible, one might assume that a Holy Bible functions only within the context of a Christian community. That is not always the case. In the culture of the United States, the Holy Bible also appears beyond the walls of churches and the homes of their adherents. The Bible, or portions thereof (e.g., the Ten Commandments), have been famously present in public ceremonies or on public buildings and/or grounds. The Bible can appear in ceremonies during which an oath is taken. Such practice was routine in courtrooms of the past but is now less frequent. Still, on 20 January 2009, when Barack Obama was inaugurated as the forty-fourth president of the United States, a Holy Bible was very much in evidence. Obama chose to take the oath of office by laying his left hand on the so-called "Lincoln Bible," the Bible that was used when Abraham Lincoln took the oath of office on 4 March 1861. News reporters waxed eloquently about the putative symbolism of this choice of Bibles. What, exactly, the choice meant, however, was not entirely clear. Was it to highlight the role of Lincoln as an emancipator who had made possible the presidency of an African American? Was it to highlight Obama's role as a leader comparable to that of Lincoln? Was it to memorialize this particular volume, which some people now call "The Lincoln and Obama Inaugural Bible"? Was it to underscore the message of freedom from enslavement that is so prominent in the Old Testament? There is no clear answer to these questions.

The particular Bible that Obama chose for this occasion was, of course, a Christian Bible. The title of this particular volume, published by Oxford University Press in 1853, was, "The Holy Bible, Containing the Old and New Testaments, Translated Out of the Original Tongues and with the Former Translations Diligently Compared and Revised, by His Majesty's Special Command." That title alone takes pain to say that what is inside the covers has been the subject of careful work. What lies between the red velvet covers matters. In the ceremony of inauguration, however, what lay inside the Bible did not matter. The Bible remained a mute religious symbol.

Here it is instructive to compare the inauguration of a president in the United States with the coronation of a monarch in England. There, too, a Christian Bible is in play. However, it appears only after the sovereign has taken the oath of office. Once that has happened, that individual is presented with a Bible. A cleric offers the following words: "Here is Wisdom; this is the Royal law; these are the oracles of God." Here there is an overt reference to the content of the book, the language of wisdom, law, and oracles. Furthermore, the act of giving the Bible to the monarch with such a description strongly implies that the monarch is supposed to govern according to the norms and values announced in such wisdom, law, and oracles. This view draws on the traditions of ancient Israel's monarchy, according to which kings were admonished to rule following the precepts of Torah.

During the inaugural moment, Chief Justice Roberts imperfectly led Senator Obama through the oath of office. At the end, President Obama said, "So help me God." Obama's hand was still on the Bible when he uttered those words. How does the Bible function in this scene? There are at least three possible answers: (1) The Bible symbolizes the presence of God. It is like the biblical ark, only this is an ark that someone can touch and still stay alive. Only the president could touch it with his bare hands. In this particular situation, it symbolizes the strength of God, whom Obama is asking for help. (2) The Bible symbolizes the power of God to bless and to curse—to help and to hinder. Obama takes the oath of office with his hand on a book that contains both kinds of words. He has just sworn, among other things, to uphold the Constitution. What if he didn't? Are we to understand that he has implicitly uttered a self-curse, that God will not help him if he does not do those things that he has sworn to accomplish? (3) This Bible is significant because it was touched by the Great Emancipator, Abraham Lincoln. It was anointed and made distinctive by his hand. Barack Obama receives some routinized charisma by taking an oath and also touching that holy book. I don't know which of these options captures the moment most fully, but I suspect portions of each were present.

Though the Bible is present in such a ritual, its significance is difficult to assay, since the Bible remains closed. It is held, even touched, but there is no commentary offered about it. It remains an iconic presence, emphasizing the gravity of a ritual. It functioned as a Holy Bible, though outside the walls of a church.

Artistic Interpretations

Second, the Christian Bible appears prominently in quite another way: as the inspiration for artistic creativity. The Bible has been interpreted in various cultural media, which can be experienced in North America. The following illustrative list identifies one example per genre:

program music	Leonard Bernstein's *Chichester Psalms*
musical	Andrew Lloyd Weber's *Joseph and His Amazing Technicolor Dreamcoat*
movie	Cecil B. DeMille's *The Ten Commandments*
play	Paddy Chayefsky's *Gideon*
opera	George Frideric Handel's *Israel in Egypt*
ballet	Ralph Vaughn William's *Job: A Masque for Dancing*
prose	Thomas Mann's *Joseph and His Brothers*
television program	Lieber, Abrams, and Lindelof's *Lost*
painting	El Greco's *The Adoration of the Shepherds*
etching	Rembrandt's *Sacrifice of Isaac*
poetry	Wilfred Owen's "The Parable of the Old Man and the Young"
comic book	Robert Crumb's *The Book of Genesis*.

I should hasten to add that the list is incomplete, since one could add mosaics, drawings, sculpture, and so forth. All of these exemplars can be viewed, heard, or read in the twenty-first century in North America.

It would be banal simply to observe that the Bible has had a significant influence on artists working in different media. It is, perhaps, better to ask what sort of influence is at work. Are artists "illustrating" the Bible text, or is there a more profound interpretation at work? Or, are they using biblical literature as an occasion to make a point about some issue that does not inhere in the biblical text? Put simply, what do artists "do" with a biblical text? In this portion of the essay, I will comment on an etching, a movie, a television show, and a comic book.

Visitors to art museums routinely encounter various media (i.e., paintings, drawings, etchings, engravings) that "illustrate" or imagine biblical scenes.[2] Visual artists have grappled with both dramatic and quiet biblical scenes. Such interpretations may be extraordinarily sensitive and perceptive. Rarely, however, do they breathe the air of a critical approach to biblical literature (and one should not expect them to do that). Interestingly, however, some do. One thinks, for example, of Rembrandt's etching *Christ Crucified between Two Thieves*, which appears in multiple states. In the first and second states, Jesus is bathed in light. The thieves are positioned on either side of him. In front of Jesus, a man kneels, his hands lifted in a religious posture. Rembrandt seems to have had the Lukan version of the crucifixion in mind: "When the centurion saw what had taken place, he praised God and said, 'Certainly this man was innocent'" (Luke 23:47 NRSV). In the fourth state, however, Rembrandt altered the scene in fundamental ways. Light gives way to dark, and the kneeling figure has disappeared, to be replaced by a large figure on horseback. Similarly, the thief on Jesus' left has been excised by hatching. Most strikingly, the clock has been moved back such that Jesus is still alive, his mouth and eyes open. The open mouth allows one to think that he speaks, perhaps the words recorded in Matthew and Mark—but not in Luke—"My God, my God, why have you forsaken me?" (Matt 27:46//Mark 15:34 NRSV). These different states of the etching attest to Rembrandt's reflection upon the crucifixion. His varied interpretations over time apparently derive from the diverse testimony about this scene in the Synoptic Gospels. In this case, Rembrandt has offered a mini-exercise in the Synoptic Problem. Here one may observe an artist wrestling with something akin to a critical interpretation of a biblical text.

---

2. I exclude from consideration here ancient art, e.g., Neo-Assyrian wall reliefs, which are part of the cultural world out of which the Bible emerged. I omit, as well, art housed in sanctuaries, since, though they are open to the public, the art still holds a religious function in a way that an altarpiece housed in "The Cloisters" does not.

The situation with Cecil B. DeMille's *The Ten Commandments* is quite different. In 1956 DeMille released his second film named *The Ten Commandments*. It is still regularly broadcast on television both in the winter holiday season and during Lent, often on "Holy Saturday." The film putatively focuses on the exodus of the Israelites from Egypt and the giving of the Ten Commandments. There are, however, a number of subtexts, interpretations created for the United States as the viewing audience. Let me cite two instances. First, before the action begins, DeMille parts the curtains and steps onto the stage to offer a prologue. In it he says, "Ladies and Gentlemen, young and old, this may seem an unusual procedure—speaking to you before the picture begins, but we have an unusual subject. The story of the birth of freedom. The story of Moses." He goes on:

> The theme of this picture is whether men ought to be ruled by God's law or whether they are to be ruled by the whims of a dictator like Rameses. Are men the property of the state or are they free souls under God? This same battle continues throughout the world today. Our intention was not to create a story but to be worthy of the divinely inspired story created three thousand years ago: the five books of Moses.[3]

One may identify two hallmarks in DeMille's speech. First, this prologue to the film offers an interpretation of the exodus relevant to the cold-war rhetoric of the 1950s. The Old Testament story of liberation from slavery has been turned into a conflict between democracy in the United States and totalitarianism in the Soviet Union. Ramesses the dictator symbolizes Russia; Moses becomes one of the United States' founding fathers. Freedom from slavery now means "free souls" in the United States. Second, DeMille includes the phrase "under God": "Are men the property of the state or are they free souls under God?" That very phrase, under God, had been introduced into the pledge of allegiance to the United States flag just two years before DeMille distributed this movie. Nascent ancient Israel becomes the prototype for American democracy—two countries "under God."

In the final scene of the film, viewers are up on a mountain in Moab with Moses. He looks out over the Israelites as they head toward the Jordan River, beyond which are majestic mountains that look more like

---

3. The speech by DeMille is printed in Alan Nadel, "God's Law and the Wide Screen: The Ten Commandments as Cold War 'Epic,'" *PMLA* 108 (1993): 416–17.

the Rockies than they do anything in Syria-Palestine. One commentator observed, "This scene replicates the familiar image of wagon trains taking 'civilization' to the West."[4] Israel, on its way to the Promised Land to dispossess the Canaanites, has been recast as nineteenth-century pioneers, ready to win the west and to decimate its native population.

A prominent biblical text, much of the book of Exodus, was on public view in *The Ten Commandments*. A cinematic director used the biblical text to create a cinematic epic that, among other things, authorized a reading of mid-twentieth-century geopolitics and a construal of the United States as a religious nation.

Presentations of biblical literature in the broader culture include far more than movies; it even involves television shows. An exceedingly popular series, *Lost*, introduced in 2004 on the American Broadcasting Network, has been known, among other things, for introducing a world that is more complicated and with greater depth than the typical televised drama. Characters are ambiguous, not simply ciphers for good or evil. Serious topics—some have called them "philosophical"—are pursued.[5]

In one episode, the Bible figures prominently. The episode (no. 210) features a character named Eko, a mysterious survivor of Flight 815. Viewers learn through a flashback that a preadolescent Eko shot and killed a man in order to save the life of his brother, Yemi. Although Eko's violent deed was spurred by good motives, this shadow of death seems to have followed him throughout his life. Yemi was later ordained as a Roman Catholic priest, and Eko grew to be feared and a successful drug lord. Indeed, it was Eko's attempt to move drugs out of his country (in order to free his people from the danger of these drugs) that would eventually place Yemi in the line of fire and end his life. Eko watched as his dying brother was pulled into a plane filled with drugs. Years later, on the island where Eko has been stranded by a recent plane crash, he finds the vine-covered, rusting remains of the plane that carried his brother. His brother's body, recognizable only by his collar and the cross he wore, is still on board.

During his time on the island, Eko has carved several biblical citations from both the Old and New Testaments onto a large stick, which

---

4. Ibid., 425.
5. See, e.g., Chris Seay, *The Gospel according to Lost* (Nashville: Nelson, 2009).

others have dubbed his "Jesus stick." Among these references is Ps 23, and it is this text that Eko recites as he burns the plane, the heroin on-board, and his brother's body in a makeshift funeral. He is joined in the recitation at verse 4 by Charlie, a heroin addict who happened to be a passenger on Eko's plane. As they recite the psalm, the episode turns to scenes of reconciliation among those on the island. Clearly the Bible plays an important role in this episode, but what sort of role?

These allusions to the Bible or biblical texts appear in an open-ended, allusive way. In episode 210, the Bible works in an almost magical fashion. When the text is recited by two characters, it has the power to affect reconciliation among those on the island who have been alienated. The words they are reciting would not naturally lead one to think that such behavior would take place. The point seems to be that any biblical words would have such an effect. Moreover, the weapon bears preternatural significance due to the biblical citations cut into it. The Bible is a talisman, able to work wonders. In the popular piety attested in *Lost*, strange and miraculous things can happen, and the Bible belongs to that strange and compelling world.

When thinking about the Bible within contemporary culture, one should also include the ways in which the Bible has been presented in visual fashion within the print medium. The tradition of illustrating or illuminating versions of the Hebrew Bible reach as far back as the sixth century C.E., as the Vienna Genesis attests. It reached a remarkable apex in printed texts with the Doré Bible and has continued up to the present day. Still, few recent translations of the Bible into English have been accompanied by illustrations, with the sketches present in the Good News Bible/Today's English Version standing as an interesting exception. Biblical texts—whether those ordered by teachers for use in classrooms or those placed in pews—are regularly devoid of illustration. Nonetheless, there is a burgeoning market for "illustrated Bibles." Instead of the traditional calligraphy and gilt, one may now find Bibles illustrated with photographs, even with figures constructed of Legos (*The Brick Testament*).[6] So, it should come as no surprise that the book of Genesis illustrated with cartoons should appear. After all, there have been interesting presentations of biblical literature á la the medium of cartoons (e.g., C. Burstein, *The Kid's*

---

6. Brendan Powell Smith, *The Brick Testament*, online: http://www.thebricktestament.com.

Cartoon Bible) for many years.[7] However, as that title indicates, most such presentations are designed for children. Not so *The Book of Genesis* by Robert Crumb.[8] His tome has been created for adult readers, as the phrase "adult supervision recommended for minors" on the cover suggests.

What, then, is *The Book of Genesis*? One answer is a "graphic novel." Others might use the phrase "underground comic," a genre with which Crumb has been associated (Fritz the Cat is one of his notable characters), a form of literature that at least some scholars claim has emerged in the past fifty years. Though graphic novels vary, illustrations normally are at least as if not more important than the printed text. In many instances, it is licit to characterize the illustrations as "cartoons," vexed though the definition of cartoon is. (Crumb speaks of himself as an "illustrator" and of the art in his book as a "comic book version" of the Bible.) If one were to refer to "classic" forms of graphic art, one should probably appeal to what Crumb has produced as a "drawing," as opposed to media such as etchings, lithographs, or engravings. In fact, Crumb's drawings in the volume look almost like etchings. His cross-hatching produced with a fine pen is not unlike that produced by an etching needle that digs in vigorously on the copper plate.

Crumb's volume offers a chapter-by-chapter presentation of text and illustrations (the text is usually presented in a cartoon-like frame), and then, in the final pages, what Crumb calls a "commentary" appears. In this commentary, again in chapter-by-chapter order (though he does not address all of the chapters), he reports his sense of what is happening in each biblical chapter. It is more of a summary than a commentary, but again Crumb seems intent on educating the reader.

Crumb has included a translation of the entire book of Genesis in the volume. In the introduction he writes, "I, R. Crumb, the illustrator of this book, have, to the best of my ability, faithfully reproduced every word of the original text, which I derived from several sources, including the King James Version, but most from Robert Alter's recent translation, *The Five Books of Moses* (2004)."

Crumb is clearly interested in helping readers understand something about the Hebrew text. To this end, he occasionally offers notes concern-

---

7. Chaya M. Burstein, *The Kid's Cartoon Bible* (Philadelphia: Jewish Publication Society, 2002).

8. Robert Crumb, *The Book of Genesis Illustrated* (New York: Norton, 2009).

ing philology in the cartoon frames. For example, when illustrating Gen 27, he writes, "'Rightly named Jacob': at birth the name *Ya'aqob* was a play on Hebrew words meaning 'Heel grabber.' Here another play on Hebrew makes the name into a verb meaning 'crooked,' with the obvious sense of devious or deceitful dealing."[9] This note is obviously very similar to one that Alter provides at virtually the same point, "At birth, Jacob's name *Ya'aqob* was etymologized as 'heel-grabber' (playing on *'aqeb*, 'heel'). Now Esau adds another layer of etymology by making the name into a verb from *'aqob*, 'crooked,' with the obvious sense of devious or deceitful dealing."[10]

Crumb's *The Book of Genesis*, though deploying a contemporary artistic idiom—the comic—forces the reader to engage the entire biblical text. The reader must confront all the scenes in Genesis, not just those deemed important, whether for artistic interpretation or for critical study. Further, Crumb has done his best to place the text in its ancient context, both by offering a vaguely Semitic profile to the cast of characters and by introducing what he takes to be the scenery of the ancient Near East.

In sum, the Bible is currently on public view in utterly diverse media. I have briefly referred to an etching, a movie, a television episode, and a comic book. Despite this incredible variety, there is at least one constant: the "reader" is consistently presented with one artist's imaginative construal of the biblical text. The museum visitor, moviegoer, television watcher, or reader is receiving "one more" commentary. Only with Crumb's *The Book of Genesis* does one actually confront the biblical text. Most audiences for these media would be made up of adults. The same is not true for that which follows.

Public Secondary Education

Third, the Bible is increasingly in public view in schools, the object of instruction in various nonparochial settings. This has been true for decades in publicly funded institutions of higher education. However, only recently has the Bible been regularly taught from a nonconfessional perspective in secondary schools.

---

9. Ibid.
10. Robert Alter, *Genesis* (New York: Norton, 1996), 142.

The Society of Biblical Literature is playing a key role in establishing policies concerning teaching of the Bible in secondary schools and has prepared a guide, *Bible Electives in Public Schools*, that includes the following sample academic goals for such courses:

- to teach students about selected books and passages of the Bible
- to familiarize students with the themes, characters, plots, narratives, and structures of the Bible
- to enjoy and appreciate the rewards of reading a biblical text closely, with the aid of secondary materials
- to teach students about the formation of the Bible, oral tradition, textual transmission and translation, and canon formation
- to familiarize students with the social, cultural, and political aspects of life reflected in biblical writings
- to appreciate the diverse interpretations of the Bible
- to understand the wide-ranging effects of the Bible on religions, culture, politics, and art
- to recognize different literary forms in the Bible
- to practice critical thinking skills.[11]

It is important to reflect upon these goals and to compare them in two ways: with resolutions passed by governing bodies concerning the teaching of the Bible in public education and with curriculum actually available for use in public secondary education.

As for the former, several states have passed guidelines for teaching the Bible in secondary schools. It is instructive to compare guidelines created by two contiguous states: Florida and Georgia. The state of Georgia passed the "Georgia Performance Standards for Literature and History of the Old Testament Era" in January 2007. The standards included this summary:

> The purpose of the course shall be to accommodate the rights and desires of those teachers and students who wish to teach and study the Old Testament and to familiarize students with the contents of the Old Testament, the history recorded by the Old Testament, the literary

---

11. Society of Biblical Literature, *Bible Electives in Public Schools: A Guide* (Atlanta: SBL, n.d.), 10, online: http://www.sbl-site.org/assets/pdfs/SchoolsGuide.pdf. This document and the standards for Georgia and Florida quoted below are available through the SBL's website at www.sbl-site.org/educational/thebibleinpublicschools.aspx.

style and structure of the Old Testament, the customs and cultures of the peoples and societies recorded in the Old Testament and the influence of the Old Testament upon law, history, government, literature, art, music, customs, morals, values, and culture. Topics may include historical background and events of the period; the history of the Kingdom of Israel; the poetry of the Old Testament; the influence of Old Testament history and literature on subsequent art, music, literature, law, and events, including recent and current events in the Middle East.[12]

The course goals are then spelled out in terms of performance standards:

B1. The student demonstrates an understanding of the major narratives, characters, stories and poetry contained in the Bible and how they are used in literature, art and music.
    B1a. Demonstrates comprehension of the variety of literary forms in the biblical text
    B1b. Identifies, analyzes and applies knowledge of structures, symbolism, motifs, and the use of language (e.g. diction, imagery, figurative language, alliteration) in biblical text
    B1c. Recognizes and traces the development of various translations of biblical text
    B1d. Understands and explains the influence of the Bible in classic and contemporary art, music and literature, including poetry, drama, and prose.[13]

Several elements are of special importance: literary issues (i.e., literary forms, literary styles), various translations, and ways in which the Bible has influenced culture, particularly various artistic media. One would imagine that courses designed to meet these performance standards would invest considerable time in exploring the media and examples mentioned above.

The guidelines for courses taught in the state of Florida are quite different and are stated in the Florida Department of Education Course Description for "Introduction to the Bible I," which was adopted in 2002.

---

12. Georgia Department of Education, "Georgia Performance Standards for Literature and History of the Old Testament Era," January 2007, online: http://www.doe.k12.ga.us/DMGetDocument.aspx/Literature%20and%20History%20of%20Old%20Testament%20Course.pdf?p=6CC6799F8C1371F60835F40D4AB1B1FB27867ED909BA92F3B9B541E3C48706D4&Type=D.

13. Ibid.

The content should include, but not be limited to, the following:
- survey of various types of literature found in the Bible
- literary analysis of chief characters, structures, and plots
- literary analysis of biblical narratives and poetry
- analysis of prophetic literature in its ancient and historical context
- historical and cultural contexts of biblical literature
- chief themes of biblical literature
- comparison of the literary forms and religious and cultural concepts in the Bible and in ancient Near-Eastern literature
- formation of biblical literature into sacred scripture
- history of interpretation in the Jewish and Christian communities
- methods of academic study of the history and literature of ancient Israel
- transmission of biblical texts and translations from antiquity to present
- impact of the Bible on Western literature, art, music, and thought.[14]

The rhetoric of these guidelines allows for attention to the cultural setting in which the Hebrew Bible was created. Such language is missing from the Georgia guidelines. The same may be said for "the academic study of the history and literature of ancient Israel." Much of what passes for biblical scholarship in college courses would probably fall under this rubric. It is present in the Florida, but not the Georgia, guidelines. The course requirements in the Florida guidelines include the following two sections:

7. Compare and contrast the literary forms of biblical writings within the context of the history and culture of ancient Israel and the literature of the non-Israelite, ancient Near-Eastern literature.
    LA.A.2.4.1   determine the main idea and identify relevant details, methods of development, and their effectiveness in a variety of types of written material.
    LA.D.1.4.1   apply an understanding that language and literature are primary means by which culture is transmitted.

---

14. Florida Department of Education, "Course Description—Grades 9–12, Adult" [Introduction to the Bible I], 2002, 2; online: http://data.fldoe.org/crsCode/912/Humanities/Humanities/pdf/0900400.pdf.

8. Demonstrate awareness of the formation of biblical literature and the process by which diverse writings came to be regarded as sacred scripture by various Jewish and Christian communities (canonization).[15]

These two sections are of signal importance. Section 7, for example, would permit a student to compare the biblical accounts of the flood with those present in the Gilgamesh Epic and the Atrahasis Myth, and section 8 would allow students to discuss various theories regarding the formation of the Pentateuch (e.g., source-critical, supplementary, and fragmentary hypotheses). Concern for "the formation of biblical literature" is markedly absent from the guidelines promulgated by the state of Georgia. These features in the Florida guidelines clearly achieve greater conformity with the SBL guidelines than do those in the Georgia document.

In sum, though states are enacting guidelines to permit and support the teaching of the Bible in secondary education, they vary significantly in their support of what one might call critical study of biblical literature.

Neither the Florida nor the Georgia guidelines mention curriculum, other than reading the biblical text. The use of a study Bible is rarely, if ever, part of the discussion. There are, however, a number of publishing initiatives in which organizations are competing to provide such resources. Some are designed for teachers, including *Teaching the Bible*, a monthly electronic journal published by the Society of Biblical Literature.[16] As one might expect, the essays are designed to provide secondary school teachers with basic information to support work in introductory courses.[17] As one might expect, these essays are fully informed by the sort of "academic study" called for in the Florida guidelines.

Curriculum designed to be put in the hands of students is quite another matter. Unfortunately, there is currently a paucity of such materials, and what is available is not of a piece with either the SBL guidelines, the Florida guidelines, or material available for teachers in *Teaching the Bible*. For example, *The Bible in History and Literature*, published by the

---

15. Ibid., 3.

16. See Society of Biblical Literature, *Teaching the Bible*, online: http://www.sbl-site.org/educational/TBnewsletter.aspx.

17. E.g., David Penchansky, "The Interpretation of Wisdom Literature in the Bible, Part 1," *TB* (February 2010), online: http://www.sbl-site.org/assets/pdfs/TB7_Wisdompt1_DP.pdf.

National Council on Bible Curriculum in Public Schools, constitutes a one-volume introduction to the Christian Bible.[18] There is minimal attention to studying the ancient Near Eastern context of the Hebrew Bible. Astonishingly, on the one page devoted to "The Genesis Flood," there is no reference to ancient Near Eastern accounts.[19] Instead, the unnamed authors point out that there are five hundred legends—they mention, among others, Aztec, Choctaw, and Inca versions—of a worldwide deluge. There is no attention given to the study of the formation of biblical material. Treatment of "The Prophets" is feeble,[20] particularly when compared with the Florida guidelines, which require that students "analyze prophetic literature in its ancient and historical context." The volume, quite simply, does not address the range of issues appropriate for study of the Bible in secondary schools. The same may be said of another comparable volume, *The Bible and Its Influence*.[21]

One can imagine an introduction to the Bible and its reception, a volume that would offer a critical introduction to the contents and the formation of the Bible and that would also address representative ways in which the Bible has been received and interpreted over the centuries. Such a volume would help explain the reason why a Bible is used as a part of a presidential inauguration in the United States; it would explore examples of good (and perhaps some bad) art that has been the subject of artistic exploration; and it would be suitable for use in a public education. Such a volume—or project—would exemplify what it means for the Bible to be on public view.

In conclusion, the Bible can be in the public view in diverse ways. First, in certain situations, the Holy Bible is closed. It functions as an iconic presence but one in which little in or about the Bible is actually said. Second, in the broader cultural world, the Bible has been interpreted

---

18. For a more detailed evaluation, see Brennan Breed and Kent Harold Richards, review of *The Bible in History and Literature*, *Religion and Education* 34 (2007): 94–102.

19. *The Bible in History and Literature* (Greensboro, N.C.: National Council on Bible Curriculum in Public Schools, 2005), 63.

20. Ibid., 156–57.

21. Cullen Schippe and Chuck Stetson, eds., *The Bible and Its Influence* (New York: BLP Press, 2005). See the critical review by Steven L. McKenzie, review of *The Bible and Its Influence*, *SBL Forum* (November 1995); online: http://sbl-site.org/Article.aspx?ArticleID=465.

imaginatively in virtually every artistic medium known to humanity. Some such interpretations bristle with insight; others offer little but well-worn commentary. Finally, the Bible is being taught in public secondary education. In this setting, the Bible is open, though it is not necessarily presented using a study Bible. Still, students can read it for themselves. Here the goals of the Society of Biblical literature, which involve, among other things, a critical reading of biblical literature and cognizance of its reception history, can align. Work on behalf of curriculum for use in such educational settings is one of the most important strategic efforts that biblical scholars can undertake in order to foster a broader understanding of the literature to which they are professionally committed. One of the great challenges facing biblical scholars is the creation of curriculum appropriate to meet the challenge of teaching the Bible in secondary education.

Bibliography

Alter, Robert. *Genesis*. New York: Norton, 1996.
Breed, Brennan, and Kent Harold Richards. Review of *The Bible in History and Literature, Religion and Education* 34 (2007): 94–102.
Burstein, Chaya M. *The Kid's Cartoon Bible*. Philadelphia: Jewish Publication Society, 2002.
Crumb, Robert. *The Book of Genesis Illustrated*. New York: Norton, 2009.
Florida Department of Education. "Course Description—Grades 9–12, Adult" [Introduction to the Bible I]. 2002. Online: http://data.fldoe.org/crsCode/912/Humanities/Humanities/pdf/0900400.pdf.
Georgia Department of Education. "Georgia Performance Standards for Literature and History of the Old Testament Era." January 2007. Online: http://www.doe.k12.ga.us/DMGetDocument.aspx/Literature%20and%20History%20of%20Old%20Testament%20Course.pdf?p=6CC6799F8C1371F60835F40D4AB1B1FB27867ED909BA92F3B9B541E3C48706D4&Type=D.
McKenzie, Steven L. Review of *The Bible and Its Influence*. *SBL Forum* (November 1995). Online: http://sbl-site.org/Article.aspx?ArticleID=465.
Nadel, Alan. "God's Law and the Wide Screen: The Ten Commandments as Cold War 'Epic.'" *PMLA* 108 (1993): 415–30.
Penchansky, David. "The Interpretation of Wisdom Literature in the Bible, Part 1." *TB* (February 2010). Online: http://www.sbl-site.org/assets/pdfs/TB7_Wisdompt1_DP.pdf.

Schippe, Cullen, and Chuck Stetson, eds. *The Bible and Its Influence*. New York: BLP Press, 2005.

Seay, Chris. *The Gospel according to Lost*. Nashville: Nelson, 2009.

Smith, Brendan Powell. *The Brick Testament*. Online: http://www.thebricktestament.com.

Society of Biblical Literature. *Bible Electives in Public Schools: A Guide*. Online: http://www.sbl-site.org/assets/pdfs/SchoolsGuide.pdf.

———. *Teaching the Bible*. Online: http://www.sbl-site.org/educational/TBnewsletter.aspx.

Part 2
New Pedagogies and the Biblical Studies Curriculum

A Republic of Many Voices:[1] Biblical Studies in the Twenty-First Century

Elisabeth Schüssler Fiorenza

Kent Richards, whose work we celebrate with this Festschrift, has made innumerable contributions to the discipline of biblical studies during his tenure as Executive Director of SBL. Others will probably detail how he stabilized and expanded SBL as a professional institution. In my reflections I want to explore one attempt to engender discussion on graduate biblical education.

Because of my experience of continuing side-lining and co-optation of critical feminist work, I had become more and more convinced that such a change would take hold only if the ethos of doctoral education was transformed. I also realized that such change could only be explored successfully if someone from the center of the discipline would collaborate in the work. Hence, I approached Kent about eight years ago with the idea of starting a seminar that would explore the present status of graduate biblical education and reflect on the necessary changes if previously excluded and still "marginalized"[2] scholarship should be recognized as central to the discourses of the discipline. I hoped to engender a public debate on the need for such change if the field of biblical studies should continue to flourish in the twenty-first century.

Despite his enormous workload and traveling schedule, Kent accepted and has worked very hard to make the seminar sessions a success and to

---

1. I have borrowed this title from William Ayers, *Teaching toward Freedom: Moral Commitment and Ethical Action in the Classroom* (Boston: Beacon, 2004), 67.

2. I am using Fernando F. Segovia's term. See Laura Nasrallah and Elisabeth Schüssler Fiorenza, eds., *Prejudice and Christian Beginnings: Investigating Race, Gender, and Ethnicity in Early Christian Studies* (Minneapolis: Fortress, 2009).

gather their intellectual fruits. We are publishing the papers of the seminars held at the international and national meetings in the hope that the resulting collection of essays will contribute to the emerging discussion on the task of the discipline in the twenty-first century.[3] However, much more work is necessary to change the discipline into a public forum and to educate future scholars in such a way that they can foster radical democratic discourses in the twenty-first century.

1. Relocating Biblical Studies

I have argued in my work that the field of biblical studies is best understood in terms of four disciplinary paradigms: (1) the religious-the*logical-scriptural paradigm, (2) the modern-scientific-historical paradigm, (3) the cultural-hermeneutic-postmodern paradigm, and (4) the rhetorical-radical-democratic paradigm. In modernity, these four paradigms for the most part have developed over and against each other. Their social-institutional home is the church or synagogue, the academy (classics or literature), and the postmodern discourses of the margins. It is striking, however, that in general the social location of biblical studies has not been the public square of democratic society. Hence, I argue that biblical scholarship must explore the democratizing potentials of the Bible, become methodologically aware of its social location in a democratic society, and reflect on its democratic sociopolitical contexts,[4] if it

---

3. See Elisabeth Schüssler Fiorenza and Kent Harold Richards, eds, *Transforming Graduate Biblical Education: Ethos and Discipline* (Atlanta: Society of Biblical Literature, 2010). The essays explore the current ethos and discipline of graduate biblical education from different social locations and academic contexts. They do so in terms of variegated experiences in graduate biblical studies and provide a critical analysis of these experiences. The majority of the essays are written either by well-known North American scholars, by scholars who are newcomers to the field, or by biblical scholars from predominantly Asian countries, because one seminar was held in Singapore but none were held in Africa or Latin America. All the contributions offer ideas about how to change graduate biblical education in such a way that it becomes a socializing power for transforming the present academic ethos of biblical studies.

4. For a the*logical perspective, see John W. De Gruchy, *Christianity and Democracy: A Theology for a Just World Order* (Cambridge: Cambridge University Press, 1995), and Cornel West, *Democracy Matters: Winning the Fight against Imperialism* (New York: Penguin, 2004). See also my article "A Discipleship of Equals: Ekklesial Democracy and Patriarchy in Biblical Perspective," in *A Democratic Catholic Church*

wants to flourish in the twenty-first century. In order to be able to do so, doctoral education needs to be newly conceptualized and situated in the "public square."

Since the Bible has had and still has enormous public influence in the U.S., it is necessary for American biblical scholarship to critically explore the impact of the Bible on American culture and life and to examine:

> what it means for Scripture to have acted as both a conservative and a radical social force, to have provided a vocabulary for both traditional deference and innovative egalitarianism, and to have been a source for both stability in the face of anarchy and freedom in the face of tyranny.[5]

The United States has understood itself from its very beginnings as a biblical nation. Law-makers assemble at the Capitol steps to sing "God Bless America," American flags grace churches and synagogues, and citizens acknowledge membership "in one nation under G*d."[6] U.S. presidents, be they Jefferson, Lincoln, Carter, or Clinton, have freely quoted the Bible. More recently, President George W. Bush deployed a strident biblical rhetoric in the interest of nationalism. For example, in his oft-quoted 9/11 anniversary speech in September 2002, Bush paraphrased John 1:4–5, saying, "This ideal of America is the hope of all mankind.... That hope still lights our way. And the light shines in the darkness and the darkness will not overcome it."[7] This paraphrase substitutes America for

---

(ed. Eugene C. Bianchi and Rosemary Radford Ruether; New York: Crossroad, 1992), 17–33.

5. Nathan O. Hatch and Mark Noll, eds., *The Bible in America: Essays in Cultural History* (New York: Oxford University Press, 1982), 8.

6. In order to indicate the brokenness and inadequacy of human language to name the Divine, I have switched in my book, *Jesus: Miriam's Child, Sophia's Prophet: Critical Issues in Feminist Christology* (New York: Continuum, 1994), from the orthodox Jewish writing of G-d, which I had adopted in *But She Said* and *Discipleship of Equals* to this spelling of G*d, which seeks to avoid the conservative malestream association that the writing of G-d provokes for Jewish feminists. For discussion of the term *God*, see Francis Schüssler Fiorenza and Gordon Kaufman, "God," in *Critical Terms for Religious Studies* (ed. Mark C. Taylor; Chicago: University of Chicago Press, 1998), 136–59.

7. Jeffrey S. Siker, "President Bush, Biblical Faith, and the Politics of Religion," *SBL Forum*; online: http//www.sbl-site.org/publications/article.aspx?ArticleID=151.

Jesus Christ, the incarnate Word of G*d, and thereby divinizes U.S. imperialism as "the light of the world."

The scriptural understanding of President Barak Obama is quite different. It is critically reflective, contextually aware, and understands the Bible as a "living word." In his book *The Audacity of Hope*, Obama explicates the hermeneutic of his reading of the Bible:

> When I read the Bible, I do so with the belief that it is not a static text but the Living Word and that I must be continually open to new revelations—whether they come from a lesbian friend or a doctor opposed to abortion. This is NOT to say that I am unanchored in my faith. There are some things that I'm absolutely sure about—the Golden Rule, the need to battle cruelty in all its forms, the value of love and charity, humility and grace.[8]

The Bible is a democratizing book. It is a collection of writings spanning the G*d-experience of many centuries, a book in which a rich plurality of "citizen" voices argue with each other, complement each other, and keep alive the vision of divine justice, care, and well-being.[9] These voices are democratically enriched by the many contexts in which they are heard and interpreted.[10] The word of G*d can only be heard as a Living Word by engaging creatively with this din of voices from very different political contexts, voices searching for freedom, equality, justice, and well-being in times of violence and empire. Such a radical democratic understanding of the Bible requires an equally far-reaching democratizing of biblical studies.

A similar point is made by the editors of *The Bible in the Public Square*. However, they argue not with reference to the struggles around the world for radical democracy but with reference to the biblical call for "reading the signs of the times":

> To read the Bible in the public square in these times is to take on a chal-

---

8. Barack Obama, *The Audacity of Hope: Thoughts on Reclaiming the American Dream* (New York: Vintage, 2008), 265.

9. See Jaroslav Pelikan, *Whose Bible Is It? A Short History of the Scriptures* (New York: Penguin, 2005).

10. For the understanding and use of the Bible in the African American community, see Allen Dwight Callahan, *The Talking Book: African Americans and the Bible*, (New Haven: Yale University Press, 2006).

lenging task. Issues of hunger, poverty, and violence are urgent and call for our response.... It follows that Biblical scholars can and do have a role to play in the public square, an ecumenical, plural, democratic space that is neither the church sanctuary nor the class room. They carry out this obligation in different ways depending on what model they employ, their own location, their audience, and their area of expertise. For all of them, however, responsible Biblical scholarship requires reading the signs of the times.[11]

In other words, rather than just learning how to interpret texts, study history, or reflect on the Bible the*logically, future biblical scholars also need to learn how to read "the signs of the times" (Matt 16:3). In order to do so, biblical scholars must become schooled in societal, ecclesial, and cultural analysis capable of naming powers of injustice and dehumanization. Such analysis must be careful, though, not to limit but rather to keep open its conception of the public.

In his book *Democracy and Tradition*, Jeffrey Stout draws attention to the problematic meaning of "the public square" if it is understood statically as a place. Instead, Stout proposes that the "public square" be understood as a dynamic "public" sphere characterized by a compelling religious vision of how citizens can reason with each other and hold each other accountable.

> One is addressing the public whenever one addresses people as citizens. In a modern democracy, this is not something one does in one place or at once. Wherever two or three citizens are gathered whom one might address as citizens, as persons jointly responsible for the common good, one is in a potentially public setting.... If you express theological commitments in a reflective and sustained way, while addressing fellow citizens as citizens, you are "doing theology" publicly—and in that sense doing public theology.[12]

Wherever two or three citizens are gathered to study the Bible, its democratizing power as the *Living Word* can be experienced. This requires an

---

11. Cynthia Briggs Kittredge, Ellen Bradshaw Aitken, and Jonathan A. Draper, eds., *The Bible in the Public Square: Reading the Signs of the Times* (Minneapolis: Fortress, 2008), 1.

12. Jeffrey Stout, *Democracy and Tradition* (Princeton: Princeton University Press, 2004), 113.

understanding that biblical studies has the function of enabling citizens to recognize that their coming together constitutes a public in which they are responsible for articulating the *Living Word* in their different sociopolitical religious contexts. Democratizing graduate biblical education would then mean that scholars recognize as the "home-spaces" of biblical studies not only the academy and the church but also democratic society with its variegated citizenship. The emerging fourth paradigm of biblical studies—an *intercultural/interreligious–emancipatory–radical democratic paradigm*—I have argued, is in the process of articulating such a radical democratic space of biblical interpretation.

However, as indicated by Dale Martin's recent study of the discipline, which is based on interviews at ten the*logical schools and surveys of other websites, the discipline is still engaged in the modern turf fight between historical-critical and the*logical-doctrinal studies. Martin points out that "the dominant method of interpretation students are taught, just about everywhere, is traditional historical criticism."[13] Michael Joseph Brown's primer, *What They Don't Tell You: A Survivor's Guide to Biblical Studies*,[14] confirms Martin's observation of the dominance of historical criticism in graduate education when he stresses again and again that biblical studies does not mean "Bible study" and warns his readers not to engage in *eisegesis*. His "rules of thumb" include, for example: "Be careful not to read your modern assumptions into ancient texts; a translation is only as good as its translator," or "An overactive imagination can get you into trouble." These rules seek to explicate the survival skills necessary for students who want to study biblical studies, while making it clear that the discipline is understood primarily in terms of historical-critical scholarship.

Neither Brown nor Martin seem to be concerned with educating graduate students to "read the signs of the times" by learning how to critically analyze their own sociopolitical cultural contextual locations and the function of the Bible in these contexts. In line with the "new traditionalists,"[15] Martin argues for a curriculum of biblical studies that places the the*logical and doctrinal function of Scripture in the church

---

13. Dale B. Martin, *Pedagogy of the Bible: An Analysis and Proposal* (Louisville: Westminster John Knox, 2008), 12.

14. Michael Joseph Brown, *What They Don't Tell You: A Survivor's Guide to Biblical Studies* (Louisville: Westminster John Knox, 2000).

15. Jeffrey Stout, who coined this term, counts among them Stanley Hauer-

at the center of the*logical education. He argues that graduate education, which is almost universally focused on the historical-critical method, needs to foster the study of premodern biblical hermeneutics and postmodern theories of text.[16]

While I agree with Martin's insistence that a critical the*logical education and sophistication is absolutely necessary for ministerial education, I do not believe that "the new traditionalism" in the*logy will solve the problem. Nor do I think that the*logical literacy should be restricted to Master of Divinity (M.Div.) students. Rather, I am concerned here with the*logical education in general and with the education of future biblical scholars and leaders in theories of interpretation, hermeneutics, and ideology critique. Unlike Brown, I am not concerned primarily with articulating ideas for surviving historical-critical biblical scholarship. Rather than attempting to persuade students to adopt the dominant historical paradigm, I seek to marshal arguments for changing graduate biblical education into a radical democratic space of critical historical inquiry, sociopolitical ethical exploration, and creative religious revisioning.

It is curious that at this point in time, when religion has again become a much researched and discussed topic, many conservative as well as many liberal and postmodern biblical scholars do not find such a reenvisioning of biblical studies and graduate biblical education in terms of public discourse to be either necessary or desirable. It seems that, even in postmodern academic approaches, the institutional dichotomy between academy and church, rather than a revisioning of the ethos of biblical studies, still takes center stage.

2. Dualistic Domain Construction: Church and Academy

For instance, in *The End of Biblical Studies*, Hector Avalos argues forcefully that biblical studies as we know it must end. He maintains that modern biblical scholarship has shown the irrelevance of the Bible for modern times.[17] But he contends that despite this proven irrelevance, a variety of scholarly disciplines sustain the illusion of the relevance of the Bible. Avalos goes so far as to state that "Bibliolatry is still what binds most bibli-

---

was, Alasdair MacIntyre, and John Milbank, who proclaim "radical orthodoxy" (see *Democracy and Tradition*, 92–179).
16. Martin, *Pedagogy of the Bible*, 29–70.
17. Hector Avalos, *The End of Biblical Studies* (Amherst: Prometheus, 2007).

cal scholars together, whether they see themselves as religious or secular, champions of Western culture or multiculturalists, evangelical Christians or Marxist hermeneuticians."[18] Moreover, modern scholarship has proven that the violence of the Bible is a product of ancient cultures whose worldviews, beliefs, and injunctions are no longer compatible with our modern and postmodern ethics and morality. To make his point that the Bible and therefore biblical scholarship is irrelevant today, Avalos shows how the main subdivisions of biblical studies (translation studies, textual criticism, archaeology, historical Jesus studies, literary criticism, and biblical theology) and their infrastructure (various universities' graduate schools, the Society of Biblical Literature, and the media-publishing complex) render the Bible irrelevant. He concludes:

> So our purpose is to excise from modern life what little of the Bible is being used and also eliminate the potential use of any sacred scripture as an authority in the modern world. Sacred texts are the problem that most scholars are not willing to confront. What I seek is liberation from the very idea that *any* sacred text should be an authority for modern human existence.... That is why the only mission of Biblical Studies should be to end Biblical Studies as we know it.[19]

As this quote shows, Avalos seems to be torn between two conflicting reasons as to why biblical scholarship as we know it must be ended. On the one hand, he stresses that biblical studies has to end because it has proven the irrelevance of the Bible. Yet, insofar as biblical studies persists in upholding some of the Bible's relevance and significance, the Bible must continue to be studied by a few agnostic scholars like him as one of the documents of antiquity, many of which have never been translated and studied and hence should receive priority over the Bible. On the other hand, Avalos argues that biblical scholars must confront the fact that the Bible is upheld as a sacred text that has authority. It is at this second point that the pathos of his argument comes to the fore. He tells us that he comes from a Pentecostal Protestant immigrant home, wanted to become a biblical scholar "to fight atheism," and in the process has come to understand that "atheism was the most honest choice" he could make.[20] As a young scholar he came more and more to the conclusion that the pur-

---

18. Ibid., 340.
19. Ibid., 342.
20. Ibid., 26.

suit of knowledge for its own sake is simply another way of describing an elite leisure pursuit. He became distressed at how few papers were actually grounded in the idea that knowledge is meant to help people to live in a better world.[21] Yet, rather than explore how biblical studies can be transformed so that they can "help people to live in a better world" and to encourage their ability to challenge the sacred authority of the Bible, he advises that, after weaning humanity from the authority of the Bible, scholars should tend to the thousands of other ancient texts that have not yet been translated. Although he asserts the irrelevance of the Bible, he still recognizes that, even though it preaches violence, the Bible still has sacred authority for innumerable people.

While I agree that it is important to identify the violence inscribed in Scriptures, I also think it is necessary to teach how to work constructively with such scriptural violence. We need to develop a critical pedagogy that teaches people who love Scripture and accord it great authority for their lives to read the Bible in a way that enables them to critically assess its ethos and vision.[22] In other words, if one defines the task of the biblical scholar only in negative terms, one is not able to answer the question of how scholarly research and teaching can serve to enhance people's lives and their desires for justice and well-being.

Taking the Bible out of the hands of people and putting it in its place alongside the ancient books that have not yet been translated does not solve the problem because such a displacement of the Bible does nothing to ensure that these other texts do not equally inscribe violence. Looking at this problem from a critical feminist perspective, such a rejection of the Bible or the Qur'an or any other Scripture or cultural classic would also mean that wo/men could claim no language, tradition, and culture, since all writings, traditions, and cultures have been elite male-determined and have promoted violence against wo/men. Rather than end biblical studies, I suggest that it is necessary to inquire into the *ends* of biblical studies.

In *Whose Bible Is It Anyway?*[23] Philip Davies, on the other hand,

---

21. Ibid., 27.
22. See also Joseph A. Marchal, "To What End(s)? Biblical Studies and Critical Rhetorical Engagement(s) for a 'Safer' World," *SBL Forum*; online: http://www.sblsite.org/publications/article.aspx?ArticleId=550.
23. Philip Davies, *Whose Bible Is It Anyway?* (2nd ed.; New York: T&T Clark, 2004).

recognizes that there is a large gap between what the public thinks biblical scholars do and what they are actually doing. Yet Davies is not so much concerned to reenvision biblical studies in terms of fostering radical democratic discourses as he is concerned with what those discourses can contribute to the life of the academy. He diagnoses the ineffectiveness of biblical studies within the academy and in the wider public and, as a remedy for this weakness, prescribes the greater academization of biblical studies as an etic, objective discipline that can take its place within the academic discourses of the humanities.[24]

Davies, like Avalos, attempts to define and establish a "genuine secular academic discipline of Biblical Studies." He sees secularism not as the opposite of religion but rather as a cultural discourse in which religious discourses are not in any way privileged. Hence, he constructs a sharp dichotomy between biblical studies and confessional the*logical studies. Like Avalos, he understands the*logical studies in a dogmatic, confessional sense and positions them as the opposite of academic, nonconfessional studies. But unlike Avalos, he postulates two independent domains— academy and church—which, in his view, must not interfere with each other but should be allowed to live alongside each other as long as they do not trespass on each other's domains.

Davies thus draws a sharp distinction between academic biblical studies as humanistic or humanities studies and confessional biblical studies as committed to Christian faith and life. In order to mark this division, he reserves the term *biblical studies* for the academic study of the Bible, whereas he argues that "Bible study," or the study of Scripture, belongs to the domain of the church. This allows him to concede that in synagogues, churches, and mosques but not in the academy, "religious discourse can reign unchallenged."[25]

The goal of "Bible study"[26] is to understand more fully the rhetorical, historical, or ideological character of the biblical text in order to affirm but not to criticize it. Such "Bible study" can be determined to be an "emic" reading, which adopts the "native" point of view, in distinction to an "etic" reading, which refers to the external description of the objective observer. In contrast to Bible studies, biblical studies as an academic

---

24. See Philip Davies, "Do We Need Biblical Scholars?" *Bible and Interpretation*; online: http://www.bibleinterp.com/articles/Davies_Biblical_Scholars.shtml.
25. Davies, *Whose Bible Is It Anyway*, 7.
26. Ibid., 11.

discipline engenders an "etic" reading that operates "outside" the canon. It is based on the presupposition that biblical writings and their reception through the centuries:

> are to be evaluated on the same terms as other known human acts of writing and reception.... The values that are adopted ... are those adopted by the critical observer and applied to other literature. The critic is free to like or dislike, to pass judgment.[27]

Consequently, Davies can uphold the right of a confessional reading, while at the same time championing a disinterested academic reading. He claims that the interest of the church and the academy are easily distinguished, since there is no confusion of what is done in the synagogue, church, or mosque and what in the academic classroom. Although Davies concedes that all discourses are in one way or the other interested, he nevertheless insists that only the etic, nonconfessional discourse of the academy has a range of evaluations and perspectives "that allow Biblical literature to interact with different value systems and to have its own varied value system compared and judged in what is analogous to a 'free market.'"[28]

In short, Davies invokes the rhetoric of unbiased, value-free, disinterested religious studies as an academic discipline in distinction to the*logical studies, which he terms confessional insofar as they are meant to affirm biblical texts because they are Scripture, not to critically investigate them. He conveniently overlooks that not only the nomenclature "Scripture" but also the classification "Bible/biblical" is already determined in and through the domain of the church, since it was the church that gathered diverse writings or scriptures into the canon of the Bible. Hence, it is curious that Davies relegates "Scripture" to the church but reclaims "Bible" for the academy. This is surprising, for one, because religious studies has sought to reclaim "Scripture"[29] as cultural artifact that must be studied as a religious-cultural document.[30]

---

27. Ibid., 12.
28. Ibid., 49
29. See Miriam Levering, ed., *Rethinking Scripture: Essays from a Comparative Perspective* (Albany: State University of New York Press, 1989).
30. Vincent L. Wimbush, ed., *Theorizing Scriptures: New Critical Orientations to a Cultural Phenomenon* (New Brunswick, N.J.: Rutgers University Press, 2008).

Such a dichotomous approach is necessary, Davies argues, because as things stand, the church cannot count on well-trained ministers, nor can the public learn about what biblical scholars do, because both inside and outside the academy, biblical scholarship is seen as a the*logical confessional pursuit. Hence, biblical scholars need to persuade both the academy and the public that they engage in a bona fide academic discipline that contributes to the intellectual life of the humanities. To do so, they have to subscribe to etic, disinterested scholarship. Like Avalos, Davies insists on the academic character of biblical studies, which serves the academy and the wider public but does not interfere with confessional studies and the*logical education. Hence, in Davies's view, we must "secularize" the Bible and biblical studies "for a secularized world."[31]

In this reading, the Bible is a product of the elite and the object of study by the academic elite. To be recognized as a part of this academic elite, biblical scholars have to study the Scriptures as a cultural document rather than as a religious one. Yet such a dichotomy between academic and confessional biblical studies not only turns the Bible into a book of the elite but also reduces the*logical studies to confessional studies. It focuses on developing a pedagogy that enables students to talk to the elites but is not able to empower them to speak to the millions of "fundamentalist" Bible readers who read the Bible in a literalist way because their ministers, pastors, and preachers taught them so. Thus both proposals—that of Avalos as well as that of Davies—deepen the dichotomy that has plagued biblical studies since the modern arrival of biblical criticism.

It must not be overlooked, however, that this dualistic domain conceptualization of the discipline as either academic or the*logical is not simply dualistic; it is an asymmetric dualistic construct that places greater value on the academic study of religion because of its alleged commitment to objectivity, value-neutrality, and the study of the Bible "for knowledge's sake." The study of religion and the Bible supposedly do not succumb to the biased interests of the*logy, which speaks from within a particular religion and is committed to a particular religious community. The*logy, in this view, cannot be truly scientific because it is not free from value commitments and interests. The*logical scholars are often reduced to "missionaries" who want to bring their audiences to commit themselves to a religious faith community. This oppositional dualistic domain con-

---

31. Davies, "Do We Need Biblical Scholars?"

struction of the field can be further illuminated and critically destabilized in and through paradigm criticism.

3. Reconceptualizing Biblical Studies

Such a dualistic conceptualization of biblical and religious studies over and against the*logical studies remains caught up in a modernist argument that does not do justice to our geopolitical situation. In a very perceptive article in the *Chronicle of Higher Education*, Stanley Fish has pointed to the breakdown of the dividing lines drawn by liberalism between academy and religion, reason and faith, truth and belief, or inquiry and revelation. Globalization and our geopolitical situation, he argues, have brought to public consciousness the fact that

> hundreds of millions of people in the world do not observe the distinction between the private and the public or between belief and knowledge and that it is no longer possible for us to regard such persons as quaintly pre-modern or as needy recipients of our saving (an ironic word) wisdom. Some of these are our sworn enemies. Some of them are our colleagues, many of them are our students.[32]

Many are seeking not only knowledge but also inspiration. He relates that when a reporter asked, after Jaques Derrida's death, what would replace high theory and "the triumvirate of race, gender, and class" in the future, he spontaneously answered "religion." Hence, there is a growing awareness that it is no longer possible for the academy to keep "the old boundaries in place" and to quarantine "the religious impulse in the safe houses of the church, the synagogue and the mosque."[33] It is no longer satisfactory to make religion the object of study. Rather, what is necessary is that academicians pay attention to students' search for inspiration and meaning. If Fish's diagnosis of the academic situation after 9/11 is correct, it will be ironic and tragic if biblical scholars continue to eschew emic biblical meaning-making and restrict themselves to etic teaching *about* the Bible and religion in order to gain academic respectability.

---

32. Stanley Fish, "One University under God?" *The Chronicle of Higher Education*, 7 January 2005; online: http://chronicle.com/article/One-University-Under-God-/45077/.

33. Ibid., 8.

Moreover, a conceptualization of biblical studies in terms of territorial dualism—as either the domain of the university or that of institutionalized religion—views the discipline in either/or terms: either as the academic study of religions or as confessional the*logical studies. Such a dualistic construction of the disciplinary ethos does not have space for a political or emancipatory approach to biblical studies that is interested in changing societal, religious, or individual mindsets. It does not conceptualize biblical studies as able to address the needs of society and the public, since biblical studies are located either in the academy or in organized religion and are not envisioned in radical democratic terms. A dualistic construction also is unable to assess the impact of biblical discourses on the democratic ethos and self-understanding of responsible citizens in society and religion. If, however, biblical studies were reconceptualized in terms of a radical democratic "republic[34] of many voices," then the dualistic domain construction of "either academy or church/institutionalized religion" could be overcome, because the exercise of full citizenship takes place in both academy and institutionalized religions as well as in society at large.

Rather than dividing biblical studies into two domains, I suggest, it is better to envision the Bible as well as biblical studies as a "republic of many voices," as a democratic religious space of debate and adjudication, as a site of struggle over meaning and ethics. The different leading parties or scholarly paradigms articulate their contributions in different ways and attract different audiences.

Thomas Kuhn's categories of "scientific paradigm" and "heuristic model" have provided a theoretical framework[35] for comprehending theoretical and practical shifts in the self-understanding of biblical studies. A paradigm expresses "the shared commitment by the members of a scientific community to a particular form of scientific practice"[36] and is characterized by conceptual coherence and common intellectual interests.

---

34. A "republic" is "a group with collective interests: a group of people who are considered to be equals and who have a collective interest, objective, or vocation (*formal*)" (*Encarta World English Dictionary*, Microsoft, 2009, s.v. "republic"; online: http://encarta.msn.com/dictionary_1861700632/republic.html).

35. Thomas S. Kuhn, *The Structure of Scientific Revolutions* (Chicago: University of Chicago Press, 1962).

36. Michael Payne, ed., *Cultural and Critical Theory* (Malden, Mass.: Blackwell, 1997), 394.

It articulates a common ethos and constitutes a community of scholars formed by its institutions and systems of knowledge.[37]

In response to the question of what kind of social-political-religious vision and self-understanding the theoretical and pedagogical practices of paradigm construction support, one has to point out that paradigm criticism in Kuhn's terms engenders competition and exclusiveness. Such a competitive model for paradigm construction, however, is not the only possible one. Paradigms as exemplary instances of theoretical frameworks and methods are not necessarily exclusive of each other. Rather, they can also be conceptualized as either existing alongside each other, or they can be seen as overlapping circles or as working in corrective interaction with each other. If paradigms are the cultural discursive practices of scholars, then they can be constructed and related to each other not only in terms of difference but also in terms of commonality. Whereas paradigm shifts as scientific revolutions are, in Kuhn's terms, characterized by "over-and-againstness," incommensurability, and exclusiveness, I have suggested that paradigms could also be conceived in terms of difference and shared common ground.

My own conceptualization of biblical studies paradigms understands them as consisting of diverse platforms or interpretive spaces. This allows one to shift the dual domain rhetoric of "either academy or religious community" to that of different interpretive spaces that overlap and interact with each other. Rather than just focusing on the paradigms of biblical studies as entities that are exclusive of each other, it is also important to emphasize those aspects and methods that are compatible with and corrective of each other. Their overlap constitutes the ever-shifting heart or "common ground" of biblical studies on the whole, whereby the incompatible elements of each paradigm—those that would be at the center in a competitive construction—become progressively decentered.

Fernando Segovia also has advocated a critical reflection on the discourses of biblical studies in terms of paradigm criticism.[38] He charts the following four paradigms in biblical studies in terms of modern and postmodern academic biblical criticism rather than in terms of the overall

---

37. David Macey, *The Penguin Dictionary of Critical Theory* (New York: Penguin, 2001), 290.

38. See also his "Pedagogical Discourse and Practices in Cultural Studies," in *Teaching the Bible: The Discourses and Politics of Biblical Pedagogy* (ed. Fernando F. Segovia and Mary Ann Tolbert; Maryknoll, N.Y.: Orbis, 1998), 137–67.

history of biblical interpretation: (1) historical criticism, which uses the text as means, was the dominant paradigm through the 1970s; (2) literary criticism, which dislodged historical criticism in the 1980s, analyzes the text as medium; (3) cultural criticism, an umbrella term that encompasses lines of inquiry such as socioeconomic and ideological analysis, Neo-Marxist, and various forms of sociological analysis, understands the text as medium and means; (4) intercultural, diasporic, or postcolonial criticism, finally, takes account of the influx of marginal voices and locates the meaning of the text in the encounter between the text and the flesh-and-blood reader.

While Segovia is constant in his delineation of the first three paradigms, he seeks again and again to name and clarify the fourth paradigm, where he now locates his work. While at first he called this paradigm "cultural studies" in order to distinguish it from cultural criticism,[39] he later qualified it as "intercultural" or "diasporic" studies, which are a part of postcolonial studies.[40] Such a fourth paradigm has become possible because of the development of interpretive and interdisciplinary postmodern, intercultural, diasporic postcolonial approaches in the academy.

Segovia correctly debunks the scientific-positivist paradigm as Western colonialist. Hence, he argues that the scientific paradigm of biblical studies in its historical and literary forms must be decentered because it has legitimized Western imperialism. Since Segovia is invested in debunking the hegemonic historical paradigm, he is not interested in highlighting its critical accomplishments. Moreover, he is compelled to omit the pre-

---

39. Fernando F. Segovia, "Introduction: 'And They Began to Speak in Other Tongues': Competing Modes of Discourse in Contemporary Biblical Criticism," in *Social Location and Biblical Interpretation in the United States* (vol. 1 of *Reading from This Place*; ed. Fernando F. Segovia and Mary Ann Tolbert; Minneapolis: Fortress, 1995), 1–32; Fernando F. Segovia, *Decolonizing Biblical Studies: A View from the Margins* (New York: Orbis, 2000), 3–52.

40. Fernando F. Segovia, "Biblical Criticism and Postcolonial Studies: Toward a Postcolonial Optic," in *The Postcolonial Bible* (ed. R. S. Sugirtharajah; The Bible and Postcolonialism 1; Sheffield: Sheffield Academic Press, 1998); idem, "Notes towards Refining the Postcolonial Optic," *JSNT* 75 (1999): 103–14; idem, *Decolonizing Biblical Studies: A View from the Margins* (New York: Orbis, 2000), 119–42; idem, "Interpreting beyond Borders: Postcolonial Studies and Diasporic Studies in Biblical Criticism," in *Interpreting Beyond Borders* (ed. Fernando F. Segovia; Sheffield: Sheffield Academic Press, 2000), 11–35; and idem, "Reading-Across: Intercultural Criticism and Textual Posture," in Segovia, *Interpreting Beyond Borders*, 59–83.

modern the*logical-religious paradigm that is considered to be beholden to the church. Such an omission of the religious-the*logical paradigm does not imply a rejection of this paradigm, however, because Segovia knows that actual "flesh-and-blood readers" are mostly located within the church and religion rather than the academy. He thereby attempts to avoid importing a "dual domain" ethos into the fourth paradigm but ultimately fails to explicitly acknowledge a place in the academy for the*logical-religious frameworks and methods. It is, however, puzzling that Segovia has, to my knowledge, never explored this omission, although it took center stage in the discussion of feminist interpretation in the 1980s and 1990s.[41]

However, the eclipse of the religious-the*logical paradigm is questionable not just in terms of feminist but also in terms of postcolonial emancipatory concerns, since both feminist and postcolonial studies derive their strength not primarily from the academy but from social-political movements for justice. Because most postcolonial and feminist biblical readers are not located in the university but in communities of faith, the religiously based paradigm of biblical studies must not be eclipsed. If it is, one restricts scholarly work to the academy and cuts off its influence on and utility for communities of faith, communities that constitute a significant part of the democratic public.

At this point it might be helpful to look at my own somewhat different construction of paradigms. I had proposed three paradigms in *Bread Not Stone: The Challenge of Feminist Biblical Interpretation*: (1) the doctrinal paradigm, which understands the Bible as the word of G*d; (2) the historical paradigm, which sees it as a book of the past; and (3) the practical-the*logical paradigm, which understands the Bible as a root-model rather than as an archetype of Christian faith and community.[42] Obviously, this form of paradigm construction is firmly located within a Christian the*logical discussion and seeks to gain distance both from the doctrinal and from the historical-positivist paradigm. With this paradigm construction I simultaneously sought both to counter the antiquarian

---

41. See Letty Russell, ed., *Feminist Interpretation of the Bible* (Philadelphia: Westminster, 1985).

42. Elisabeth Schüssler Fiorenza, *Bread Not Stone: The Challenge of Feminist Biblical Interpretation* (Boston: Beacon, 1984), 25–33. This chapter was a revised form of "For the Sake of Our Salvation: Biblical Interpretation and the Community of Faith," in *Sin, Salvation and the Spirit* (ed. D. Durken; Collegeville, Minn.: Liturgical Press, 1979), 21–39.

ethos of biblical studies and to relocate academic biblical interpretation within the public of engaged and dialogical communities of faith. Ecclesiastical as well as academic biblical interpretation should once again serve the people.

Almost fifteen years later, in *Rhetoric and Ethic*, I revisited and renamed as follows the four paradigms of interpretation that I had sketched out in *Bread Not Stone*: (1) the doctrinal-fundamentalist paradigm; (2) the scientific-historical paradigm; (3) the hermeneutic-(post)modern paradigm; and (4) the rhetorical-emancipatory paradigm.[43] This reformulation was undertaken in light of the discussions that had been engendered by postmodern and various emancipatory approaches in biblical studies. In the meantime, the fourth paradigm has developed into a rich and strong party in biblical studies, although it is still often relegated to the margins in doctoral studies.

A comparison with Segovia's paradigm construction shows that we differ formally only with respect to the first paradigm, since my four basic paradigms take the premodern paradigm of interpretation into account, whereas Segovia's paradigm construction is restricted to the academy. Although we use a different nomenclature for the fourth paradigm, I believe we are envisioning a similar restructuring of biblical studies. In light of the "dual domain" discussion, I would like to broaden my understanding of the first paradigm further by stressing that biblical studies as academic studies are not only scientific, cultural, and emancipatory studies but also religious and the*logical studies. In addition, scientific and cultural-emancipatory, like religious-the*logical studies, may not be restricted to the questions and interests of the academy. They, too, must become radical democratic studies responsible to all the people.[44]

In doing so, one needs to be careful not to import the "dualistic domain" construction of the field. Whereas in Segovia's model, this is done by omitting the religious-the*logical paradigm, I have done so in previous attempts by labeling the first paradigm of interpretation as "doctrinal" rather than as religious-the*logical.[45] However, such a labeling does not do justice to the wide-ranging reach and sophistication of this

---

43. Elisabeth Schüssler Fiorenza, *Rhetoric and Ethic: The Politics of Biblical Studies* (Minneapolis: Fortress, 1999), 31–56.

44. Lori Anne Ferrell, *The Bible and the People* (New Haven: Yale University Press, 2008), discusses the Bible's profound impact on readers over the centuries.

45. See my *Rhetoric and Ethic*, ch. 2.

paradigm. It also unwittingly promotes the "dualistic domain" conception that eliminates religious discourses from academic biblical studies, on the one hand, and critical-historical/hermeneutical-emancipatory discourses from the biblical interpretation of communities of faith, on the other.

4. Intellectual and Moral Accountability

Instead of splitting the field into two irreconcilable domains, I suggest, one needs to articulate the accountability of biblical studies: the accountability to the academy and its commitment to excellence, the accountability to religious communities and their commitment to truth and justice, the accountability to the search of individuals for meaning and well-being, the accountability to the wider society and its public interests as well as to the ideals of democracy, human rights, and radical equality around the globe.[46]

For biblical studies to practice these responsibilities, its self-understanding needs to shift from an objectivist, scientist, or dogmatist ethos to a critical-constructive rhetoric of inquiry. Such a rhetoric of inquiry pays special attention to the argumentative discourses of scholarship and their theoretical presuppositions, social locations, investigative methods, and sociopolitical functions. Since the space of rhetorical discourse is the public and political realm, a rhetoric of inquiry does not need to suppress but rather is able to investigate the sociopolitical frameworks, cultural perspectives, modes of argumentation, and symbolic universes of religious texts and biblical interpretations.[47] It is able to explore the notion of ethos and ethic not only in epistemological-rhetorical but also in pedagogical-didactic terms.

To that end, the exploration of a pedagogy of participation and critical argument in graduate biblical studies, as well as the development of a collaborative model of graduate biblical education, is necessary in order to displace the competitive dualistic model of the academy, on the one

---

46. See Charles Tilly, *Democracy* (New York: Cambridge University Press, 2007); and Thomas Banchoff, ed., *Democracy and the New Religious Pluralism* (New York: Oxford University Press, 2007).

47. For an exploration of rhetoric as argumentation, see Anders Eriksson, Thomas H. Olbricht, and Walter Übelacker, eds., *Rhetorical Argumentation in Biblical Texts* (Emory Studies in Early Christianity; Harrisburg, Pa.: Trinity Press International, 2002).

hand, and the individualistic-privatized model of spiritual biblical reading, on the other. An emancipative model of teaching and learning can conceive of the task of the biblical interpreter in rhetorical-emancipative terms.[48] Rhetoric is aware that texts seek to persuade and to argue; they are address and debate rather than objective statement and value-free description.

In this model the biblical scholar does not have the task of "popularizing" and "applying" the results of research so that they can be appropriated by the general reader. Rather, a critical feminist rhetorical understanding of biblical studies shifts attention away from biblical interpretation construed as an ever-better explanation of the meaning of the text. It sees biblical interpretation and education as a forum of debate and conversation, a space for becoming conscious of structures of domination and for articulating visions of radical democracy and well-being (salvation) that are inscribed in our own experience as well as in those of biblical texts. Hence, it is necessary to take biblical interpretation out of the hands of positivist scholarship *and* out of the privatized spiritual realm of the individual solitary reader. In order to democratize biblical studies, we need to constitute graduate biblical education as a *forum*, a "republic of many voices," and a space of possibility where the *ekklēsia*, the radical democratic assembly of biblical scholars, students, and general readers, can debate and adjudicate the public and personal meanings of the scriptures in their sociopolitical contexts and ours. I want to thank Kent for all his work toward this goal.

Bibliography

Avalos, Hector. *The End of Biblical Studies*. Amherst: Prometheus, 2007.
Ayers, William. *Teaching toward Freedom: Moral Commitment and Ethical Action in the Classroom*. Boston: Beacon, 2004.
Banchoff, Thomas, ed. *Democracy and the New Religious Pluralism*. New York: Oxford University Press, 2007.
Brown, Michael Joseph. *What They Don't Tell You: A Survivor's Guide to Biblical Studies*. Louisville: Westminster John Knox, 2000.

---

48. For the development of biblical studies as rhetorical studies, see my *Rhetoric and Ethic*.

Callahan, Allen Dwight. *The Talking Book: African Americans and the Bible*. New Haven: Yale University Press, 2006.
Davies, Philip. "Do We Need Biblical Scholars?" *Bible and Interpretation*. Online: http://www.bibleinterp.com/articles/Davies_Biblical_Scholars.shtml.
———. *Whose Bible Is It Anyway?* 2nd ed. New York: T&T Clark, 2004.
De Gruchy, John W. *Christianity and Democracy: A Theology for a Just World Order*. Cambridge: Cambridge University Press, 1995.
Eriksson, Anders, Thomas H. Olbricht, and Walter Übelacker, eds. *Rhetorical Argumentation in Biblical Texts*. Emory Studies in Early Christianity. Harrisburg, Pa.: Trinity Press International, 2002.
Ferrell, Lori Anne. *The Bible and the People*. New Haven: Yale University Press, 2008.
Fiorenza, Francis Schüssler, and Gordon Kaufman. "God." Pages 136–59 in *Critical Terms for Religious Studies*. Edited by Mark C. Taylor. Chicago: University of Chicago Press, 1998.
Fish, Stanley. "One University under God?" *The Chronicle of Higher Education* (7 January 2005). Online: http://chronicle.com/article/One-University-Under-God-/45077/.
Hatch, Nathan O., and Mark Noll, eds. *The Bible in America: Essays in Cultural History*. New York: Oxford University Press, 1982.
Kittredge, Cynthia Briggs, Ellen Bradshaw Aitken, and Jonathan A. Draper, eds. *The Bible in the Public Square: Reading the Signs of the Times*. Minneapolis: Fortress, 2008.
Kuhn, Thomas S. *The Structure of Scientific Revolutions*. Chicago: University of Chicago Press, 1962.
Levering, Miriam, ed. *Rethinking Scripture: Essays from a Comparative Perspective*. Albany: State University of New York Press, 1989.
Macey, David, ed. *The Penguin Dictionary of Critical Theory*. New York: Penguin, 2001.
Marchal, Joseph A. "To What End(s)? Biblical Studies and Critical Rhetorical Engagement(s) for a 'Safer' World." *SBL Forum*. Online: http://www.sbl-site.org/publications/article.aspx?ArticleId=550.
Martin, Dale B. *Pedagogy of the Bible: An Analysis and Proposal*. Louisville: Westminster John Knox, 2008.
Nasrallah, Laura, and Elisabeth Schüssler Fiorenza, eds. *Prejudice and Christian Beginnings: Investigating Race, Gender, and Ethnicity in Early Christian Studies*. Minneapolis: Fortress, 2009.

Obama, Barack. *The Audacity of Hope: Thoughts on Reclaiming the American Dream.* New York: Vintage, 2008.
Payne, Michael, ed. *Cultural and Critical Theory.* Malden, Mass.: Blackwell, 1997.
Pelikan, Jaroslav. *Whose Bible Is It? A Short History of the Scriptures.* New York: Penguin, 2005.
Russell, Letty, ed. *Feminist Interpretation of the Bible.* Philadelphia: Westminster, 1985.
Schüssler Fiorenza, Elisabeth. *Bread Not Stone: The Challenge of Feminist Biblical Interpretation.* Boston: Beacon, 1984.
———. *But She Said: Feminist Practices of Biblical Interpretation.* Boston: Beacon, 1992.
———. "A Discipleship of Equals: *Ekklesial* Democracy and Patriarchy in Biblical Perspective." Pages 17–33 in *A Democratic Catholic Church.* Edited by Eugene C. Bianchi and Rosemary Radford Ruether. New York: Crossroad, 1992.
———. "For the Sake of Our Salvation: Biblical Interpretation and the Community of Faith." Pages 21–39 in *Sin, Salvation and the Spirit.* Edited by D. Durken. Collegeville: Liturgical Press, 1979.
———. *Jesus: Miriam's Child, Sophia's Prophet: Critical Issues in Feminist Christology.* New York: Continuum, 1994.
———. *Rhetoric and Ethic: The Politics of Biblical Studies.* Minneapolis: Fortress, 1999.
Schüssler Fiorenza, Elisabeth, and Kent Harold Richards, eds. *Transforming Graduate Biblical Education: Ethos and Discipline.* Atlanta: Society of Biblical Literature, 2010.
Segovia, Fernando F. "Biblical Criticism and Postcolonial Studies: Toward a Postcolonial Optic." Pages 39–65 in *The Postcolonial Bible.* Edited by R. S. Sugirtharajah. The Bible and Postcolonialism 1. Sheffield: Sheffield Academic Press, 1998.
———. *Decolonizing Biblical Studies: A View from the Margins.* New York: Orbis, 2000.
———. "Interpreting beyond Borders: Postcolonial Studies and Diasporic Studies in Biblical Criticism." Pages 11–35 in *Interpreting Beyond Borders.* Edited by Fernando F. Segovia. Sheffield: Sheffield Academic Press, 2000.
———. "Introduction: 'And They Began to Speak in Other Tongues': Competing Modes of Discourse in Contemporary Biblical Criticism." Pages 1–35 in *Social Location and Biblical Interpretation in the United*

States. Vol. 1 of *Reading from This Place*. Edited by Fernando F. Segovia and Mary Ann Tolbert. Minneapolis: Fortress, 1995.

———. "Notes towards Refining the Postcolonial Optic." *JSNT* 75 (1999): 103–14.

———. "Pedagogical Discourse and Practices in Cultural Studies." Pages 137–67 in *Teaching the Bible: The Discourses and Politics of Biblical Pedagogy*. Edited by Fernando F. Segovia and Mary Ann Tolbert. Maryknoll, N.Y.: Orbis, 1998.

———. "Reading-Across: Intercultural Criticism and Textual Posture." Pages 59–83 in *Interpreting beyond Borders*. Edited by Fernando F. Segovia. Sheffield: Sheffield Academic Press, 2000.

Siker, Jeffrey S. "President Bush, Biblical Faith, and the Politics of Religion." *SBL Forum*. Online: http//www.sbl-site.org/publications/article.aspx?ArticleID=151.

Stout, Jeffrey. *Democracy and Tradition*. Princeton: Princeton University Press, 2004.

Tilly, Charles. *Democracy*. New York: Cambridge University Press, 2007.

West, Cornel. *Democracy Matters: Winning the Fight against Imperialism*. New York: Penguin, 2004.

Wimbush, Vincent L. ed. *Theorizing Scriptures: New Critical Orientations to a Cultural Phenomenon*. New Brunswick, N.J.: Rutgers University Press, 2008.

Teaching the Biblical Languages: Time for a Rethink?

David J. A. Clines

Most of us teach the biblical languages in the way we were taught them, which is to say, with an emphasis on grammar and parsing, much memorization, and all students in a class working at the same pace. This is, when you come to think about it, a pretty shocking state of affairs. To be sure, not much has changed about the biblical languages since most of us were students, twenty or thirty (or more) years ago, but a very great deal has changed about everything else in education: the philosophy and styles of education, a greater awareness of education as a collaborative process, and, above all, the students themselves. We do not live in the sixties, seventies, or eighties of the twentieth century any more—not even in the twentieth century at all! I will not begin by saying that it is time for a change, only that it is, unquestionably, time for a rethink. Every generation should reconsider its praxis. This essay, offered to Kent Harold Richards as a lifelong enthusiast for reflection on the quality of teaching in our field, aims to take note of some recent developments that challenge current practice, such as:

1. Emphasis on student-centered learning rather than teacher-oriented teaching
2. Knowledge versus skills
3. Recognition of the variety of learning styles
4. Establishment of planned outcomes for language learning
5. Increasing pressures of other disciplines on the theological curriculum
6. The potential impact of electronic resources on learning

I need to say at the beginning that I am not thinking in this essay about teaching the biblical languages to our best students, the ones who will go on to become academics and teachers of biblical languages themselves. It hardly matters how they are taught; they are so good they can probably teach themselves. I am thinking of the 90 percent of students who are good, average, and below-average students, in an M.Div. program, for example, who are currently learning Hebrew and/or Greek within the context of a degree in theology. What should we be offering them? What should we be requiring from them?

Student-Centered Learning

The biggest change that has taken place during my own career as a teacher of biblical studies has been the transition from teaching to learning as the focus of our endeavors. This is not a transition that has occurred everywhere; it has not even been heard of everywhere. In places where it has taken place, however, a dramatic change has happened in the classroom: if one looks into such a classroom, what one sees is no longer a teacher teaching students but students learning, with the assistance of teachers. It is a major difference of perspective, one that foregrounds the importance of the learners—for whose sake of course the classroom exists—rather than the importance of the teachers. It is the learners' needs, abilities, progress, and future that are paramount, not the subject and its demands or the teacher and his or her performance. In this scenario, the teacher has given up the role of the sage on the stage in favor of that of the guide by the side. Though the teacher brings into being the learning experience, the teacher has become more of a facilitator of student learning than an expert passing on knowledge.

What impact has the transition from teaching to learning had on our handling of the biblical languages? Let me offer an example as a kind of litmus test for whether one's classroom is a traditional one or a reformed one. Traditional teachers, like the teachers we ourselves had (on the whole), believed (and still believe), among many other things, that a student of Hebrew must learn (by heart) the forms of the regular verb. Some will settle for nothing less than the forms of all the verbs, regular and irregular, but let us just say, the regular verb. Now learning the regular verb includes learning the forms of the Hophal, does it not? Not many teachers of elementary Hebrew know, I wager, that the Hophal occurs fewer than 400 times in the Hebrew Bible. There are some 74,000 verbs in the Hebrew Bible; thus, only one in every 185 verbal forms is a Hophal.

There are some 300,000 words in the Hebrew Bible; therefore, one has to read 750 words of Hebrew, on average, before one encounters a Hophal. That means that if one reads five chapters of the Hebrew Bible, one is likely to bump into as many as—two Hophals. Why, I ask, have we been making our students learn all the forms of the Hophal when it is so rare? Would not a student-centered learning approach take a cost–benefit view of the matter?

Knowledge versus Skills

The traditional view of teaching's purpose has been to impart knowledge. The second biggest educational change that has taken place during my career has been the recognition that the impartation of knowledge, though necessary and desirable at many levels, is not generally appropriate for higher education. Here we want our students to gain understanding rather than knowledge and to learn how to do things rather than to learn stuff. The purpose of higher education has come to be recognized as not so much to acquire knowledge as to know how to deploy knowledge.

Every one of our classroom hours in which our students practice thinking, learn how to solve problems, and enquire after knowledge are all hours that will develop them as mature adults. They are not hours that will have to be revised for an exam, for when one *knows how to do* something (as distinct from *knowing* something) one does not forget it.

Now, sad to say, learning the biblical languages is not an activity that teaches people how to think or develops understanding. Because it is largely, in its traditional forms at any rate, a matter of learning by heart and of the re-presentation of already-known knowledge, it is something of an anomaly in a program of higher education. Of course, we all want students to know something at least about the languages in which the Bible was written, but I have never heard it acknowledged that language learning is intellectually of second-order value in a theology degree, by comparison with many of the subjects that expand the minds of students today. It is essentially an uncritical enterprise, to be honest, and what we want most for our students is that they should develop skills in critical thinking.

On the other hand, the time is ripe for considering how to upgrade the intellectual value of language teaching and learning, by transforming it from a process of acquisition of facts to the acquiring a set of skills in handling a biblical text. We might think, for example, of a problem-based approach to the biblical languages, of making the grammar subordinate to the vocabulary, of evaluation of modern translations of the Bible in the light of the originals. Only by so doing can we make the learning of languages a worthy component of a degree program.

Recognition of the Variety of Learning Styles

As the student learning experience has moved to center stage, one result has been the growing awareness of the variety of learning styles that actual learners have and deploy. I have never encountered a classroom in which different groups of students were taught separately because of their dramatically different preferences as learners, but I think it is a shame that everyone should be forced into the one mold as learners.

The three main learning styles are visual, aural, and physical (kinesthetic). I myself am a visual learner. I cannot remember people's names until I have seen them written; that is why I spend a great deal of time at congresses peering at people's name badges. Last year, my wife and I enrolled in a course in elementary Mandarin. I wanted to experience again the difficulties of learning a foreign language, and I certainly had my wish. I did very well at memorizing the characters and their pin-yin transliterations. The teacher expected us to learn by conversation, however, and introduced new words orally, which I could not remember because I had not yet seen them written. I found the experience so painful that I dropped out of the course. Yet, my wife, who is an aural learner, thrived on this method and completed the whole course. I could have done as well if there had been room for my learning style!

The first thing every teacher of the biblical languages should do with a class, in my opinion, is to give students a diagnostic test on their preferred learning style and then shape the course according to the needs of the class. In that way, the individuality of each student will be respected, and students will not be terrified. They may have to adapt to some learning styles other than their own preferred one, but they will be able to feel comfortable most of the time.

Outcomes

A feature of the developing focus on the student learning experience has been in recent decades a movement toward defining intended outcomes of a course of study, including all the units within it.

When we say what the outcomes of a course are, we state what students will be able to do at the successful completion of the course—what they will be able to understand, explain, evaluate, and apply. The focus is on the students' achievement. It is not, of course, a statement of what students will *know*, though there will be an increase in knowledge, but of the capacities, skills, and know-how that students will be able to deploy. Stating outcomes is fair to students, since it gives them some assurance of the benefit of the course. It is also helpful to teachers, since it compels them to think through the purposes and intentions of their course.

The interesting thing is that I have yet to see even a half-satisfactory statement of outcomes of a biblical languages course, and, even worse, there appears to be no debate about the subject. Students on a M.Div. program in some institutions may be expected to spend a quarter or even a third of their time on language learning, but no one seems to know why. Some statements of outcomes one hears are banal or vague, such as "the student will be able to read the Hebrew and Greek originals with the help of a dictionary." What does one mean by "read," and why should that be a desirable outcome? Does one mean that the student will be personally able to translate a chapter of the Bible? What exactly is the point of that when there are already more than enough translations of the Bible in existence? Will the student be able to do a better job than the whole expert panel that produced the NRSV, for example? Surely not.

Why are there no studies of the actual uses graduates make of their seminary or university education in the biblical languages? If a tenth of one percent of the effort that goes into teaching the biblical languages were spent on properly researching what happens to students after graduation, we might all be shocked by the results, I dare say, judging from the anecdotal evidence with which we are all familiar. Some serious thinking might emerge about what outcomes for language study might make sense; perhaps we would even question the wisdom of giving a significant share of the curriculum to language study at all.

Pressures on the Curriculum

Supposing we are agreed that every student in a theological degree program should study Greek and Hebrew. We know that such language learning is only one of a host of subjects competing for a place in the curriculum. What mechanism exists, what considerations should apply, for resolving the competing claims?

It is not rational to attempt to justify teaching the biblical languages on the ground that we have always done so or on the strength of assertions that every proper course in biblical studies must include the biblical languages. The only rational approach must be through a review of proposed outcomes. What are the intended purposes of the degree course? What benefits does each unit of study have for the students in realizing the overall intentions of the course?

If the outcomes for the M.Div. course were simply to prepare the next generation of teachers of the biblical languages and to ensure the progress of biblical research, there would be little doubt that Greek and Hebrew must have a very significant place. That cannot be the desired outcome, however, for the members of the class as a whole, most of whom will not end up as teachers of the subject. If the overall outcome of the course should be to equip students for a career in ministry, for example, it becomes very difficult to justify a program of study that will probably have very little place in that career. Even in my own department of biblical studies, whose outcomes are not vocational and whose remit is exclusively the Bible, without any of the traditional theological disciplines, the many current claims on the curriculum are much easier to justify than the biblical languages for the majority of students. How can a person be a graduate in biblical studies, I am constantly asking, without a deep appreciation of feminist criticism, postcolonial criticism, structuralist exegesis, deconstruction, ideological criticism, psychoanalytic criticism, and experience of how these methods impact on the interpretation of the biblical texts? None of these methods existed when I began my study of the biblical languages, but now they are indispensable elements of contemporary biblical studies. Make adequate room for these disciplines, and the biblical languages would be squeezed into such a tiny space that they would hardly seem worthwhile. Can four classroom hours a week for the biblical languages for twenty weeks, let us say, lead to any appropriate outcomes? And if not four hours a week, which may be about half the student's time in the classroom, but two hours a week, what would be the outcomes? If that should be all the time the biblical languages can be afforded in the curriculum, we really do need to rethink what kind of outcomes might be feasible.

Each year at the SBL Annual Meeting I take a look at new grammars of biblical Hebrew (there are several each year!). I am always looking for one that will make Hebrew easier, not more difficult. Year-by-year, my impression is, however, they get more and more complex, dragging in every little exception, elaborating analysis of the syntax beyond the useful and the necessary and, I presume, deterring all but the most determined students. When will someone write a grammar called *Hebrew without Tears*, an introduction to Hebrew in ten hours, say, that majors on comprehension and understanding rather than on memorization, that gives students experience of things they can do with Hebrew themselves rather than overwhelming them with masses of data?

Electronic Resources

In the last fifteen years, with the advent of the Internet and of Bible search programs, the intellectual context for the study of the biblical languages has been transformed. Nonetheless, we have yet to see—as far as I know—any program of study of the biblical languages that systematically draws upon the electronic resources now available. People are saying that, because of the ubiquity of the Internet, everyone born after 1985 thinks differently from the older generations. I do not know about that, but I do know that, for example, memorization, which was a staple of pre-electronic language learning, becomes less and less important as instant access to all kinds of knowledge is available to the students of today.

Suppose that one is introducing students to Hebrew verbs. Nowadays, one does not have to make the students memorize a list of forms; one can help them to find out for themselves what they need to know. For example, one may have them find all the Qal perfect third masculine singular verbs in Gen 1–3 using Accordance, BibleWorks, or Logos software, matching the verses and highlighted words retrieved against their English translations. One may have them identify the forms the verbs exhibit and see how many such forms there are in the whole of the Hebrew Bible, then do the same exercises for the feminine forms. Where do the verbs come in the sentences? One does not tell them any of this; one enables them to find it out for themselves. They will surely have a much better chance of remembering what they have discovered for themselves, compared with what they have been told on the authority of the teacher.

Recommendations

I end by making ten recommendations of my own, but these particular points are not as important as the challenge I am inviting readers of this essay to meet—which is to rethink whatever one is doing as a teacher of the biblical languages.

1. Throw away textbooks and design a course in which every class has the students' interests, needs, and abilities in the forefront.
2. Abandon the idea of the whole class moving at the same speed. Develop schemes for independent learning.
3. Minimize memorization.
4. Focus on understanding rather than knowledge.
5. Give students things to do. Have them learn the alphabet by typing the letters (kinesthetic learning!). Have them find out how constructs are used by discovering all 1,824 construct expressions in Psalms (in Accordance/BibleWorks/Logos). Let them handle old Bibles.
6. End the fetishization of grammar. Give as much time to vocabulary and semantics as to grammar. Get students to find out how dictionaries of the biblical languages differ from one another.
7. Give every student experience of dealing with different versions of the Bible, discerning which variants are meaningful, and, when possible, recognizing the reasons for their differences.
8. Use interlinear translations constantly.
9. Enable every student to have a sense of achievement in biblical languages every week.
10. Enable students to imagine how they will use their experience of Greek and Hebrew when they have forgotten everything they learned by heart in their course.

The SBL in the Undergraduate Classroom: Pedagogical Reflections

Elizabeth Struthers Malbon

For many undergraduate students in biblical studies classes, there is a major contextual shift in the way of approaching the Bible: from church sermons and faith-based Bible study groups interested in applying "Bible lessons" to their lives, to academic classrooms that focus on understanding ancient literary documents in their complex historical and cultural contexts of origin and transmission. I am most familiar with this situation in a large state university, my own teaching context—as well as my own undergraduate and graduate student context, but I am aware that the situation also occurs in smaller, private colleges and universities and in some church-related colleges and universities.[1] I have found various resources

---

1. See Barbara E. Walvoord, *Teaching and Learning in College Introductory Religion Courses* (Hoboken, N.J.: Wiley-Blackwell, 2008), and Mitchell G. Reddish, "Teaching Biblical Studies: Fact and Faith," *SBL Forum* 2/6 (2004); online: http://sbl-site.org/Article.aspx?ArticleID=40. Reddish points out that a private university like his, Stetson, with a historical connection to a religious tradition and a mission statement that explicitly encourages "appreciation for the spiritual dimension of life," may offer the professor more freedom in discussing issues of faith in the classroom than either state universities or some church-related institutions. Almost as an illustration of this point, see J. Bradley Chance (of William Jewell College), "Faith and the Discipline in the Classroom: A Crucial Dialectical Relationship," *SBL Forum* 5/3 (2007); online: http://sbl-site.org/Article.aspx?ArticleID=642. However, see also Mark S. Cladis, "The Place of Religion in the University and in American Public Life," *Sound* 91 (2008): 389–416, who argues that "By means of the skills and virtues of public engagement, the critical and 'protected' space of the religious studies classroom can be maintained while also permitting expressions of a student's religious identity and experience insofar as it is an attempt to contribute to the intellectual inquiry of the topic at hand ... [and] that scholars of religion should distinguish between the regret-

of the Society of Biblical Literature—from books to people—extremely useful in helping undergraduate students of the New Testament make this contextual transition as they learn to appreciate the biblical scholarship the SBL seeks to foster.

Because of the importance of context in biblical studies, for the student as well as for the studied, I must first introduce briefly my present teaching context. Since 1980 I have taught at Virginia Polytechnic Institute and State University (Virginia Tech), a large, comprehensive, state university (although less and less of our funding is supplied by the state). The teaching of religious studies—and biblical studies—here is more than fifty years old, although the name of the academic unit through which this teaching occurs has changed six times since my arrival. For many years I have taught each spring (without a teaching assistant) an introductory New Testament class enrolling over one hundred students, so some challenges of scale have been added to the usual challenges of the subject matter. In addition, in the fall of most years I teach an upper-level New Testament course for twenty to thirty students, alternating between "Jesus and the Gospels" and "Paul and His Interpreters." Occasionally I am able to teach an upper-level "Topics in Biblical Studies" class as a small (five to eleven students) undergraduate seminar. It is these courses, but especially the introductory New Testament class, that will serve here to exemplify how the Society of Biblical Literature is an important presence in my classroom—primarily in the form of books, but also in the form of people, my SBL colleagues near and far.

The SBL in Books

Crucial to any biblical studies course is a study Bible (or perhaps several study Bibles). As an undergraduate, I grew to appreciate—and depend upon—*The New Oxford Annotated Bible, Revised Standard Version*,[2] and as a teacher I assigned it as a required text. When the New Revised Standard Version was released, I was disappointed with the level of updating in the introductions and annotations of *The New Oxford Annotated Bible,*

---

table student practice of privileging experience and the potentially valuable practice of students expressing nonprivileged life experience, religious or otherwise" (405–6).

2. *The New Oxford Annotated Bible, Revised Standard Version* (ed. Herbert G. May and Bruce M. Metzger; New York: Oxford University Press, 1962, 1973).

*New Revised Standard Version.*³ So when *The HarperCollins Study Bible, New Revised Standard Version* became available in 1993,⁴ I was an early adopter. I was not disappointed. It did take me a while to learn where often-read passages were (right-hand column of a left-hand page, for example!), but I find the introductions to the New Testament books to be extremely compact and well-written summaries of current scholarly interpretations and the footnotes to open up not only the Jewish world of the biblical intertext but also the contemporary Hellenistic world. I call the attention of my students to the names of the scholars who have written these introductions and notes, where appropriate mentioning other work by these scholars. I want to personalize biblical scholarship for my students, to let them hear a bit of the scholarly conversation that is ongoing, to prepare them to listen for scholars when they appear on PBS, NPR, the History Channel, and in various forms online.

Although I encourage students to read more than one translation and point out to them how doing so reminds us of the limits of all translations, I do require the NRSV for my New Testament courses; it is a translation new and strange for some and old and familiar for others. I joke that students cannot have too many translations of such an important book and that if they ever want to "swear on a stack of Bibles," they should just come to my office. I also require, in both introductory and upper-level New Testament classes, not just any NRSV edition but *The HarperCollins Study Bible*. When occasional resistance is offered at this point, I comment that "to sign up for this course suggests that you have a serious interest in the Bible, so I'm sure you will want to start (or perhaps continue) building your personal Bible reference library."

Like many New Testament scholars, I have, over the years, sampled a number of New Testament textbooks from the ever-growing supply. Some I have never tried in my state-university situation because of their explicit or implicit stance within the Christian faith. Some I have never tried because they are too long or too demanding for my intelligent but not

---

3. *The New Oxford Annotated Bible with the Apocryphal/Deuterocanonical Books, New Revised Standard Version* (ed. Bruce M. Metzger and Roland E. Murphy; New York: Oxford University Press, 1991).

4. Wayne A. Meeks et al., eds., *The HarperCollins Study Bible, New Revised Standard Version, with the Apocryphal/Deuterocanonical Books* (New York: HarperCollins, 1993). Now Harold W. Attridge, ed., *The HarperCollins Study Bible: Revised Edition* (San Francisco: HarperSanFrancisco, 2006).

bookish students to read. Some I have used for a couple of years before trying something else. Always I have learned something from the selected textbook; always something is changed in my teaching as a result. But always I am looking for something else.

Since its appearance in 1985, I had found the *Harper's Bible Dictionary* a convenient and informative personal and professional resource, and it became my most recommended book to colleagues and friends who asked me questions about the Bible.[5] It was not, however, until the spring of 2002 that I realized that the dictionary, in its revised form as *The HarperCollins Bible Dictionary* (1996),[6] could serve the students in my introductory New Testament class equally well in place of a textbook. Yes, it is long, but my students do not read the entire dictionary, and individual entries vary in length from a few lines to several pages (occasionally more), shorter than textbook chapters. In addition, the range of authors presents a variety of writing styles that avoids the sometimes sleep-inducing homogeneity of some textbooks. In fact, reading a collection of entries from the dictionary for each class session fits quite well with my students' habits of gathering information and interpretation in bits and bytes, in Googling this and looking up that.[7] In addition, I encourage students not to sell the study Bible and Bible dictionary for a pittance at the end of the term but to keep them on hand for looking things up in their future encounters with the Bible. Many do, and my subversive attempt to encourage life-long learning is rewarded.[8] Even before the course is over, a number of students talk with me about some nonassigned entry they read out of curiosity or because it came up in a nonacademic setting. They seem to appreciate having such a resource at the ready, and it reminds

---

5. Paul J. Achtemeier et al., eds., *Harper's Bible Dictionary* (San Francisco: Harper & Row, 1985).

6. Paul J. Achtemeier et al., eds., *HarperCollins Bible Dictionary* (rev. ed.; San Francisco: HarperSanFrancisco, 1996).

7. As I was drafting this section, I received an e-mail from the SBL office about a survey as part of the planning for developing a website intended for general audiences and named "The World of the Bible: Exploring People, Places, and Passages." So maybe one day my metaphor of bits and bytes will become literal for SBL-sponsored information as well.

8. I recently received a thank-you note from a former student, now a seminary graduate and an associate pastor, which read in part, "As I was pulling my *HarperCollins Bible Dictionary* off the shelf today for my sermon prep, I thought of you and your class and how invaluable it was to me."

them, in a way a textbook they can "finish" does not, that there will always be more to learn.

Textbooks seem to give students the false impression, from which good textbooks try to dissuade them, that a subject, such as the New Testament, can be "covered" in a semester. But, like many New Testament professors, I focus more on how to approach the New Testament as a scholar, what questions to ask about its context, and how its meaning has been and can be interpreted. Although I would not go so far as R. Timothy McLay, who argues—seriously but rhetorically—that "content is irrelevant," like him I am more concerned to encourage critical thinking about the Bible than to "cover" the content of the New Testament or the content of New Testament scholarship.[9] For this reason, *The HarperCollins Study Bible* and *The HarperCollins Bible Dictionary* serve me and my students well in place of a textbook on the New Testament, even one of the many excellent textbooks written by SBL members. Although I assign specific articles to be read for most assignments, students develop the habit of "looking it up," of finding out more on their own, and of dealing with differences in what they discover.

Since I use a study Bible and a Bible dictionary instead of an integrative textbook in my large introductory New Testament class, I myself must, in my organization of the class and in class sessions, offer students ways of integrating the complex and diverse material of the New Testament and its equally complex and diverse interpretation. From the beginning of the course I introduce key concepts that can aid in this process of integration: presuppositions, context, author/text/audience, and interdisciplinarity.[10]

On the first day of class, I introduce the word *presuppositions* as one

---

9. R. Timothy McLay, "The Goal of Teaching Biblical and Religious Studies in the Context of an Undergraduate Education," *SBL Forum* 4/8 (2006); online: http://sbl-site.org/Article.aspx?ArticleID=581.

10. Compare the four "major analytical categories" used by Alan Lenzi to help students "organize and interpret the detailed data" they are learning about the Hebrew Bible: (1) Composition. Hebrew Literature: Becoming Careful Readers; (2) Conversation. Israelite Society: Discerning and Appreciating Diversity; (3) Cultural Embeddedness. The Ancient Near East: Putting Data in a Broader Context; (4) Construction of Authority. Israelite Ideology: Understanding the Rhetoric of Persuasion. See Alan Lenzi, "Confessions and Reflections: What Can the Bible Do for the Liberal Arts?" *SBL Forum* 5/1 (2007); online: http://sbl-site.org/Article.aspx?ArticleID=611.

of my favorite words. Presuppositions are usually unstated, I explain, but in this class we will make a point to look for them in ourselves, in our text (the New Testament), and in our textbooks (the study Bible and Bible dictionary). So, as part of my truth-in-advertising introduction to the course, I explain three presuppositions of my teaching, each in the form of a continuum: cognitive–affective, past–present–future, and teaching–learning. Near the close of the first class, having touched on the scope of the course and the scope of the New Testament, I mention two presuppositions of the New Testament itself, two aspects assumed by the New Testament but not explicitly stated: community of faith and historical context. At this point in the first class session, the importance of the presupposed historical context is becoming clear to students. However, the first aspect, that New Testament materials are written for communities of faith, makes for an especially interesting discussion, since I have just moments earlier explained that our class is not a community of faith. I point out that, just as we read silently and study Shakespeare's plays in ways he never intended yet with profit to ourselves, so we can also read and study the materials of the New Testament in ways their human authors never imagined. I remind them that we are not the primary audience of either Shakespeare or Paul.

On the second class day we examine the presuppositions of our textbooks. On that day students turn in a short written "reflection" on the first reading assignment: "Introduction to *The HarperCollins Study Bible*" and "To the Reader" (the translators' introduction) in *The HarperCollins Study Bible* and the "Preface" to *The HarperCollins Bible Dictionary*. In class, students are asked to write for one minute on this topic: What does the preface to *The HarperCollins Bible Dictionary* suggest about its presuppositions? Some, of course, give me a blank stare at first, but, as a prompt, I show on the screen the first and last two sentences of the preface:

> The purpose of this dictionary is to make more widely available, and to an audience of nonspecialists, the results of the best of current biblical scholarship. … A whole world awaits exploration in these pages. The scholars of the SBL invite the readers of this dictionary to share that adventure with them.[11]

---

11. *HBD*, xix and xxii.

I ask for several volunteers to read what they have written (and only what they have written). Usually it does not take any further prompting to bring into the discussion both the academic approach (biblical scholarship) and the academic attitude (exploration, adventure), and it is good for students who are being introduced to academic study of the Bible to see this attitude in a positive way. When a volunteer reader makes a comment about the presuppositions of the Bible dictionary, I ask him or her, "What is your textual evidence?"—thereby also introducing this important aspect of how biblical scholars examine the presuppositions of texts. As a second example, I ask, "Would it be easy to get Professor Malbon to give you a make-up exam? What is your textual evidence from the syllabus?" Thus I am able to introduce the concept of presuppositions in a user-friendly way—before we get to more freighted questions such as pseudonymity. When we move to Paul's letters, I begin the discussion of each letter with the same first question: "What's the occasion?"—that is, what occasion is presupposed by this letter? Actually, after following this procedure for a couple of letters, my first question becomes "What's the first question?" And they know.

A second key concept or organizing principle for my class is context. On the first day of class students are given a brief writing assignment (usually just one paragraph) to complete for the second day: "A rule of thumb for biblical scholars is 'Read the text in context; don't use the text for a pretext.' What do you think scholars mean by this? What elements of the context of the New Testament do you think are important for its interpretation? Why?" This assignment serves as the "Entrance Statement"; it is required but not graded, and it is compared with the student's reply to the same prompt as the "Exit Statement" at the end of the course as a part of "Outcomes Assessment" for the course. These initial statements always show plenty of room for improvement, which is not inappropriate at the beginning of a class. After a semester of reading Bible dictionary entries such as "biblical criticism," "Judea," "Pharisees," "Gnosticism," "midrash," "Women in the NT," "slavery in the New Testament," "homosexuality," "Sepphoris," "Teacher of Righteousness," nearly all students write more completely and complexly about the importance and challenges of reading the text in context.

In class on the second day I explore the concept of context more metaphorically by means of two analogies. First, I ask each student to think of a misunderstanding or surprise she or he has experienced in the process of learning a foreign language or traveling or living in a foreign country.

I wait just a moment for lots of smiles to appear, and some laughter, then ask for several smiling people to share their experiences briefly. Then I ask them to consider how that experience could occur when studying the New Testament. Second, I show a clip of an early scene of the movie *The Gods Must Be Crazy*—the scene in which the pilot of the small plane drops an empty Coke bottle out the window, and it is discovered by an indigenous African group living below. If you are not familiar with this classic dramatic comedy, you have a treat in store. If you are familiar with it, then you will understand how most of the humor of the movie depends upon the disjunction between "our" concept of the Coke bottle as litter and "their" concept of the Coke bottle as a gift from the gods. After my students have laughed at the scenes, I ask them, "Why do you think I showed you this movie clip?" The most direct answer I have ever received is this: "The Bible is a Coke bottle." We discuss how, in our context, we are the ones who may receive the Bible as a gift from the gods without knowing anything about its originating context. Someone might find our unknowing reactions humorous. I also mention explicitly the scene of the fighting over the Coke bottle and the harm it does to a little girl when the elder tries to throw it back up to the gods. Students easily acknowledge that there has been fighting over the Bible and that it has been used for harm as well as for good. I also say a word about metaphors, analogies, and other types of figurative language, about how they will recur in our New Testament material, from Paul's allegory of the olive tree to the parables of Jesus, about their heuristic value and their very real limits.[12] Again, I am trying to make a way for students to build on what they have already learned in order to transition to an academic approach to the New Testament. I am trying both to make the familiar (New Testament) strange and to make the strange (academic study of the New Testament) familiar. *The HarperCollins Bible Dictionary* has a similar purpose: "to make more widely available, and to an audience of nonspecialists, the results of the best of current biblical scholarship."[13]

Of course, it is not just the text that has a context, or, rather, mul-

---

12. Eric Daniel Barreto, "The Bible Is Like … Or is It?" *SBL Forum* 6/1 (2008); online: http://sbl-site.org/Article.aspx?ArticleID=744, describes an activity of asking students to complete the sentence, "The Bible is like…" Then he invites them to share their metaphors and explore their strengths and weaknesses as a way of encouraging them to consider their mental images of the Bible.

13. *HBD*, xix.

tiple contexts; all readers have contexts as well. I explain to my students that they are not being asked to ignore, much less renounce, any religious contexts in which they might also read the text (although no such contexts are required for this course); rather, they are being asked to add another way of reading that focuses on historical, literary, and religious contexts of the ancient Mediterranean world. I am asking them not to be schizophrenic but sophisticated. I point out that they are complex people and they do this all the time; for example, they knew, even without my mentioning it, to behave differently in my class than they do at a football game. I also try to honor students' contexts as students by offering weekly quizzes and weekly writing assignments on a points-earned basis, with a generous margin for occasional illness or simply a bad week. With over one hundred students, I cannot manage weekly "excuses" and "make-ups," so I give students both the opportunity and the responsibility to manage these choices on their own.

A third key concept or organizing principle for my class is the relationship between author, text, and audience. My students have a harder time with the postmodern concept that none of these three are separable entities, but the continuum (they are accustomed to that term) is of heuristic value for the class in learning to separate various questions. We consider, at the beginning of the course, three foci that we might have in approaching the New Testament:[14]

Author	What did the text mean in its historical context?
Text	How does the text mean as a literary work?
Audience	What does the text mean to me or us, to our faith?

By the end of the first class day, students are well able to answer that the first two questions, not the third, will be the shared foci of our class.[15] I have also found it advisable to warn students that they will likely learn

---

14. SBL members will recognize the serious limits inherent in this oversimplification but, I hope, will also be aware of—and likely share—my need for it in this context.

15. For an explicit emphasis on this third question in terms of "awareness of our own social and self-texts [that] also keeps before students the idea that it is they who are constructing interpretations, or interpretive texts," see Chance, "Faith and the Discipline in the Classroom"; see note 1 above on Chance's teaching context. See also J.

less than they hope about the personal life of the individual "authors" of the New Testament books, a subject in which they are frequently quite interested, and more than they imagine about the general historical context, even some reasons why we cannot know so much about "individual authors" from the ancient world.

We do, however, think seriously about the ancient audience. I point out that I use the term "audience" rather than "reader" to stress the oral delivery and reception of New Testament materials. We consider what is presupposed about the audience in each of Paul's letters. We explore how each of the Gospels presupposes a somewhat different audience. I try to communicate the distinction between the time of a story's telling and the time about which it tells. Help is provided by an analogy to a television series that is well known through reruns: *M.A.S.H.* I ask, "About which war is this story told?" Someone always knows: the Korean conflict. "Which war was more current at the time of its first telling?" Someone always knows: the Viet Nam war. I have to say very little else to get across the point, which I then apply to the Gospels as stories told about Jesus but in a later time, to a later audience, with other agendas and needs in mind. I also show a number of paintings by artists of several nationalities of scenes unique to Luke's Gospel that allow students to see at a glance how the artist has painted his or her own audience into the picture. The author of Luke, of course, does something similar in writing—something not quite so easy for all students to see.[16]

A fourth key concept or organizing principle for my class is interdisciplinarity. Although biblical studies (and, indeed, religious studies) is inherently interdisciplinary, explicit attention to this aspect became more important when my department was called the Center (later the

---

Bradley Chance and Milton P. Horne, *Rereading the Bible: An Introduction to the Biblical Story* (Upper Saddle River, N.J.: Prentice Hall, 2000).

16. See the interesting discussion of "transfer learning" by Frank Ritchel Ames, "Critical Methods and Guarded Minds," *SBL Forum* 2/2 (2004); online: http://sbl-site.org/Article.aspx?ArticleID=219. Transfer learning, closely allied with the discovery-learning approach of Jerome Bruner, involves students' exploration and discovery of abstract principals that can be applied to other areas of learning. Ames describes a classroom activity of exploring William Hogarth's painting *The Graham Children*, then helping students transfer what they learn from interpreting art to the analogous discipline of biblical interpretation as a way of overcoming students' initial resistance to biblical scholarship.

Department) of Interdisciplinary Studies (1995–2009). In introducing the concepts of presuppositions and context on the first day of class, I ask students to consider the implications of the embedded contexts of our class:

Virginia Polytechnic Institute and State University	What type of approach to the Bible is entailed in a state university?
College of Liberal Arts and Human Sciences	In what sense is academic study of the New Testament liberating?
Formerly, Department of Interdisciplinary Studies	How is biblical studies interdisciplinary?
Or now, Department of Religion and Culture	How does biblical studies help us understand the interrelations of religion and culture?

However, even with the restructuring and name change of my department, I still raise the question of interdisciplinarity explicitly in an early class.

I suggest that two presuppositions of our New Testament introduction class are a community of scholars (in explicit contrast to the community of faith presupposed by the New Testament) and interdisciplinarity. I present (on screen, although students also have a printed copy) the following two definitions of interdisciplinarity.

> Of course, multi-disciplinary courses can be created by the successive juxtaposition of several disciplines which seek to comprehend the "same" thing. But when no attempt is made to make a coherent and imaginative synthesis, you do not have a genuine interdisciplinary course. Interdisciplinary thinking is a kind of thinking whereby the incompleteness and limits of each disciplinary view are partially corrected by the other, with the result that a new and broader vision is brought before the mind.[17]

> Interdisciplinary courses are really about such matters as recognizing contrasting perspectives; learning how to synthesize, think critically,

---

17. Allie Frazier, "The Interdisciplinary Heart of Liberal Studies," in *The Tradition in Modern Times: Graduate Liberal Studies Today* (ed. Charles B. Hands; Lanham, Md.: University Press of America, 1988), 60–61.

and reexamine the world that we take for granted; empowering students to tackle meaningful but complex issues; weaning students from dependence on experts without dismissing expertise; and teaching students to value disciplines as powerful sources of insight while becoming aware of the nature of their various limitations.[18]

Certainly these two definitions of interdisciplinarity, especially the second one, bring up a number of learning objectives that I regard as crucial for my students. It has been my experience that assigned readings from *The HarperCollins Study Bible* and *The HarperCollins Bible Dictionary* do indeed help students learn how to synthesize, think critically, and reexamine the biblical world as it is distinctive from the world they take for granted. These resources in students' hands also help empower them to tackle meaningful but complex issues of New Testament interpretation with growing independence, weaning students from dependence on the professor as "the" expert without dismissing expertise and, in fact, with increasing appreciation for the expertise of a community of scholars in conversation. Toward the end of the term (when some students are actively looking for "more points"), I give a "reflection" assignment that allows students to choose one of the following longer Bible dictionary articles: "Bible and Western art," "Bible and Western literature," "economics in NT times," "historical geography of the Bible," "sociology of the NT," or "theology, New Testament." My students appreciate the opportunity to choose a discipline that interests them and explore what it may have to say about the New Testament. By this point in the semester they are also more able to value disciplines—and a variety of disciplines and approaches—as powerful sources of insight while becoming aware of the nature of their various limitations.

Following the introduction of the definitions of interdisciplinary by Frazier and Newell, I borrow liberally from the introductory chapter of SBL member Russell Praegent's textbook, *Engaging the New Testament: An Interdisciplinary Introduction*,[19] for a breath-taking overview of a range of approaches to the New Testament—from the historical-critical method,

---

18. William H. Newell, "Designing Interdisciplinary Courses," in *Interdisciplinary Studies Today* (ed. Julie Thompson and William G. Doty; New Directions for Teaching and Learning 58; San Francisco: Jossey-Bass, 1994), 43.

19. Russell Pregeant, *Engaging the New Testament: An Interdisciplinary Introduction* (Minneapolis: Fortress, 1995).

to social-scientific criticism to source, form, and redaction criticism, to explicitly literary approaches from reader response to deconstruction. As my students begin to show panic, I point out that this is like an open house for a dorm or apartment complex: Too many names and faces to keep straight! Don't worry; what is necessary will be sorted out later; enjoy the party. I even use a PowerPoint presentation background with confetti. When surveying the Synoptic Gospels, I concentrate on narrative criticism for Mark (my primary research interest, which I do not hide from students), play a recording of several songs from the musical *Godspell* in association with Matthew, and show images of a number of paintings of scenes unique to Luke, pointing out that story, music, and art can enliven our understanding of many New Testament books in myriad ways.

I conclude our class discussion on interdisciplinarity by introducing the term *hermeneutics* (which they recognize from the assigned article in the *HBD*), asking first what they know about the Greek god Hermes. Their knowledge of his winged sandals and his role as messenger help them understand and remember that this strange-sounding discipline of the theory of interpretation entails the familiar activity that happens when an audience understands a text and communicates/interprets its meaning. I emphasize to students that we will not, as a class, have time to explore every approach introduced, although we will further investigate a number of them, but the crucial point is that we all interpret when we read. All reading is interpretation. The goal for beginning biblical scholars, for example, my introductory New Testament class, is to become more aware of our own presuppositions and those of others and to appreciate the diversity and richness of both the New Testament and scholarly approaches to the New Testament. It is a goal well supported by the combined efforts of members of the Society of Biblical Literature in *The HarperCollins Bible Dictionary*, who wish "to make more widely available the results of the best of current biblical scholarship" and who regard this "exploration" of a "whole world" as an "adventure."[20] With that spirit of adventure comes responsibility for beginning the journey. I close with a video clip from the movie *Dead Poets Society*, the courtyard scene where the English teacher is encouraging his students to take the initiative to explore their own ways of walking, a clear metaphor for their own ways of thinking, reading, and interpreting literature—and living their lives. I end

---

20. *HBD*, xix and xxii.

the scene with the disapproving look of the headmaster from the window above, and we reflect briefly on what might get in the way of such initiative for any of us.

My students are not, of course, biblical scholars, and few of them will ever become such, which is a good thing, since the world can only accommodate so many of us. But they are the interested nonspecialists of the target audience of *The HarperCollins Bible Dictionary*. I think it was at a writing-across-the-curriculum workshop years ago when a colleague not in religious studies asked me, "Are you teaching producers or consumers?" I suspect I underappreciated the business metaphor at first, but the question proved to be a richly clarifying one for me. For the most part, I am teaching "consumers" of biblical scholarship, not "producers" of it, and this realization has informed my revision of writing assignments especially but also my overall approach to meeting students' needs rather than following old habits. Since most of my students, especially in my large introductory New Testament class, are not religious studies majors and are not planning to enroll in graduate school in religious studies after graduation, I have found the traditional "research paper" or "term paper" less valuable for them than more frequent, more focused, and shorter writing assignments that ask them, for example, to list ways in which their world differs from the New Testament world and how this might make a difference in their work in this course, or to state and argue for an opinion on the authorship of a disputed Pauline letter, or to evaluate critically a website on a biblical subject. In relation to this image of students as consumers or producers, it is interesting to note the comment of John Dart, who writes for *Christian Century*:

> In fact, news professionals and teachers have similar goals: Both deal with an ever-changing audience—whether they are students, readers or TV viewers. For every consumer with a genuine desire to learn, we know there are just as many who are only casually interested. We both prefer to address the avid learner, but we'd be fools not to do our best for the newly curious and others with minimal knowledge.[21]

Nevertheless, the majority of my students are connected with the Christian tradition in one or more of its myriad forms and in a variety of

---

21. John Dart, "Biblical Research Findings for the Public," *SBL Forum* 4/7 (2006); online: http://sbl-site.org/Article.aspx?ArticleID=567.

ways, and some intend to go to seminary and become leaders of Christian congregations. I point out to all my students that, as participants in a full-semester academic course on the New Testament, they will likely have more training in biblical scholarship than the majority of persons they meet in their lifetimes. I do this not to make them cocky (by the end of the course, most have a healthy sense of how little they know in relation to what could be known) but to help them see the responsibility that the privilege of study brings. For example, knowing, as they do, something of the ancient historical and societal contexts of the anti-Semitic and/or anti-Judaic strands in the New Testament itself, they must be the ones to bring up this issue among their peers and to raise the ethical question of whether such strands must be continued in yet another era by those who value these texts.[22] In this, as Dart notes, there is another similarity between reporters and professors:

> Religion news writers and Bible scholars become equally excited if their investigations allow them to conclude, "We believed before that a familiar biblical figure, place or practice meant this, but now we have new studies that tell us differently. And here is why it is significant for Bible understanding and to issues today."[23]

Professors are even more excited if we are able to assist our students in arriving at such a conclusion on their own!

All analogies break down at some point, as does the consumer/producer analogy with biblical studies students. Once when I was presenting scholarly arguments for the pseudonymity of Ephesians in my introductory New Testament class, a student called out, "I'm not buying it." I called back, "I'm not selling it." I explained that I was telling, not selling. No student is required to share the majority opinion of New Testament scholars, I noted, but everyone in the class is required to be familiar with such opinions. Furthermore, I encouraged everyone who disagreed to take the opportunity to become more aware of his or her reasons for dis-

---

22. See Joseph A. Marchal, "To What End(s)? Biblical Studies and Critical Rhetorical Engagement(s) for a 'Safer' World," *SBL Forum* 4/6 (2006); online: http://sbl-site.org/Article.aspx?ArticleID=550, who argues that "In order for biblical studies to retain its critical place, then, it must elucidate and engage the historical heritage of how biblical arguments have been used toward oppressive ends. This reflects a process frequently extolled in Schüssler Fiorenza's work, that of a rhetoric of inquiry."

23. Dart, "Biblical Research Findings."

agreeing. Since we read Paul's letters first—the only way I have ever found actually to teach students that they were written first—we come upon the troubling issue of pseudonymity early on. Later, when we are reading the Gospels, I have an opportunity to give an example of a situation in which I disagree with the majority of scholars: I present the two-source hypothesis, then ask students to think of any other theoretical models to explain the Synoptic relationships; after they come up with a few, I explain why I am a nonbeliever in Q but rather a believer in Markan priority without Q, the Farrar-Goulder-Goodacre hypothesis. They are inevitably intrigued by the state of the argument, and they know quite a bit from reading about it in the Bible dictionary ("Synoptic Problem, the," "Q," "M," "L"). Yet, the consumer-not-producer analogy remains helpful because most of my students will not be making independent analyses of the Synoptic problem; they do, however, gain confidence in deciding for themselves how convincing they find various scholarly arguments to be, and, most important, they become accustomed to the fact that scholars do not always agree with each other because of the complexities of studying and interpreting ancient documents. I was delighted one year at my students' reactions to news about the Gospel of Judas, not "Wow, this is amazing! What has been kept from us?" but "Hmm. Another discovery. This is going to provide an interesting debate." Their basic resources have been a study Bible and a Bible dictionary that do not hide the ongoing debate that characterizes biblical scholarship.

The SBL in People

In addition to relying on these two important SBL-sponsored books, I share with my upper-level New Testament students each fall my anticipations and reflections on the SBL Annual Meeting so that they have a peek at the scholarly world focused on the Bible in its various contexts. In 2009, I was able to relate to my "Paul and His Interpreters" class an even stronger interpretation of the olive tree allegory that we had explored earlier in the term after hearing Mark Nanos's SBL paper on "'Broken Branches': A Pauline Metaphor Gone Awry?" Even before the 2009 SBL meeting I had sent an e-mail note to my frequent SBL Pauline tutor, Jerry Sumney, with "a Paul question for you that can't wait till New Orleans," a good question asked by a student on the basis of what I had taught him but for which I had no good answer. Jerry sent a thorough and thoughtful reply within eight hours, which I printed and read in class the next day. My students were impressed that I have such good scholarly friends, and so am I. They are also experientially aware that biblical scholarship is an ongoing conversation, which is an important learning objective of mine.

Occasionally SBL members have participated more directly in my courses, in person or via e-mail or video conferencing. In October 2009 our newly restructured and renamed Department of Religion and Culture brought Bart Ehrman to campus as the Hammond Lecturer, and, in addition to his public address and a graduate seminar, he spoke with my undergraduate seminar on the Gospel of Mark about "Secret Mark." Soon after, I heard an intriguing session on Secret Mark at the SBL meeting (Psychology and Biblical Studies session on "The Secret Gospel of Mark, Sex, Death, and Madness: The Psychodynamics of Morton Smith's Proposal") and was able to report back on that to my class without having to explain the whole situation. In 1999, I arranged for a dozen SBL Markan scholars to be in e-mail contact with my small undergraduate seminar on "Reading the Gospel of Mark" for the week in which we were reading each scholar's work; every scholar whom I invited participated in this electronic question-and-answer experience. In 2004, I was able to arrange two video conferences between a group of sixteen Honors reading group students from the large New Testament class and the authors of works they were reading: we communicated with SBL members John Gager about *Reinventing Paul* and David Barr about *Tales of the End: A Narrative Commentary on the Book of Revelation*.[24] We also had e-mail exchanges that year with Marcus Borg and N. T. Wright about *The Meaning of Jesus: Two Visions*,[25] even though both SBL members were traveling quite a bit at the time.

The idea for the video conference with John Gager was first discussed at a chance meeting in an elevator at an SBL meeting. But one of my favorite SBL elevator stories is about my similar meeting with William Lane Craig, whom I knew only from the firecracker book (have students read it, then jump back and watch the fireworks!) *Will the Real Jesus Please Stand Up?*[26] in which the transcript of a debate on the resur-

---

24. John G. Gager, *Reinventing Paul* (New York: Oxford University Press, 2000); David L. Barr, *Tales of the End: A Narrative Commentary on the Book of Revelation* (Santa Rosa, Calif.: Polebridge, 1998).

25. Marcus J. Borg and N. T. Wright, *The Meaning of Jesus: Two Visions* (New York: HarperCollins, 1999).

26. *Will the Real Jesus Please Stand Up? A Debate between William Lane Craig and John Dominic Crossan* (ed. Paul Copan; Grand Rapids: Baker, 1998).

rection of Jesus between Craig and Dominic Crossan is followed by four powerful essays representing the "two sides" of the debate. I was using the book in an interdisciplinary studies class called "Looking for Jesus" that focused on various approaches to interpreting Jesus—from the quest for the historical Jesus, to this theological debate, to Jesus movies. Noticing Dr. Craig's nametag in the elevator, I introduced myself quickly and told him my class was reading this book; he kindly stepped off on my floor to finish the conversation. He was surprised to learn that most of my students entered the class with ideas much closer to his than to Crossan's. My class was excited to hear about the conversation, and a few weeks later a student learned from her parents that Craig also had mentioned the surprising elevator conversation in an e-mailing. Thus my students have learned, through their mediated contact with SBL members, not only that biblical scholarship is a conversation, but also that it is a spirited yet cordial conversation.

It is not accidental that the footnotes to this essay are liberally sprinkled with essays from the online *SBL Forum* for, after my attention was called to one relevant article by an editor of this volume, I searched for other articles and was delighted with what I found. I now have an increased awareness of this additional way that the SBL can be present in my classroom, through the pedagogical suggestions and reflections of my SBL colleagues. Soon I will be embarking on preparing an online graduate course designed especially for public school teachers, "The Bible and U.S. Public Schools." I have already felt the support of the SBL in several ways for this project: (1) the book sponsored and published by the SBL, *Teaching the Bible: Practical Strategies for Classroom Instruction*;[27] (2) the SBL resource page, "The Bible in Public Schools" (http://www.sbl-site.org/educational/thebibleinpublicschools.aspx); (3) the SBL session on "Teacher Experiences with the Bible and World Religions in the High School Classroom" at the 2008 SBL meeting, organized by SBL staffer Moira Bucciarelli; and (4) especially the strong letter of support sent on very short notice by Kent Harold Richards at my request when, as I was proposing this course, questions were raised about whether there is really a need for teachers to learn about how to deal with the Bible in language arts and social-studies classes in public schools. Kent said yes most convincingly.

---

27. Mark Roncace and Patrick Gray, eds., *Teaching the Bible: Practical Strategies for Classroom Instruction* (SBLRBS 49; Atlanta: Society of Biblical Literature, 2005).

Thus I anticipate being able to help introduce the SBL into some additional public school classrooms (it is already there) where it can assist both teachers and students in addressing the challenging questions that arise when the Bible and biblical traditions come up, as they frequently do in the study of the history and literature of our nation and the world. At a "Research 1" land-grant university, which is my teaching context, connections between research and teaching and engagement with the community are important and encouraged; the resources of the SBL—both books and people—make these connections easy for me to share with students in the undergraduate classroom as I engage them in biblical studies as a way of exploring the biblical scholarship the SBL aims to foster.

Bibliography

Ames, Frank Ritchel. "Critical Methods and Guarded Minds." *SBL Forum* 2/2 (2004). Online: http://sbl-site.org/Article.aspx?ArticleID=219.

Achtemeier, Paul J., et al., eds. *The HarperCollins Bible Dictionary*. San Francisco: HarperSanFrancisco, 1996.

———. *Harper's Bible Dictionary*. San Francisco: Harper & Row, 1985.

Attridge, Harold W., ed. *The HarperCollins Study Bible: Revised Edition*. San Francisco: HarperSanFrancisco, 2006.

Barr, David L. *Tales of the End: A Narrative Commentary on the Book of Revelation*. Santa Rosa, Calif.: Polebridge, 1998.

Barreto, Eric Daniel. "The Bible is Like … Or is It?" *SBL Forum* 6/1 (2008). Online: http://sbl-site.org/Article.aspx?ArticleID=744.

Borg, Marcus J., and N. T. Wright. *The Meaning of Jesus: Two Visions*. New York: HarperCollins, 1999.

Chance, J. Bradley. "Faith and the Discipline in the Classroom: A Crucial Dialectical Relationship." *SBL Forum* 5/3 (2007). Online: http://sbl-site.org/Article.aspx?ArticleID=642.

Chance, J. Bradley, and Milton P. Horne. *Rereading the Bible: An Introduction to the Biblical Story*. Upper Saddle River, N.J.: Prentice Hall, 2000.

Cladis, Mark S. "The Place of Religion in the University and in American Public Life." *Sound* 91 (2008): 389–416.

Copan, Paul, ed. *Will the Real Jesus Please Stand Up? A Debate between William Lane Craig and John Dominic Crossan*. Grand Rapids: Baker, 1998.

Dart, John. "Biblical Research Findings for the Public." *SBL Forum* 4/7 (2006). Online: http://sbl-site.org/Article.aspx?ArticleID=567.

Frazier, Allie. "The Interdisciplinary Heart of Liberal Studies." Pages 60–61 in *The Tradition in Modern Times: Graduate Liberal Studies Today*. Edited by Charles B. Hands. Lanham, Md.: University Press of America, 1988.

Gager, John G. *Reinventing Paul*. New York: Oxford University Press, 2000.

Lenzi, Alan. "Confessions and Reflections: What Can the Bible Do for the Liberal Arts?" *SBL Forum* 5/1 (2007). Online: http://sbl-site.org/Article.aspx?ArticleID=611.

Marchal, Joseph A. "To What End(s)? Biblical Studies and Critical Rhetorical Engagement(s) for a 'Safer' World." *SBL Forum* 4/6 (2006). Online: http://sbl-site.org/Article.aspx?ArticleID=550.

May, Herbert G., and Bruce M. Metzger, eds. *New Oxford Annotated Bible, Revised Standard Version*. New York: Oxford University Press, 1962, 1973.

McLay, R. Timothy. "The Goal of Teaching Biblical and Religious Studies in the Context of an Undergraduate Education." *SBL Forum* 4/8 (2006). Online: http://sbl-site.org/Article.aspx?ArticleID=581.

Meeks, Wayne A., et al., eds. *The HarperCollins Study Bible, New Revised Standard Version, with the Apocryphal/Deuterocanonical Books*. New York: HarperCollins, 1993.

Metzger, Bruce M., and Roland E. Murphy, eds. *New Oxford Annotated Bible, with the Apocryphal/Deuterocanonical Books, New Revised Standard Version*. New York: Oxford University Press, 1991.

Newell, William H. "Designing Interdisciplinary Courses." Pages 35–51 in *Interdisciplinary Studies Today*. Edited by Julie Thompson and William G. Doty. New Directions for Teaching and Learning 58. San Francisco: Jossey-Bass, 1994.

Pregeant, Russell. *Engaging the New Testament: An Interdisciplinary Introduction*. Minneapolis: Fortress, 1995.

Reddish, Mitchell G. "Teaching Biblical Studies: Fact and Faith." *SBL Forum* 2/6 (2004). Online: http://sbl-site.org/Article.aspx?ArticleID=40.

Roncace, Mark, and Patrick Gray, eds. *Teaching the Bible: Practical Strategies for Classroom Instruction*. SBLRBS 49. Atlanta: Society of Biblical Literature, 2005.

Walvoord, Barbara E. *Teaching and Learning in College Introductory Religion Courses*. Hoboken, N.J.: Wiley-Blackwell, 2008.

"Psalms Are Not Interesting": Learner-Centered Approaches to Teaching Biblical Poetry and the Psalms

Charles William Miller

"I like Revelation, and the Book of Daniel, and Genesis and Samuel, and a little bit of Exodus, and some parts of Kings and Chronicles, and Job, and Jonah."

"And the Psalms? I hope you like them?"

"No, sir."

"No? Oh, shocking! I have a little boy, younger than you, who knows six Psalms by heart; and when you ask him which he would rather have, a gingerbread nut to eat, or a verse of a Psalm to learn he says: 'Oh! the verse of a Psalm! angels sing Psalms,' says he; 'I wish to be a little angel here below'; he then gets two nuts in recompense for his infant piety."

"Psalms are not interesting," I remarked.[1]

I have found that many of the students who enroll in my introductory Hebrew Bible class share little Jane Eyre's attitude toward the Psalms. They, too, believe that "Psalms are not interesting." In fact, with few exceptions, they come to class with the predisposition to find all poetry boring (not just the Psalms), so that when I mention that approximately one third of the Hebrew Bible is composed of poetry and that we will spend a significant amount of class time examining these poetic passages, there is

---

1. Charlotte Brontë, *Jane Eyre* (London: Penguin, 1996), 42.

usually a collective sigh.² After several years of wondering how I might instill in my students the same appreciation for (if not the love of) classical Hebrew poetry that I enjoy, I finally hit on a practical idea that has worked remarkably well in all of my classes.³ This essay describes the set of practices that I now employ in the classroom to introduce students to biblical poetry and to the basic literary genres found in the Psalms.⁴

Background and Context

I have taught courses on the Bible for several years in many different contexts: both at institutions within the United States and in the South Pacific; at a denominational seminary, an interdenominational theological college, and a private university. Presently, I find myself at a state-funded public university, teaching in a department that houses both philosophy and religion. The University of North Dakota (UND) is situated in a small city located on the vast northern prairies of the upper Midwest—only miles from the Canadian border. Except for the highly regarded aerospace program and the nationally renowned collegiate hockey team, there is little to draw students from outside of the geographical area. The region is sparsely populated, with the major industries in the area being agricul-

---

2. My students are not alone in their negative (or apathetic) attitude toward poetry. A National Endowment for the Arts survey in 2004 revealed that only 12 percent of the United States public chooses to read or listen to poetry. This was down from 19.8 percent in 1992 (*Reading at Risk: A Survey of Literary Reading in America* [Research Division Report 46; Washington, D.C.: National Endowment for the Arts, 2004], 22).

3. For similar approaches to teaching poetry in the classroom, see Craig M. Rustici, "Sonnet Writing and Experiential Learning," *College Teaching* 45 (1997): 16–18; Linda Young, "Portals into Poetry: Using Generative Writing Groups to Facilitate Student Engagement with Word Art," *Journal of Adolescent & Adult Literacy* 51 (2007): 50–55; and Rolf A. Jacobson, "Teaching Students to Interpret Religious Poetry (and to Expand Their Avenues of Thinking)," *TThRel* 7 (2004): 38–44.

4. It seems appropriate to contribute an essay to Kent Richards's Festschrift that focuses on a practical aspect of classroom pedagogy, since it was in his classroom, as one of his students, that I experienced first-hand what it means to create learning environments that promote significant student learning. His championing of teaching excellence and educational innovation, both as a classroom educator and as the Executive Director of the Society of Biblical Literature, has influenced immeasurably my own teaching career, as well as the professional lives of many others within the United States and across the globe.

tural in nature. The vast majority of students who attend UND are from small rural farming communities that tend to emphasize traditional conservative American values such as family, religion, and patriotism. There is very little ethnic, cultural, or religious diversity at the university. Each year brings greater heterogeneity to UND, although enrollment at the university remains above 90 percent for white Euro-American, almost all of whom primarily self-identify as Christian. There are, of course, many exceptions to this profile, but more often than not, when I survey the students in one of my courses, the demographics support these data.[5] One can readily discover the influence of Christianity in the region by noting that, even though this is a state-sponsored/funded institution, few of the students (or their parents) see any problem with having Good Friday and Easter Monday as university holidays.

The introductory Hebrew Bible course is taught each fall semester and has an enrollment of forty students, primarily first- and second-year students and typically eighteen or nineteen years old. Many students take the course believing it should be easy since they already know what the Bible says or that it will be similar to the Sunday school classes they attended as a child. They are usually disabused of this idea on the first day of class, although for some it lingers much longer. I have been teaching the course for over ten years and do not teach it as a survey of the literature and history of the Hebrew Bible. I focus instead on issues of interpretation—especially in regard to the importance of recognizing the different literary types contained in the Bible and the way those genres impact reader expectations. For this reason, I usually do not use a standard textbook but instead require students to purchase a study Bible (most recently, the *New Oxford Annotated Bible*[6]); at times, I have had them also buy the *Eerdmans*

---

5. In my most recent introductory Hebrew Bible course (fall 2009), for example, of the forty-one students enrolled in the class, all were white Euro-Americans, and only one did not self-identify as Christian (either formerly during childhood or presently as an adult).

6. *New Oxford Annotated Bible: New Revised Standard Version with the Apocrypha* (ed. Michael D. Coogan; 3rd ed.; Oxford: Oxford University Press, 2007). Although I have used other study Bibles (e.g., Harold W. Attridge, ed., *The HarperCollins Study Bible: Revised Edition* [San Francisco: HarperSanFrancisco, 2006] or *The Jewish Study Bible: Featuring the Jewish Publication Society Tanakh Translation* [ed. Adele Berlin and Marc Zvi Brettler; Oxford: Oxford University Press, 2004]), I usually return to the *NOAB* because students seem to find it easier to understand and, therefore, prefer it to the others.

Dictionary of the Bible.[7] We begin the semester with discussions of canon, text/translation, and social location—both of the texts and of the readers. From there we begin an exploration of genre, focusing first on narratives and then moving to poetry. After these introductory matters have been addressed, the rest of the semester is spent examining examples of different types of literature: law, history, prophecy, and so forth. The discussion of classical Hebrew poetry comes during the first third of the course.

For the most part, my experience of teaching the introductory Hebrew Bible course has been very rewarding. I find that many of the students who enroll in my classes are often highly motivated. They come to class to learn more about a book that they consider to be significant to their personal faith and, therefore, worthy of serious study.[8] The source of their motivation, however, can also become a problem. By the time these students come to my class, they have previously had several years of experience with the Bible. They have already been "trained"—both formally (within a particular religious community) and informally (within a family or among friends)—in how to approach the study of the Bible.[9] These learned preunderstandings are rarely based on self-conscious, critical reading practices; rather, they often rely on unexamined ideas about what the text "ought" to say. Therein lies the problem: not the preun-

---

7. David Noel Freedman, ed., *Eerdmans Dictionary of the Bible* (Grand Rapids: Eerdmans, 2000).

8. On the issue of "conservative" students in the "liberal" classroom, see Marit Trelstad, "The Ethics of Effective Teaching: Challenges from the Religious Right and Critical Pedagogy," *TThRel* 11 (2008): 191–202.

9. Many of the students who take my Bible courses are members of religious communities that have little connection to the world of academics. It is too easy to forget that what I might see as faulty thinking, or wrong-headedness, is, in fact, perfectly appropriate to their community. This important insight is articulated by Kenneth Bruffee, when he writes about students, "They talked, wrote, and behaved in a manner that was perfectly correct and acceptable within the community they were currently members of. The way they talked, wrote, and behaved was 'incorrect' and unacceptable, we found ourselves saying, only in a community that they were not—or were not yet—members of. The community that the students were not yet members of and were asking to join by virtue of committing themselves to attend college was of course the (to them) alien community of the 'literate' and the 'college educated'" (*Collaborative Learning: Higher Education, Interdependence, and the Authority of Knowledge* [Baltimore: Johns Hopkins University Press, 1993], 17).

derstandings or the experiences per se but the fact that they are largely unexamined.[10]

Most biblical studies instructors would acknowledge that the students' preunderstandings present a problem, regardless of whether they arise from a particular religious community or are gleaned from the culture at large. However, few instructors can deal with the problem adequately in the traditional introductory course. The reason for this is that the focus in those courses is commonly on content: what texts are actually contained in the Bible and what scholars say about those texts. This emphasis on the transference of knowledge from the teacher to the student is characteristic of a teacher-centered model of education.[11] I have found that, when one focuses on content alone, students can reproduce that content in exams, papers, or other assignments, but they have often gained no real understanding of the basic reading strategies necessary responsibly to interpret a biblical text for themselves. They can tell me, for example, how Hermann Gunkel interpreted a specific psalm and even identify the method he used to interpret it. Nevertheless, Gunkel's views do not affect their own; furthermore, they are unable to employ his method themselves when confronted with another similar psalm. In other words, there is no real engagement with either the method or with the text. Knowledge remains merely information, and that information has no existence or relevance apart from the narrow confines of a particular course.[12]

---

10. The problem of unexamined preunderstandings is not confined to students but is also an issue for the instructor. See Khosrow Bāgheri, "A Hermeneutical Model for Research on the Evaluation of Academic Achievement," *New Thoughts on Education* 1 (2005): 5–12.

11. The most widely known and, perhaps, the best critique of teacher-centered approaches comes from Paulo Freire, in his *Pedagogy of the Oppressed* (New York: Seabury, 1970). See, e.g., his definition of the "banking" method of education: "Education thus becomes an act of depositing, in which the students are the depositories and the teacher is the depositor. Instead of communicating, the teacher issues communiqués and makes deposits which the students patiently receive, memorize, and repeat. This is the 'banking' concept of education, in which the scope of action allowed to the students extends only as far as receiving, filing, and storing the deposits" (58). See, as well, the now-classic response to teacher-centered education in Maryellen Weimer, *Learner-Centered Teaching: Five Key Changes to Practice* (San Francisco: Jossey-Bass, 2002).

12. It is not merely a problem that students are unable to extend knowledge beyond a specific course, but, as Donald Finkel points out, they are unable to retain

Over twenty-five years ago the National Institute of Education stated: "There is now a good deal of research evidence to suggest that the more time and effort students invest in the learning process and the more intensely they engage in their own education, the greater will be their growth and achievement, their satisfaction with their educational experience, their persistence in college, and the more likely they are to continue their learning."[13] This statement, of course, echoes the work of many of the educators who were writing in the decades prior to the 1984 report (including such diverse thinkers as John Dewey and Paulo Friere, whom I will discuss below). The idea that students learn best through active engagement has become a truism, and all learner-centered pedagogies take such a perspective for granted. Nonetheless, it is not an easy task to move from acceptance of the concept to putting the concept into practice.[14] This essay offers one possible way of actively engaging students in learning about classical Hebrew poetry and the genres found in the Psalms.

In an attempt to deal with the problem of unexamined preunderstandings and facile learning that does not truly engage the student, I have moved away from the content-driven model of introductory courses (What should the student know?) to one that focuses on skills (What

---

that knowledge for future reference (*Teaching with Your Mouth Shut* [Portsmouth, N.H.: Heinemann, 2000]). Finkel writes, "But how many could pass those same exams (without any subsequent preparation) five years later? If this question seems unreasonable, ask yourself what justifies all those hours spent composing lectures, delivering them, taking notes, studying those notes, and taking exams. If all these efforts do not aim to produce any significant, lasting learning, then what is their point? Five years is not long to expect significant learning to last" (3). Grant Wiggins suggests using a "backward design" in planning and organizing courses. Instructors should begin by thinking about what they want students to value and/or remember one or two years after the course has ended (*Educative Assessment: Designing Assessments to Inform and Improve Student Performance* [San Francisco: Jossey-Bass, 1998]).

13. National Institute of Education, *Involvement in Education* (Washington, D.C.: Department of Education, 1984), 17.

14. For those interested in a practical workbook helpful in transforming teacher-centered courses into learner-centered ones (in whole or in part), see Phyllis Blumberg, *Developing Learner-Centered Teaching: A Practical Guide for Faculty* (San Francisco: Jossey-Bass, 2009). Blumberg's book is based on the five dimensions of learner-centered education as identified by Maryellen Weimer in *Learner-Centered Teaching*: balance of power, function of content, role of the teacher, responsibility for learning, and purposes and processes of evaluation.

should the student be able to do?). Moreover, I have come to see the knowledge and the experiences that students bring to class not as a detriment to their learning experience but as a foundation upon which they can construct new knowledge.[15] In an effort to help students think about how their backgrounds might affect the way they read the Bible, as well as to give me insight into who is taking the course, I begin the semester with two exercises: one a homework assignment and the other an in-class activity. The first assignment of the semester is a "letter to the professor." Students are asked to write me a personal letter in which they describe their religious/nonreligious background, identify where and how they have read and studied the Bible previously, and reflect critically on how their past experiences with the Bible might influence how they approach the Bible in this particular course.[16]

During the first or second class meeting, I use another exercise to help the students and me think about the preunderstandings they bring to the course. I ask students to make a list of everything they know about the Hebrew Bible. Each student shares the list in a small group, together the group combines all the lists into one, and then they prioritize the lists from the most important to least important item. Finally, groups write their top three items on the board, and I query each group about their

---

15. The significance of employing student experience in the construction of new knowledge is one of the basic elements of constructivist pedagogies. See, e.g., George W. Gagnon Jr. and Michelle Collay, *Designing for Learning: Six Elements in Constructivist Classrooms* (Thousand Oaks, Calif.: Corwin, 2001), esp. 17–34; and Kathy L. Schuh, "Knowledge Construction in the Learner-Centered Classroom," *Journal of Educational Psychology* 95 (2003): 426–27.

16. I have also used "social location" inventories, where students identify specific aspects of their life (e.g., gender, economic background, race, and so forth), then describe how each of those particular situations might affect their reading of the Bible. In my context, these sorts of inventories work much better with advanced students, in upper-level courses, than they do with beginning students. The personal letter appears to be less threatening and equally effective in provoking the younger students to reflect on the issue. For examples of inventories, see Norman K. Gottwald, "Framing Biblical Interpretation at New York Theological Seminary: A Student Self-Inventory on Biblical Hermeneutics," in *Social Location and Biblical Interpretation in the United States* (vol. 1 of *Reading from This Place*; ed. Fernando F. Segovia and Mary Ann Tolbert; Minneapolis: Fortress, 1995), 251–61; and F. V. Greifenhagen, "The Social Location of the Reader," in *Teaching the Bible: Practical Strategies for Classroom Instruction* (ed. Mark Roncace and Patrick Gray; SBLRBS 49; Atlanta: Society of Biblical Literature, 2005), 16–17.

choices and the assumptions that led to the group's decision. By the end of the class period, I have learned about some of the preunderstandings that the students bring to class, and the students have begun to comprehend how their assumptions affect the decisions that they make in regard to the study of the Bible.[17]

These two exercises offer a great deal of background information about what the students are bringing to class, which information I then employ to adjust my semester teaching plans, so that I can make use of their previous experiences, as well as their learned preunderstandings. Because my educational concern has moved away from thinking exclusively about how best to transfer information from teacher to student, I am now free to reflect on how students process the information they encounter in class. Instead of merely focusing on subject coverage, I now think in terms of creating meaningful learning experiences. Students' appreciation of biblical poetry is one of the areas that has benefited from this alternative approach to teaching.

Poetry and Parallelism

Throughout the semester I make use of video clips, art, and music to illustrate the ways in which the Bible continues to influence our contemporary culture, as well as to offer examples of how the process of interpreting the Bible is an ongoing practice taking place at many cultural sites.[18] I begin our exploration of classical Hebrew poetry by playing samples of popular music.[19] Because this is a normal part of their classroom experience, the students are prepared to work with this medium. As the music plays, the

---

17. Charles William Miller, "Teaching Tactics: Make a List of What You Know About...," *TThRel* 13 (2010): 53.

18. For many helpful teaching/learning exercises that highlight the relationship of the Bible and culture, see Mark Roncace and Patrick Gray, eds., *Teaching the Bible through Popular Culture and the Arts* (SBLRBS 53; Atlanta: Society of Biblical Literature, 2007). An excellent overview of the problem of culture and text (including religious texts), written with beginning students in mind, is included in Mallory Nye, *Religion: The Basics* (2nd ed.; London: Routledge, 2008), 152–81.

19. In the following descriptions of classroom exercises (both in regard to parallelism and lament), I do not make reference to the amount of time required for any individual activity. Instead, for the sake of convenience, I have telescoped everything together into one process. The time spent on any exercise will vary according to the particular class and how quickly the students in that class are able to catch on.

words to the music are shown on a screen at the front of the classroom. I next ask the students to explain what it is about the words to this music that would cause many listeners to consider it "poetry." The students, working together, have little trouble identifying answers to this question, including, for example, rhythm, rhyme, and typography (of the written text); sometimes someone will comment on the structural patterns that he or she observes. It is rarely difficult to get a room full of students talking about the music or to get them to begin making some initial steps toward an elementary literary analysis of what they have heard.

The basic connection between the structure of a song and that of a poem, which might seem obvious to many, can be a major revelation to an eighteen or nineteen year old who gave less than full attention in a high school literature class. I use this initial exercise to engage the students in a preliminary and simple critique of poetic structures by asking them to draw on their own experiences with music and then to use that experience to make the first initial steps toward developing their own understandings and definitions of poetry and poetic structures. The students find themselves, therefore, reconstructing their experience in a manner that makes it meaningful in a completely new context.[20]

After the discussion of music and poetry, I introduce to them two classic English language poems, both of which most students have encountered at some point in their educational experience or within their broader cultural context.[21] Although I have in the past varied my choices, I find that now I almost always use Robert Frost's "Stopping by the Woods on a Snowy Evening" and Walt Whitman's "O Captain, My Captain."[22]

Sometimes I move rather rapidly through these units. At other times, it takes a considerably longer amount of time before students are able to understand the concepts.

20. The idea of reconstructing experience as central to the educational experience appears in John Dewey, "My Pedagogic Creed," where he comments, "I believe that education must be conceived as a continuing reconstruction of experience; [and] that the process and the goal of education are one and the same thing" (*Dewey on Education* [ed. R. D. Archbambaum; Chicago: University of Chicago Press, 1974], 434). See, as well, Joe L. Kincheloe, *Critical Constructivism* (New York: Lang, 2005), 4.

21. It was Kent Richards who first suggested to me that I include simple examples of American poetry when I introduce classical Hebrew poetry to students (e-mail, 12 February 1999).

22. Frost's "Stopping by the Woods on a Snowy Evening" was originally published in Frost's Pulitzer Prize winning collection of poetry, *New Hampshire: A Poem with Notes and Grace Notes* (New York: Henry Holt, 1923), but it is widely available

I ask students to use the observations they made about the poetic components of the music to explain why these new texts are poems. This transfers the knowledge constructed from their previous experience to another similar learning situation.[23]

Frost works very well because there is an obvious, albeit unusual, rhyming pattern (aaba/bbcb/and so forth), which the students are very excited to discover. The meter (iambic tetrameter) is equally apparent when it is read aloud, even though few students will be able to identify the name of the metrical pattern. Moreover, new poetic elements are introduced (e.g., the use of metaphor, image, and personification) and easily discerned by the students. One can also discuss the way poetic structure influences the reader toward certain interpretive possibilities (repetition of the final lines and the breaking of the rhyming pattern). It is not unusual for students to become engaged in a debate over the "meaning" of this poem and, thereby, begin to experience the excitement that critical analysis can generate. As students come to find the poetic structures of the Frost poem understandable, I switch to Whitman's poem in an effort to problematize the easy connection of a poem to a "list" mentality of poetic components. Whitman's rhymes are less regular and his meter not as easily determined. On the other hand, the poem is rich in imagery, personification, and metaphor. Furthermore, "O Captain, My Captain" offers a valuable illustration of how the knowledge of the historical background of a poem (Lincoln's assassination, in this case), although not necessary for constructing meaning, can nonetheless enrich the reader's understanding of the poem. It is also possible to show students how that historically bound text can gain a new life when the historical circumstances are similar to the original (e.g., as when this poem was used after the assassinations of both President John F. Kennedy and, interest-

---

in numerous anthologies.Many students recognize Walt Whitman's "O Captain, My Captain" from the movie *Dead Poet's Society* (Peter Weir, director, Tom Schulman, screenplay , Touchstone Pictures, 1989), which starred Robin Williams. The poem first appeared in the *Saturday Press* (4 November 1865) and has been anthologized regularly.

23. On the transfer of knowledge, see David N. Perkins and Gavriel Salomon, "Transfer of Learning," in *The International Encyclopedia of Education* (ed. Torsten Husen and T. Neville Postlethwaite; 2nd ed.; 12 vols.; New York: Pergamon, 1994), 6453–55. See, as well, Frank Ritchel Ames, "Critical Methods and Guarded Minds," *SBL Forum*; online: http://sbl-site.org/Article.aspx?ArticleID=219.

ingly, Prime Minister of Israel Yitzhak Rabin). By the time the students complete their encounter with these two poems, they have a fairly good, although very basic, grasp of how English language poetry operates and what to look for when reading a poem. At this point, the students are prepared for an introduction to classical Hebrew poetry.

I next place the text of Ps 104 on the screen and ask students to explain how one could recognize this text as poetry. How is it similar to and different from the poems they have already read? As in the preceding exercises, I want students to use what they have previously learned, so that their learning experience both deepens and broadens. That is to say, students must draw on their newly formed ideas about what makes a text poetry and use those ideas to understand and to explain another set of texts that are quite different from what they have already encountered. Students begin by searching for rhyme, or meter, but are always frustrated in their efforts. They quickly pick up the imagery and metaphorical language but recognize that these literary devices are not enough to argue that this text is a poem. Since repetition (of sounds, lines, words) have already been an important part of the class discussion, it is not unusual for a few students to notice the parallel structure of the poetic lines. This does not happen every time, but it does occur often enough that I do not feel the need to rush the process. I allow them the time and freedom to reflect on the problem. When the recognition of parallel lines does occur (with or without some prompting), it provides me the opportunity to give them a very general overview of semantic parallel structures, restricting the discussion to the so-called synonymous, antithetic, and synthetic types.[24]

At this point I have students work in small groups to complete a worksheet (appendix 1). They are provided with an initial phrase or sentence but must write a second line to complete the poetic (parallel) line. They then write their completed lines on the board, and the class as a

---

24. I recognize that this is an overly simplistic approach to this very complex literary device. Nonetheless, one must begin somewhere, and this tripartite division does work well within the beginning classroom. I also suggest, for those students who are interested, that they consult one of the excellent introductory books on classical Hebrew poetry, such as Robert Alter, *The Art of Biblical Poetry* (New York: Basic, 1985); David L. Petersen and Kent H. Richards, *Interpreting Hebrew Poetry* (GBS; Minneapolis: Fortress, 1992); and J. P. Fokkelman, *Reading Biblical Poetry: An Introductory Guide* (Louisville: Westminster John Knox, 2001).

whole critiques their work: Are these lines really synonymous? antithetic? On the worksheet, I always include one line from the Bible in each category, so that they can compare how close they come to the line from the biblical poem. It is rare that the parallel lines come out very well the first time, but it is quite common for students to understand why the lines are not quite parallel. At this stage, the class as a whole can begin to revise the lines to make them better. The last aspect of their assignment is that they must write a three-line poem structured according to classical Hebrew poetry style and describing their experience at UND.[25] As before, they share their results with the rest of the class, and the class together critiques the poems. By the end of this exercise, students have come to understand both the theoretical and practical aspects of parallel structures. Their assignment is then to focus on a poem from the Bible and analyze the text, employing all that they have learned about what makes a text a poem, including parallel structures, metaphor/simile, images, and so forth. Once they have completed their analysis, I employ their new knowledge about semantic parallelism to introduce other aspects of parallel structures, including grammatical and morphological parallelism.[26]

Genre and Lament

From very early in the semester, I emphasize the role genre identification plays in interpreting biblical texts.[27] Students have already encountered

---

25. I have also had one group write a line and give it to a second group, who must write the next line, then they write the first line of the next parallelism and pass it on to another group—a competition begins in terms of which group can produce the best first line and/or second line.

26. For advanced students interested in pursuing the more technical aspects of classical Hebrew poetry, I recommend Adele Berlin, *The Dynamics of Biblical Parallelism* (rev. ed.; Grand Rapids: Eerdmans, 2007); and W. G. E. Watson, *Classical Hebrew Poetry: A Guide to Its Techniques* (rev. ed.; JSOTSup 26; Sheffield: Sheffield Academic Press, 1995).

27. When I first introduce the issue of genre, I regularly assign John Barton's discussion of "literary competence" (*Reading the Old Testament: Method in Biblical Study* [rev. ed.; Louisville: Westminster John Knox, 1997], 8–19). It is one of the more accessible introductions to the role that genre plays in biblical interpretation. It is important to point out that my emphasis in this introductory course is on "genre theory," not on "form criticism," as traditionally understood. Two helpful collections of essays focusing on "genre pedagogy" in general are Ann M. Johns, ed., *Genre in the*

several different prose genres and have come to understand how genre affects both the way a text is written and how it is read.[28] As students discover for themselves what makes a poem a poem, they are, at the same time, learning to differentiate between the broad genre categories of prose and poetry. The next objective of the course is to introduce them to specific poetic genres. In what follows, by way of example, I will describe how I use lament literature as the students' gateway to understanding and interpreting the genres found in Psalms. My choice to begin with laments is based on the fact that they represent the largest number of psalms in the collection (approximately 40 percent), and, more importantly, students, regardless of their religious background, can usually relate very personally to the subject matter of conflict, threat, and loss.

When I introduce individual lament poems, I begin, as was the case with poetry, by using music. This time I bring two or three examples of the blues, projecting the words on a screen as I play the songs.[29] The first

---

Classroom: Multiple Perspectives (Mahwah, N.J.: Erlbaum, 2002); and Aviva Freedman and Peter Medway, eds., *Learning and Teaching Genres* (Portsmouth, N.H.: Boynton/Cook, 1994). For the beginning student, see also the following introductions to the study of biblical genres: James L. Bailey and Lyle D. Vander Broek, *Literary Forms in the New Testament: A Handbook* (Louisville: Westminster John Knox, 1992); D. Brent Sandy and Ronald L. Giese Jr., eds., *Cracking Old Testament Codes: A Guide to Interpreting the Literary Genres of the Old Testament* (Nashville: Broadman & Holman, 1995); Marshall D. Johnson, *Making Sense of the Bible: Literary Type as an Approach to Understanding* (Grand Rapids: Eerdmans, 2002); and Margaret Nutting Ralph, *And God Said What? An Introduction to Biblical Literary Forms* (rev. ed.; Mahwah, N.J.: Paulist, 2003).

28. Genre theory, as with most literary concepts, is a highly contested idea. The following monographs offer a range of approaches to the subject, including both literary and linguistic: Northrop Frye, *The Anatomy of Criticism* (Princeton: Princeton University Press, 1957); Alistar Fowler, *Kinds of Literature* (Oxford: Oxford University Press, 1982); John M. Swales, *Genre Analysis* (Cambridge: Cambridge University Press, 1990); and Garin Dowd, Lesley Stevenson, and Jeremy Strong, eds., *Genre Matters: Essay in Theory and Criticism* (Chicago: University of Chicago Press, 2006).

29. One of the blues masters I usually include is Mississippi Fred McDowell (1904–1972). His style of eliding sections of the song (forcing the listener to provide the appropriate word or phrase) is an excellent way to introduce students to this important literary technique (which they have already encountered in classical Hebrew poetry but may not have noticed). Listen, for example, to his recording of the Big Joe Williams classic "Baby, Please Don't Go"; McDowell does not sing the final word of the first two lines, but includes it in the third ("Baby, please don't.../ Baby,

thing students must do is to make an argument to support the contention that these songs are "poetry." This exercise is completed quickly, since almost all of the students have internalized and integrated a basic conception of what poetry is and are able to apply that concept to a new situation. I then initiate the discussion of genre by asking the students to explain why these songs are "blues" music. That is to say, how does one differentiate this type (genre) of music from other types? The question gives the students another opportunity to draw on their prior learning experiences, so that they can use what they had previously discovered about identifying prose genres to work with a new poetic genre.[30]

The students usually start with content, which is, of course, obvious in the name of the genre, but also in much of the subject matter. To problematize this overly easy identification, however, I include one sample that, although sharing the expected structure of a blues song, does not have the anticipated content. In this way, it is difficult for students to rely solely on subject matter in making a decision about genre. All of the sample music is highly structured (aaab or aab lines), so that the students become aware of the importance of the structure of the music in determining if a song is blues or not. If the class is fortunate enough to have someone in the classroom who is a musician familiar with the blues, then students are introduced to the specific chord structures and progressions that are a part of the music. The most difficult aspect of the discussion is identifying the function of the blues. Students often want to think in terms of the entertainment value of music rather than an emotional or ideological purpose. The idea that the blues might be a way, not of transcending the pain, but rather of keeping the pain alive, is often foreign to the students.[31] As is the case when music is used

---

please don't... / Baby, please don't go"). The fourth and concluding line omits the entire final phrase ("Back to New Orleans ... [you know I love you so]"). The listener is required to provide the missing words/phrases and, thereby, one could argue, becomes a participant in the music. McDowell's rendition of this song can be heard on *I Don't Play No Rock 'n' Roll* (Capitol Records, 1969; produced by Tommy Couch; recorded at Malaco Sound Recording Studio, 8–11 September; reissued as a CD, 2001).

30. Students are taught to distinguish among genres by focusing on content, structure, and function (Ronald L. Giese, "Literary Forms of the Old Testament," in Sandy and Giese, *Cracking Old Testament Codes*, 5–28).

31. Ralph Ellison comments, "The blues is an impulse to keep the painful details and episodes of a brutal experience alive in one's aching consciousness, to finger its

to introduce poetry, students become very involved in these discussions and can easily offer examples of contemporary music that employs similar content, the same line structure, and/or serve a similar function as that of the blues.

When I make the switch from blues to lament, I place on an overhead both Ps 13 and Ps 54, so that students can compare and contrast the two poems. I ask students how these two psalms are similar to the music they have just heard.[32] As with the earlier discussion of blues, they begin by noticing the similarity of content but also observe the poetic structures (parallelism) that exist within the poems. I remind them, if necessary, that, with blues, there is a basic underlying structure that transcends the poetic line and ask whether they see any structural similarities between these two poems. Often students, working together, will pick out most of the important components of the lament structure (invocation, complaint, petition, motivation, confession of trust, and vow of praise), although they might not have the technical vocabulary to identify those parts by name. By discerning the constituent parts of the genre on their own, students become active "meaning-making" agents rather than passive "meaning-receiving" entities.[33] The process of discovery the students pursue, as they develop their personal agency in regard to the critical reading of biblical literature, serves to empower and to motivate them to be committed to their own learning.[34]

---

jagged grain, and to transcend it, not by the consolation of philosophy but by squeezing from it a near-tragic, near-comic lyricism" (*Shadow and Act* [New York: New American Library, 1964], 78).

32. For other practical approaches to introducing students to lament literature, see Roncace and Gray, *Teaching the Bible*, 198–203. Although primarily targeting high school teachers and students, Nancy Lee offers suggestions for relating lament to contemporary events in two brief articles: "Biblical and Contemporary Lament: Examples and Resources," *Teaching the Bible* (February 2010); online: http://www.sbl-site.org/assets/pdfs/TB7_LamentContemporary_NL.pdf; and "Lament in the Bible and in Music and Poetry across Cultures Today," *Teaching the Bible* (February 2010); online: http://www.sbl-site.org/assets/pdfs/TB7_LamentMusic_NL.pdf.

33. L. Dee Fink, *Creating Significant Learning Experiences: An Integrated Approach to Designing College Courses* (San Francisco: Jossey-Bass, 2003), 104–10.

34. Ira Shor has commented, "To help move students away from passivity and cynicism, a powerful signal has to be sent from the very start, a signal that learning is participatory … students are people whose voices are worth listening to, whose minds can carry the weight of serious intellectual work, whose thought and feeling

After students complete this activity, it is easy for me to fill out whatever parts of a lament they might have missed or, better yet, to nuance the students' own observations. At this point I help them enlarge their knowledge base by bringing into the discussion further examples of both communal and individual laments and asking students to reflect on how these are similar and different in regard to content, structure, and function. I have found that Lam 5 is very effective in helping the students understand the way a poet will frustrate the expectations of the reader to make a point. Certain aspects of the anticipated components of the lament are left out, shortened, and/or extended. This poem serves as an excellent example of how structure is important to meaning. Finally, I ask groups of three students to write a lament poem consisting of six to ten parallel lines and employing all of the structural components of an individual lament. The responses, I must admit, can be rather disappointing at times.[35] Nonetheless, when the poems are projected on a screen and are critiqued by other students, the discussion can become very serious indeed. It is rare that a badly written lament does not significantly improve over the course of the critique. Once they complete their analysis, I then use their new knowledge about the structural basis of the lament to introduce them to other types of poems found in the Psalms.

Assessment

The final issue is, of course, whether or not these exercises are effective in promoting student learning. To answer this question, I assign students to write a short essay (appendix 2).[36] They are asked to enter an imaginary

---

can entertain transforming self and society" (*Empowering Education: Critical Teaching for Social Change* [Chicago: University of Chicago Press, 1992], 26).

35. During the 2001fall semester, the class addressed the genre exercises in early October. The events of 9/11 were still at the forefront of the students' consciousness, so that much of the poetry produced that day, although perhaps not technically excellent, was very emotionally moving—a very powerful evocation of sorrow and loss.

36. I originally used the essay as a stand-alone assignment immediately after completing the units on parallelism and lament (appendix 2). For the past few years, however, I have altered the assignment and included it as a question on the final exam. Since the final exam is usually several months after the conclusion of the relevant units, it offers a better possibility of assessing whether or not the students have retained what they learned earlier in the semester about classical Hebrew poetry and its genres.

world in which they are noted biblical scholars who have been given a recently discovered text from an archaeological dig. The unidentified text (Ps 51, which was not introduced or discussed in class) is typographically in the form of a narrative when they receive it, so they must break down the text into its parallel lines, as well as mount an argument that it is a lament poem. Students who have completed the assigned readings for the course and who have attended class during the days when we worked on these topics have little difficulty in adequately completing this assignment. Those who did only the reading and missed class usually have problems even knowing where to begin.[37]

I note, moreover, that, for the rest of the semester, whenever the students encounter classical Hebrew poetry (e.g., in the prophetic literature), they are quick to recognize the parallelism of the lines and to use their knowledge to help them interpret the passages they are assigned. It is especially gratifying to see those same students making a connection between what they learned in the introductory class and other courses, say, with the prayer of Mary in Luke 1.

Conclusion

I have shared in this essay a successful strategy that I use to engage students in the construction of knowledge concerning classical Hebrew poetry and the genres found in the book of Psalms. It is a means to free them from the banking model of education to one that equips them for a lifetime of learning and the appreciation of the poetic arts, generally, and the Hebrew Bible, specifically. The most important goal of a liberal education, it seems to me, is to transform and liberate students from viewing the world in the same way they did when they entered the class. Content (information) is important and is, obviously, a significant aspect of

---

37. Over the past four years, when this assignment has been used as a part of the final exam, 127 students have responded to the question. For 89 percent of the exams, the student did significantly better on this essay question than on any other. Of the 11 percent who did not do as well, in all but two cases the students did not attend class on the days when the parallelism and lament exercises were completed but had (I assume) only read the written assignments for that day. These data suggest that the parallelism and lament exercises are effective methods for student learning. On the other hand, a follow-up study asking the students to complete a similar essay question one or two years after the completion of the course would offer better evidence.

all of the introductory Hebrew Bible classes I teach, but, to be honest, it is something students can gain on their own if they are really interested. Skills associated with critical reading and thinking, the capacity to reconstruct prior experience into new knowledge, and the ability to adapt knowledge to new situations are best learned in the context of a classroom where students are actively engaged in their own learning. As Paulo Freire reminds us, "For apart from inquiry, apart from the praxis, men [and women] cannot be truly human. Knowledge emerges only through invention and re-invention, through the restless, impatient, continuing, hopeful inquiry men [and women] pursue in the world, with the world, and with each other."[38]

Bibliography

Alter, Robert. *The Art of Biblical Poetry*. New York: Basic, 1985.
Ames, Frank Ritchel. "Critical Methods and Guarded Minds." *SBL Forum*. Online: http://sbl-site.org/Article.aspx?ArticleID=219.
Attridge, Harold W., ed. *The HarperCollins Study Bible: Revised Edition*. San Francisco: HarperSanFrancisco, 2006
Bāgheri, Khosrow. "A Hermeneutical Model for Research on the Evaluation of Academic Achievement." *New Thoughts on Education* 1/2 (2005): 5–12.
Bailey, James L., and Lyle D. Vander Broek. *Literary Forms in the New Testament: A Handbook*. Louisville: Westminster John Knox, 1992.
Barton, John. *Reading the Old Testament: Method in Biblical Study*. Rev. ed. Louisville: Westminster John Knox, 1997.
Berlin, Adele. *The Dynamics of Biblical Parallelism*. Rev. ed. Grand Rapids: Eerdmans, 2007.
Berlin, Adele, and Marc Zvi Brettler, eds. *The Jewish Study Bible: Featuring the Jewish Publication Society Tanakh Translation*. Oxford: Oxford University Press, 2004.
Blumberg, Phyllis. *Developing Learner-Centered Teaching: A Practical Guide for Faculty*. San Francisco: Jossey-Bass, 2009.
Brontë, Charlotte. *Jane Eyre*. London: Penguin, 1996.

---

38. Freire, *Pedagogy of the Oppressed*, 58.

Bruffee, Kenneth. *Collaborative Learning: Higher Education, Interdependence, and the Authority of Knowledge.* Baltimore: Johns Hopkins University Press, 1993.

Dewey, John. "My Pedagogic Creed." Pages 434–37 in *Dewey on Education.* Edited by R. D. Archbambaum. Chicago: University of Chicago Press, 1974. Reprint of *School Journal* 54 (January 1897): 77–80.

Dowd, Garin, Lesley Stevenson, and Jeremy Strong, eds. *Genre Matters: Essay in Theory and Criticism.* Chicago: University of Chicago Press, 2006.

Ellison, Ralph. *Shadow and Act.* New York: New American Library, 1964.

Fink, L. Dee. *Creating Significant Learning Experiences: An Integrated Approach to Designing College Courses.* San Francisco: Jossey-Bass, 2003.

Finkel, Donald. *Teaching with Your Mouth Shut.* Portsmouth, N.H.: Heinemann, 2000.

Fokkelman, J. P. *Reading Biblical Poetry: An Introductory Guide.* Louisville: Westminster John Knox, 2001.

Fowler, Alistar. *Kinds of Literature.* Oxford: Oxford University Press, 1982.

Freedman, Aviva, and Peter Medway, eds. *Learning and Teaching Genres.* Portsmouth, N.H.: Boynton/Cook, 1994.

Freedman, David Noel, ed. *Eerdmans Dictionary of the Bible.* Grand Rapids: Eerdmans, 2000.

Freire, Paulo. *Pedagogy of the Oppressed.* New York: Seabury, 1970.

Frost, Robert. *New Hampshire: A Poem with Notes and Grace Notes.* New York: Henry Holt, 1923.

Frye, Northrop. *The Anatomy of Criticism.* Princeton: Princeton University Press, 1957.

Gagnon, George W., Jr., and Michelle Collay. *Designing for Learning: Six Elements in Constructivist Classrooms.* Thousand Oaks, Calif.: Corwin, 2001.

Giese, Ronald L. "Literary Forms of the Old Testament." Pages 5–28 in *Cracking Old Testament Codes: A Guide to Interpreting the Literary Genres of the Old Testament.* Edited by D. Brent Sandy and Ronald L. Giese Jr. Nashville: Broadman & Holman, 1995.

Gottwald, Norman K. "Framing Biblical Interpretation at New York Theological Seminary: A Student Self-Inventory on Biblical Hermeneutics." Pages 251–61 in *Social Location and Biblical Interpretation in the United States.* Vol. 1 of *Reading from This Place.* Edited by Fernando F. Segovia and Mary Ann Tolbert. Minneapolis: Fortress, 1995.

Greifenhagen, F. V. "The Social Location of the Reader." Pages 16–17 in *Teaching the Bible: Practical Strategies for Classroom Instruction*. Edited by Mark Roncace and Patrick Gray. SBLRBS 49. Atlanta: Society of Biblical Literature, 2005.

Jacobson, Rolf A. "Teaching Students to Interpret Religious Poetry (and to Expand Their Avenues of Thinking)." *TThRel* 7/1 (2004): 38–44.

Johns, Ann M., ed. *Genre in the Classroom: Multiple Perspectives*. Mahwah, N.J.: Erlbaum, 2002.

Johnson, Marshall D. *Making Sense of the Bible: Literary Type as an Approach to Understanding*. Grand Rapids: Eerdmans, 2002.

Kincheloe, Joe L. *Critical Constructivism*. New York: Peter Lang, 2005.

Lee, Nancy. "Biblical and Contemporary Lament: Examples and Resources." *Teaching the Bible* (February 2010). Online: http://www.sbl-site.org/assets/pdfs/TB7_LamentContemporary_NL.pdf.

———. "Lament in the Bible and in Music and Poetry across Cultures Today." *Teaching the Bible* (February 2010). Online: http://www.sbl-site.org/assets/pdfs/.TB7_LamentMusic_NL.pdf.

McDowell, Mississippi Fred. *I Don't Play No Rock 'n' Roll*. Capitol Records, 1969. Produced by Tommy Couch. Recorded at Malaco Sound Recording Studio, 8–11 September. Reissued as a CD, 2001.

Miller, Charles William. "Teaching Tactics: Make a List of What You Know About...." *TThRel* 13 (2010): 53.

National Endowment for the Arts. *Reading at Risk: A Survey of Literary Reading in America*. Research Division Report 46. Washington, D.C.: National Endowment for the Arts, 2004.

National Institute of Education. *Involvement in Education*. Washington, D.C.: Department of Education, 1984.

Coogan, Michael D., ed. *New Oxford Annotated Bible: New Revised Standard Version with the Apocrypha*. 3rd ed. New York: Oxford University Press, 2007.

Nye, Mallory. *Religion: The Basics*. 2nd ed. London: Routledge, 2008.

Perkins, David N., and Gavriel Salomon. "Transfer of Learning." Pages 6453–55 in *The International Encyclopedia of Education*. Edited by Torsten Husen and T. Neville Postlethwaite. 2nd ed. 12 vols. New York: Pergamon, 1994.

Petersen, David L., and Kent H. Richards. *Interpreting Hebrew Poetry*. GBS. Minneapolis: Fortress, 1992.

Ralph, Margaret Nutting. *And God Said What? An Introduction to Biblical Literary Forms*. Rev. ed. Mahwah, N.J.: Paulist, 2003.

Roncace, Mark, and Patrick Gray, eds. *Teaching the Bible through Popular Culture and the Arts*. SBLRBS 53. Atlanta: Society of Biblical Literature, 2007.
Rustici, Craig M. "Sonnet Writing and Experiential Learning." *College Teaching* 45 (1997): 16–18.
Sandy, D. Brent, and Ronald L. Giese Jr., eds. *Cracking Old Testament Codes: A Guide to Interpreting the Literary Genres of the Old Testament*. Nashville: Broadman & Holman, 1995.
Schuh, Kathy L. "Knowledge Construction in the Learner-Centered Classroom." *Journal of Educational Psychology* 95 (2003): 426–42.
Shor, Ira. *Empowering Education: Critical Teaching for Social Change*. Chicago: University of Chicago Press, 1992.
Swales, John M. *Genre Analysis*. Cambridge: Cambridge University Press, 1990.
Trelstad, Marit. "The Ethics of Effective Teaching: Challenges from the Religious Right and Critical Pedagogy." *TThR* 11 (2008): 191–202.
Watson, W. G. E. *Classical Hebrew Poetry: A Guide to Its Techniques*. Rev. ed. JSOTSup 26. Sheffield: Sheffield Academic Press, 1995.
Weimer, Maryellen. *Learner-Centered Teaching: Five Key Changes to Practice*. San Francisco: Jossey-Bass, 2002.
Wiggins, Grant. *Educative Assessment: Designing Assessments to Inform and Improve Student Performance*. San Francisco: Jossey-Bass, 1998.
Young, Linda. "Portals into Poetry: Using Generative Writing Groups to Facilitate Student Engagement with Word Art." *Journal of Adolescent & Adult Literacy* 51 (2007): 50–55.

Appendix 1: Writing Classical Hebrew Poetry

PART A: In each example below, the first line of the parallel structure appears. Complete the poem by writing a second line that represents the type of relationship suggested by each heading.

1. Synonymous parallelism: line B repeats line A in similar words

    A Go home to the land you love
    B Return _____

    A The city glows like a jewel at dawn
    B The town _____

    A Make the lightning flash and scatter them
    B Send out _____

2. Antithetic: line B repeats line A but with opposing words

    A The mountains rise to the heavens
    B [But] the valley _____

    A Smooth as silk is the surface of the lake
    B [But] the ocean _____

    A The wealth of the rich is their fortress
    B [But] the poverty _____

3. Synonymous or Antithetic

    A The leaders of the world are mighty
    B _____

    A Books are the door to understanding
    B _____

    A Well meant are the wounds a friend inflicts
    B _____

PART B: Write a short poem, in classical Hebrew style, that focuses on your experience at this university. It should contain at least three pairs of parallel lines.

Appendix 2: Reading Poetry

In this essay you will focus on biblical poetry. Printed immediately below this paragraph is the text you will use for this essay. Since I am interested in your own observations and reflections, I have provided the text for you. Do not use a Bible or any other resources to do your analysis. Work only from this text and/or your notes from the class. You should begin your analysis by carefully and closely reading the following text:

> Have mercy on me, O God, according to your steadfast love; according to your abundant mercy blot out my transgressions. Wash me thoroughly from my iniquity, and cleanse me from my sin. For I know my transgressions, and my sin is ever before me. Against you, you alone, have I sinned, and done what is evil in your sight, so that you are justified in your sentence and blameless when you pass judgment. Indeed, I was born guilty, a sinner when my mother conceived me. You desire truth in the inward being; therefore teach me wisdom in my secret heart. Purge me with hyssop, and I shall be clean; wash me, and I shall be whiter than snow. Let me hear joy and gladness; let the bones that you have crushed rejoice. Hide your face from my sins, and blot out all my iniquities. Create in me a clean heart, O God, and put a new and right spirit within me. Do not cast me away from your presence, and do not take your holy spirit from me. Restore to me the joy of your salvation, and sustain in me a willing spirit. Then I will teach transgressors your ways, and sinners will return to you. Deliver me from bloodshed, O God, O God of my salvation, and my tongue will sing aloud of your deliverance. O Lord, open my lips, and my mouth will declare your praise. For you have no delight in sacrifice; if I were to give a burnt offering, you would not be pleased. The sacrifice acceptable to God is a broken spirit; a broken and contrite heart, O God, you will not despise. Do good to Zion in your good pleasure; rebuild the walls of Jerusalem, then you will delight in right sacrifices, in burnt offerings and whole burnt offerings; then bulls will be offered on your altar.

For this essay, you will be asked to enter into an imaginary world in which you are a noted scholar of biblical poetry. Recently, in an archaeological dig in Israel, an archaeologist discovered the text printed above written on an ancient clay tablet. She has brought it to you for study and analysis. You immediately recognize that it is a lament poem and are very excited about the possibility of writing an article about this text. It is this brief article that you will turn in to me as your second essay. The article you will write is for a general but educated audience who probably does not know anything about the formal characteristics of either biblical poetry or the structure of a lament poem. Your first task will be to divide the text into the appropriate parallel structures/lines. After you have completed that task, you should then number each line, so that, throughout your paper, your citations of the text will be to the appropriate line number (as was the case in your previous essay). Please include a copy of your lineation of the poem (with line numbers) as an appendix to your paper. The essay itself will offer an argument for why this text should be considered a poem and offer reasons for why you have identified the poetic lines as you have. The essay will also need to convince your reader that this is a particular type of poem, namely, a lament poem. This can only be accomplished by developing an argument that persuades the reader that this poem fits the expected structure of a lament poem—although perhaps not exactly. As with all good essays, I would expect an introduction (which includes a thesis statement), a good middle (where you develop your arguments to support the thesis statement), and a conclusion (where you summarize what you have written).

Part 3
Studies in Methods and Contexts

Revisiting the Composition of Ezra-Nehemiah: A Prolegomenon

Tamara Cohn Eskenazi

Introduction

In his book *Map Is Not Territory,* Jonathan Z. Smith writes, "The historian's task is to complicate not to clarify. He strives to celebrate the diversity of manners, the variety of species, the opacity of things. He is therefore barred from making a frontal assault on his topic. Like a pilgrim, the historian is obliged to approach his subject obliquely. He must circumambulate the spot several times before making even the most fleeting contact."[1] As the

---

1. Jonathan Z. Smith, *Map Is Not Territory: Studies in the History of Religions* (Chicago: University of Chicago Press, 1978), 290. I was introduced to Jonathan Z. Smith's insightful "definition" of the historian's task by my late husband, J. William Whedbee, who, had his life not been cut short, would have added his own inimitable voice to those who honor and celebrate Kent Harold Richards in this volume. I mention Smith's description of the historian's challenging task because it beautifully captures Kent's approach to life and learning. Kent Harold Richards is a teacher, scholar, and leader who respects, celebrates, and nurtures diversity, ever attuned to the opacity of things and to what must remain complex. Those of us who have had the privilege of working closely with Kent are all too aware of the care, sensitivity, wisdom, and competence that he brings to his tasks. In his role as the Executive Director of Society of Biblical Literature, he has widened the context of biblical studies and generated a genuine international conversation in which new voices can be heard. One is forever grateful to him for his immeasurable contribution to our field. In this essay, I wish to reflect on scholarly questions that were sparked by his own teachings when, some thirty years ago (!), I first became his student, and he inspired me to explore Ezra-Nehemiah. I will be examining, within this paper, the "international" context for the composition of Ezra-Nehemiah. In so doing, I wish to honor Kent Harold Richards for placing biblical scholarship in its international context. Fit-

title of Smith's book indicates, a map is not territory. Maps are, however, helpful. In what follows, I draw a map of diverse paths for understanding the composition of Ezra-Nehemiah. Discerning how Ezra-Nehemiah was composed is significant both for interpreting the postexilic and Hellenistic eras, as well as the book's messages. Such an exploration can be postponed when one uses literary approaches or canonical ones, but it cannot be dispensed with for long.² In addition, theories of Ezra-Nehemiah's com-

---

tingly, a version of this paper was delivered at a conference on "Judah and the Judeans in the Fourth Century B.C.E," held in Münster, 12–15 August 2005. I thank the organizers of the conference, Rainer Albertz and Oded Lipschits, for the invitation to the conference and for the opportunity to discuss the subject with the participants.

2. There is an unfortunate tendency among some scholars to misunderstand or denigrate literary approaches to biblical texts as somehow less urgent, "serious," or "scientific" in comparison with historically oriented inquiries. The following comment is a case in point: "Obviously, one can and should use *the final text* for theological purposes in the Synagogue or the Church, but this should clearly be separated from historical questions" (Juha Pakkala, *Ezra the Scribe: The Development of Ezra 7–10 and Nehemiah 8* [BZAW 347; Berlin: de Gruyter, 2004], 11–12; emphasis added). However, the final form of a text *is* historical datum. It is the only ascertainable datum in most cases. Therefore, serious analysis of a text must begin here. The final form tells us what was acceptable to an author or a community at a particular time and what meanings were being conveyed at that time. It is thus important to begin phenomenologically, with what we have, before moving to the more speculative "data" and hypothesizing about how a text came to be this way. For this, and other reasons, it is insufficient to relegate the literary interpretation of the final form to "theological purposes in the Synagogue and the Church" or to suppose that "this should clearly be separated from historical questions" (Pakkala, *Ezra the Scribe*, 12). Instead, an evaluation of the final form needs to be a starting point of a scholarly and "scientific" inquiry, even when we disagree as to the precise time of the final form. Literary approaches such as found in Michael W. Duggan, *The Covenant Renewal in Ezra-Nehemiah (Neh 7:72b–10:40): An Exegetical, Literary and Theological Study* (SBLDS 164; Atlanta: Society of Biblical Literature, 2001), and in my own *In an Age of Prose: A Literary Approach to Ezra-Nehemiah* (SBLMS 36; Atlanta: Scholars Press, 1988) aim to illustrate the results one may achieve from these kinds of starting points. Such efforts are less speculative than the "abstraction of the text's factual development" (Pakkala, *Ezra the Scribe*, 12). While I do not share the view that all source or redactional analyses of biblical texts are tantamount to trying to unscramble the omelet (to borrow Robert Alter's felicitous phrase), I am repeatedly amazed when scholars fail to read the received text and interpret it in its own historical context before speculating on its layered history. Moreover, it is surprising how often the results of redactional expositions depend on prior assumptions about historical contexts, themselves constructed

position are relevant for understanding the compositional possibilities of other biblical books, given the literary activities in the postexilic and early Hellenistic eras to which most scholars date this book. Thus anything we can say about Ezra-Nehemiah also contributes to the debates about the formation of other biblical books, especially, perhaps, the Torah/Pentateuch, given that its editing is believed to coincide roughly with the time of Ezra-Nehemiah.

Theories about the composition of Ezra-Nehemiah continue to proliferate, with no consensus in sight; and the growth in scholarly literature makes it possible, and even necessary, to review and assess theories about the compositional layers of Ezra-Nehemiah.[3] After a brief review of current compositional models for Ezra-Nehemiah, this essay will focus on what ancient sources from Mesopotamia and Greece tell us about the composition of "histories" in antiquity. Such a comparative survey can provide information about models that were current in the ancient world when Ezra-Nehemiah was composed and, thus, what these nonbiblical models might contribute to the theories about Ezra-Nehemiah's composition.

In light of the importance of the issues, it is frustrating to state at the outset that this essay concludes without claiming a definitive answer to how and when Ezra-Nehemiah was composed. This result is not due to a lack of cogent hypotheses on the subject. Rather, the reverse: we are blessed with several compelling, at times mutually exclusive, hypotheses. These hypotheses unambiguously show several different connections between the book and history that extend from the fifth to the third centuries B.C.E. As a result, scholars are able to construct or invoke different models for Judah in the Persian period and a range of different compositional histories for Ezra-Nehemiah. Recent archeological and epigraphic studies do not resolve this problem (despite the tremendous expansion of knowledge) because their conclusions, taken together, can support any one of these hypotheses.

---

via the literature a scholar is trying to unpack, yet without careful attention to what the literature is conveying.

3. Although divided into two books in most English-language Bibles, Ezra-Nehemiah was preserved in the earliest extant sources as a unified work attributed to Ezra. On the unity of Ezra-Nehemiah, see Eskenazi, *In an Age of Prose*, as well as the essays in Mark J. Boda and Paul L. Redditt, eds., *Unity and Disunity in Ezra-Nehemiah: Redaction, Rhetoric, and Reader* (Hebrew Bible Monographs 17; Sheffield: Sheffield Phoenix Press, 2008).

What have we got, then? Almost all scholars acknowledge the authenticity of the so-called Nehemiah Memoir (however conceived); thus the fifth century is a common denominator for one layer of Ezra-Nehemiah. Many acknowledge decisive formation in the fourth century but fluctuate between Persian and Hellenistic formation as the more decisive context; some assume a Hellenistic layer as late as the second century (depending on when one dates Daniel and Esther). In reviewing these options for Ezra-Nehemiah, I do not intend to complicate the subject; it is complicated enough. Instead, after describing how four representative scholars address this question,[4] I will circumambulate in order to find a standing place outside the debates from which to perceive the subject, if not more clearly, then at least differently.

Each of the four hypotheses summed up here works adequately as an explanation of much in Ezra-Nehemiah; each also reflects a different understanding as to the manner in which texts were composed and the likely motivation of the authors/editors. I have selected these four representative works with the understanding that the many other proposals either resemble these in some fundamental features or depend on them. Moreover, I chose these four because each makes a distinct contribution that, in an important sense, does not depend primarily on its theoretical underpinning. In other words, these specific interpretations offer valuable insights into plausible dynamics at work in Ezra-Nehemiah, even if or when the compositional theory remains uncertain.

Four Theories of Composition

H. G. M. Williamson

Hugh Williamson has proposed a particularly effective (and influential) way to think of Ezra-Nehemiah as a fourth-century composition.[5] He identifies three basic stages.

(1) The writing of two sources, the so-called Ezra Memoir and the Nehemiah Memoir, are more or less contemporary with the events. Wil-

---

4. The key term is "representative" in that the approach that each of the four scholars uses is distinct from the others but is at the same time shared by other scholars in Ezra-Nehemiah studies.

5. H. G. M. Williamson, *Ezra, Nehemiah* (WBC 16; Dallas: Word, 1985). See also idem, "The Composition of Ezra i–vi," *JTS* 34 (1983): 1–30.

liamson accepts the authenticity of the Nehemiah Memoir (roughly Neh 1–7 and parts of 12:27–43 and 13:4–31) as Nehemiah's (or someone under his direction[6]) and thinks the Ezra material (Ezra 7–8, Neh 8 and Ezra 9–10, with this as the likely original sequence), similarly, goes back to Ezra.[7]

(2) The combining of the Ezra Memoir and Nehemiah Memoir with other sections to form Ezra 7:1–Neh 11:2 (ca. 400 B.C.E.). The motivation for this stage was the desire to show a unity of the work of the two reformers.

(3) The adding to Ezra 7–Neh 13 of Ezra 1–6, which was derived largely from the Aramaic sources, the earlier Memoirs, Ezra 7–Neh 13, additional documents, and Hag–Zech 8, and also included the late stratum of Chronicles. This section constitutes the final stratum of the book.[8] According to Williamson, the final editor or author was a propriestly writer who left the sources largely unchanged.[9] The date of the final form is early Hellenistic period, around 300 B.C.E. The connection with "current events" that Williamson postulates for the final section is the emergence of the Samaritan temple. The organizing principle is a typology that begins with the exodus and concludes with the first temple.

The authors lived decades apart but combined what were isolated events into a continuity and organized some of the material in the form of parallels to these prior events (which is especially true of the Nehemiah material). Williamson suggests that the authors "stood in particular amongst the successors of Ezra and Nehemiah themselves and thus have had an interest in providing an introduction to the account of their work."[10] He states: "A history of the composition must, therefore, begin with the combination of the Ezra and Nehemiah memoirs."[11] A guiding motivation for this composition, according to Williamson, is the ongoing conflict with neighbors. Ezra-Nehemiah's authors/editors compose to suggest that reform work was a product of unity (even though the Ezra and Nehemiah worked separately). Williamson sees no need for an intermediate editor between the sources and the final editor of Ezra 1–6. The author is bound by the sources and working from them. Editorial

---

6. Williamson, *Ezra, Nehemiah*, xxiv.
7. Ibid., xxxi.
8. Ibid., xxxiii–xxxv.
9. See esp. Williamson, "Composition of Ezra i–vi," 28.
10. Ibid.
11. Williamson, *Ezra, Nehemiah*, xxxiv.

comments are limited, and the author's work is based on contemporary practices. It is Williamson's observation that contemporary practices are relevant that propels my search for empirical models and sends me back to ancient Near Eastern and Greek sources (see below).

Joseph Blenkinsopp

Joseph Blenkinsopp describes a process that largely mirrors the sequence of events that the book narrates.[12] Like Williamson, he maintains: "The account of the first return has been drawn selectively from various sources that include Aramaic documents, Haggai and Zechariah, etc. The Xerxes and Artaxerxes material was inserted in a manner not inconsistent with ancient writings, with a resumptive repetition to mark the insertion."[13] The mention of "selectively" is important because Blenkinsopp supposes, as does Williamson, that the writers/author had actual documents, some of them authentic, from which he or they excerpted relevant material. Nonetheless, where Williamson sees a dependency of Ezra 1–6 on the later chapters, Blenkinsopp links these early chapters with the author of Chronicles and considers them earlier than the rest of the book.[14] As a continuation of Chronicles, this stage marks a revival after the low point of destruction and exile, a cycle resembling the move from Ahaz to Hezekiah and so on. "The weight of the evidence is therefore against Williamson's hypothesis."[15]

Stage two, according to Blenkinsopp, is the combining of the Ezra material, which was available to the author/editor, with some lists. The Memoir thus existed as a source, with the third-person material either derived from the same source or yet another source. Acknowledging the hypothetical nature of any conclusion about the Ezra "memoir," or, as he calls it, "memorandum," Blenkinsopp sees no reason to doubt its authenticity and considers that material in Ezra-Nehemiah to have been excerpted from a more extensive source.[16] The abrupt end of Ezra's story possibly masks some controversy concerning the failure of Ezra. More-

---

12. Joseph Blenkinsopp, *Ezra-Nehemiah: A Commentary* (OTL; Philadelphia: Westminster, 1988).
13. Ibid., 40–41.
14. Ibid., 44.
15. Ibid.
16. Ibid., 46.

over, Neh 8 most likely preceded Ezra 9 and represents the original sequence of events (not simply textual adaptation or sources), in which the reading of the Torah preceded the separation of foreign wives.[17]

Nehemiah 7:5–10:40 is the final major link in the narrative, with chapter 10 as the latest.[18] These have been inserted and separate an earlier unity of Neh 1:1–7:4 and 11:1.

Blenkinsopp emphasizes parallels with "late Egyptian autobiographical votive texts addressed to God and deposited in a temple."[19] As for the Nehemiah Memoir, Blenkinsopp notes that the building of the wall, which, in time, accounts for only some fifty-two days out of twelve years, receives disproportionate space, constituting about half of the Nehemiah Memoir. "This would most naturally suggest that only excerpts from a larger work have been preserved."[20]

Yonina Dor

Yonina Dor concentrates on the compositional history of Ezra 9–10 but suggests that the principles she describes apply to the rest of Ezra-Nehemiah as well.[21] She looks at the vocabulary and disjunctions in Ezra 9–10 to identify strata and to place them in their historical context. Without attempting to describe her method here, let me sum up her conclusions. She identifies three main sources: the prayer in Ezra 9; the short description of the gathering with Shechaniah in 10:2–6; and the long account of the gathering in the rain concluding with a list of those intermarried (Ezra 10:7–44). She points to repetitions with different vocabulary between the two sections of Ezra 10 and suggests that they come from different hands.

In general, Dor claims that the three sources are organized according to their relevance to their authors' worlds. The third and longest among them, the public gathering in the rain, during which Ezra addresses the people as a whole (Ezra 10:7–44), is the earliest narrative and preserves details of traditions from a period close to the actual occurrence of the events. The short narrative placed just before it (Ezra 10:2–6) also evi-

---

17. Ibid., 45.
18. Ibid., 46.
19. Ibid.
20. Ibid., 47.
21. Yonina Dor, "The Composition of the Episode of the Foreign Women in Ezra IX–X," *VT* 53 (2003): 26–47.

dently preserves historical details, but it was written by another author and from a certain distance in time. It is a militant-separatist revision of the earlier source. Ezra's prayer in chapter 9 is an independent work. Its "outlook" and "spirit" differ from those in the two other sources. The third author placed it at the beginning to redirect the meaning of the earlier sources that follow. This speech reflects a later period and a more moderate approach, coming after the controversy in the period of Ezra had died down, and its daring-dramatic ideas failed to be realized by the expulsion of the foreign wives. Dor writes that "the prayer left its impression by conveying the principled outlook that one was to refrain from mixed marriages."[22] Dor considers the long episode in Ezra 10 to be reasonably accurate as a description of Ezra's work in the fifth century: "Over the course of time, and from the view point of various composers, the separatist position changed: the first change was in the direction of extremism, expressed in the short narrative," namely, the message of Shechaniah in 10:2–4.[23] However,

> A second change was in the direction of moderation, and towards a deeper, more inclusive approach. Deeper and more inclusive—because it is grounded in ideological positions anchored in traditions of the Torah, and because it includes both men and women, its horizon is historically broader and not only contemporary, and it relates to general relations with the Gentiles and not only to marriage; moderate—because its message is realistic and more doable than that of its predecessor: namely, that one is to refrain *ab initio* from mixed marriage, but that existing families are not to be broken up.[24]

Thus, according to Dor, tough positions regarding mixed marriages pertained only to the earliest stages of the revitalizing of Judah and Jerusalem.

Dor claims that her linguistic analysis is a model for exploring the composition of other units in the book, "both smaller and larger." Ezra's prayer already embodies the same compositional approach "when it uses known linguistic formulae from the Torah, extracting from them a *halakhic* midrash bearing a new ideological dimension."[25] Similarly, the composition of Ezra-Nehemiah as a whole may be explained as the edit-

---

22. Ibid., 46.
23. Ibid.
24. Ibid.
25. Ibid., 47.

ing of fragments, documents, and sources according to the religious, historical or other outlooks of the author-editor, whose perspective she claims to have uncovered by means of her analysis.[26] In her longer exposition of the subject, Dor employs anthropological criteria to comprehend the social dynamics behind the textual presentation and thereby brings to the study of Ezra-Nehemiah a lens not sufficiently employed elsewhere.[27]

JACOB L. WRIGHT

There is initially a family resemblance between Jacob L. Wright and Dor in the way that they focus on similar linguistic and ideological phenomena, such as seams in the narrative (even if in different chapters), but beyond that they go in opposite directions.[28] Wright adds yet another different and compelling analysis of Ezra-Nehemiah to those listed before. According to Wright, "the Nehemiah Memoir has gradually developed from a short building report into an account of Judah's Restoration, which in turn provided the theological impulses for the literary maturation of Ezra-Neh."[29]

Wright argues that a greatly truncated Nehemiah Memoir came first and that Ezra 1–6 was written next to complement the Nehemiah Memoir. Ezra 7–8 was composed later, expressly to bridge the gap between the two accounts and to redirect the story of the rebuilding.[30] Wright identifies many more layers of compositional history and three main stages of additions to the Nehemiah Memoir building report. The Nehemiah Memoir provoked, according to Wright, the composing of Ezra 1–6 as an attempt to broaden the interpretation of the reconstruction and tone down Nehemiah's critique of the priesthood in the Nehemiah Memoir.[31] Ezra 7–8, as a middle position, was inserted to nuance the messages by combining the content of Ezra 1–6 and the form of Nehemiah Memoir.[32] The final major

---

26. Ibid.
27. Dor's fuller discussion is found in Yonina Dor, "The Theme of the Foreign Women in Ezra-Nehemiah" [Hebrew] (Ph.D. diss., Hebrew University, 2001).
28. Jacob L. Wright, *Rebuilding Identity: The Nehemiah Memoir and Its Earliest Readers* (BZAW 348; Berlin: de Gruyter, 2004).
29. Ibid., vii.
30. Ibid., 94.
31. Ibid., 5–6.
32. Ibid., 5.

stage included Ezra 9–10 and Neh 8–10. These chapters view Nehemiah's work more positively and limit the role of priests. Wright maintains that tension regarding the priesthood and the temple drove the interpretive choices taken by a coterie of writers/editors who sought to retain earlier voices but reshaped the story of Israel gradually to express different ideologies. The book in its final form is Hellenistic, reflecting back on the Persian period as a model for how to live within an empire. More of its features belong to this Hellenistic era.

Wright invests the processes themselves with historical value that is lacking in other compositional theories. His concept is markedly different from those proposed by Williamson, Blenkinsopp, and others who are working with a version of a "documentary hypothesis" model, namely, the splicing of major blocks of sources. Wright, instead, considers Ezra-Nehemiah to be "a *creatio continua*,"[33] with the text undergoing a kind of "maturation process": earlier voices are heard as new generations also contribute their insight by gradually adding to the text and, in that way, also contributing to the reconstruction of Jewish life. The process he describes is akin (I think) to what Michael Fishbane claims for the Hebrew Bible in general.[34] Although both the manner with which Wright reaches his conclusion and the nature of his phenomenological approach to the text differ from Fishbane's, it nonetheless seems that both would agree that,

> Exegesis rises out of a practical crisis of some sort.... There is ... something of the dynamic of "tradition and the individual talent" here—where the tradition sets the agenda of problems which must be creatively resolved or determines the received language which may be imaginatively reworked. The strategies vary from textual annotation, literary allusion, and types of analogical or synthetic reasoning. They include also the ethical, legal or even spiritual transformation of textual content.[35]

Fishbane states further that

> [o]ne may say that the entire corpus of Scripture remains open to these invasive procedures and strategic reworkings up to the close of the

---

33. Ibid., 3.
34. Michael Fishbane, "Inner Biblical Exegesis: Types and Strategies of Interpretation in Ancient Israel," in *Midrash and Literature* (ed. G. H. Harmant and S. Budick; New Haven: Yale University Press), 19–37.
35. Ibid., 34.

canon in the early rabbinic period, and so the received text is complexly compacted of teachings and their subversion, of rules and their extension, of topoi and their revision. Within ancient Israel, as long as the textual corpus remained open, Revelation and Tradition were thickly interwoven and interdependent.[36]

There is also a notable similarity between Wright's approach and that of the "supplementary hypothesis" proposed by Alexander Rofé, among others.[37] Rofé writes: "According to the Documentary Hypothesis there originally existed independent and discrete documents, which were gathered and assembled by a later editor."[38] The "supplementary hypothesis," in contrast, "prefers to see the formation of biblical literature as a gradual developmental process: layer on layer, stratum on stratum, continuing until the works reached their canonical form."[39]

Conclusions

Each of the four sets of arguments is compelling in a number of ways. Each of the theories is largely consistent internally and plausible for different stages in the history of the Judahite community. Their cogency does not, however, settle the issue conclusively, because one could defend any one of the models equally and challenge each of them in turn. We are left with a number of probable theories for interpreting the compositional history of Ezra-Nehemiah, as well as the history of the eras. Importantly, each theory represents a different understanding of how ancient writers, editors, or scribes approached their task. Each also understands differently the purposes of the editorial or redactional activities. Can we adjudicate among them? I do not think we can come to a consensus on this matter because all the theories are both cogent and plausible. Furthermore, we lack external evidence with which to weigh the options. For that reason I begin to circumambulate, following Jonathan Z. Smith's suggestion. My

---

36. Ibid., 36. I am not sure, however, whether Wright would credit scribes with the supplements.

37. Alexander Rofé, "Joshua 20: Historico-Literary Criticism Illustrated," in *Empirical Models for Biblical Criticism* (ed. Jeffrey H. Tigay; Philadelphia: University of Pennsylvania Press, 1985), 131–48.

38. Ibid., 144.

39. Ibid.

goal is to see what known practices in antiquity from nonbiblical sources, preferably contemporary with Ezra-Nehemiah, might contribute to the discussion.[40]

Nonbiblical Examples of Compositional Processes

To place the theories about the composition of Ezra-Nehemiah in a wider context, I briefly look at other types of ancient texts and the evidence about their composition. I will focus on both Jeffrey H. Tigay's work on the Gilgamesh Epic and the Greek historians as useful sources.

The Gilgamesh Epic

More fortunate than Ezra-Nehemiah scholars, Tigay can follow the formation of the Gilgamesh Epic through over 1,200 years of editorial work.[41] Tigay, therefore, recommends the use of models, such as the formation of the Gilgamesh Epic, for the study of biblical texts. The purpose is not to speculate about a genetic relation between different traditions but to examine "common-sense techniques which developed independently among the transmitters of literary traditions when they were faced with

---

40. The plethora of late biblical writings such as Esther, Daniel, First Esdras, and the LXX manuscripts of these books, including the Alpha text of Esther, supports the plausibility of each of the theories concerning the composition of Ezra-Nehemiah. See studies of the redaction of the Esther traditions, in which the Alpha Text, along with the LXX, prompt various conclusions about Jewish editorial practices in the Persian and Hellenistic eras. Kristin De Troyer, *The End of the Alpha Text of Esther: Translation and Narrative Technique in MT 8:1–17, LXX 8:1–17, and AT 7:14–41* (SBLSCS 48; Atlanta: Scholars Press, 2000), offers a comprehensive summary of centuries of scholarship on the different versions. See also David J. A. Clines, *The Esther Scroll: The Story of the Story* (JSOTSup 30; Sheffield: JSOT Press, 1984); Michael V. Fox, *The Redaction of the Books of Esther: On Reading Composite Texts* (SBLMS 40; Atlanta: Scholars Press, 1991); and Karen H. Jobes, *The Alpha-Text of Esther: Its Character and Relationship to the Masoretic Text* (SBLDS 153; Atlanta: Scholars Press, 1996). Conclusions about the transmission of the Esther traditions include observations that would confirm aspects of each of the four of the theories about Ezra-Nehemiah's composition. These studies enrich the investigation but do not adjudicate among them.

41. Jeffrey H. Tigay, "The Evolution of the Pentateuchal Narratives in the Light of the Evolution of the *Gilgamesh Epic*," in Tigay, *Empirical Models for Biblical Criticism*, 21–52.

similar tasks."⁴² Tigay observes: "as long as the main use of analogues is to show what is realistic, even distant analogues will have a heuristic value if they were produced under conditions comparable to those underlying biblical literature, especially if our knowledge of how they developed is empirical rather than hypothetical."⁴³ Using Tigay's results, based on his search for empirical models, I ask: How did people writing in a comparable genre think about what they were doing, and what do we actually know about what they were doing?

Tigay identifies four stages in the formation of the Gilgamesh Epic, each with its own range of activities, beginning roughly in 1500 B.C.E.⁴⁴ (1) The first stage is composed of Ur III Sumerian sources. (2) The second stage consists of the Old Babylonian version(s) in Akkadian, where material was integrated, showing selective use of sources, but with no attempt to preserve everything. This layer also shows a readiness to add material.⁴⁵

(3) The third stage is characterized as follows:

> In contrast to the freedom with which the Old Babylonian formulated the text of the epic, and modified its contents, subsequent revisions of the epic left enough similarities in outline and wording to show that the later versions are textually related to the Old Babylonian version. Though the editors of these versions made their own creative contributions to the epic … they were clearly transmitting in revised form a text that was essentially the work of an earlier author."⁴⁶

Tigay indicates here that there is no single third stage but rather several. Standardization took centuries.

(4) In the fourth stage, not much updating of language exists. However, some of the changes include an important detail for our consideration, namely, the addition of prologues.⁴⁷ Greater inconsistencies point to later material.⁴⁸

The text shows, according to Tigay, incomplete revision: the "he" and

---

42. Jeffrey H. Tigay, "Introduction," in Tigay, *Empirical Models for Biblical Criticism*, 18.
43. Ibid., 19.
44. Tigay, "Evolution of the Pentateuchal Narratives," 34.
45. Ibid., 37.
46. Ibid., 38–39.
47. Ibid., 41.
48. Ibid., 46.

"I" material is not always integrated, a feature to keep in mind in light of the turns between "he" and "I" in Ezra-Nehemiah. In concluding the essay, Tigay approvingly cites Moshe Greenberg: "Plasticity and integrative capability are characteristic of early stages of transmission; rigidity and unassimilability, characteristic of the quasi-canonical status of the material in the time of redaction."[49]

For Tigay, the chief contribution of such data to biblical studies lies in their heuristic value in helping to test the appropriateness of a certain method of analysis that has characterized biblical criticism for the past couple of centuries. His study confirms that each of the practices presumed or proposed by theories concerning the composition of Ezra-Nehemiah indeed "characterizes literary development and transmission in the Ancient Near East."[50] His study, however, does not help to settle which one of the four views presented is the most plausible.

Greek Historiography

Greek sources help even less in deciding which model for Ezra-Nehemiah is most plausible. They do, nevertheless, shed sobering—and very valuable—light on some assumptions that scholars make in interpreting what is "common-sense" for an ancient author. Examples from Greek historiography, from Herodotus in the fifth century B.C.E. to the Hellenistic era, including the early Roman period, are valuable in that they give us access to ancient writers who speak about their methods, as it were. These provide us with certain concrete examples that challenge some important presumptions about what an ancient author would or would not do. Obviously, Greek historiography differs from Ezra-Nehemiah, even though it is contemporaneous with Ezra-Nehemiah (however dated). It is valuable, nonetheless, because it discloses actual practices.

In reviewing the contributions from the classics, first we must note

---

49. Moshe Greenberg, "The Redaction of the Plague Narrative in Exodus," in *Near Eastern Studies in Honor of William Foxwell Albright* (ed. H. Goedicke; Baltimore: Johns Hopkins University Press, 1971), 245; cited by Tigay, "Evolution of the Pentateuchal Narratives," 45.

50. Tigay, "Evolution of the Pentateuchal Narratives," 51. One can of course argue conversely as well: a rapport between Tigay's conclusions and biblical studies is sometimes the result of adopting his conclusions. For a recent example, see Pakkala, *Ezra the Scribe*, 23 n. 3, where Pakkala's argument is based explicitly on Tigay's work.

key differences. Here are some aspects that sharply differentiate Greek historiography from Ezra-Nehemiah. (1) The obvious contrast between Ezra-Nehemiah and Greek authors is the prominence of named authors in these Greek writings. In the fifth century, the anonymity of authorship, as reflected in the *Odyssey* and *Iliad*, is replaced by clear ascriptions to individual authors.[51] However, Greek historiography resembles Ezra-Nehemiah (and contrasts with the Gilgamesh Epic) in that individuals other than kings place themselves in the accounts they write. It is no longer simply kings who commemorate their activities. In a sense, the fact that the so called "Ezra Memoir" and "Nehemiah Memoir" are cast as attributable to an individual author (in contrast to anonymous biblical books such as Samuel and Kings) somewhat bridges the distance between the two genres. (2) Greek historical writings increasingly narrow their scope to military events. (3) Greek historical writings are much longer than biblical works dealing with historical material. (4) Greek historians explicitly describe their goals.

Yet, or perhaps therefore, some useful information about how historians perceived their task in the centuries before the common era is also provided by the literature from Greece. Here are ten features that are important for biblical scholars to consider in studying the composition of Ezra-Nehemiah.

(1) One of the best-known insights that Greek historiography provides is the ambiguity of ending in both Herodotus and Thucydides. Classicists continue to debate whether the books' endings are lost or whether, as some argue, the books' endings, as we have them, are original, concluding abruptly either because the author intended it this way or because the author simply never got any further. These seemingly inconclusive endings challenge how we think about a proper ending in ancient sources.

(2) More important, because it is so clear, is Thucydides' famous statement about the speeches in his work:

> In the history I have made use of set speeches.... I have found it difficult to remember the precise words used in the speeches which I listen to myself and my various informants have experienced the same difficulty; so my method has been, while keeping as closely as possible to the gen-

---

51. Individual authors, such as Hesiod, are preserved from an earlier period, but their work does not take the form of historically oriented prose writing.

eral sense of the words that were actually used, *to make the speakers say what, in my opinion, was called for by each situation.*[52]

That composing speeches was an honorable practice for even the historian considered the most "objective" and "accurate" has obvious ramifications for thinking about speeches in Ezra-Nehemiah, such as the prayers.

(3) Less familiar but also important is the observation that almost all Greek historians, down to the age of Polybius (second century B.C.E.), were concerned with contemporary history or near-contemporary history. "Even the few histories that began in the distant past ... brought the narrative down to the present, which received the greatest emphasis and the most extensive treatment."[53] This holds true also for histories of cities that were carried down to the author's lifetime. Polybius (writing in Greek) says why this is the case: the distant past seemed less relevant and less certain because no reliable sources were available for it. Only later, and under the pressure of Roman control, did Greek historians and other writers turn their attention to earlier traditions; they did so because writing about the present had become dangerous since it was perceived as sedition. Thus, new accounts about Troy appear only when Greece has come under Roman domination.

(4) Also important is the data we garner concerning additions. In one case where we know of revisions, they were made by the original author, Polybius, twenty-two years later.[54] Polybius revised his introduction in a minor way (announcing that he is revising; 3.1–5), but added ten chapters in order to bring the narrative to the latest significant events in his own time: the fall of Carthage and Rome's conquest of his own Achaean homeland (books 30–40; see 3.4).[55] This indicates the freedom to change both the beginning and the end of a previously completed work.

(5) When we know of revisions of individual passages, they are minimal. An anecdote sheds an interesting light: when Polybius confronted Zeno of Rhodes, identifying errors in Zeno's work and suggesting correction, Zeno (says Polybius), "gave friendly reception to my comments" (16.20ff.). But Zeno also "pointed out that since his history was already

---

52. Thucydides, *The Peloponnesian Wars* (trans. Rex Warner; Baltimore: Penguin, 1965), 1.22 (p. 24); emphasis added.
53. Torrey James Luce, *The Greek Historians* (London: Routledge, 1997), 142.
54. Ibid., 140.
55. Ibid.

published, corrections to what was now in the public domain were no longer possible."[56] The anecdote indicates that for the one author, corrections were useful and welcome, and to another, publication precluded changing the work.

(6) From Xenophon and other fourth century Greek historians, we learn that the tendency was to begin their accounts where predecessors stopped (rather than engage in revisions, compilation, etc.). Sometimes these accounts began with a slight overlap so as not to begin in mid-episode—a feature that would please those colleagues who (unlike me) date Ezra-Nehemiah after Chronicles (with Cyrus's Edict, as such, an overlap).

(7) Challenges to earlier or competing models of the same events were usually explicit rather than oblique. Writers directly expressed their differences, at times through digressions. They did not revise their predecessors' work in order to communicate their own opinions.

(8) Consistency is not as firmly established as one would expect. Polybius's portrait of Philopoemen in his biography differs from the one in his histories.[57] Since the same author's description of an individual in one work is in tension with the same author's description in another work, we have to be even more cautious in how we interpret inconsistencies.

(9) Our assumption as to what is a fitting beginning and what reveals an editorial hand could be challenged by the fact that Xenophon begins his *Hellenica* with what one classicist terms "one of the oddest openings in literature,"[58] namely, "After these events, Themochares came from Athens not many days later with a few ships."[59] Nothing is said concerning what "these [preceding] events" might be!

(10) In 36.12 Polybius interrupts his narrative to say that the frequent references to himself result from the fact that he was personally involved in the events he depicts but—and this is important for Ezra-Nehemiah, given the alternation between first- and third-person accounts in Ezra 7–10—that he deliberately varied these references to himself by using different forms of reference, namely, using "Polybius," "I," or "we."[60] This practice, it seems to me, throws a monkey wrench in some of the discussions about the role of first- and third-person material in Ezra-Nehemiah.

---

56. Ibid., 129.
57. Polybius, *The Histories*, 10.21.
58. Luce, *Greek Historians*, 102.
59. Ibid.
60. Ibid., 128–29.

Conclusions

The empirical model that Tigay describes for the Gilgamesh Epic confirms the realistic nature of compositional histories, such as those proposed by Williamson, Blenkinsopp, Dor, and Wright. Greek historiography, however, complicates, rather than clarifies, our ability to adjudicate among these models. Practices of Greek historians force us to be even more tentative in our conclusions because they challenge some of the seemingly logical presumptions that we bring to a text when drawing conclusions about its history. These reflections on the composition of ancient texts, then, serve as a prolegomenon for expanding the conversation about the composition of Ezra-Nehemiah and, perhaps most importantly, for exploring what is gained and what is conveyed by Ezra-Nehemiah when we interpret its messages based on one or the other of the possible compositional theories.

The presence of first-person, seemingly "autobiographical," material in Ezra-Nehemiah makes it useful to consider also the Greek autobiographies and biographies. Apparently Greek biography and autobiography emerged alongside of historiography in the fifth century but was always distinguished from it. I chose to limit this essay to historical writings both because of space limitations and because, according to Arnoldo Momigliano, the direction of influence in the writing of biography and autobiography was from east to west.[61] Nevertheless, additional study of such works will further augment our sense of what was, in fact, considered "reasonable" for writers to do in the ancient world. It will, therefore, advance our sensibilities in reviewing the composition of Ezra-Nehemiah

---

61. Momogliano writes: "Autobiography was in the air in the Persian period of the early fifth century.... Autobiography was a well-cultivated literary genre in various countries of the Persian Empire, from Egypt to Assyria. Both Jews and Greeks reformed their political culture and redefined their national identity in relation to the Persians. We may therefore wonder whether it is a matter of pure coincidence that in the fifth century Nehemiah and perhaps Ezra wrote autobiographies in Judea while Ion wrote his autobiographical memoirs in Chios. Nehemiah's autobiography was a novelty in Judea just as much as Ion's autobiographical notes were a novelty in Greece" (*The Development of Greek Biography* [Cambridge: Harvard University Press, 1993], 15). Biblical scholars are more reluctant to call Nehemiah's "Memoir" an autobiography, but given that it is embedded in a larger narrative, the broader canvas calls for examination, which is what the theories of composition reviewed are able to accomplish.

and other Persian period and Hellenistic biblical writings. For this reason as well, the present essay is to be regarded as a prolegomenon.

BIBLIOGRAPHY

Blenkinsopp, Joseph. *Ezra-Nehemiah: A Commentary*. OTL. Philadelphia: Westminster, 1988.
Boda, Mark J., and Paul L. Redditt, eds. *Unity and Disunity in Ezra-Nehemiah: Redaction, Rhetoric, and Reader*. Hebrew Bible Monographs 17. Sheffield: Sheffield Phoenix Press, 2008.
Clines, David J. A. *The Esther Scroll: The Story of the Story*. JSOTSup 30. Sheffield: JSOT Press, 1984.
De Troyer, Kristin. *The End of the Alpha Text of Esther: Translation and Narrative Technique in MT 8:1–17, LXX 8:1–17, and AT 7:14–41*. SBLSCS 48. Atlanta: Scholars Press, 2000.
Dor, Yonina. "The Composition of the Episode of the Foreign Women in Ezra IX–X." *VT* 53 (2003): 26–47.
―――. "The Theme of the Foreign Women in Ezra-Nehemiah" [Hebrew]. Ph.D. diss. Hebrew University, 2001.
Duggan, Michael W. *The Covenant Renewal in Ezra-Nehemiah (Neh 7:72b–10:40): An Exegetical, Literary and Theological Study*. SBLDS 164. Atlanta: Society of Biblical Literature, 2001.
Eskenazi, Tamara Cohn. *In an Age of Prose: A Literary Approach to Ezra-Nehemiah*. SBLMS 36. Atlanta: Scholars Press, 1988.
Fishbane, Michael. "Inner Biblical Exegesis: Types and Strategies of Interpretation in Ancient Israel." Pages 19–37 in *Midrash and Literature*. Edited by G. H. Harmant and S. Budick. New Haven: Yale University Press.
Fox, Michael V. *The Redaction of the Books of Esther: On Reading Composite Texts*. SBLMS 40. Atlanta: Scholars Press, 1991.
Greenberg, Moshe. "The Redaction of the Plague Narrative in Exodus." Pages 243–52 in *Near Eastern Studies in Honor of William Foxwell Albright*. Edited by H. Goedicke. Baltimore: Johns Hopkins University Press, 1971.
Jobes, Karen H. *The Alpha-Text of Esther: Its Character and Relationship to the Masoretic Text*. SBLDS 153. Atlanta: Scholars Press, 1996.
Luce, Torrey James. *The Greek Historians*. London: Routledge, 1997.
Momigliano, Arnoldo. *The Development of Greek Biography*. Cambridge: Harvard University Press, 1993.

Pakkala, Juha. *Ezra the Scribe: The Development of Ezra 7–10 and Nehemiah 8*. BZAW 347. Berlin: de Gruyeter, 2004.
Rofé, Alexander. "Joshua 20: Historico-Literary Criticism Illustrated." Pages 131–48 in *Empirical Models for Biblical Criticism*. Edited by Jeffrey H. Tigay. Philadelphia: University of Pennsylvania Press, 1985.
Smith, Jonathan Z. *Map Is Not Territory: Studies in the History of Religions*. Chicago: University of Chicago Press, 1978.
Thucydides, *History of the Peloponnesian War*. Translated with an introduction by Rex Warner. Baltimore: Penguin, 1965.
Tigay, Jeffrey H. "The Evolution of the Pentateuchal Narratives in the Light of the Evolution of the *Gilgamesh Epic*." Pages 21–52 in *Empirical Models for Biblical Criticism*. Edited by Jeffrey H. Tigay. Philadelphia: University of Pennsylvania Press, 1985. Repr., Eugene, Ore.: Wipf & Stock, 2005.
Williamson, H. G. M. "The Composition of Ezra i–vi." *JTS* 34 (1983): 1–30.
———. *Ezra, Nehemiah*. WBC 16. Dallas: Word, 1985.
Wright, Jacob L. *Rebuilding Identity: The Nehemiah Memoir and Its Earliest Readers*. BZAW 348. Berlin: de Gruyter, 2004.

Rome and the Early Church: Background of the Persecution of Christians in the First and Early Second Centuries

Paul J. Achtemeier

There is clear evidence in various New Testament writings that the early church understood itself as having undergone persecutions from the beginning.[1] Given the fate of Jesus at the hand of both Romans and Jews, that will come as no surprise. If the "founder" of the Christian movement was rejected and suffered, then it is not astonishing that those who followed him will have undergone a similar fate.[2] Indeed, that fate is reflected in many passages in the New Testament as a whole, ranging from the most general kind of reference to those that are quite specific.

In order to assess the kind of environment within the Roman Empire reflected in such passages, it will be useful first to examine that environment. We will restrict ourselves to the period from about 50 to 125 C.E. That will then give us a basis to inquire into the kinds of policies the various New Testament references to suffering appear to presume. We turn, then, to examine Roman policies and attitudes toward non-Roman religions, toward *collegia*, and finally toward the imperial cult.

In seeking to determine Roman policies toward non-Roman religions, it is necessary to observe some caveats. First, since all too often erroneous notions about when and why official Roman persecution of non-Roman religions occurred, it will be necessary to undertake a careful examination of Roman policy on these questions. That will show that many of

---

[1]. It is a pleasure to contribute to a Festschrift honoring Kent Harold Richards, my good friend and longtime colleague in the Society of Biblical Literature.

[2]. For Jesus' predictions of that fate, see Matt 24:9; Luke 6:33, 21:16–17; John 15:19.

these notions are based more on historical imagination than historical fact. A second caveat to be noted is the need to avoid the assumption that, once a policy was announced or a practice instituted in Rome or in some province, it was from that point on enforced equally in all provinces throughout the empire. Even when considering broad lines of policy, it is necessary to note that different emperors followed different policies and that different regions saw differing applications of various policies being pursued at any given time. Broad assumptions must therefore be constantly tested against the evidence we have.

We will first investigate the Roman attitude toward non-Roman religions and the impact that would have had on Christianity. Second, we will investigate the Roman attitude toward *collegia*, since Christianity will probably have appeared to the Roman mind to fit the form of *collegium* rather than religion. Third, we will look at the general attitude in the Roman Empire toward social nonconformity and see to what extent Christianity may also have fallen within that purview.

Christianity as a Religion

Fundamentally, Roman policy toward the practice by non-Roman peoples of non-Roman religions was one of tolerance. Dionysius of Halicarnassus notes that those non-Roman masses who had migrated to Rome "are under every necessity of worshipping their ancestral gods according to the customs of their respective countries."[3] Again, Suetonius noted that even Augustus "treated with great respect such foreign rites as were ancient and well established."[4] If observance of such foreign religious customs, provided they posed no threat to Roman hegemony, were appropriate for foreigners for whom they were ancestral, they were not appropriate for Romans, any more than Roman religious customs were appropriate for foreigners. For example, the emperor Trajan writes to the legate Pliny that "the ground of a foreign city is not capable of receiving [the] kind of consecration which is conferred by our laws."[5] In other words, what is religiously appropriate in Rome is not appropriate elsewhere. Such tolerance, however, was not always practiced. Suetonius tells us that Tiberius

---

3. *Ant. rom.* 2.19.3, Cary. All translations, unless otherwise noted, are taken from the Loeb Classical Library series.
4. *De vita* 2.93, Rolfe.
5. Pliny, *Ep.* 10.50, Hutchinson.

"abolished foreign cults, especially the Egyptian and the Jewish rites, compelling all who were addicted to such superstitions to burn their religious vestments and all their paraphernalia."[6] Whether that applied beyond the bounds of the city of Rome is not made specific. It does, however, indicate that policy often depended on a given emperor.

Of more importance to the Roman attitude toward Christianity is the Roman attitude toward the Jewish religion, since the two were related, and on occasion identified, in this period. That attitude ranged from protection to irritation to suppression. Julius Caesar, for example, granted Jews certain privileges regarding the practice of their religion, practices that were then reaffirmed by succeeding emperors, with the exception of Caligula. Despite such policies, however, there was an abiding distaste for Jewish religious practices. Juvenal thought they worshiped "nothing but the clouds and the divinity of the heavens," they saw "no difference between eating swine's flesh … and that of man," they practiced circumcision, and, flouting Roman law, they instead "learn and practice and revere the Jewish law, and all that Moses committed to his secret tome."[7] Tacitus reports that they rest on the seventh day because of indolence, have "base and abominable customs … owe their persistence to their depravity," and are loyal to one another but "toward every other people … feel only hate and enmity."[8] On occasion this distaste was translated into official policy. As noted above, Tiberius at one point forbade the practice of Egyptian and Jewish rites and banished large numbers of people who practiced them. Claudius either "did not drive [the Jews] out of Rome but ordered them, while continuing their traditional mode of life, not to hold meetings"[9] or in fact "since the Jews constantly made disturbances at the instigation of Chrestus [sic] he expelled them from Rome."[10] Vespasian, and then Titus, following the Jewish war, levied a tax specifically on them, the *fiscus Judaicus*.[11] Nevertheless, certain privileges that had previously been granted to the Jews were continued.

This distaste, inspired largely by Jewish exclusivity, was transferred to Christians, who suffered additionally from the fact that they could plead

---

6. *De vita* 3.36, Rolfe.
7. *Sat.* 14.95–109, Ramsey.
8. *Hist.* 5.5, Moore; this is only a partial list of his complaints against the Jews.
9. So Dio Cassius, *Hist. rom.* 60.6, Cary.
10. Suetonius, *De vita* 5.25.4, Rolfe; cf. Acts 18:2.
11. It was then continued under Domitian (Suetonius, *De vita* 8.12.2).

no ancestral customs for their religious practices. Yet despite that, official Roman tolerance for foreign religions could also apply to the Christians. Trajan's unwillingness to "lay down a specific rule which would have universal application" with respect to the Christians, reported on by Pliny, illustrates this point.[12]

Christianity as *Collegium*

Roman attitudes toward organized groups also played a role in their reaction to Christianity. Such groups, given a variety of names—*collegium, corpus, universitas, sodalitas, sodalicium, societas*, and, if its purposes were political, *hetaeria*—were associations of individuals who gathered to promote some common interest. That interest could be commercial, religious, social, cultural (e.g., musicians, artists), sport, age (youth, elderly), or even geographic origins or local neighborhoods. Often sponsored by a prominent citizen, and with a god or gods as tutelary deities, the members paid regular dues, attended monthly meetings often accompanied by a meal, and elected officers to maintain order. Because they served such a variety of purposes, such *collegia* existed in large numbers; although a few types were officially recognized—primarily professional and burial societies[13]—inscriptional evidence shows only a small minority had received official permission to exist.[14]

Because there were so many such societies in existence apart from official sanctions, they presented a constant problem for the governing authorities. As early as the second century, measures were taken to restrain them; the steps taken in Rome in 186 B.C.E. to control the followers of Bacchus fall under this kind of action. In 64 B.C.E. the senate, fearing that such gatherings would turn into political groups, that is, *hetaeria*,[15] banned all such gatherings, a ban subsequently lifted in 58 B.C.E. But the problem did not disappear. Sounding a theme that would be regularly repeated, Julius Caesar "dissolved all guilds, except those

---

12. Pliny, *Ep.* 10.97, Hutchinson.
13. See Peter Herrmann et al., "Genossenschaft," *RAC* 10:109–19 (professional societies) and 102–3 (burial societies).
14. See Ernest G. Hardy, *Christianity and the Roman Government: A Study in Imperial Administration* (London: Allen & Unwin, 1925), 131.
15. See Herrmann et al., "Genossenschaft, 92, 112.

of ancient foundation."[16] Augustus, under the *lex Julia*, "disbanded all guilds, except such as were of long standing and formed for legitimate purposes."[17] While Caligula had allowed such groups to re-form, Claudius again "disbanded the clubs."[18] Claudius's brother Nero, because of fights at a gladiatorial game instigated by the Pompeians, banned all their assemblies for ten years, "and the associations [Latin *collegia*] which they had formed illegally were dissolved."[19] Finally, Trajan allowed such groups to meet if they existed in places that still enjoyed their own laws.[20] In other situations, however, as in the case of a society formed to fight neighborhood fires, Trajan told Pliny they were not to be allowed, since "whatever title we give them, and whatever our object in giving it, men who are banded together for a common end will all the same become political associations [*hetaeriae*] before long."[21] Apparently this conviction also led to Pliny's mistrust of Christians, who, lacking the characteristic marks of a religion—temple, ancestral deities, ancient cultic rites with (hereditary) priesthood—looked more like a *collegium*, even a *hetaeria*, than a religion. The varied ethnic origins of Christians would have raised further suspicions. For that reason Pliny allowed Christians to hold morning assemblies, but not their evening meetings, which included meals, and hence made the group appear more like a *hetaeria*.[22]

Christianity and the Imperial Cult

Prior to the third century, when the Roman emperor Decius made participation in the imperial cult part of a demonstration of loyalty to Rome, one cannot speak of an official Roman policy regarding the cult of the emperor. In the period with which we are concerned, according divine honors to an emperor depended on what the various emperors would permit or, less frequently, require. Further, participation in such cultic activity was more frequent in provinces, especially Asia Minor, than in Rome itself.

---

16. Suetonius, *De vita* 1.42.3, Rolfe.
17. Suetonius, *De vita* 2.32.1, Rolfe.
18. Dio Cassius, *Hist. rom.* 60.6.6, Cary.
19. Tacitus, *Ann.* 14.17, Moore.
20. Pliny, *Ep.* 10.92, 93.
21. Pliny, *Ep.* 10.34, Hutchinson.
22. Cf. Pliny, *Ep.* 10.96.

The movement to attribute divine honors to a given emperor obtained some headway under Julius Caesar, although in Suetonius's judgment, he "allowed honors to be bestowed on him which were too great for mortal man ... temples, altars and statues beside those of the gods, a special priest, an additional college of the Luperci.... In fact there were no honors which he did not receive or confer at pleasure."[23] Greater impetus was given to this movement with the accession of Augustus and the stability and peace that it brought with it. Augustus, however, resisted divine accolades, not even permitting his children and grandchildren to address his as "dominus."[24] "He further forbade any one to worship him or offer him any sacrifice (and) checked the many excessive acclamations accorded him."[25] In the provinces, however, he permitted temples to himself, for example in Spain and in Asia.[26]

Tiberius followed Augustus in this policy, declaring, after a delegation from Further Spain had requested permission to erect a temple in his honor, that, "following the precedent already sealed by his (the deified Augustus) approval, with all the more readiness that with the worship of my self was associated veneration of the Senate," he granted the request.[27] Claudius, on the other hand, "forbade any one to worship him or to offer him any sacrifice."[28] Trajan also expressed his unwillingness to allow the creation of "an awe of my person by severe and rigorous measures."[29] Martial celebrated Trajan's modesty in this regard, writing, "I am not about to speak of 'Lord and God'.[30] ... There is no Lord here, but a commander-in-chief and the most just of all senators, through whom rustic, dry-haired Truth has been brought back from the house of Styx."[31] This reticence to address emperors as gods, despite Domitian's demand that he be addressed as "dominus et deus noster" ("our Lord and God"),[32] remained

---

23. *De vita* 1.76.1, Rolfe.
24. Suetonius, *De vita* 2.53.
25. Dio Cassius, *Hist. rom.* 60.4, Cary.
26. Tacitus, *Ann.* 1.78; 4.37.
27. Tacitus, *Ann.* 4.37–38, Moore.
28. Dio Cassius, *Hist. rom.* 60.5.4, Cary.
29. Pliny, *Ep.* 10.82, Hutchinson; see also 10.9.
30. Probably a reference to Domitian.
31. *Epigr.* 10.72, Ker.
32. See such references in Martial, *Epigr.* 5.8: "Phasis ... was praising the edict of our Lord and God"; Quintilian, *Inst.* 4, preface 5: "calling to my aid all the gods and Himself before them all (for his power is unsurpassed) and there is no deity that looks

through the beginning of the second century C.E. Tacitus, referring to the city of Rome, could declare as a rule that "the honor of divinity is not paid to the emperor until he has ceased to live and move among men."[33]

In the provinces, on the other hand, particularly in Asia Minor, it was rather different. All the emperors mentioned above had divine honors paid to them, sometimes with their approval, sometimes without. This was the case for two reasons. First, it provided for Rome a convenient way to let various cities demonstrate their loyalty to the empire, since the attitude to the cult reflected the attitude to Rome, and was so interpreted.[34]

Second, it allowed the provinces to fit the political reality of their subjugation to Rome into the context of their Greek culture, which provided a framework for subjugation in the form of cultic reverence for the gods. In that way the imperial cult allowed leading families of the various cities to maintain cultural continuity in light of their radically altered political situation. By making the emperor a deity, they understood political subjugation in terms of the subjugation of cultic adherents to their gods.[35] The cult flourished, therefore, in the provinces not so much as a way to honor individual emperors but as a way for local indigenous authorities to maintain cultural stability and control in a situation of political subjugation.

For this reason, disobedience to the cult of the emperor challenged not only Roman power and authority; it was rather a challenge to the social fabric of the community itself. It thus threatened to bring to naught the cultural continuity represented by the cult itself. Pressure to conform to cultic practices would therefore be greater from local authorities than from the Roman overlords. "The imperial cult ... enhanced the dominance of local elites over the populace, of cities over other cities, and of Greek over indigenous cultures. That is, the cult was a major part of the web of power that formed the fabric of society."[36]

---

with such favor upon learning." See also Martial, *Epigr.* 9.66; Suetonius, *De vita* 8.13.2; Dio Chrysostom, *Or.* 45.1.

33. *Ann.* 15.74, Moore.

34. See above, note 27. So also, e.g., Tacitus (*Ann.* 4.36), who reports that neglect of the cult of Augustus in a Phrygian town was coupled immediately with a charge of abuse against Roman citizens.

35. S. R. F. Price argues persuasively for this thesis in *Rituals and Power: The Roman Imperial Cult in Asia Minor* (Cambridge: Cambridge University Press, 1984).

36. Ibid., 248.

In that situation, Christian unwillingness to bow before statues of emperors, seen as idols, and an unwillingness to confess as "lord and god" an emperor instead of Jesus Christ would bring negative social pressure to bear on them. As we shall see, such social pressure is probably much more responsible for the kind of persecution reflected in the New Testament than any official policy of Rome and its emperors.

We shall now turn to consider persecution of Christians, first as empire-wide under the rubric of official Roman policy, then as more local expressions of persecution.

Persecution of Christianity

When one speaks of general persecution of the Christians in the Roman Empire of the late first and early second centuries C.E., the most likely scenario is assumed to be persecution under the edict of a given emperor. More specifically, scholars have tended to place such persecutions under the reigns of Nero, Vespasian, Domitian, and Trajan. We must examine each of these periods, to see what evidence there is for a general, official persecution of Christians.

1. Nero (54–68): While the emperor Claudius expelled Jews from Rome because of disturbances "at the instigation of Chrestus" (*impulsore Chrestus*),[37] there is no indication he persecuted Christians as Christians. It is in the reign of Nero that the first evidence of such a specific persecution surfaces. Tertullian writes that "Nero was the first to rage with the imperial sword against this school [i.e., Christianity]."[38] Tacitus accounts for Nero's persecution as an attempt to shift blame for the fire in Rome from himself to the Christians: "To scotch the rumor, Nero substituted as culprits and punished with the utmost refinement of cruelty a class of men, loathed for their vices, which the crowd styled Christians."[39] Suetonius, while omitting mention of the fire, confirms as the reason for persecution the fact that Christians were "a class of men given to a new and mischievous superstition."[40]

---

37. Suetonius, *De vita* 5.25.4, Rofe. "Chrestus" has generally been understood to mean "Christus," at least since the time of Tertullian.
38. *Apol.* 5.3; Eusebius identifies Nero and Domitian as "the only emperors ... to slander our teaching" (*Hist. eccl.* 4.26.9, Glover).
39. *Ann.* 15.44, Moore.
40. *De vita* 6.16, Rolfe.

If in fact the main motive for Nero's persecution of the Christians was to shift blame for the fire in Rome,[41] it would explain why there is no evidence, even in those who did not mention the fire (e.g., Suetonius), that these persecution extended beyond the bounds of the city of Rome. While Nero's acts would surely have encouraged a negative view of Christians, there is no evidence for an empire-wide persecution. References to suffering in Christian literature will therefore not have originated in some empire-wide condemnation of Christians in the middle of the first century.

2. Vespasian (69–79): The Roman victory over the Jewish revolt and the resulting destruction of Jerusalem, with its temple, led Vespasian to attempt to head off any further uprisings by eliminating descendants of David. As Eusebius reports, "Vespasian, after the capture of Jerusalem, ordered a search to be made for all who were of the family of David, that there might be left among the Jews not one of the royal family."[42] While, as Eusebius further reports, this unleashed a persecution against the Jews, there is no mention that it extended to Christians as well. Vespasian's tolerance and moderation were noted by Tacitus,[43] and Eusebius reports that "Vespasian had planned no evil against us."[44] Thus there is no evidence of any kind of official persecution of Christians during Vespasian's reign.

3. Domitian (81–96): Suetonius notes that early in his reign Domitian "was equally free from any suspicion of love of gain or of avarice, both in private life and for some time after becoming emperor; on the contrary he often gave strong proofs not merely of integrity, but even of liberality."[45] Very soon, however, "he turned to cruelty,"[46] putting to death "many senators, among them several ex-consuls,"[47] and seizing "the property of the living and the dead ... everywhere on any charge brought by any accuser."[48] In such a situation, it is not surprising that Christians

---

41. The fire consumed a large portion of Rome that was occupied by tenements and that Nero had coveted, but been unable to obtain, as an area on which to build a grand palace. Because the fire consumed that area, suspicion for its origins fell on Nero.
42. *Hist. eccl.* 3.12.1, Lake.
43. *Hist.* 4.42.
44. *Hist. eccl.* 3.17, Lake.
45. *De vita* 8.9.1, Rolfe.
46. *De vita* 8.10.1, Rolfe.
47. *De vita* 8.8.2, Rolfe.
48. *De vita* 8.12.1, Rolfe.

also fell victim to Domitian, even some of them within the royal family. Eusebius relates that "in the fifteenth year of Domitian, Flavia Domitilla, who was the niece of Flavius Clemens, one of the consuls at Rome at that time, was banished with many others to the island of Pontia" because of her testimony to Christ.[49] Part of the problem for Christians was Domitian's desire to be addressed as "Deus et dominus noster" ("our God and Lord"),[50] something Christians would clearly resist, but for which he was also condemned by others as well.[51]

While there was thus widespread persecution of Christians under Domitian, his persecutions obviously were not limited to them. He also at one point "banished all the philosophers from the city and from Italy."[52] Rather, persecutions appear to be part of his larger policy of suppressing all opposition, real or imagined, to his rule and self-imputed divinity. Such persecution was also spasmodic[53] and lacked the persistence and organization necessary to label it an "official persecution." Nerva (96–98), who succeeded Domitian, brought an end to Domitian's excesses, including persecuting Christians, and recalled those who had been banished (including Christians), but his rule was short-lived.

4. Trajan (97–117): The exchange of letters between Trajan and Pliny the Younger, whom Trajan had sent as legate to Bithynia to help restore order to the administrative and fiscal chaos that had developed there, gives us a good insight into the official Roman attitude to Christians in this period.[54]

Pliny's letter was occasioned by the fact that some people had been denounced to him as Christians, that he had conducted some trials, and that he had then written to Trajan for confirmation of how he had pro-

---

49. *Hist. eccl.* 3.18.4, Lake.

50. Suetonius, *De vita* 8.13.2.

51. E.g. Martial, *Epigr.* 10.72, Pliny, *Pan.* 2.3, praising Trajan, notes "times are different and our speeches must show this.... nowhere should we flatter him as a divinity and a god," reflecting Pliny's distaste for Domitian's pretenses.

52. Suetonius, *De vita* 8.10.3, Rolfe; see also Pliny, *Ep.* 3.11 "when the philosophers were expelled from Rome."

53. See J. B. Bauer, "Der erste Petrusbrief und die Verfolgung unter Domitian," in *Die Kirche des Anfangs: Festschrift für Heinz Schürmann zum 65. Geburtstag* (ed. Rudolf Schnackenburg et al.; ETS 38; Leipzig: St. Benno, 1977), 513–27.

54. Pliny's letter to Trajan concerning Christians (*Ep.* 10.96) and Trajan's reply (*Ep.* 10.97) are chiefly in view here. Unless otherwise noted, the summaries presented are drawn from these two letters.

ceeded and for advice on how to proceed further. It is clear from Pliny's letter that, while he knows trials against Christians have taken place and that some crimes were associated with the title "Christian," he knows of no general policy that is to govern his action. Trajan replies that (a) there is no such general policy regarding Christians and that (b) Trajan is unwilling to lay down any general rule(s) to cover how Christians are to be treated.

In response to the accusations, Pliny had conducted hearings in which a thrice-repeated confession of being a Christian brought death, but more for obstinacy and inflexible stubbornness ("pertinaciam ... et inflexibilem obstinationem") than for anything else. Those who were willing to appeal to the gods and to adore and sacrifice to an image of Trajan and curse Christ, were released—procedures that Trajan approved. Lastly, Pliny reported that, while Christians were morally and politically harmless, the danger of their "perverse and immoderate superstition" ("superstitionem pravam, immodicam") was that it led large numbers of people to abandon normal participation in temple worship and sacred festivals. Trajan responded that, while confessed Christians were to be punished, anonymous accusations were not to be pursued, and no search for them was to be undertaken. In short, no general persecution was to be instituted.

We may now draw some conclusions regarding persecution of Christians in the latter decades of the first and early decades of the second centuries C.E. Clearly there was no official empire-wide persecution of Christians during this period. While Nero's persecution was surely "official" in the sense that the emperor undertook it, it was nevertheless local, affecting only Christians in Rome. Domitian certainly put a number of Christians to death, but the reasons seem more individual suspicions of disloyalty (unwillingness to participate in official functions) than the persecution of a "religion." Domitian's general cruelty to those who had no relation to the Christian faith shows clearly enough that his "persecutions" reflected more his general attitude and policy than any intention to subjugate members of a religion. Trajan, in his answer to Pliny, clearly revealed his unwillingness to institute any kind of official attempt to seek out and destroy Christians, just as Pliny's question makes clear enough that to that point no such official policy had been instituted. One cannot therefore assume the existence of any official, empire-wide policy of persecuting Christians in the period under consideration.

What our evidence also makes clear, however, is that Christians did in fact suffer spasmodic officially instigated periods of persecution. The principal legal basis of that kind of persecution appears to have been, not an empire-wide decree issued by emperor or senate, but rather a procedure known as *coercitio*, under which local authorities had at their disposal the power to decree and enforce punishments primarily intended to maintain public order.[55] It allowed the Roman magistrate the widest latitude in all aspects of its application, from gathering evidence to establishing punishment. Pliny obviously exercised such authority when he proceeded to inquire about Christians, to try them, and to punish them.[56] This procedure is probably reflected in Acts 16:19–24 and 1 Pet 3:15. It was apparently the type of judicial action most often employed by provincial magistrates, and it was the form most often used in our period to visit official punishment on members of the Christian community.[57]

Perhaps an even greater threat faced by Christians was the attitudes of the general populace toward them. Tacitus notes that as early as the reign of Nero, they "were convicted, not so much on the count of arson as for hatred of the human race" (*odium humani generis*). Tacitus describes Christians as "a class of men, loathed for their vices, whom the crowd styled Christians. Christus, the founder of the name, had undergone the death penalty in the reign of Tiberius, by sentence of the procurator Pontius Pilate,[58] and the pernicious superstition was checked for the moment, only to break out once more, not merely in Judea, the home of the disease, but in the capital itself."[59]

This reputation was based primarily on their unwillingness to take part in general religio-cultural activities such as the festivals held regularly in the cities of Asia Minor, as well as in cities throughout the empire. Christians were accused of offending the gods by their behavior and by bringing the disfavor of the gods upon the communities where they lived.[60] In addition, Christians brought about negative economic effects by

---

55. K. J. Neumann has a detailed discussion of this policy in "Coercitio," PW 4.1:201–4.

56. *Ep.* 10.96.

57. So Neumann, "Coercitio," 203–4; see also William L. Schutter, *Hermeneutic and Composition in I Peter* (WUNT 2/30; Tübingen: Mohr Siebeck, 1989).

58. An example of *coercitio*, rather than official Roman policy. See the discussion of that term above.

59. *Ann.* 15.44, Moore.

60. See Apuleius, *Metam.* 14; Tertullian, *Apol.* 10; the twin charges of treason and sacrilege show that religious and civil offenses were regarded as one and the same. See

their activities. Pliny reports that, as a result of his crackdown on Christians, "there is a general demand for sacrificial animals, which for some time past have met with but few purchases."[61] A similar economic effect is reflected in Acts 16:19–24 and 19:24–27. Christians were thus regularly accused not only of antisocial activities but even of criminal behavior. For example, Minucius Felix asks: "Why have they no altars, no temples, no recognized images? Why do they never speak in public, never meet in the open, if it be not that the object of their worship and their concealment is either criminal or shameful?"[62] As a result, even the name "Christian" came to be associated with such antisocial activities.[63]

Conclusions

As we have seen, there is no evidence for an official, empire-wide period of persecution from the latter decades of the first to the early decades of the second centuries C.E., the period within which the New Testament was written. As a result, we cannot assign the references to suffering in the New Testament to such an official persecution. This is not to deny that Christians underwent persecution by officials of the Roman Empire. The death of Jesus on a Roman cross, the Roman means of execution for non-Roman citizens, is sufficient in itself to demonstrate that. Further general New Testament references to such persecutions are evident: Matt 10:17–18; Luke 21:12; Rev 1:10; 17:14; Acts 16:22; 22:22–29; 2 Cor 6:5; 11:32; 1 Pet 4:12, to name but a few. But these, as we have seen, are in the nature of the application of *coercitio* by local officials rather than examples of an empire-wide policy.

That Christians were also persecuted because they set themselves apart from others and would not participate in the normal activities expected of those who resided in Roman provinces is also evident: general nonparticipation, Acts 19:26–27; 1 Pet 4:4; unwillingness to participate in

---

also Marta Sordi, *The Christians and the Roman Empire* (trans. A. Bedini; Norman: University of Oklahoma Press, 1986), 5, 203.

61. *Ep.* 10.96, Hutchinson.
62. *Oct.* 10.2, Rendall. See also Tertullian, *Apol.* 2.5–20.
63. So Tertullian, *Apol.* 2.18: "So when in every detail you treat us differently from all other criminals ... you can gather that the gravamen of the case is not any crime but a name" (Glover).

idolatry, 1 Cor 10:14, 20; general accusation of Christians as wrongdoers, 1 Pet 2:12; 3:16–17, among other references.

Hatred of Christians because of the name, specifically because of their reverence for Jesus, is also evident in the New Testament: Matt 24:9; Luke 6:33; 21:16–17; John 15:18; 2 Cor 12:10; Heb 13:13; 1 Pet 4:14; Rev 12:17; 13:10, again to cite a few. In fact, there are some references to the fact that suffering is simply the lot of the Christians in their society: 1 Thess 3:3; 1 Pet 4:16; 5:9 to name but three.[64]

All of these New Testament references to the suffering of Christians reflect an environment of hostility toward them within the world in which they lived, a hostility that occurred over wide areas of the Roman Empire. Nevertheless, they appear from the evidence to be episodic and to have broken out at different times in different areas. Not all of Paul's letters, for example, contain such explicit references to suffering or hatred by others for their faith. The persecutions reflected in these New Testament writings therefore seem to be the result of outbreaks of local and regional hatred rather than due to some sort of continuous official Roman policy to persecute Christians in all part of the empire at all times.

Bibliography

Baur, J. B. "Der erste Petrusbrief und die Verfolgung unter Domitian." Pages 513–27 in *Die Kirche des Anfangs: Festschrift für Heinz Schürmann zum 65. Geburtstag*. Edited by Rudolf Schnackenburg et al. ETS 38. Leipzig: St. Benno, 1977.

Butler, H. E., et al., trans. *Quintilian*. 4 vols. LCL. London: Heinemann, 1921.

Cahoon, J. W., et al., trans. *Dio Chrysostom*. 5 vols. LCL. London: Heinemann, 1932–1951.

Cary, Earnest, et al., trans. *Dio Cassius*. 9 vols. LCL. London: Heinemann, 1914–1927.

———, trans. *Dionysius of Halicarnassus*. 7 vols. LCL. Cambridge: Harvard University Press, 1937–1950.

---

64. For a more detailed account of the evidence in the New Testament, the reader may consult Richard J. Cassidy, *Christians and Roman Rule in the New Testament: New Perspectives* (Companions to the New Testament; New York: Herder & Herder, 2001).

Cassidy, Richard J. *Christians and Roman Rule in the New Testament: New Perspectives.* Companions to the New Testament. New York: Herder & Herder, 2001.
Gaselee, S., et al., trans. *Apuleius.* 2 vols. LCL. London: Heinemann, 1965.
Glover, T. R., et al., trans. *Tertullian.* LCL. London: Heinemann, 1931.
Hardy, Ernest G. *Christianity and the Roman Government: A Study in Imperial Administration.* London: Allen & Unwin, 1925.
Herrmann, P., J. H. Waszink, K. Colpe, and R. Kotting. "Genossenschaft." *RAC* 10:81–135.
Hutchinson, W. M. L., et al., trans. *Pliny the Younger.* 2 vols. LCL. London: Heinemann, 1915.
Ker, Walter Charles Alan, et al., trans. *Martial.* 2 vols. LCL. London: Heinemann, 1919–1920.
Lake, Kirsopp, et al., trans. *Eusebius.* 2 vols. LCL. London: Heinemann, 1926–1932.
Moore, Clifford H., et al., trans. *Tacitus.* 5 vols. LCL. London: Heinemann, 1925–1937.
Neumann, K. J. "Coercitio." *PW* 4.1:201–4.
Price, S. R. F. *Rituals and Power: The Roman Imperial Cult in Asia Minor.* Cambridge: Cambridge University Press, 1984.
Ramsey, G. G., et al., trans. *Juvenal.* LCL. London: Heinemann, 1918.
Rendall, Gerald H., et al., trans. *Minucius Felix.* LCL. London: Heinemann, 1931.
Rolfe, J. C., et al., trans. *Suetonius.* 2 vols. LCL. London: Heinemann, 1914.
Schutter, William L. *Hermeneutic and Composition in 1 Peter.* WUNT 2/30. Tübingen: Mohr Siebeck, 1989.
Sordi, Marta. *The Christians and the Roman Empire.* Translated by A. Bedini. Norman: University of Oklahoma Press, 1986.

Do You Feel Comforted? M. Night Shyamalan's *Signs* and the Book of Job

J. Cheryl Exum

Early morning. Graham Hess, a farmer in Bucks County, Pennsylvania, wakes from his sleep with a jolt. The house is quiet. He is in the bathroom brushing his teeth when he hears a distant high-pitched scream. He looks in the children's room, and they are not there. Again a scream, and Graham's brother, Merrill, starts out of his sleep. Together they rush through the tall stalks of corn in the field, calling for the children, Morgan and Bo. The dogs are barking, the children are uneasy. In the middle of the field is a 500-foot crop circle. "I think God did it," says Morgan.[1]

"I think God did it" is not a throwaway line. M. Night Shyamalan's 2002 science-fiction film *Signs* is as much about God as it is about the invasion of the earth by extraterrestrials who, virtually overnight, create giant crop circles around the world. A clue is provided by the film's title, with its double meaning. Signs are crop signs, the geometrical markings made by the aliens to navigate by. Signs are also miracles, evidence of God's intervention in human affairs, a connection that the film itself makes.[2]

In terms of genre, *Signs* is best described as a science-fiction thriller. The sense of eeriness and foreboding created by the opening credits, the music, and the first scene, described above, grows as people are forced to accept the fact that the signs are not a colossal hoax. But *Signs* eludes

---

[1]. It is a pleasure to offer this paper in a volume honoring Kent Harold Richards, who, in his role as Executive Director of the Society of Biblical Literature, has done so much to foster biblical scholarship and to encourage new approaches such as that represented here.

[2]. See the dialogue between Graham and Merrill cited below.

easy classification. Like many of Shyamalan's films, it deals with seemingly ordinary people and what happens to them in abnormal circumstances.[3] According to Shyamalan, who both wrote and directed *Signs*, the movie is also about faith.[4] Viewers, too, have drawn attention to the film's religious dimension.[5] The story revolves around the Hess family and their response, over the course of a few days, to incredible and terrifying events as they swiftly unfold. Mel Gibson stars as Graham—I will call him Graham, though everyone in the film wants to call him "Father"—a former minister who left the church when his wife was killed in a freak automobile accident. He resumes his ministry when his children—and the world—are spared and the invaders depart. Does his journey from faith to rejection of God—even to the point of refusing to allow his family to pray—and then back to his earlier way of life and a restored relationship to God have anything to do with the book of Job? Graham's crisis of faith could be compared to Job's challenge to traditional piety when he accuses God of perverting justice and insists on his own integrity. Both Graham and Job suffer losses that disrupt their initial harmonious relationship with God, both wrestle with God in their own ways, and both are restored at the end.

No doubt the similarities are, to borrow a key concept from the film, coincidences. I am not suggesting that the book of Job inspired *Signs* or even that this film is about the same issues as Job.[6] Job is a classic, a profound literary masterpiece.[7] *Signs* is the work of an established director

---

3. E.g., in *The Lady in the Lake* a spirit from another world appears in a condominium swimming pool, and the residents, who initially find the idea absurd, join to help her return. In *The Sixth Sense* we learn only at the film's end that the psychiatrist trying to help a young boy who sees dead people is, himself, dead. *The Village* deals with the fear of the unknown and its effect on the residents, but the village itself turns out to be something different from what it seems.

4. Rebecca Murray, "Keeping the Faith in 'Signs,'" About.com; online: http://movies.about.com/library/weekly/aa072902a.htm. Like Hitchcock, whose influence on his oeuvre is obvious, Shyamalan likes to appear in his films; in *Signs* he plays Ray Reddy, the neighbor responsible for Graham's wife's death. Shyamalan is also known for his surprise endings.

5. See, among other sites, the comments at http://www.horrorwatch.com/reviews/movies/signs.shtml and http://brothersjudd.com/index.cfm/fuseaction/reviews.moviedetail/movie_id/63/Signs.htm.

6. It is not, e.g., about retribution or the wonders of the cosmos.

7. See, e.g., the Testimonia in David J. A. Clines, *Job 1–20* (WBC 17; Dallas: Word, 1989), ix; and idem, *Job 38–42* (WBC 18B; Nashville: Thomas Nelson, 2010), ix–x.

and boasts major stars (Mel Gibson as Graham, Joaquin Phoenix as his brother Merrill) who, along with Rory Calkin and Abigail Breslin as the children, give credible performances. One of Shyamalan's stronger films, it received generally positive reviews and did well at the box office.[8] It is a good film but not a great film, and its religious outlook, unlike Job's, is simplistic. Still, there are similarities between the film *Signs* and the biblical book of Job that make comparison both worthwhile and, I hope, illuminating. Job is about the relationship of God to the universe (clearly God is not concerned with justice; does he care about human beings and what they do?) and about human dissatisfaction with the way the universe is run.[9] One could say that *Signs* is about these issues, too; it just deals with them differently. In one important respect, Job and *Signs* are uncannily similar. They both raise the question, the possibility, of an inhospitable, unaccommodating universe, and the plot resolutions they provide beg the question.

The first part of this essay will discuss some of the more general or, if you prefer, more superficial, points of comparison between *Signs* and the book of Job. I will then turn to the question of endings, where, in spite of differences, the simpler resolution offered by *Signs* brings into relief the existential angst, "the ultimate disharmony of existence,"[10] that the epilogue of Job cannot adequately account for or explain away or reduce to something else.

---

8. See, e.g., the reviews posted at http://www.metacritic.com/movie/signs (not all the links are active, but the citations from them give a good idea of the critics' responses); see also http://en.wikipedia.org/wiki/Signs_(film).

9. Job is an individual, not a representative of humanity in general. Not everyone can expect to have his or her complaints answered in a theophany. Still, there is something universal about Job as he grapples with questions about suffering and fairness and the way the world operates. Comparison with another, in this case iconic, film, *The Wizard of Oz*, highlights the ambivalent portrayal of God; see Tod Linafelt, "The Wizard of Uz: Job, Dorothy, and the Limits of the Sublime," *BibInt* 14 (2006): 94–109, repr. in *The Bible in Film/The Bible and Film* (ed. J. Cheryl Exum; Leiden: Brill, 2006), 94–109.

10. The phrase is Karl Jaspers's, in *Tragedy Is Not Enough* (trans. H. A. T. Reiche, H. T. Moore, and K. W. Deutsch; Boston: Beacon, 1952), 45.

Does Job Serve God for Naught?

Readers of the book of Job know more than Job knows. Because we are privy to the scene in heaven in the prologue, we know that what happens is a test; it has nothing to do with retribution, the reward of the righteous and punishment of the wicked, which is the issue for Job and his friends. Viewers of the film, in contrast, do not have a privileged point of view; we see things through the eyes of the Hess family, particularly Graham. What happens to Graham is not a test, and God in the film is not a character who puts in a personal appearance, as he does in the book, though the people in the film find it easier to believe in God's existence than, initially, in that of extraterrestrials.[11] But the genuine theological question that gives rise to the test—does Job (or anyone, for that matter) serve God for naught?—is a question of great consequence for the film as much as it is for the book of Job. Is there a selfless piety? Do people worship God apart from what they get out of it? Whereas the answer of the book is not straightforward, the answer of the film is clearer: Graham does not serve God for naught, it would seem. When his wife is killed (we discover the details only over the course of the film, mainly through flashbacks), he leaves the church and turns his back on God. Just as Job takes his suffering as a personal attack, accusing God of persecuting him—"If I have sinned, what is it to you...? Why have you made me your target?" (7:20)—Graham takes the death of his wife personally. "Don't do this to me again! Not again," he tells God, when he thinks he is about to lose his son as well, "I hate you!" Although the film does not show him praying to God to spare his wife's life, we soon come to realize that he blames God for taking his wife away from him. At what may be the family's last supper, he refuses to let them pray, declaring, "I am not wasting one more minute of my life on prayer, not *one* more minute."

Both Job and Graham are angry at the god they have so faithfully served for not behaving as they believe God should behave. Whereas Graham will not waste his time on prayer, Job is "full of talk," as Zophar

---

11. Graham struggles against the dawning recognition that the extraterrestrial invasion is not a hoax. "Hundreds of thousands have flocked to synagogues, temples, and churches," a television reporter informs us (there is no mention of mosques), once the true nature of the threat becomes known. "God be with us all," he adds, and one wonders if the extraterrestrials are asking (their) god's blessing. Graham, though he has turned away from God, does not stop believing in God's existence (see below).

puts it. He insists, in the face of his friends' increasingly accusatory arguments, that, whatever his faults, he does not deserve all the calamities that God has brought upon him, and he accuses God of mismanaging the universe. He demands a trial so that he can argue his case before God, even though he knows one cannot contend with God and win (9:3, 14–20). Both men hold fast to their integrity. Job will not meekly accept the way God treats him: "He will kill me, I have no hope. Yet I will argue my cause to his face" (13:15). Graham will not turn to God, even in a time of dire need, when the earth is about to be destroyed. He is just as stubborn as Job is about maintaining his position.[12]

Meanwhile, Job's friends and Graham's, who disapprove of their new, antagonistic attitudes to God, endeavor to get them to change their way of thinking. Job's three friends, Eliphaz, Bildad, and Zophar, who come to comfort him, keep insisting that Job is wrong to accuse God and that, if he is righteous, God will restore his fortunes. Elihu, too, wants to set Job straight. Graham's fellow townspeople do not want to acknowledge his new-found nonreligious stance. To his consternation, they continue to call him "Father," from his friend the sheriff, to the young woman who works in the pharmacy and makes him hear her confession, to the neighbor responsible for his wife's death. "Please stop calling me 'Father,'" "It's not 'Father' anymore," he has to keep telling them. His son is upset by the change in his father, who seems to have lost his ability to cope and to offer his children the support they need,[13] but the strongest criticism comes from his brother Merrill. Merrill wants Graham to "pretend to be like you used to be" and "give me some comfort." After a terrifying night during which the family escapes hostile aliens by boarding themselves in the cellar, he demands that Graham change:

---

12. Job is more concerned with his integrity than his losses. In one sense, Graham is the reverse of Job: he loses his faith, in effect "cursing" God, when his wife dies. Though he loses his wife, his children are spared. Job loses his children, and does not seem to put much store in the fact that his wife is spared, calling her a foolish woman (2:10) and condemning her to physical abuse if he is proved guilty (31:10).

13. At one point his son wishes his uncle Merrill were his father because he offers more assurance, and, when Graham refuses to let them say a prayer, he says, "I hate you." Perhaps he is accusing his father of not having enough faith when he follows this up with, "You let Mom die." It is clear he does not mean what he says in this outburst, and the scene ends with Graham crying, Morgan going over to hug him, and Graham grabbing the whole family into a hug.

There are a lot of things I can take, and a few that I can't. What I can't take is when my older brother, who's everything that I want to be, starts losing faith in things. I saw that look in your eyes last night. I don't ever want to see that look in your eyes again.

Graham, like Job, has stood firm against criticism of his posture until now. He nods his head and says okay, but he cannot change what he believes just because his brother wants him to any more than Job can genuinely repent just because his friends call for it. Ultimately what brings about a change in Graham, as in Job, is a *deus ex machina*, unexplainable though not unexpected in terms of the plot development: in Job's case, the appearance of God; in Graham's, it is not so much the appearance of extraterrestrials as their hasty, unanticipated departure.

Is It Possible That There Are No Coincidences?

God's speeches to Job from the tempest constitute the turning point of the poem. Job has made his final, impassioned declaration of innocence (Job 29-31), and God answers him from the tempest,[14] overwhelming him with questions, as Job predicted he would (9:16-20), and holding before him the vision of a terrifyingly beautiful but morally unintelligible universe. In *Signs*, an alien invasion sets the stage for Graham's renewed faith and return to God, which does not takes place, however, until the film's end, when Morgan, near death from an attack by an alien left behind when the main force departed, revives. Earlier in the film, in a key scene between Graham and Merrill that takes place when the lights of unidentified crafts begin to appear in the sky, we discover how Graham, and perhaps the film, looks at the world.

Merrill:	Some people are probably thinking this is the end of the world.
Graham:	That's true.
Merrill:	Do you think it could be?
Graham:	Yes.
Merrill:	How can you say that?
Graham:	That wasn't the answer you wanted?

---

14. If the Elihu speeches properly belong before Job's defense; see David J. A. Clines, *Job 21-37* (WBC 18A; Nashville: Thomas Nelson, 2006), 709, 711 *et passim*.

Merrill:	Can't you pretend to be like you used to be—give me some comfort.
Graham:	People break down into two groups when they experience something lucky. Group number one sees it as more than luck, more than coincidence. They see it as a sign, evidence, that there is someone up there, watching out for them. Group number two sees it as just pure luck, a happy turn of chance. I'm sure that people in group number two are looking at those fourteen lights in a very suspicious way. For them, the situation is a fifty-fifty. Could be bad, could be good. But deep down, they feel that whatever happens, they're on their own. And that fills them with fear. Yeah, there are those people. But there's a whole lot of people in group number one. When they see those fourteen lights, they're looking at a miracle. And deep down, they feel that whatever's going to happen, there will be someone there to help them. And that fills them with hope. See, what you have to ask yourself is what kind of person are you? Are you the kind that sees signs, sees miracles? Or do you believe that people just get lucky? Or look at the question this way: Is it possible that there are no coincidences?

Possibly at this point Shyamalan wishes to distance himself from these alternatives, or perhaps he wants simply to inject a humorous vein, for Merrill offers a ludicrous explanation of why he believes in miracles (or maybe Shyamalan is aiming at realism by showing us the kind of silly thing one sometimes says in a critical situation). Merrill tells Graham about an opportunity he had to kiss a woman at a party: he paused to take his chewing gum out of his mouth, at which point she vomited all over herself.

Merrill:	I knew the second it happened, it was a miracle. I could have been kissing her when she threw up. That would have scarred me for life. I may never have recovered. I'm a miracle man. Those lights are a miracle.
Graham:	There you go.
Merrill:	So, which type are you?
Graham:	Do you feel comforted?
Merrill:	Yeah. I do.
Graham:	Then what does it matter?

But it does matter. Graham, who is still coming to terms with his wife's death some six months earlier, tells Merrill for the first time her dying words, "see" and "swing away." These words were sparked by a random memory of one of Merrill's baseball games that popped into her head, Graham explains, caused by nerve endings in her brain firing as she died. And so he discloses, after all, what he really believes: "There is no one watching out for us, Merrill, we are all on our own."[15] As Graham sees it, the alternative to no one watching out for us is that there are no coincidences, which Merrill's example takes to its extreme. But Merrill is not alone in believing there are no coincidences. Just before she dies, Graham's wife tells him, "It was meant to be," and the remorseful neighbor who caused her death takes the same view: "It had to be at that right moment, that ten, fifteen seconds when I passed her walking. It's like it was meant to be."[16]

Although the book of Job is not so simplistic in its theological outlook, according to the doctrine of retribution so vehemently defended by Job's friends, what happens to people is not coincidence but rather the result of their thoughts and acts. Even if retribution does not come swiftly, in the end the righteous will get their just reward, and the wicked will be punished. The suffering, the misery, the evil, and the inexplicable in the world can thus be understood as part of an inscrutable, larger plan for the good.

> Think now, who that was innocent ever perished?
> Where were the upright ever cut off? (Eliphaz, Job 4:7)

> Surely the lamp of the wicked is snuffed out,
> the flame of its fire does not shine. (Bildad, Job 18:5)

> the exulting of the wicked is short,
> and the rejoicing of the godless but for a moment.
> Though their height ascend to the heavens,
> and their head reach to the clouds,
> they will perish for ever like their dung....

---

15. Interestingly, the title of the book Morgan is reading about aliens, arguing—correctly, it turns out—that there are others in the universe, is *We Are Not Alone*. The book, of course, is not referring to "someone up there watching out for [us]."

16. He fell asleep at the wheel, something he had never done before, and ran into her, pinning her between the truck and the tree and severing her body. In flashbacks we see Graham arrive at the scene and speak to her before she dies.

> Their children will beg from the poor,
> and their hands will give back their wealth.
> Their bones are full of youthful vigor,
> but it will lie down with them in the dust. (Zophar, Job 20:5–11)
>
> Far be it from God to do wickedness,
> and from the Almighty to do wrong.
> For what humans do, he pays them back,
> and sees that they get what their conduct deserves. (Elihu, 34:10–11)

Job, too, believes in the doctrine of retribution, though he begins to question it. He believes that his intense suffering is unwarranted—his conduct merits reward, not punishment—and he castigates God for not giving him his due. He wants retribution and he wants it now, not later.

> Know then that God has put me in the wrong,
> and closed his net around me.
> If I cry out, "Violence!" I am not answered;
> I call aloud, but there is no justice. (19:6–7)

> How often is the lamp of the wicked snuffed out,
> and how often does their ruin come upon them? ...
> Does God store up their iniquity for their children?
> Let him punish the guilty, and let them know it.
> Let their own eyes see their destruction,
> and let them drink the anger of the Almighty.
> For what do they care for their household after them,
> when the number of their months comes to an end? (21:17-21)

In the end, Job receives from God twice as much as he had before (42:10). It could be argued that the epilogue to the book of Job confirms the doctrine of retribution, though the argument of the poem would suggest otherwise. Or, is Job's restoration to good fortune a coincidence?

Do You Feel Comforted?

What causes Job and Graham to change their minds, to abandon their oppositional stance toward God? A major conundrum for the interpretation of the book of Job is whether or not, in the light of what God has revealed about the design of the universe in the divine speeches, or in response to the fact that the master of this universe has deigned to appear to him, Job repents, as number of translations have it[17]—in which case the question must be, of what does he repent? It cannot be of what he has said about God, at least not entirely, since no less an authority than God himself informs us that Job has spoken "right" of him (42:7).[18] Or, does Job not repent of anything at all? His words in 42:6 can be translated, "I foreswear dust and ashes," the symbols of mourning,[19] or "I submit, and I accept consolation for my dust and ashes."[20] Job ceases to press his suit against God because he has come to understand that justice, and thus retribution, is not the principle upon which the world is founded.[21] He may

---

17. "I despise myself, and repent in dust and ashes" (NRSV, RSV, NIV); "I abhor myself, and repent in dust and ashes" (KJV, ASV); "I melt away; I repent in dust and ashes" (NEB). JPS, "I recant and relent, Being but dust and ashes" strains the sense of the Hebrew.

18. According to Newsom, the contradiction between Job's obscuring God's design by words without knowledge (38:2) and his speaking what is right of God is impossible to reconcile (Carol A. Newsom, "The Book of Job," *NIB* 6:634). It seems to me more likely that, as Clines argues (*Job 38–42*, 196-97), although God reproaches Job for focusing solely on justice, he commends Job for recognizing that the world is not governed by justice; the friends, in contrast, were wrong in maintaining that God governs the world in terms of retributive justice. It is unlikely that God is referring only to Job's replies in 40:4-5 and 42:2-6, since Job hardly seems to have said enough of substance about God here to merit the assessment "right" (196). David Robertson, who argues that Job's repentance is "tongue in cheek" and that he does not mean any of it, points out a number of things that Job has said about God that are true: that God is arbitrary, elusive, inhumane, God's wisdom is folly, God perverts justice, and even if he were given a chance to make his case to God, God would overwhelm him in a tempest and cause him to condemn himself, although he is blameless (9:16-20) (David Robertson, "The Book of Job: A Literary Study," *Sound* 56 [1973]: 446-69; idem, *The Old Testament and the Literary Critic* [Philadelphia: Fortress, 1977], 33-54).

19. Dale Patrick, "The Translation of Job xlii 6," *VT* 26 (1976): 369-71.

20. Clines, *Job 38–42*, 174-75. Newsom lists five major options for translating 42:6 and points out that how one understands this verse depends on how one interprets the rest of the book ("The Book of Job," 628-29; see also, Samuel E. Balentine, *Job* (Macon, Ga.: Smyth & Helwys, 2006), 693-95.

21. Clines comments, "Job will withdraw his suit not because he has lost his case but because, given the attitude of his opponent, he finally despairs totally of ever winning it—and even of having it heard" (*Job 38–42*, 181). Cf. Edwin M. Good, who takes "I despise and repent of dust and ashes" to mean that Job repents of repentance; that is, he renounces the entire religious structure of guilt and innocence (*In Turns of Tempest: A Reading of Job with a Translation* [Stanford, Calif.: Stanford University Press,

be impressed by the "marvels [God] has lavishly scattered throughout the universe,"[22] but he has no choice but to accept the world the way it is and to get on with living as best he can.

Another crucial, and more undecidable, question is posed by the epilogue to Job: Why does God restore Job's fortunes? Suddenly we encounter a god very much interested in human affairs and what is "right" and who considers Job his "servant" (four times in 42:7–8)—the same god who brought so much misfortune upon Job (42:11) without cause (2:3). Does God restore Job's fortunes because he repents? Would that not confirm the principle of retribution? After all, his friends have been telling him that he needs to repent to win God's favor. Is Job restored because he prays on behalf of his friends? The efficacy of prayer would be a perfect ending for *Signs*, but it comes as something of a surprise in Job.[23] Job's intercession on behalf of his children (1:5) was no more effective than Graham's prayers for his wife to live, so what makes this prayer different?[24] Does Job have a choice? Must he pray for his friends, who have maligned him throughout much of the book and who have not spoken what is "right" of God? Is Job's restoration his reward for passing what we know from the prologue is a test? Is it "an act of grace?"[25] Or is restoring to Job more than he had lost God's way of paying compensation for the wrong he has done to

---

1990], 375–78, 383); and Norman C. Habel, who understands "I retract and repent of dust and ashes" as Job's withdrawal of his suit because God's appearance to him vindicates his innocence and is "clear evidence of his good will," thus making it futile to pursue a case based on the principle of retribution (*The Book of Job* [OTL; London: SCM, 1985], 575–76, 579, 582–83 [citation from 582]).

22. Édouard Dhorme, *A Commentary on the Book of Job* (trans. Harold Knight; Nashville: Thomas Nelson, 1984), 647.

23. If, as Balentine (*Job*, 712–13) suggests, Job's prayer should be for the sake of both God and the friends, since it prevents God from dealing reprehensibly with the friends, imagine the irony of an ending to *Signs* in which Graham prays for the sake of the god who once let him down by not answering his prayer. Clines wonders if having to pray for his friends is another test that Job must undergo in order to be restored (*Job 38–42*, 199–200).

24. One difference is that we know in advance that it will be accepted, and, assuming his friends tell him what God has said to them (for God does not address Job in the epilogue), so does Job. Another is that, rather than focusing on himself as Job has been doing, this time he does something on behalf of others. As Clines points out (*Job 38–42*, 199), it is unlikely that a contrast is meant between the inefficacy of Job's sacrifices in 1:5 and the efficacy of his prayer in 42:10.

25. Habel, *The Book of Job*, 584.

Job?²⁶ Has Job undergone some inner transformation that the poet leaves for us to surmise? Is restoration a serendipity, something that simply happens regardless of anything Job does? In other words, if from the poem we have learned our lesson that justice is not the principle upon which the world is founded, we will not see Job's restoration in the epilogue as validating the doctrine of retribution. But it is hard not to, isn't it? Perhaps the poet relates Job's restoration to give us a happy or satisfying ending,²⁷ to make the poem more orthodox, or to make the book more intellectually engaging by leaving loose ends to needle us rather than tying them up in a tidy package.²⁸

Fewer questions are posed by Graham's conversion. *Signs* presents Graham's existential dilemma—either there are no coincidences or we are all on our own—rather starkly and lets viewers down when it resolves the question too easily. After a night in the cellar, a night they fear they will not survive, the Hess family hears on the radio that the aliens have been defeated and have departed in haste, leaving some of their wounded behind. Morgan has suffered a severe asthma attack and needs his medicine, so they cautiously make their way upstairs to the living room. Everything seems to be in order. Graham and Merrill leave the room briefly. When they come back, they find an alien holding Morgan. Graham, Merrill, and Bo watch, petrified, as it releases a poisonous gas into his face. At this point, there is a flashback, as Graham remembers his wife's dying words and asks himself if it is possible that there are no coincidences. She had told him to see. He looks around the room and spies the baseball bat hanging on the wall, a souvenir of a minor league record Merrill once set. She told him to tell Merrill to "swing away." And so he does: "Swing away, Merrill. Merrill, swing away." Merrill takes the bat and hits the alien in the small of the back, causing it to drop Morgan. Graham grabs his son and rushes outside. Merrill and Bo watch anxiously as Graham gives him an epinephrine injection. Morgan is not dead. "That's why he had asthma," says Graham. "It can't be luck. His lungs were closed.

---

26. Clines, *Job 38–42*, 202.
27. What happened to Job, his suffering, was not a coincidence according to the prologue, where we see Job's fate decided in the divine council.
28. I find the book of Job wonderfully self-deconstructing: the poem says that retribution does not work; the prose folktale suggests it does. See David J. A. Clines, "Deconstructing the Book of Job," in *What Does Eve Do to Help? And Other Readerly Questions to the Old Testament* (JSOTSup 94; Sheffield: JSOT Press, 1994), 106–23.

No poison could get in." Whereas, after his wife's death, Graham could not, would not, accept the possibility that there are no coincidences, now, in the face of this evidence, he does. Morgan opens his eyes and asks, "Did someone save me?" "I think someone did," replies Graham, amid tears.

Graham, it seems, has changed his mind about coincidences and, like other characters in the film, decided that things are meant to be. It cannot be luck. He has become the kind of person who sees signs and miracles. The implications of this position, however, are troubling: his son has asthma so that he can survive the alien attack; he has to lose his wife in order not to lose his son. It seems a high price to pay. Nor can Job's new sons and daughters compensate for the ones he lost, who cannot be replaced so easily as sheep, camels, oxen, and donkeys.[29] Ironically, when Graham believed that prayer could save his wife, he did not get what he prayed for, but when he refuses to pray, to waste even one more minute of his life on prayer, he gets what he wants. Does this sound at all like Job, who believes in the doctrine of retribution but does not receive his just reward for his righteous life, yet, when he recognizes the fallacy of retribution, gets what looks suspiciously like a reward?

Like the book of Job, *Signs* has an epilogue. The scene has shifted from summer to winter. We see snow falling through the bedroom window. Graham enters the room, wearing his ministerial collar. Laughter can be heard from somewhere in the house as he leaves the room. All's well with the world. Or is it?

The epilogue to *Signs* is like the epilogue to Job in a number of ways. It is brief, the hero is no longer defiant, and he is restored to his previous way of life. Whether or not Job's harmonious relationship to God is reestablished, we cannot be sure. Is Job simply going through the motions of piety, having resigned himself to a grand design he cannot comprehend? Can we really be sure about Graham? Neither protagonist says anything about the change in himself,[30] and neither the film nor the biblical book offers much clarification. Through its conspicuously disquieting ending, *Signs* sheds particular light on the book of Job. It is surprising that the aliens depart so unexpectedly. Reports say a primitive method was found

---

29. We should not forget the servants, some slaughtered by the Sabeans, some killed by the Chaldeans, and others burned alive by a fire from heaven (1:15–17).

30. The only speech in the epilogue to the book is God's (42:7–8), and it is not even addressed to Job. There is no speech in the epilogue to *Signs*.

to defeat them, though no one knows the details.[31] Apparently they are susceptible to water, which burns them. They may no longer pose a threat, but what is to prevent them from returning? All they need is some nifty waterproof spacesuits, which should be no problem for a civilization that can build spaceships.[32] In fact, the possibility of their return is raised by the book about extraterrestrials that Morgan has been reading. It explains that, if extraterrestrials invade the earth and are defeated, they will probably return with full forces hundreds or even thousands of years later. Why not sooner? So the question viewers are left with at the film's end is, can a restored Graham feel secure in such a universe? Similarly, we might ask, can a restored Job trust God again? Who knows what further debates might arise in the divine council? God could decide to test Job another time. Or, in a world where catastrophes simply happen, calamity could strike again.

Both *Signs* and the book of Job make us aware of the precarious lot of humanity in a world that is now and then bewildering and unaccommodating. In spite of its "happy ending," the book of Job's refusal to minimize the possibility of cosmic indifference to human misfortune is one of the things that make Job a tragic figure—for Richard Sewall, "the towering tragic figure of antiquity."[33] The resolution is simply not sufficient in either power or conviction to transform the book into a comedy.[34] The questions

---

31. As noted above, God's appearance to Job and the aliens' departure are turning points in the book and film. Why the aliens depart is not entirely clear. Nor is it entirely clear why God appears to Job. In an important study, Tsevat proposed that Job's oath in Job 31 compels God to respond, either by bringing the curses upon Job (which would be tantamount to conviction) or not bringing the curses upon Job (which would amount to acquittal) or by responding personally to the oath; see Matitiahu Tsevat, "The Meaning of the Book of Job," *HUCA* 37 (1966): 73–106, esp. 77–79; repr. in *Studies in Ancient Israelite Wisdom* (ed. James L. Crenshaw [New York: Ktav, 1976], 341–74, esp. 345–7; see also Edwin M. Good, "Job and the Literary Task: A Response," *Sound* 56 (1973): 470–84; and idem, *In Turns of Tempest*, 314.

32. With their superior intelligence, it is odd that the aliens are unable to break into the Hess's house and that they can be locked in cupboards.

33. Richard B. Sewall, *The Vision of Tragedy* (New Haven: Yale University Press, 1980), 9. On the terror of the Joban universe, see Timothy K. Beal, *Religion and Its Monsters* (London: Routledge, 2002), 47–56.

34. Another thing that makes Job tragic is not so much his suffering as his struggle to know the cause of his suffering and his refusal to accept blame; see J. Cheryl Exum, *Tragedy and Biblical Narrative* (Cambridge: Cambridge University Press,

that the book of Job raises about suffering, about God's interest in human beings, and about cosmic intelligibility are questions it resolves only aesthetically, not thematically.[35] Indeed, Job is so fascinating, in part, for the very reason that it resists the efforts of readers to find simple or straightforward answers and to resolve or reduce its vision of the cosmos into a harmonious, reassuring whole. Tragedy, observes Sewall, "is not for those who cannot live with unsolved questions or unresolved doubts."[36] It may be comforting to know that we humans are not the measure of all things but only part of a vast, complex, wonderful and terrible universe, and that we suffer without cause. But how comforting is a god who tests?

Signs, too, displays resistance to resolution. As one viewer puts it, "[T]here is real reconciliation.... However, it is all left very cryptic. There's no mention of God. We are left to draw our own conclusions based on whatever we believe."[37] Both Job and Graham suffer from what George Steiner sees as an essential ingredient of tragedy, "the intolerable burden of God's presence."[38] Is there, for either of them, a prospect of harmony with their world or, more precisely, with God as constructed by the poet of Job and by M. Night Shyamalan? On what is it founded? The epilogues to both *Signs* and Job leave readers and viewers with a vague feeling of uncertainty. Or look at the question this way: Do you feel comforted?

1992), 11–13 *et passim*. For a sophisticated reading of Job as comedy, see J. William Whedbee, *The Bible and the Comic Vision* (Minneapolis: Fortress, 2002), 221–62. Northrop Frye's observation that Athena's appearance at the end of the *Eumenides* does not turn the *Oresteia* into a comedy but rather clarifies its tragic vision applies *mutatis mutandis* to Job (*Anatomy of Criticism* [New York: Atheneum, 1966], 209).

35. On this understanding of tragedy as resolving the tension of the tragic vision aesthetically, while leaving it thematically unrelieved, see Murray Krieger, *The Classic Vision* (Baltimore: Johns Hopkins University Press, 1960), 4–8, 36–39; idem, *The Tragic Vision* (Baltimore: Johns Hopkins University Press, 1960), 2–4; and idem, "The Tragic Vision: Twenty Years After," in *Tragedy: Vision and Form* (ed. Robert W. Corrigan; 2nd ed.; New York: Harper & Row, 1981), 42–46.

36. Sewall, *The Vision of Tragedy*, 5.

37. Matthew Hudswell, "M Night Shyamalan's 'Signs,' Starring Mel Gibson," *Facing the Challenge*, http://www.facingthechallenge.org/signs.php.

38. George Steiner, *The Death of Tragedy* (New York: Oxford University Press, 1980), 353.

Bibliography

Balentine, Samuel E. *Job*. Macon, Ga: Smyth & Helwys, 2006.
Beal, Timothy K. *Religion and Its Monsters*. London: Routledge, 2002.
Clines, David J. A. "Deconstructing the Book of Job." Pages 106–23 in *What Does Eve Do to Help? And Other Readerly Questions to the Old Testament*. JSOTSup 94. Sheffield: JSOT Press, 1994.
———. *Job 1–20*. WBC 17. Dallas: Word, 1989.
———. *Job 21–37*. WBC 18A. Nashville: Thomas Nelson, 2006.
———. *Job 38–42*. WBC 18B. Nashville: Thomas Nelson, 2010.
Dhorme, Édouard. *A Commentary on the Book of Job*. Translated by Harold Knight. Nashville: Thomas Nelson, 1984.
Exum, J. Cheryl. *Tragedy and Biblical Narrative*. Cambridge: Cambridge University Press, 1992.
Frye, Northrop. *Anatomy of Criticism*. New York: Atheneum, 1966.
Good, Edwin M. *In Turns of Tempest: A Reading of Job with a Translation*. Stanford, Calif.: Stanford University Press, 1990.
———. "Job and the Literary Task: A Response." *Sound* 56 (1973): 470–84.
Habel, Norman C. *The Book of Job*. OTL. London: SCM, 1985.
Jaspers, Karl. *Tragedy Is Not Enough*. Translated by H. A. T. Reiche, H. T. Moore, and K. W. Deutsch. Boston: Beacon, 1952.
Krieger, Murray. *The Classic Vision*. Baltimore: Johns Hopkins University Press, 1960.
———. *The Tragic Vision*. Baltimore: Johns Hopkins University Press, 1960.
———. "The Tragic Vision: Twenty Years After." Pages 42–46 in *Tragedy: Vision and Form*. Edited by Robert W. Corrigan. 2nd ed. New York: Harper & Row, 1981.
Linafelt, Tod. "The Wizard of Uz: Job, Dorothy, and the Limits of the Sublime." *BibInt* 14 (2006): 94–109. Repr. as pages 94–109 in *The Bible in Film/The Bible and Film*. Edited by J. Cheryl Exum. Leiden: Brill, 2006.
Newsom, Carol A. "The Book of Job." *NIB* 6:319–637.
Patrick, Dale. "The Translation of Job xlii 6." *VT* 26 (1976): 369–71.
Robertson, David. "The Book of Job: A Literary Study." *Sound* 56 (1973): 446–69.
———. *The Old Testament and the Literary Critic*. Philadelphia: Fortress, 1977.

Sewall, Richard B. *The Vision of Tragedy*. New Haven: Yale University Press, 1980.
Steiner, George. *The Death of Tragedy*. New York: Oxford University Press, 1980.
Tsevat, Matitiahu. "The Meaning of the Book of Job." *HUCA* 37 (1966): 73–106. Rep. as pages 341–74 in *Studies in Ancient Israelite Wisdom*. Edited by James L. Crenshaw. New York: Ktav, 1976.
Whedbee, J. William. *The Bible and the Comic Vision*. Minneapolis: Fortress, 2002.

Canaan, Land of Promise: An Ecological Reading of Genesis 10:15–20 in Context

Norman Habel

Over the years I have often addressed Christian groups and asked the pointed question: What was God doing in Australia before the Europeans came? I asked them whether God was waiting for Captain Cook to discover the country or for the first missionaries to arrive. I suggested their theology might allow for a God who created, or even played with, a platypus. I found that few had ever really explored the question of God's presence and purpose in a distant land of indigenous peoples.

Now, in appreciation for the work of Kent Harold Richards and his role in supporting ecological hermeneutics as part of the SBL agenda, I would like to pursue an ecological reading, in context, of a rather forgotten text: Gen 10:15–20. To do so, I would like to commence by framing a question similar to that posed above. What was God doing in Canaan before the Israelites, "the people of God," arrived? Or, to put the question another way, Who is the Canaan of this text?

The principles and process of contemporary ecological hermeneutics are enunciated in the SBL Symposium Series volume entitled *Exploring Ecological Hermeneutics*,[1] a publication encouraged by Richards. Ecological hermeneutics, however, is an evolving skill, and recent explorations have led to an appreciation of habitat as an important dimension of this hermeneutic.[2]

---

1. Norman Habel and Peter Trudinger, eds., *Exploring Ecological Hermeneutics* (SBLSymS 46; Atlanta: Society of Biblical Literature, 2008).

2. In this context, we are especially indebted to the work of Lorraine Code, *Ecological Thinking: The Politics of Epistemic Location* (Oxford: Oxford University Press, 2006), 25.

Beyond the strictly biological and geological interdependency we experience, this habitat called Earth is also a complex world of interacting presences that impinge upon us from birth to death, forming and transforming us as Earth beings, social beings, and thinking beings. From the presence of a towering mountain or the sight of a threatening storm to the delicate wing of a butterfly or the so-called weeds that invade our garden, we are enveloped by environmental influences that mold our minds, our spirits, and our culture.s Habitat speaks of the place where the material, social, natural, and spiritual interact creatively.

In this study, I plan to explore, briefly, dimensions of Canaan as a habitat, taking the relevant text of Gen 10 as my point of departure.

Canaan the Cursed

The first dilemma we face is that the context of Gen 9 has biased many a reader before even reaching the text in question. After Ham "sees" his father's nakedness, whatever that might ultimately mean, Noah wakes from his drunken state and pronounces a curse on his grandson Canaan: "Cursed be Canaan, the lowest of slaves shall he be to his brothers!" (Gen 9:25). So the vivid story of Noah's drunkenness, Ham's actions, and Canaan's curse tend to blind the reader to the distinctive portrait of Canaan in Gen 10. The first time we meet Canaan, he is cursed and apparently destined to be a slave. What hope is there for Canaan?

Significantly, this curse and related texts influenced the people who came to promised lands like Australia. Australian Aborigines were said to be cursed, to have lost the image of God, and to live like animals that could be hunted down and destroyed. Harris records the attitude of a number of early European settlers:

> it was not simply that "like the Hittites, and the Jebusites and the Aboriginal Canaanites, they had been left to the natural consequences of not retaining the knowledge of God" but that of all people in that condition, the Aborigines were judged to be on "the lowest scale of degraded humanity."[3]

---

3. John W. Harris, *One Blood: 200 Years of Aboriginal Encounter with Christianity: A Story of Hope* (Sydney: Albatross, 1990), 30.

What happens to Canaan the grandson of Noah in Gen 9 tends to hinder our capacity to empathize with Canaan the land. The text of Gen 10, however, I would argue, reflects a very different tradition about a land whose voice deserves to be heard without the curse of Gen 9 ringing in our ears.

Canaan the Promised Land

The other factor that is likely to influence our reading of Gen 10 is the extensive range of passages relating to the promised land in Deuteronomy and Joshua. On the one hand, Canaan is described as a good land

> with flowing streams, with springs and underground waters, welling up in valleys and hills, a land of wheat and barley, of vines and fig trees and pomegranates, a land of olive trees and honey, a land where you may eat bread without scarcity, where you will lack nothing. (Deut 8:7–9 NRSV)

The impression is given here that God was in Canaan preparing a land of plenty for the incoming people of Israel. The focus lies on God preparing the land and then giving this land to a chosen people. The role of Canaan as a specific habitat molding the generations before Israel arrives is generally ignored.

On the other hand, Canaan is described as a land inhabited by seven nations, identified as the Hittites, the Girgashites, the Amorites, the Canaanites, the Perizzites, the Hivites, and the Jebusites. Nothing is said about the relation of Canaan to these people. The implication seems to be that the habitat of Canaan fostered false gods. The question of what God was doing with these peoples in a land promised to Israel is totally ignored.

Rather, a promise is given that these peoples will be cleared from "the land" (Deut 7:1). Canaan, the habitat for these peoples for centuries, is left without a chance to defend her role in nurturing these peoples. Instead, because they worship other gods than YHWH, they are, according to Deuteronomy, to be destroyed in case they intermarry with Israelites and lead them to worship false gods. The question of what God was doing in Canaan among these seven nations remains unanswered.

The promise of Canaan is cited in Joshua as a charter that justifies the invasion of land, the conquest of the Canaanites, and the allocation of the land to Israelite families. The granting and allocation of land seems to be portrayed as equivalent to a legal grant of property.[4] The Joshua narrative grounds ancient Israel's claim to land in both divine right and legal authority. Canaan is viewed as *terra nullius*, a land without legal inhabitants. Her rights are denied. Her very identity as a nurturing habitat is ignored.

How is this divine right interpreted? After visiting the obliging Canaanite Rahab and returning to Joshua, the spies announce what amounts to a divine verdict on the situation: "Truly YHWH has given all the land into your hands" (Josh 2:24). In other words, the narrator claims that ancient Israel can possess the land as a grant by divine right. Evidence of this forthcoming possession is that the inhabitants have been transformed into weaklings "melting with fear."

Ancient Israel's divine right to the promised land is also interpreted as a right to conquer, kill, and destroy. In fact, this process goes so far as to "devote to YHWH by destroying" (*ḥerem*). Destroying all cities, lives, and livestock is viewed by the primary narrator as a mandate from YHWH to dedicate the conquest to YHWH. A devastated land is apparently all that will remain after YHWH has been satisfied with destruction in his name. Anyone, like Achan, who dares to defy this mandate, is burned alive.

Perhaps the story of the killing fields of Canaan can be summarized in the recurring line: "[Joshua] struck it with the edge of the sword, and every person in it he utterly destroyed that day!" (Josh 10:30, 32, 35, 39). The outcome of these campaigns is summarized as a total conquest that corresponds to God's promise. Joshua takes "the whole land according to what the Lord has spoken to Moses" (11:23). Canaan is here the land God promised to assign to Joshua's people by conquest, destruction, and killing. The promised land in the book of Joshua is a land flowing not only with milk and honey but with blood and brutality. The voice of this land is suppressed beneath shouts of conquest.

---

4. Harry Orlinsky, "The Biblical Concept of the Land of Israel: Cornerstone of the Covenant between God and Israel," in *The Land of Israel: Jewish Perspectives* (ed. Lawrence A. Hoffman; University of Notre Dame Center for the Study of Judaism and Christianity in Antiquity 6; Notre Dame, Ind.: University of Notre Dame Press, 1986), 27–64.

Canaan, a Primal Habitat

If we now turn to the text of Gen 10 and set aside the ideologies of Gen 9, Deuteronomy, and Joshua, we may discern another legend of Canaan.

Genesis 10 is usually described as a genealogy listing the descendants of the sons of Noah. With the introduction of Canaan in verse 15, however, the pattern changes. While the first two names listed are the individuals Sidon and Heth, those that follow are peoples: the Jebusites, the Amorites, the Girgashites, the Hivites, the Arkites, the Sinites, the Arvadites, the Zemarites and the Hamathites. The territory of Canaan is then described as extending from Sidon in the north to Lasha in the south.

This Gen 10 tradition offers an alternative portrait of peoples, cultures, and nations expanding across Earth without necessarily being in conflict or subordinating one group to another. Throughout this genealogy of Ham, Canaan is not cursed but is portrayed as an ancestor whose progeny also seems to spread across particular domains of Earth as part of a natural process of selection. For Canaan, "after the flood" means peoples moving into her territories and developing distinctive cultures.

According to Cassuto, "The purpose of this list is not to tell us that a racial kinship existed between the peoples and tribes enumerated therein, but only to indicate who were the inhabitants of the country called in the Torah, the land of Canaan, and thereby define the boundaries of the land that was assigned to the children of Israel."[5] But is this reference to Canaan in Gen 10 simply an anticipation of the promised-land legend, a mere definition of her boundaries?

The peoples and locations incorporated in the legend of Canaan, I would contend, need not be viewed simply as denoting the boundaries of a land yet to be invaded by the Israelites. Rather, Canaan is identified as a habitat where several cultures and ethnic groups emerge. As a habitat, Canaan is the material, social, and spiritual context where people of diverse cultures are nurtured. Canaan the person merges with Canaan the land, a home for all kinds of Canaanites with diverse languages, families, and customs. Canaan is here a primal habitat creating cultures, not a polluted land whose cultures deserve to be cleared. Further, I would suggest,

---

5. Umberto Cassuto, *From Adam to Abraham: A Commentary on the Book of Genesis* (trans. Israel Abrahams; 2 vols.; Jerusalem: Magnes, 1964), 2:209.

this Canaan legend preserved the memory of God's presence and involvement in Canaan long before the Israelites arrived.

There is no indication here that the languages and cultures nurtured by Canaan are to be condemned because they worshiped deities other than YHWH. Canaan, moreover, is portrayed as the location where languages and cultures emerged quite independent of the Babel legend, which claims all languages emanated from the tower of Babel episode.

The fact that the land of Canaan also shelters and nurtures peoples of non-Canaanite origin suggests that Canaan is a land where other peoples were welcome. Canaan is depicted as a host to more than Canaanites. As a host country, Canaan here has a positive image, a territory open and diverse. In short, Canaan is a land of promise for several peoples in this text, not just for one!

A rich understanding of Canaan as a primal spiritual habitat is something sensed by some indigenous Australians. They experienced the language of missionaries who spoke of the promised land intended for Europeans but said little about the spirituality of the indigenous inhabitants or of the land itself. If Australia is indeed "Canaan" for the incoming peoples, then it is time to affirm God's presence in this land by sharing her habitat with its indigenous inhabitants rather than treating her as *terra nullius* and conquering her as Joshua did.[6]

Canaan, a Host Country

Like other peoples, Terah decides to migrate to Canaan with this son Abram and his nephew Lot. They settle in Haran until Terah dies. Thereupon, Abram travels to Canaan and passes through the land until he reaches Shechem. As the narrative recalls briefly and without comment, "The Canaanites were in the land" (Gen 12:6).

At various points in the Abraham legends, mention is made of YHWH promising the land of Canaan to Abraham's offspring, thereby anticipating a promised-land ideology. Is there any indication that the Canaan Abraham enters is consistent with the tradition in Gen 10 that reflects Canaan as the nurturing host?

This ideology of land as host country associated with Canaan in the Abraham narrative is one that I identified some years ago. This host orien-

---

6. See appendix 2 in Rainbow Spirit Elders, *Rainbow Spirit Theology: Towards an Australian Aboriginal Theology* (Melbourne: HarperCollins Religious, 1997).

tation is to be sharply distinguished from a range of other land ideologies elsewhere in the Hebrew Scriptures.[7]

Canaan welcomes Abraham. Canaan is the host, the potential habitat and home for Abraham and his family. Canaan is the host, and Abraham is the guest along with a "rich" entourage of livestock and goods (Gen 13:2). The first conflict Abraham experiences is not with Canaan or the Canaanites but with his nephew Lot, who agrees to separate and enjoy a different region of the land.

The legend of Gen 14 is quite remarkable in this context. Abraham is a guest in the host land of Canaan but is also described as an ally of locals who is ready to fight for them against invading armies from the east. Canaan is a land where guests and hosts have bonded before YHWH is identified.

The most striking expression of Canaan as host, however, takes place after the battle with the invaders. Abraham and the king of Sodom are met by Melchizedek, king of Salem. As a priest, he welcomes them with bread and wine, an obvious ritual of hospitality and public welcome. Melchizedek is Canaan personified. Even more significant, perhaps, is the blessing of Melchizedek: "Blessed be Abram by El Elyon, maker of heaven and earth" (Gen 14:19). This is not the place to debate the origin of the name El Elyon, a name for God that is later identified with YHWH (14:22). Abraham clearly recognizes this God, the God of Canaan in this context, as the creator. El Elyon represents the spiritual dimension of the land, the host country, the habitat of Jebusites and other peoples.

Here Canaan is not the land to be invaded and cleansed because it is polluted with pagan gods. Here Canaan is also God's abode. What was God doing in Canaan before the grand invasion of Joshua? Welcoming Abraham—and much more! God was creating peoples and habitats, cultures and covenants.

Canaan, a Covenant Land

Another passage in the Abraham tradition that is relevant here is the covenant with Abimelech. In spite of his prior relations with Abraham, Abimelech recognizes that God is with Abraham, a stranger and guest in

---

7. Norman Habel, *The Land Is Mine: Six Biblical Land Ideologies* (OBT; Minneapolis: Fortress, 1995), 115–33.

the land, and he states: "as I have dealt loyally with you, you will deal loyally with me and the land where you have resided as an alien" (Gen 21:23). Abimelech asks for covenant loyalty from Abraham in all future relations. The ecological significance of this text, however, has largely been ignored. Abimelech, the Canaanite host who appears to have some sensitivity to the land where Abraham is residing, asks for loyalty not only to Abimelech as host but also to the very land where Abraham resides as an alien. The technical term for loyalty here is *ḥesed*, a term that frequently refers to covenant loyalty and faithfulness. Abraham is asked to have the same relationship with the land as he does with fellow humans with whom he makes a covenant. In other words, Abraham makes a covenant with Canaan—the host country as well as the host people.

Later, when there is a dispute about a local well, this relationship leads to a formal covenant with sacrificed animals and a formal oath (21:25–34). Once again it is the Canaanite God El, here designated El Olam, that Abraham recognizes in Beersheba, where he plants a tamarisk tree. This tree becomes part of the covenant site, the symbol of God's presence in the land when Joshua arrives.

When ancient covenants were made, components of nature were often called upon to witness the covenant. Joshua calls upon a stone to witness his covenant with God (Josh 24:27). Canaan, in this Abraham legend, is not only a witness to the covenant but a party to the promise of loyalty. And this Canaan seems to be consistent with the Canaan in the tradition we have traced from Gen 10. What might the voice of this Canaan be as promised-land ideologies of later writers became dominant?

The Voice of Canaan

Daniel Hillel, in his recent work, *The Natural History of the Bible*, speaks of five principal ecological domains in Canaan, "the rainfed (relatively humid) domain, the pastoral (semi-arid) domain, the riverine domain, the maritime (coastal) domain, and the desert domain."[8] Each of these domains may well nurture distinct habitats. The region of wells that Abraham and Abimelech share is clearly one such habitat. The diverse range of peoples named in Gen 10:15–20 suggests that Canaan provided a diversity

---

8. Daniel Hillel, *The Natural History of the Bible: An Environmental Exploration of the Hebrew Scriptures* (New York: Columbia University Press, 2006), 14.

of social and spiritual habitats long before the arrival of Israel. Canaan was indeed a land of promise and formation for many peoples, not just for one.

What might be the voice of Canaan in this tradition? What if we now empathize with the primal habitat called Canaan?

> I am Canaan. I am a land of promise for many peoples. I have provided a primal habitat for cultures to emerge beside the sea, in my hills, and on my deserts. I have springs, rivers, and underground streams. I am a fertile home for those who bond with me and share my resources.
>
> Peoples have interacted with my environment for thousands of years, from the day humans knew me as home. They have discerned the spiritual in my domains and the sacred in my mountains. They knew the spiritual in my midst as El, the Creator. I am Canaan, a host country for peoples to share and celebrate the Creator.
>
> I was a host country who welcomed strangers like Abraham and Sarah. I made a covenant with Abimelech and Abraham. I nurtured the children of Abraham together with many other peoples. They are all my children and know my spirit.
>
> Why, if I am a land of promise for many peoples who share me in peace, should I become the promised land for but one people? Why?
>
> So what was God doing in my midst before the Israelites arrived? Creating a land of promise for many peoples to share!

Bibliography

Cassuto, Umberto. *From Adam to Abraham: A Commentary on the Book of Genesis*. Translated by Israel Abrahams. 2 vols. Jerusalem: Magnes, 1964.

Code, Lorraine. *Ecological Thinking: The Politics of Epistemic Location*. Oxford: Oxford University Press, 2006

Habel, Norman. *The Land Is Mine: Six Biblical Land Ideologies*. OBT. Minneapolis: Fortress, 1995.

Habel, Norman, and Peter Trudinger, eds. *Exploring Ecological Hermeneutics*. SBLSymS 46. Atlanta: Society of Biblical Literature, 2008.

Harris, John W. *One Blood: 200 Years of Aboriginal Encounter with Christianity: A Story of Hope*. Sydney: Albatross, 1990.

Hillel, Daniel. *The Natural History of the Bible: An Environmental Exploration of the Hebrew Scriptures*. New York: Columbia University Press, 2006.

Lemche, Niels Peter. *The Canaanites and Their Land: The Tradition of the Canaanites*. JSOTSup 110. Sheffield: JSOT Press, 1991.

Orlinsky, Harry. "The Biblical Concept of the Land of Israel: Cornerstone of the Covenant between God and Israel." Pages 27–64 in *The Land of Israel: Jewish Perspectives*. Edited by Lawrence A. Hoffman. University of Notre Dame Center for the Study of Judaism and Christianity in Antiquity 6. Notre Dame, Ind.: University of Notre Dame Press, 1986.

Rainbow Spirit Elders. *Rainbow Spirit Theology: Towards an Australian Aboriginal Theology*. Melbourne: HarperCollins Religious, 1997.

Revising the Myth of the "Biblical Family": Reflections on Issues of Methodologies and Interpretive Ideologies*

Athalya Brenner

Disclaimer: Preliminary General Considerations

It seems advisable to start by advancing several disclaimers, especially when the topic discussed is as loaded, emotionally as well as academically, as is the topic of "the family" or "families."

First, every so often a return to basics seems in order. By this I mean, within the context of this contribution, that reconsideration of a basic concept should be undertaken, accounting for possible academic biases and interpreters' personal tendencies and needs, even when opinions have already progressed from hypothesis to dogma. This is necessary for every reflection on past scholarship, especially when disrespect to previous chains of knowledge is not intended, and, indeed, disrespect is not my intention when I criticize earlier scholarship. On the contrary, a "post" position, as in postmodern scholarship and the like, strongly implies a debt to predecessors.

Second, to readers who will wonder what my general frame of reference is: in my view, the Hebrew Bible/Old Testament (hereafter HB) is

---

* This essay is offered to Kent Harold Richards in appreciation of how he "fathered" the Society of Biblical Literature for many years. This work is based on a much shorter paper delivered at a conference in UNISA, Pretoria, South Africa, in September 2009 and repeated with modifications at the International Meeting of the Society of Biblical Literature in Tartu, Estonia, July 2010, and in the ABIB (Association of Brazilian Biblical Studies) at the Metodista University of São Paulo, Brazil, in September 2010.

part of the classical world and should be studied alongside the New Testament, if it is to be used for understanding itself and the Judaisms and Christianities that grew out of it and after it. As is almost a consensus among scholars nowadays, most parts of the HB acquired their final or near-final form—the form in which the HB has been reproduced from just before the beginning of the Common Era and is known until today—not earlier than the late sixth to early fifth centuries Before the Common Era and centuries later. For many texts, processes of compilation, editing, and literary reproduction continued well into the Greco-Roman period and were ultimately accomplished concurrently with the creation of the New Testament, if not until the advent of printing. Granted, events and ideologies depicted in the HB chronologically antedate those in the New Testament and later Judaic texts; hence, it is customary to illustrate biblical texts by reference to older, ancient Near Eastern sources from Mesopotamia, Egypt, "classical" Greece, and the like. However, in view of the HB's complex history of editorial activity and transmission, and its newer, later positioning by especially European scholars, another view is perhaps timely. Furthermore, I will claim below that HB interpreters were influenced by notions gleaned from classical texts of the last centuries B.C.E. and especially the first two centuries C.E., projecting those notions onto the HB "myth screen," so to speak—a practice much less admitted or weighted than the outspoken search for ancient Near Eastern cognates.

Lastly, this essay represents preliminary reflections on an ancient topic. Undoubtedly, more work than will be undertaken here is necessary. Moreover, if the discussion will be reopened, then perhaps the confessed brief and tenative nature of this essay can be forgiven.

THE "HOUSE OF THE FATHER" IN THE HEBREW BIBLE: AN INTRODUCTION

Most scholars agree that the normative, minimal, nuclear family unit in the HB is the *bêt 'āb*, בית אב, "house of the father." This is a cornerstone idea, rarely questioned, and a prerequisite for defining the social order in HB times as "patriarchal." It, therefore, would seem appropriate to investigate the semantics of this freely used idiom before problematizing the extralinguistic concept it presumably designates; first, however, I will address the accepted theory.

The range of the basic Hebrew term *bayit*, בית, is quite wide: from the physical, architectural, and spatial to the conceptual and abstract. When *bayit* is used in the HB, it may serve as the semantic equivalent of the English "house," that is, as a geographical site, secular (domicile, living quarters) or religious (place of worship); as a "household," both for location and human unit; as a "kin unit," or as a "social unit, community," variously identified as smaller or bigger—from our "family" to our "clan" to our "tribe" to specific "houses" of descent and interests, that is, dynasties or even communities. It so happens that the Greek οἶκος and οἰκία may seem to cover the same semantic ground, roughly speaking. In Latin, though, the situation is a little different, with much less interchange between *domus* and *familia*—the latter term, as many people agree today, indicating more "household" as a sociolegal term than our "family." That the semantic range seems to be different between Hebrew and Latin—a target language used to transmit the HB for centuries, thus coloring the meaning of the source term for worshipers, clergy, and scholars—seems inescapable in a Western world where Latin, in its various developing forms, has served as a lingua franca and where much scholarship emanated from study of the so-called classics.

The Israeli scholar Shunia Bendor published his monograph *The Social Structure of Ancient Israel* in 1986,[2] and since then it has been customary in HB studies to define the basic/smallest structure of Israelite society as governed by the father and to call it *bêt 'āb*, "house of the father." We are told that, much like the Roman *paterfamilias*, the alpha male dominated "his" group, so named. The group's typical members were father, mother, children, and perhaps a third generation vertically, and other blood kin and additional nonagnatic members horizontally. The alpha male had powers and responsibilities regarding survival and economy but also regarding worship, ethics, and social responsibility. His household group, the equivalent of our "family," combined with others of its sort and size to create "families," Hebrew *mišpāḥâ*, משפחה, "clan" for us now, which in turn combined into a "tribe," *šēbeṭ*, שבט. According to Bendor, and as accepted by most scholars, this hierarchical structure persisted from more agrarian times and places into more complex social organizations and into urbanity, in various metamorphoses, from the entry into Canaan in the later half of the second millennium B.C.E., to the end of the monarchy (sixth century B.C.E.) and beyond. It is worth noting that,

---

2. Shunia Bendor, *The Social Structure of Ancient Israel: The Institution of the Family (*bēt 'āb*) from the Settlement to the End of the Monarchy* (Jerusalem Biblical Studies 7; Jerusalem: Simor, 1986; English translation, Winona Lake, Ind.: Eisenbrauns, 1996).

in Bendor's description, there is no space for our "nuclear family" (two vertical generations, parents and children, mostly kin-related), and our term "family" is applied to the entity known for most of us as "extended family" or "clan." When reflecting anew upon this description of a social construction, widely accepted by scholars today, I do so in order to assess its usefulness, to attempt to trace the origins of several ideological biases that appear to have motivated it and to offer some direction for future discussion.

The Term *Bêt 'Āb* and What It Actually Signifies

The noun phrase *bêt 'āb* appears in the HB many times: with suffixes, as a grammatical singular, and, as time goes by, also in the plural or double plural ("house/s of the fathers"). A representative list from many types of biblical genres and texts, from the First Temple period to the Second Temple period and into the Hellenistic period, is to be found on Bendor's first introductory page. However, if we look at his examples, a simple survey from Gen 12:1 (Abraham) and beyond the HB to John 14:2 in the New Testament, we find that, more often than not the designation *bêt 'āb* points mostly to either a location or to a male list compiled for some "male" purpose, such as the military list of Num 1:2, which reads: "Take a census of the whole Israelite community by the clans of its *ancestral houses*, listing the names, every male, head by head" (JPS). Yet despite the contention that a *bêt 'āb* is the "father's house," there is a tendency in contemporary translation to neutralize it into an "ancestral house" or "family" (whereas older translations, such as the Dutch *Statenvertaling* or the King James Version or the American Standard Version of 1901, just as examples, retain the "father's house"). I am not here fully denying the presumed basically patriarchal nature of Israelite and Judahite societies over the ages, as those societies recorded themselves in their writings. All that I am trying to say is that, as a minimal social organization, the *bêt 'āb* is neither inclusively valid nor as precisely definable as Bendor and his many followers claim, unproblematically. Things are not as tidy as that. The term's semantic range is much too broad; it may refer to a nuclear agnatic social group as well as to a bigger one, and the translations, their modern and postmodern gender-inclusive tendencies notwithstanding, perhaps reflect this better than biblical scholars by modifying a linguistically "wrong" rendering of *bêt 'āb* into a more socially correct understanding of "homestead" instead of "father's house."

Alternate Structures, Variations and Variety: The "Mother's House"

Moreover, the biblical texts themselves contain more than just traces evidencing social structures other than those governed by "fathers." Such structures, as they appear in the biblical texts, seem to be minority structures quantitatively. What seems a minority structure in hindsight might, however, have been more common or greater in quantity at one time. As is well recognized nowadays, memory may be real, but it also might be manufactured, ideologically biased, and streamlined to conform to a writers' wishes. This hardly needs exemplifying, in general as well as in relation to social situations.[3] In other words, both the biblical insistence on the dominance of the father in his house and in the wider social structure, as well as interpreters' acceptance of this picture as totally valid for biblical times and beyond, might be a combination of propaganda and wishful thinking.

We have four HB references to the בית אם, *bêt 'ēm*, "the mother's house" (Gen 24:28; Ruth 1:8; Song 3:4; 8:2). Reading these texts in their contexts, in each instance and as compared with the "father's house," the *bêt 'āb*, the "mothers' houses" might indeed be designations of a location, for instance, of female living quarters, a circle within the circle of the physical *bêt 'āb* space; however, in the absence of the father/Father figure, an absence that is common to all four texts, a competing and contemporaneous institution might be indicated here.

Carol Meyers discusses the term *bêt 'ēm*, including in her discussion of passages from Proverbs, where it is clear, though no "mother's house" is mentioned per se, that women and woman figures such as the Wisdom figure, the "Other Woman" (both in various passages, Prov 1–9), or the Woman of Valor (Prov 31) do have "houses" of some description, spatial and/or social. Part of her conclusion is:

> To consider once more our term "mother's house", we may say that its appearance may be startling in an androcentric document such as the Bible, but its existence as a meaningful term in Israelite society should not be unexpected. It may be rare and surprising in a male-dominated

---

3. See, e.g., the essays in Mieke Bal, Jonathan Crewe, and Leo Spitzer, eds., *Acts of Memory: Cultural Recall in the Present* (Hanover, N.H.: University of New England Press, 1998).

written word, but would not have been so in life as lived at the time. As anthropologists have discovered, the male-oriented, formal record of a society does not map onto "informal reality", in which women are also powerful actors in daily affairs and family decisions.[4]

I would like to press Meyers's line of reasoning forward and argue as follows. For me it is beyond doubt that, at certain times and places at least, and perhaps more often than we know, female households did exist not only as "informal" arrangements, as Meyers claims, but also as self-standing regular social units. This was so even if the arrangement was far from satisfactory for its participants, or presented as such, and even if "they," those participants in such households, do not receive generous press. Rahab, a "whore" from Jericho, owns a house and successfully looks after her relatives (Josh 2 and 6) and saves them from extermination. Who would deny that this is the behavior of a responsible family head? Two women share a household, spatially and otherwise, and give birth to sons, then come to King Solomon for judgment (1 Kgs 3): even if the biblical writers label them—here, too—as "whores," we may stop and inquire what the two women have done, apart from having no protective males in their lives, to deserve that label. What makes their respective establishment less than a "household" or a "family," where the next generation is nurtured, in a better or worse manner, depending on the mother's attitude? Good or bad, both women are mothers. Why not call their house, where they live according to their witness on their own, with no man in the house, a "mother's house"? The same applies to households run by widows: they are seen as poor and in need of protection, but does this negate the fact that they run a "household," as in the Elijah and Elisha stories (1 Kgs 17; 2 Kgs 4)? Or, in the case of Naomi, who turns out—in spite of her presentation and self-presentation as a poor and helpless widow—to be a land owner whose land is sold, or "redeemed," without adequate reason given (Ruth 4:3), much to the interpreters' consternation? In these stories widows care for their children as well as for themselves. They undergo hardships, and they are depicted as stereotypes of the needy in the absence of male bread-winners. Several of them are narrated as poor and lacking food. They may not be brilliant as kin-sustainers. They may have preferred to be married,

---

4. Carol Meyers, "Returning Home: Ruth 1.8 and the Gendering of the Book of Ruth," in *A Feminist Companion to Ruth* (ed. Athalya Brenner; FCB 3; Sheffield: Sheffield Academic Press, 1993), 113.

as Naomi prefers for Ruth (3:1–3) and as Ruth herself seems to prefer (3:9), but does this mean that widows are not family heads? Is Naomi not a family head until she chooses to relinquish the role in favor of Boaz?

"Alternate" Structures, Variations, and Variety: Other Groups

In the books of Samuel and at the beginning of 2 Kings, "sons of the prophets" are mentioned as primarily male groups. Although females are recorded as their wives (2 Kgs 4), it is clear that the "sons" constitute a social entity that only our bias prevents us from calling a "family," that is, a socially amalgamated group with a self-authored identity and purpose, sharing a location and/or organization, whether it includes kin connections or not. Once it is admitted that kin relations are not the only members of a "family," "house," or "household," there is no reason to exclude the "sons of the prophets" from being defined as a family of sorts. True enough, the designation itself assumes a parental hierarchy from father/Father to son, but this hierarchy is best viewed not only as an imitation or metaphor of a real kin "father's house" but rather as an alternate mode that does not necessarily exclude marital and productive heterosexual relations.

Further, what about fraternity-governed social units, as seems to be the case in Gen 24 as well as Song 1 and 8? Is it accidental that a female's blood brothers are mentioned in three out of the four occurrences of "mother's house" in the HB? Furthermore, in the fourth occurrence, in the book of Ruth, although Boaz is not a brother, he still is presented as a male kin-in-law! In spite of available anthropological material from the Mediterranean basin, where it is customary for brothers to uphold the honor/shame matrix linked with the sexual behavior of their female relatives, especially their sisters, and even violently so, fraternal family organizations in the HB are usually waived aside as a meager minority as against the usual patriarchal order or as a default situation after the father's death.

Indeed, on further inquiry we find that the situation in the HB is in fact quite complex. On the one hand, there are descriptions of heterosexual cells focused on reproduction and economical survival, ostensibly led by a father or father figure. On the other hand, if we stick to the "house" (*bayit*) definition for the nuclear or minimal social unit, and take seriously designations of individuals as "sons" or the like, not remaining content with viewing those designation as "just a metaphor" (which is never a clever interpretive move), then female-dominated reproductive as well as same-sex nonreproductive households emerge from the textual shadows. Ultimately, even Bendor limits his observations to the First Temple period, that is, not beyond the beginning of the sixth century B.C.E. Now let us move on to look at another literary source: legal prescription or the so-called biblical laws.

Legal Prescriptions versus "Reality"

In matters of reconstructing the sociology of ancient times according to the scriptures of the interested parties who wrote them, care should always be exercised, not only about nascent ideologies, but also because we often read so-called "legal" or "juridical" texts as evidence of praxis. This is not always the case: privileging such "legal" texts as more trustworthy over and above narrative texts, regarding them as factual and the narrative as more fictive or as imaginative, disregards the often wishful or authoritative nature of "juridical texts." Juridical texts, whether biblical, Mesopotamian, Egyptian, Greek, Roman, or whatever, are neither innocent nor necessarily reflective of "reality" at any time and at any place. Moreover, the need to legalize patriarchy in emphatic terms, much like the need to outlaw human killing and similar sociopathic modes of behavior, may stem from anxiety as much as from actuality. The veracity of near-total patriarchy is suspect at best, even if—in ancient Mediterranean cultures—it is presented not only as the norm but also as by far the major basic social arrangement.

Influence of (Re)constructed Roman Law and Post–Industrial Revolution Concepts on Bible Interpretation

I would like to advance the notion that our views of "biblical" and other "ancient" families are much influenced by Western post–Industrial Revolution perceptions of the family, nuclear or cell family, extended family, and the like. As living spaces and conditions changed, as premodern then modern Western urbanization developed, as the middle classes gained more and more ground, perceptions of what "families" were, or rather of what they should have been, were increasingly projected onto the past. We have developed a basic family model of a married couple—father and mother—plus children, perhaps also half a cat and a quarter of a dog, and ideally its own living quarters; such families, quite simply, seldom existed in the ancient worlds. In the HB, there is no trace of a marriage ceremony or proper marriage documentation, apart from half a formula here or there. Is this an oversight? Perhaps, but then perhaps not, since in the Greek worlds knowledge of marriage contracts and ceremonies is also scant.[5] There is enough evidence for female-male partnerships being concluded on the basis of kin, spatial, and economic arrangements, to be sure; there is enough evidence for judging that marriage's first purpose, in ancient Athens as in ancient Israels (I use the plural deliberately, bearing in mind that "Israel" or "Israels" are constructs), was reproduction, a close second production, and that the family—whatever its form and membership—was hierarchical and regulated parenthood and inheritance. There is plenty of evidence for financial concerns, often justified by kin genealogies and relations, and professional continuity in the forms of guilds. But an idealized picture of the "family" as a basis for social activity, the equation of a marriage hierarchy with a male household marriage partner governing (almost) every family, with a married couple or more than one couple as the nucleus of and synonym for a "family," seems to me as too exclusive a construct. I am not the only one to think that this is the case. One instance is Mark 3:31–35:

> Then his mother and his brothers came; and standing outside, they sent to him and called him. A crowd was sitting around him; and they said to him, "Your mother and your brothers and sisters are outside, asking for you." And he replied, "Who are my mother and my brothers?" And looking at those who sat around him, he said, "Here are my mother and my brothers! Whoever does the will of God is my brother and sister and mother." (NRSV)

It is easy and perhaps tempting to understand this passage as Jesus' rejection of his biological family, but since we have enough evidence in the Bible that families were not biological only and that apparently the understanding of "family" was different, we may want to appreciate this reported pronouncement not as a rejection but as a nonrevolutionary (re)definition anchored in the praxis of the Greco-Roman male world, with a difference: the "sisters" are included as well as the "brothers." Jesus is not rejecting his biological kin group; he is affirming that "family" is not only

---

5. See Sarah B. Pomeroy, *Families in Classical and Hellenistic Greece: Representations and Realities* (Oxford: Oxford University Press, 1997), 220.

biological. The answer to the question as to whether this is a revolutionary statement or an acknowledgement of current practice depends on how we visualize "families" of the past as much as on how we wish to visualize Jesus' radicality.

REASSESSMENT: WHAT IS THE *BÊT 'ĀB*, WHAT ARE "BIBLICAL FAMILIES"?

In a collection of articles published in *Family and Family Relations as Represented in Early Judaisms and Early Christianities: Texts and Fictions*,[6] the contributors to and editors of that volume tried to show that in ancient Israels "families" were varied and many. Here I am trying to take this notion a step or two further.

First and foremost, let us redraw attention to a reversal: the understanding that a fundamental human unit, according to the HB, is heterosexual and essentially a unit of reproduction, and only then a unit of production, as in Gen 1–3, can be put on its head. In a reversal, a fundamental human (social) unit will have its first interest as production for sustenance, with reproduction as just one facet of that necessity. The existence of professional biblical "guilds"—from textile workers to priests and scribes and builders and singers and professions in between, much as in ancient Athens and in Roman cities,[7] as well as in other ancient Near Eastern countries—supports this notion further. Males as well as females inherited professions, but also acquired them, and even a "household" was not limited to biological kin relationships. That genealogical kin relationships were invented, that the human world was perceived as emanating from a single primordial couple, does not belie the understanding that "families" were more, and less, than "households" (governed by a dominant male or otherwise, as the case might have been). Let us stop here again and remember the wide ranges of the Hebrew term *bayit*.

There are also other considerations that come to the fore if and when biblical texts are carefully studied—and let me point out once more that, according to many scholars, many of the biblical texts, even those that describe the world's beginnings, date in their present form to the so-called Persian period at their earliest, which means not earlier than the Athe-

---

6. Jan Willem van Henten and Athalya Brenner, eds., *Family and Family Relations as Represented in Early Judaisms and Early Christianities: Texts and Fictions* (Studies in Theology and Religion 2; Leiden: Deo, 2000).

7. Pomeroy, *Families in Classical and Hellenistic Greece*.

nian period and probably later than that (see my disclaimer above). A common denominator to most biblical texts is indeed the wishful attempt to describe an alpha male, a father, as heading a household and having a public and cultic function as well. This might or might not have been true for agrarian societies, not necessarily earlier than other forms of societies. In such Agrarian societies, even though it is not expressed in the extant texts, women might have indeed commanded group economic resources.[8] The real difference, however, is spatial: in urban societies, where "households" transformed into other and more professional interest groups, the situation changed. Moreover, even the most orthodox claims that the "father's house" was the basic biblical family unit do not allege that the unit governed social/spiritual obligations per se; for instance, worship responsibility is attributed to unit chiefs, mostly men, but is soon taken over by office-holders.

From the very beginning, the Hebrew god is depicted as a father: a single and unnatural male parent, no doubt, as is clear from both creation stories in Genesis. No woman/goddess is involved in this unnatural parenthood. Later on, in the Prophets, he becomes husband to his wife/people as well. Again, no natural heterosexual liaison is indicated by this hyperbole. Do these images testify to the primacy of a patriarchal family model in ancient Israels, in any period? This is a possibility, but it is equally possible that the metaphors, many images of male parenthood and husbandhood, exclusive of female participation, are born out of regulatory desire. Entertaining this option might upset the (re)construction of ancient Israelite social norms, but it may also open the way for another vision, for if procreation and the role of women are largely absent from genealogies such as in Gen 5, and if in 1 Chr 1–9 only traces of female genealogies are retained,[9] these absences do not indicate a lack of knowl-

---

8. See further Carol Meyers, "Everyday Life: Women in the Period of the Hebrew Bible," in *The Women's Bible Commentary* (ed. Carol A. Newsom and Sharon H. Ringe; Louisville: Westminster John Knox, 1992), 244–51; idem, "Returning Home," 85–114; and idem, *Discovering Eve: Ancient Israelite Women in Context* (Oxford: Oxford University Press, 1988).

9. See Ingeborg Löwisch's Ph.D. dissertation work, undertaken at the University of Utrecht, on female genealogies, especially in 1 Chr 1–9 and in comparison to a contemporary documentary film investigating a partly Jewish "female family." A sample of her work can be found in Ingeborg S. Löwisch, "Genealogies, Gender, and the Politics of Memory: 1 Chronicles 1–9 and the Documentary Film *mein Leben Teil*

edge of reproductive biology. Rather, the absences, or deletions, indicate ideologies of male supremacy that might or might not have been paramount in biblical times and, who knows to what extent, down to the late Hellenistic era. Such ideologies seem to have been essential for the writers of the biblical texts and for their desired mode of life. At the same time, such presentations strengthen the feeling that our habitual definitions of "families," based as they are on kin and heterosexual relations and a notion of overarching patriarchy, are slightly or more than slightly unsuitable for describing what "families" meant in the ancient worlds.[10]

Additional Models: Possibilities of Multiple Constructions and Sociospiritual Families

That there were nonpatriarchal families, or small social units headed by females, in biblical times and places seems beyond doubt. That their number seems small by comparison to the patriarchal norm may be the result of tendentious writing by males. At any rate, traces as recounted above, or in the story of Zelophehad's daughters (Num 27; 36) or the short mentions of stories about women as genealogical figureheads in 1 Chr 1–9, evidence this state of affairs. What I would like to suggest here is to go one step further than merely pointing to what might be construed as well-known exceptions to a patriarchal rule, that is, to go back to basics and look anew at materials relating to the basic human organizations in ancient Near Eastern, Hebraic, Hellenistic and Roman, early Jewish, and Christian societies, usually defined as patriarchal.

In the Hebraic worlds as depicted in the HB, male groups of sons of the prophets, priests and other cult officials, scribes and teachers, and so on existed side by side with reproductive and productive resource-governing units. It suits us to call the former "guilds," "communities,"

2," in *Performing Memory in Biblical Narrative and Beyond* (ed. Athalya Brenner and Frank H. Polak; Bible in the Modern World 25; Sheffield: Sheffield Phoenix Press, 2009), 228–56.

10. That homosexuality and bestiality are forbidden (as famously and in no generous terms as in Lev 18:22–23 and 20:13, 15–16) probably stems from the presumed damage to human reproduction from such practices, as well as to male anxiety of gender-bender and human-animal exchange roles. This, however, is the topic for another article altogether. Suffice it to note here that the apparent homophobia betrays a real anxiety that, in its turn, deconstructs patriarchal supremacy further.

"professions," or "classes" and the latter "families," since the former are productive, whereas the latter are both productive and reproductive. This division may, however, be perhaps misleading. If we remember that (1) not every "family" member is a blood kin; (2) propaganda aside, not every family is reproductive; (3) not every family is heterosexual, at least not always; (4) every family remains a productive unit, or attempts to remain such, in order to sustain itself and continue its existence; and, finally, (5) belonging to a group is a matter of identity and memory, and those can be chosen, manufactured, and manipulated, then a vista opens to other views and other definitions. In that case, both groups, the productive/reproductive and the productive, were "families." An individual—especially a male individual—could have and may have belonged simultaneously to a reproductive/heterosexual family dedicated to survival in the sense of biological self-generation and economics *and* to an economical and sociospiritual family that more often than not was a same-gender unit: a case of dual family identity, if you will. Certainly, there always was slippage between the sociospiritual and production modes; that social roles and professions were presented as hereditary supports that view. However, and this seems important to me, later social developments such as same-gender (male) rabbinic Torah study and same-gender celibate groups appear less explicable if we do not read the signs early on, the signs that insist that our contemporary (postmodern) term "family" is too limited to describe the dual-tiered reality of ancient times, biblical and otherwise.

Some Modes of Spiritual/Intellectual Families

As we progress in time toward the Common Era, when rabbinic Judaisms developed alongside nascent Christianities, and vice versa, various social groups, typically male, emerge. Sages and students of Torah spend long periods away from their marital obligations and spouses. Essenes founded male centers in the north and the south, although they may make a place for women and children, at the margins of their communities, so it seems.[11] Disciples, mostly male, follow Jesus, regardless of kin or marital

---

11. See Flavius Josephus, especially in *War* 2.119–161, also in *Antiquities* 18.18–21 and elsewhere; Philo, *Apology*, 12.75–87; Pliny, *Natural History*, 5.73. For a convenient summary of scholarly positions and discussion of the Essenes' attitude to marriage and procreation (although his conclusions are often disputed), as in Jose-

family ties. Females in Rome begin forming households that eventually institute monastic ways of life. The basic metaphors for all these social organizations are hierarchical and identical with those of the "natural," that is, biological or reproductive family: father, mother, children, other kin. Is this simply a metaphor or transference? Or is it further evidence that "family" is not "just a metaphor" and substitute term for biological facts but a reality of expression over and beyond the reproductive/economic unit we would like to define as such? In other words, should we not consider the possibility that in later Israel, as in Athens and Rome, at least privileged males had a dual familial identity, a reproductive/economic family membership as well as a contemporaneous economical/spiritual/intellectual identity, and that both identities were as important, and as basic? They were social markers, not to be distinguished as "familial" as against "communal," or private as against public. Moreover, as we have seen, this was also possible for women, in a more limited way—at least for elite women or for very poor or marginal ones.

Again: In the Name of the Father; Or, the Egg and the Chicken, by Comparison to the Greco-Roman Worlds

In this essay I have tried to reconsider the current practice of romantization and idealization of the "biblical family" so that the term suits what seems like the needs of current Western societies. That the concepts of "families" or, worse still, "the family" as we sociologically define it does not work for ancient civilizations is clear, even if reworked according to what we imagine as the appropriate (past) *Zeitgeist*. Memories of those times are manufactured: at best, near authentic; at worst, inexplicable. Our definitions are at best inadequate and at worst confessionally, emotionally, or academically biased: *confessionally*, since the basic biblical call for reproduction as the family's raison d'être is confused with heterosexual marriage as the basis for reproduction and allowed theological and moral authority, discounting matters of choice and reality then and

---

phus's and the other relevant ancient texts, see Steve Mason, "What Josephus Says about the Essenes in His *Judean War*"; online: http://orion.huji.ac.il/orion/programs/Mason00-1.shtml. A shorter version is available in print, idem, "What Josephus Says about the Essenes in His *Judean War*," in *Text and Artifact in the Religions of Mediterranean Antiquity: Essays in Honour of Peter Richardson* (ed. Stephen G. Wilson and Michel Desjardins; Waterloo, Ont.: Wilfrid Laurier University Press, 2000), 434–67.

now, by women and by men; *emotionally*, since parenthood is romanticized as a natural, biologically motivated wish, especially for females; and *academically*, since the classical Roman (Augustan) model has influenced many scholars, classically trained, to extend it to other societies in antiquity. Feminist criticism, in its zeal, largely, if not always, and paradoxically foregrounded patriarchy while, at the same time, spending too little time in questioning, not its values—this has been done arduously!—but the details of its historical veracity beyond the matriarchal paradigm. At any rate, explaining how (mostly, typically, male) groups belonged at one and the same time both to marital families *and* to mono-sexual designated families cannot be done without reference to the conjecture that individuals, at least privileged males and some privileged and underprivileged women, could and did see themselves as belonging to two family units or hierarchies at the same time.

We now finally come down to the question: What about love as motivation for family membership? To which we can answer: the story of heterosexual love in the HB is sad and limited. Outside the Song of Songs (a great exception), females may love other females (Ruth loves Naomi) but not male spouses. Only Michal loves a male, David; usually males love females (Isaac and Rebekah; Jacob and Rachel). Women love their children; males also love their offspring. Proverbs recommends to "sons" that they should love a personified female Wisdom as an erotic mistress, and later Jewish students and sages love the Torah as a desired mistress, spending as much or more time in the house(hold?) of Torah than with their marital families, although rabbis are not exempt from marriage and reproduction/production. Jesus' disciples prefer him to other concerns. Perpetua of the milky breasts chooses martyrdom over her baby. To conclude, a dual identity sometimes requires a choice, preference of the one love object, the one concurrent identity, over the other. Nonetheless, dual identity and commitment seems to have remained in the Mediterranean region throughout antiquity and beyond.

Bibliography

Bal, Mieke, Jonathan Crewe, and Leo Spitzer, eds. *Acts of Memory: Cultural Recall in the Present*. Hanover, N.H.: University of New England Press, 1998.

Bendor, Shunia. *The Social Structure of Ancient Israel: The Institution of the Family (bēt 'āb) from the Settlement to the End of the Monarchy*. Jerusalem Biblical Studies 7. Jerusalem: Simor, 1986; English translation, Winona Lake, Ind.: Eisenbrauns, 1996.

Brenner, Athalya, and Jan Willem van Henten, eds. *Family and Family Relations as Represented in Early Judaisms and Early Christianities: Texts and Fictions*. Studies in Theology and Religion 2. Leiden: Deo, 2000.

Löwisch, Ingeborg S. "Genealogies, Gender, and the Politics of Memory: 1 Chronicles 1–9 and the Documentary Film *mein Leben Teil 2*." Pages 228–56 in *Performing Memory in Biblical Narrative and Beyond*. Edited by Athalya Brenner and Frank H. Polak. Bible in the Modern World 25. Sheffield: Sheffield Phoenix Press, 2009.

Mason, Steve. "What Josephus Says about the Essenes in His *Judean War*." Online: http://orion.huji.ac.il/orion/programs/Mason00-1.shtml. A shorter version is available in print in "What Josephus Says about the Essenes in His *Judean War*." Pages 434–67 in *Text and Artifact in the Religions of Mediterranean Antiquity: Essays in Honour of Peter Richardson*. Edited by Stephen G. Wilson and Michel Desjardins. Waterloo, Ont.: Wilfrid Laurier University Press, 2000.

Meyers, Carol. *Discovering Eve: Ancient Israelite Women in Context*. Oxford: Oxford University Press, 1988.

———. "Everyday Life: Women in the Period of the Hebrew Bible." Pages 244–51 in *The Women's Bible Commentary*. Edited by Carol A. Newsom and Sharon H. Ringe. Louisville: Westminster John Knox, 1992.

———. "Returning Home: Ruth 1.8 and the Gendering of the Book of Ruth." Pages 85–114 in *A Feminist Companion to Ruth*. Edited by Athalya Brenner. FCB 3. Sheffield: Sheffield Academic Press, 1993.

Pomeroy, Sarah B. *Families in Classical and Hellenistic Greece: Representations and Realities*. Oxford: Oxford University Press, 1997.

Clandestine Relationship: An Approach to the Song of Songs*

Pablo R. Andiñach

The activity of thinking theologically in situations of marginalization, the struggle for human rights, and the reality of countries burdened by unjust debts never sought exercises us in the hermeneutics of suspicion. From this perspective, one attends to what is expressed and what is not expressed; one privileges the other side of the text, the semantics of the negative, the voice of the other. The historical experience of marginalization better prepares for bias than for systemic clarity, and the experience motivates one to seek behind words things only expressed in the darkness and at a distance. This hermeneutics of suspicion is not, however, only applied to the external reality—in this case, the biblical text—but also to our own understanding of theology, of meaning. To those who think theologically from the margins, it seems that God not only calls to liberate those things one desires to liberate and those that deserve to be liberated, but also those other things that one usually sets aside and forgets, that one does not recognize as belonging to oneself. The Song of Songs invites the reader to be freed from the hypocrisy wrapped around sexuality, and it does this through the voice of a woman who does not accept the norms and stereotypes that male society has assigned her. She pronounces the revolutionary phrase,

I am black and beautiful. (1:5)[1]

---

* This essay is, to a large extent, an extract from Pablo Andiñach, *Cantar de los Cantares, El fuego y la ternura* (Buenos Aires: Lumen, 1997; in Portuguese: *Cântico dos Cânticos* (Petrópolis: Vozes-Sinodal, 1998). A Spanish version of the essay with modifications is forthcoming (*Acta Poética* 31 [2010]).

1. Quotations of the Bible in this essay are from the NRSV.

From this point she strikes with force against the rigid structures of her time and ours. She wants to liberate women and men from the chains of prejudice so that they may meet, touch each other, and look straight into the face of the other. This is achieved, if we know how to find under the dust of the years the correct key that will open her text.[2]

To establish a strategy for reading is a delicate task, for it presupposes that the interpretation that follows will be influenced by the approach. It is also necessary to mention that it is very difficult for a text to be approached with only one reading strategy; this not only refers to the richness of the whole text and its polysemy but also to the richness of the reader's vital experience—both diverse and contradictory—through which one reads and interprets the text at hand. In the Song of Songs, we discover that the text itself suggests four clues for reading that are complementary and illuminating, and the erotic is present in diverse forms in each:

(1) *The opposition between the singular and the multiple.* This opposition is evident in aspects of the text such as the affirmation of personal love and the rejection of depersonalized sexuality or preservation of one's own body for the loved one and denial of this body to other people or other possible relations.

(2) *A critique of the Solomonic model of sexuality.*[3]

(3) *The value of the loved one as body.* This contrasts with another value in which possessions embellish the body and in which riches and furniture are exalted.

---

2. The contemporary critical thinking on sexuality is never-ending. Three seminal works express the conflict and the difficulties of the erotic in our life and society: Emmanuel Levinas, *Totality and Infinity: An Essay on Exteriority* (Pittsburgh: Duquesne University Press, 1969), especially 254–86; Michel Foucault, *The History of Sexuality* (3 vols.; New York: Vintage, 1980–1986); and Paul Ricoeur, "La maravilla, lo errático, el enigma," in *La Sexualidad* (Barcelona: Fontanella, 1979), 9–21. The work of Richard Davidson, *Flame of Yahweh: Sexuality in the Old Testament* (Peabody, Mass.: Hendrickson, 2007), is a massive volume that includes a bibliography for Song of Songs (545–632).

3. See Pablo R. Andiñach, "Crítica de Salomón en el Cantar de los Cantares," *Revista Bíblica* 53 (1991): 129–56.

(4) *The need to read the Song of Songs from woman's point of view.* The linguistic structure of the book itself suggests that the author is a woman, and her perspective is present in each of the poems.[4]

Song of Songs and Genesis 2–3

In her important book on sexuality in the Old Testament, Phyllis Trible reads Song of Songs as an answer to Gen 2–3.[5] From her perspective, creation is described in the text as the development, in four stages, of Eros. The first stage begins with the creation of human beings. The second describes the planting of the garden, where human beings will live. In the third, animals are created as companions that inhabit and share the garden. The highlight of the narrative is the fourth episode, with the creation of sexuality. The subsequent expulsion of the first human couple from this erotic place, and the closure of the garden, which is jealously guarded by cherubim with a threatening sword, prevents all access to this original erotic space. Trible suggests that the text of Song of Songs redeems this expulsion and again opens up the way to pleasure and the enjoyment of the senses.[6] If the narrative of Gen 2–3 does not offer any possibility of opening up the garden of sexuality, another garden is constructed—Song of Songs—where Eros will be celebrated. This book by Trible is original and interesting when it offers an analysis of the texts that support these ideas. However, we can point to a difficulty. The problem with Trible's interpretation rests not in its logic but rather in the reading of these works together. Genesis does not suppose the need—or hidden desire—of returning to that primitive state, nor does Song of Songs allow us to understand that it is raising creation-related questions or restoring that which was lost.[7] Genesis 2:4–4:26 is a unit that we can call the first

---

4. David J. A. Clines questions the role of women in the Song of Songs, concluding that her role is subordinate to the role of the man. His starting point is that the Song of Songs describes women from the male perspective. Clines assumes this viewpoint but does not defend it, which, in my understanding, makes it lose, to a large extent, the feminine richness of the text (*Interested Parties: The Ideology of Writers and Readers of the Hebrew Bible* [JSOTSup 205; Gender, Culture, Theory 1; Sheffield, JSOT Press, 1995], 120–21).

5. *God and the Rhetoric of Sexuality* (OBT 2; Philadelphia: Fortress, 1978), 144–65.

6. Ibid., 144.

7. Athalya Brenner points to the differences of these texts and shows interesting

period of creation, and it narrates the history of the heavens and earth (see 2:4a) where transgressions ("sins") are part of the "original" everyday living. In the text, God's attributes (e.g., eternal existence, authority over people, among others) are not secondary acts in the development of humanity; rather, they are understood as inherent to humanity's first and only nature. There is no state of perfection and freedom to which we can return, be it in the realm of justice or sexuality. Moreover, this distinct conception is reflected in the translation of the Hebrew word גן: a garden is a place for enjoyment of free time and for fun. I prefer to translate גן as "orchard," a place where we have to work and so enjoy its produce, where the fruit of human labor contributes to the well-being and harmony of those who work.[8]

In Song 7:10 there is an allusion to Gen 3:16, not as restitution of a time past, but rather with the intention of correcting the Genesis text by widening the reading of contrasting traditions:

I am my beloved's,
And his desire is for me. (Song 7:10)

Your desire shall be for your husband
And he shall rule over you. (Gen 3:16)

In Gen 3:16 the erotic is established as an inclination of woman to man, needing a man to satisfy her sexual desire,[9] which supposes a form

---

points of divergence (*The Song of Songs* [OTG; Sheffield, JSOT Press, 1989], 83). See also, Clines, *Interested Parties*, 115–16.

8. See Pablo R. Andiñach, "Génesis," in *Comentario Bíblico Latinoamericano I: Pentateuco y textos narrativos* (ed. Armando Levoratti; Estella: Verbo Divino, 2004), 374.

9. It is a mistake to interpret this passage as if woman's erotic desire was a punishment for disobedience and a sign of subjection to men. I prefer to interpret it as a sign of human character and bodily diversity, of the divine existence to which the human couple aspired: disobedience would have its prize: "[Y]ou will be like God" (Gen 3:5). George W. Coats indicates that this unity is not a curse but rather establishes a new relation between man and woman different from the intimate and binding relation of Gen 2:23–24 (*Genesis, with an Introduction to Narrative Literature* [FOTL 1; Grand Rapids, Eerdmans, 1983], 56). Gerhard von Rad also rejects the idea of a curse and prefers to speak of it as an announcement that on woman's life will fall "severe afflictions and terrible contradictions" (*Genesis: A Commentary* [trans. John H. Marks; OTL; Philadelphia: Westminster, 1961], 90).

of domination and subjection on his part.[10] This condition of woman has its male parallel in the curse on the land and the need for men to work to produce what is necessary for living (vv. 17–19), but there is no mention of male eroticism. So the sensitivity of the author of Song of Songs corrects this idea by indicating that man, as well, needs woman as object of his eroticism, and, in consequence, he is also subject to her. What is now revealed in Song of Songs is that the erotic drive addressed to the other is not exclusive to woman; it also lives in the male as directed to woman.

What should be noticed is that while the Genesis text is etiological and intends to produce an account of human behaviour based on the answer of God when faced with the disobedience of the human couple, Song of Songs celebrates this mutual drive and there is no connotation of punishment for disobedience, or any intention to respond to the subjection proper to the human condition. It is a primary act not related to a previous one that conditions it. From the perception of sexuality in Song of Songs, there is a liberation of pleasure from the bonds to which it has been subjected when considering it a consequence of something else—in this case, a stain on conduct—aggravated by the double and different signification: punishment to woman, guardian of the fulfilment of this punishment to the male.

Let us turn to other cases. The poem of 8:5 is constructed around a brief dialogue between the couple:

HIM: Who is that coming up from the wilderness
leaning upon her beloved?

HER: Under the apple tree I undressed[11] you.
There your mother was in labor with you;
there she who bore you was in labor.

---

10. Note that the woman's inclination toward the man in Gen 3:16 is placed after and not before the reference to pregnancy and giving birth. This order indicates that her inclination is not related to procreation but rather to the desire for pleasure that generates submission to the loved one. The complementing of Gen 2:23 is now revealed as suffering for woman and as "the will of God." It is to this last statement that the Song of Songs responds. See Severino Croatto, *Crear y amar en libertad: Estudio de Génesis 2:4–3:24* (Buenos Aires: La Aurora, 1986), 143–44.

11. NRSV: "awakened."

The words of the man are repeated as a refrain (3:6; 6:10), relating the woman to the desert. In this case, it is the symbol of a rare and exotic place, attractive because it is enigmatic.[12] The woman's answer refers to a new scene: under an apple tree. The Hebrew verb עור has two meanings. The first meaning is "to awake," which is used by most translators in this verse. The second is "to undress."[13] The choice between these meanings cannot be a matter of mere statistics; rather, it must be determined by the literary context of the passage and the overall work. In this unit, the conception of the male and the time of his birth are the issue. Both of these events take place naked and express central moments of erotic life. If the intention is one of referring to the sexual union, then it is more appropriate to translate it as "I undressed you." In this way one emphasizes the central role of the young woman in the activity. It is she who undresses him to enjoy his body.

The absence of any reference to the father—notably absent in all of Song of Songs—again places the accent on the woman's perspective, and given this perspective, it is striking that there is no textual basis for thinking of Song of Songs as relating eroticism and sexuality to maternity. In a culture in which fertility was central to the value of the life of a woman, these poems make it evident that pleasure is justified in itself, which includes the playing of two bodies and the tenderness of caresses. It is not the external and consequent element—procreation—that gives meaning to the kissing, the pleasure of giving of oneself, and the receiving of fullness. Conception is only mentioned on one other occasion in the Song

---

12. A mechanical interpretation of this passage must be avoided, where "desert" is understood as a place of purification, an encounter with God, or a memory of exodus as some sort of paradigm. These possibilities may be correct in other places in the Old Testament but not here, where there are no recurring signs given of the need for purification or the evocation of times past as more benign. See Raymond J. Tournay, *Quand Dieu parle aux hommes le langage de l'amour* (Paris: Gabalda, 1982), 65.

13. The Heb. root עור refers to the concept of "awake," but in some contexts it has the meaning of "undress" (e.g., Hab 3:9). The root is also related to ערר (e.g., Isa 23:13; 32:11), whose relationship is built on the weakness of their consonants. It is also found in words such as ערירי, "stripped," "childless," "undressed of children" (Gen 15:2; Jer 22:30). From the root ערה ("to be naked") comes ערוה ("nakedness") usually with the negative meaning of impudicity (e.g., Lam 1:8; Ezek 16:37). However, in this case, the radical ה hides a ו and becomes עור, which is close to my proposed translation. Maybe we need to recognize that the text is playing with these ambiguities and concepts "awake"/"undress."

of Songs (3:4). In this case it is the woman's conception, and this is mentioned to indicate the place where the woman and the man have already met to make love. In this sense it is a closed place where sexuality has already been exercised and where the woman's eroticism is evoked.

Another text is the poem of 2:16–17, which is voiced by the woman:

My beloved is mine and I am his;
he pastures his flock among the lilies.

Until the day breathes
and the shadows flee,
turn, my beloved, be like a gazelle
or a young stag on the cleft mountains.

The initial stanza is repeated in 6:3 and 7:11. The first line expresses the exclusive and profound union of the couple. The semantic structure is compressed and demonstrates a high capacity for poetic concision. In the second line, lilies are an allusion to woman herself and to her sexuality. For this reason the image of a shepherd—whose task it is to lead the flock over diverse geographical landforms—is used to refer to the mutual relationship and to their love-play.

The second verse is suggestive. It takes place at night when she is alone waiting for him to come back to her bed.[14] The clandestine nature of the meeting is evident in the need for it to take place while shadows may still hide it. There have been interpretations of the expression "the mountains of Bether" that suggest it alludes to woman's pubis, although in Josh 15:59 (LXX) there is mention of this as the name of a small village. Faithful to poetic language, we must consider that the correct reading evokes both realities: the mount south of Judah, where a gazelle grazes, is an image of the long-awaited movement of the man over the woman's body. In this way the poem is an invitation to re-create, or to make effective, the desire expressed in the first verse. It is not the first place in Song of Songs where hills are mentioned. "Hill of frankincense" (4:6) and "mountain of spices" (8:14), both in the singular, are images of exotic and aromatic

---

14. Michael V. Fox suggests that all of Song of Songs happens at night and secretly (*The Song of Songs and the Ancient Egyptian Love Songs* [Madison: University of Wisconsin Press, 1985], 145).

places associated with the sexual organs. What enhances this interpretation in 2:17b is the plural "mountains." In this case, it is possible to extend the allusion in the text to include places of pleasure. We must not forget that mountains can also be images of the breasts or of the repeated curvatures of her body. When one reads love poems, it is not necessary for each word to find a reference. What is important is that a climate is created by the recurrence of images. A gazelle covering the mounts here evokes the image of the woman being caressed by her loved one.[15]

In another poem (2:3) the woman is referred to in relation to her playing with the body of the man:

> As an apple tree among the trees of the wood,
> so is my beloved among young men.
> With great delight I sat in his shadow,
> and his fruit was sweet to my taste.

In the narrative, it is she who covers the man's body as one who climbs the tree, seeking its fruit and delighting in it.

The man also gives expression to his love in various poems. In 7:6–9 he does so this way:

> How fair and pleasant you are,
> O loved one, delectable maiden!
>
> You are stately as a palm tree,
> and your breasts are like clusters.
> I say I will climb the palm tree
> and lay hold of its branches.
> O may your breasts be like clusters of the vine,
> and the scent of your breath like apples,
> and your kisses like the best wine
> that goes down smoothly,
> gliding over lips and teeth.

---

15. See Nicolás de la Carrera, *Amor y erotismo del Cantar de los Cantares* (Madrid: Nueva Utopía, 1998). Carrera analyzes Song of Songs from a psychological and pleasure perspective. Many moments of the book are considered simply as amorous reflections that are justified by simply and wonderfully being there.

In the previous poem (7:1–6), the man describes the woman while she is dancing. She danced with her feet and moved to the rhythm of the music. In contrast to that poem, on this occasion she is seen as static, remaining in one place and within a framework of serenity that is represented as firmly rooted like a palm tree. The passion of man is here expressed by comparing her lines to the curvature of the palm trunk. He climbs to the heights to take hold of the cluster of dates, evoking an image of her breasts. The man searches for her, and, as many times before when he has climbed trees in search of dates, he now is seeking her to taste her lips and breath. Many are the images evoked in these verses. The man must make the effort to reach her. He must climb, he must collect in his hands the fruit and then take it into his mouth. Poetry does not require us to define a concept but rather to participate in a climate of love and eroticism created by both of them.

In this poem the woman indicates the way she would like to be treated. It must not be read as if all women would like this form of relationship nor as a paradigm for the correct and gentle male. It is a testimony, not an archetype. It does not pretend to establish a paradigm of either pleasure for women or behavior for men. It simply seeks to demonstrate that she enjoys being desired.[16] In Song of Songs, neither the man nor the woman are stereotypes of people or models to be followed.

She Is the Author

The reader may have realized already that we refer to the author of Song of Songs as "she." This would not need any justification if it were not for our own narrow-mindedness that finds it strange to imagine that a woman could be the author of this work in the Bible. As a matter of fact, it would need a long justification to explain how a man could have written a collection of poems in which the dominating sensitivity is clearly feminine and the body that is exalted is mainly male. Though many commentaries mention the "androcentric" character of Song of Songs, they do so without paying much attention to the fact that their later analyses contradict this affirmation. We believe that they are entrapped in a certain intellectual

---

16. Such is the analysis of much of the excellent work by Carey Ellen Walsh, *Exquisite Desire: Religion, the Erotic, and the Songs of Songs* (Minneapolis: Fortress, 2000).

inertia and have not attempted a careful reading of the text in relation to the issue.

It is necessary to discard the idea of Solomonic authorship. Although 1:1 seems to say that Solomon is the author, other information within the book conspires against this conclusion: David is named in such a way that it is difficult to accept that the author is talking about his father (4:4). The text reports that "Solomon had a vineyard" (8:11), an expression that presupposes that the author is neither Solomon nor a contemporary of Solomon. The author rejects Solomon's riches, and does with harsh words, contrasting his one vineyard with Solomon's many vineyards (8:12). From a linguistic point of view, the title (1:1) does not correspond to the rest of the work. There the Hebrew word *'asher* is used, which is foreign to the tongue in which the rest of Songs is written. This indicates an independence from the rest of the text. The painful reality of the attribution of Solomonic authorship is that along the way the name of the woman who authored this text was lost.

The idea that a woman wrote Song of Songs is sustained on internal elements. In the poems, it is the woman's voice that is the main one; she carries the conceptual initiative in the majority of cases; she enters in dialogue with the women chorus; he never does; and the voice of the woman opens and closes the book.

There are other elements that can be taken into account. In Song of Songs we find the only example in biblical literature in which a woman is spokesperson for herself, that is to say, a woman whose voice is not mediated by any other author.[17] The woman in Song of Songs speaks directly in first person:

Let him kiss me. (1:2)

I am black and beautiful. (1:5)

Her feelings, thoughts, and actions are not transmitted by another person, as is the case in Ruth or Esther; rather, it is her own voice that speaks to readers.

---

17. See Renita Weems, "Song of Songs" in *The Woman's Bible Commentary*, (ed. Carol Newsom and Sharon Ringe; London: Westminster, 1995), 156.

To these arguments one must add that in two instances the voice of the man is mediated by the woman. This means that her voice tells what he says:

My beloved speaks and says to me:
"Arise my love...." (2:10–14)

I slept, but my heart was awake.
Listen! My beloved is knocking.
"Open to me, my sister, my love...." (5:2)

We need to point out that the inverse case—her voice mediated by the man—does not take place anywhere in the book. We have already mentioned the reference in 7:11 to the sexual desire that leads man to woman and forces him to seek her. Song of Songs responds to that text from a woman's perspective. Carey E. Walsh, in a recent book, points out that "[i]t is, first of all, shocking that an entire biblical book is devoted to women's desire," then to consider that, at a minimum, it counter-effects the vast amount of thinking that opposes women's desire, while, at a maximum, it is definitively a subversive text.[18]

To conclude, we should mention that these arguments do not imply that we have to affirm an author in the modern sense of the word, that one hand wrote each and every one of the poems. In antiquity this was an exception. What was current was that some person would collect previous texts, transmitted by tradition, and would group them in the light of a new theological and social situation, generally adding fresh material composed by their own hand. It is in this way that our woman provided Song of Songs with a particular woman's touch.

Literary Aspects

A text that possesses the erotic condition as one of its semantic centers cannot avoid reflecting this in its literary aspects. There has been much debate about whether or not Song of Songs possesses an internal literary structure or if its poems are grouped haphazardly. Neither alternative seems to be fully convincing. It is not easy to prove the existence of struc-

---

18. Walsh, *Exquisite Desire*, 4.

turing elements among the poems. It has been suggested that a structuring element may be a leitmotif, such as "O daughters of Jerusalem," or other such phrases, which are repeated in various poems. The difficulty rests in understanding the value of such structures. Moreover, the diversity and reoccurrence of images, as well as where they appear, do not seem to fit into rigid structures.

Other authors have suggested that the order of the poems is quite by chance and that the book is simply an anthology united by stanzas. There has been an effort to describe the work as a linear drama in which a (woman) shepherd who is in love with a simple (male) shepherd is sought by Solomon. This narrative creates a rivalry between these two men and a conflict for her, between true love and her duty as a subject before her powerful king. In my understanding, these options for a narrative structure do not bear fruit, and I find it more useful to discover, in the sequence of poems, a subtle network of words and themes that connect one with another.[19] In some cases one unit is the answer to a previous one (e.g., 1:5–8 relates to 1:9–17); in other cases the units relate to each other by the use of a common word (e.g., "mother" relates 8:1–4 with 8:5). They may refer to objects and common places ("wine," "vineyard" in 1:2–4 and 5–8). They can multiply occurrences, though the constant element is that there are no strict links but rather an ordinary succession that opens up space for imagination and taste.[20] The semantic relations offer little by way of a visible structure, though they do provide coherence to the poetical language. A too rational and rigid structure would have betrayed the spirit of the message. In this sense, one can say that the erotic has more to do with the pleasure of reading and its references than to a message that is articulated and discernible. What is needed is a different level of interpretation where it is possible to postulate that the primary message being promoted is the right to love and its sexual expression.

The literary genre is part of the erotic of the text. I describe it as the poetry of human love, and this must be clarified due to the fact that, for a long time, Song of Songs was considered a nonerotic text, or at least resignified eroticism: a love text that focused on the relationship between sublime figures such as the Messiah and God, Israel and God, the church and the Messiah, and so forth. It was love, it was erotic, and it was human,

---

19. See Andiñach, *Cantar de los Cantares*, passim.
20. This is the emphasis of Weems ("Song of Songs," 157).

but not between human beings. Evidence from the text, however, indicates human love, and for this reason it was difficult to understand and justify its belonging to both the Jewish and Christian canon. The problem that arose was the need to explain the presence in the canon of secular and erotic poems in which the name of God is not found and where there are no allusions to liturgical practice or to the foundational events basic to the faith of Israel. Its value was questioned, as was its inclusion in the Bible. In contrast, we find that Sir 47:17 (ca. 220 B.C.E.) refers to Solomon's "songs," and the Septuagint includes Song of Songs among its books. When Aquila, Simachus, and Theodotion produced their own translations of the Hebrew texts into Greek, they included Song of Songs in their work, testifying this way to its acceptance and place in the Jewish canon by the year 180 C.E. This discussion has its justification. It is Rabbi Akiba, a leading rabbi of the Jewish community after 70 C.E., who established the prohibition against the use of Song of Songs in private festivities and restricted its liturgical and religious use.[21] These restrictions offer evidence that the poems were known and used outside religious circles, probably as erotic songs to provoke the sexual excitement of participants. I also believe that this was a primary use and gave origin to the poems. The alternative spiritual and allegorical readings saved them from being excluded from the canon, although it distorted the sense.

Ethics and Beauty

In Song of Songs we find an ethic that questions the morals of the society of its time—and, in many ways, of our times—concerning the erotic and sexuality. The poems create tension between the legitimacy of love in the decision of lovers to unite without any need of authorizing social sanction and a strong link of faithfulness that assures the continuity of the relationship and a mutually exclusive belonging. The couple does not regularly live together. They meet to make love in hidden or private places, places where they cannot be seen (1:4–7; 2:4,14; 3:4; 4:8; 5:5; 7:12–13; 8:1). The

---

21. In part this is explained by the words of R. Akiba: "He who tunes his voice singing Song of Songs in the place where a party is to be held, and this way turns it into a secular song, will have no place in the coming world" (t. Sanh. 12:10), and "No one in Israel can say that Song of Songs stains one's hands. Because all the world is not as valuable as the day in which Song of Songs was given to Israel; because all the Writings are holy, but Song of Songs is the Holy of Holies" (t. Yad. 3:5).

author indicates that this situation is related to the brothers of the young woman, who hide her and preserve her for marriage to a man who will provide a hefty dowry (see 8:8–9). The author despises the act of buying love with money and expresses distain in 8:7, a reference to the dowry system and the handing over by men of their daughters or sisters. This may not be the only reason for the lover's clandestine relationship, but the possibility of eloping together is a constant theme:

> Come my beloved,
> let us go forth into the fields
> and lodge in the villages; …
> There I will give you my love. (7:12–13)

Faced with this freedom of feelings and the body, of Eros exposed in its vital potential, it is necessary to oppose an equivalent force that frames and limits their love so that it can act positively within the erotic economy, socially constituted and accepted by the other. The author finds a wonderful answer: this force is the exclusiveness of mutual belonging. The love they have for each other is not open to other actors. He calls her "a garden locked" (4:12) for other men. She calls him "my beloved is mine" (2:16), and when the other women want to share him, she stops this by saying "my beloved has gone down to his garden … my beloved is mine" (6:1–3). This issue reaches its climax in the poem where she says:

> Set me as a seal upon your heart,
> as a seal upon your arm. (8:6–7)

This way of claiming is to make public what is a hidden relationship, confirming it with a visible and indelible mark.

These poems are, at the same time, a source of aesthetic and erotic resources, not common in much of universal literature. It requires poetical sensitivity to value the more daring images, such as when the man compares the woman to "a mare among Pharaoh's chariots" (1:9). Here we must remember that the most beautiful of all mares was chosen for the monarch. Or when she says "your nose is like a tower of Lebanon" (7:4). This reminds us that a nose was an important sign of a strong personality, and so this becomes the highest praise, more than mere physical beauty. In Song of Songs we come across many comparisons with animals: breasts as gazelles (4:5); hair black as a raven (5:11); white teeth as a flock of ewes" (6:6). The author also refers to landscape to describe love and lovers: the beloved is like an apple tree (2:3); she is a "beautiful city" (6:4), a lily among brambles (2:2). Neither are smells absent, so she describes her loved one as fruit that is sweet to her taste (2:3), and she is nard giving forth her fragrance for her beloved (1:12–14). In 4:11 he describes her mouth distilling milk and honey. Their bodies are exalted with images taken from nature. Her body is at various times compared to a vineyard, a fertile and aromatic land (1:6; 8:12), and a garden (5:1; 6:2). The body of the man is compared with animals, aromatic spices, stones, tree trunks. Concerning his legs, she evokes "Lebanon, choice as the cedars" (5:15).

Another resource used by the author is repetition. In various poems, she repeats complete or partial phrases such as "I adjure you, O daughters of Jerusalem..." (2:7; 3:5; 5:8; 8:4) and "my beloved is mine and I am his" (2:16; 6:3; 7:11). If we consider the simple images, we could count dozens of repetitions. Rather than a structure, these repetitions express a fundamental intuition concerning love between lovers: the fact that this love must be expressed and constantly renewed. These poems do not respond to a legal logic by which something that has been expressed once remains forever. On the contrary, in these poems what has been affirmed must be renewed and validated with each encounter and—as happens with each caress—repetition does not tire, rather it is an invitation to claim and expect more, each time.

Theological Discourse

Ignorance and poetic insensitivity, added to the need to find a religious explanation for the poems, led many to imagine a hidden theology behind the images and metaphors of Song of Songs. This allowed for the creation of an allegorical understanding needed to assure a theology that otherwise could not be justified and that was indispensable for preserving the canonicity of the book. I prefer valuing what is said in the text and feel challenged to understand its significance. Two theological elements will be noted: The first is the negative role attributed to Solomon. When the author portrays Solomon negatively, she sides with a particular understanding of the history of Israel and of what God blesses and rejects. The model of an impersonal relationship, which is virtually slave-driven and founded on polygamy, in which the king is the greatest Israelite hero, is denounced in the poems. Solomon is described as a frivolous and an aggressive king (3:6–11), in contrast to the love of the couple:

> Look it is the litter of Solomon
> Around it are sixty mighty men ...
> all equipped with swords
> and expert in war,
> each with his sword at his thigh
> because of alarms by night. ...
> King Solomon made himself a palanquin. ...
> its interior was inlaid with love.
> Daughters of Jerusalem, come out. (3:6–11)[22]

This poem contrasts with the description of the bodies of the lovers in Song of Songs. Here the king is described as a piece of furniture, of his soldiers and of the number of women that live in his bed. It says nothing about his love or his feelings. For the author of Song of Songs, this man could never offer a model of sexuality in common with her ideas. She loves a body and expects her body to be loved, not her possessions. She demands the possibility of deciding for herself, of not being pushed into anonymous sex with a man of power but without a face. While the king fears the night, for its dangers and alarms, and is surrounded by bodyguards, she waits with passion:

> Upon my bed at night
> I sought him whom my soul loves.... (3:1)

> I slept but my heart was awake. (5:2)

The negative description of the king allows for a clearer emphasis on the positive value of love and sexuality in the couple. They come together because they love each other, and that fact is more important than any form of social or political power. Even more, they challenge the Solomonic model when they denounce, in a subtle but explicit way, a love that can be bought with money:

---

22. Solomon is not a hero in this poem; rather, he is undervalued when described in his frivolity, his lack of love, and in contrast to the simplicity and sensitivity of the young lovers. See Andiñach, *Cantar de los Cantares*, 96–104.

If one offered for love
all the wealth of one's house,
it would be utterly scorned. (8:7)

This purchasing of love was common practice in the court society. It was not related, in this case, to prostitution but rather was used to pay for favors and political agreements through the handing over of daughters for marriage.

There is a liberating theology in Song of Songs. We must search for it when taking a stand concerning the social place for truthful and sincere love—in particular the place of women—within the dynamics of a society that represses erotic feelings or at least denaturalizes them. Society channels erotic feelings into a structure in which women are subject to men, through forced marriages or marriages decided by others (8:8–9). This is the same society that offers approval to the man for wanting to break off a relationship with a woman when she rejects money (8:12). This collection of poems declares that God has another place in life for love and eroticism. It is when faced with the face of the other that we begin on this way.

Bibliography

Andiñach, Pablo R. *Cantar de los Cantares, El fuego y la ternura*. Buenos Aires: Lumen, 1997.

———. "Crítica de Salomón en el Cantar de los Cantares," *Revista Bíblica* 53 (1991): 129–56.

———. "Génesis." Pages 363–420 in *Comentario Bíblico Latinoamericano, 1: Pentateuco y textos narrativos*. Edited by Armando Levoratti. Estella: Verbo Divino, 2004.

Brenner, Athalya. *The Song of Songs*. OTG. Sheffield: JSOT Press, 1989.

Carrera, Nicholás de la. *Amor y erotismo del Cantar de los Cantares*. Madrid: Nueva Utopia, 1998.

Clines, David J. A. *Interested Parties: The Ideology of Writers and Readers of the Hebrew Bible*. JSOTSup 205; Gender, Culture, Theory 1. Sheffield: JSOT Press, 1995.

Coats, George W. *Genesis, with an Introduction to Narrative Literature*. FOTL 1. Grand Rapids: Eerdmans, 1983.

Croatto, Severino. *Crear y amar en libertad: Estudio de Génesis 2:4–3:24*. Buenos Aires: La Aurora, 1986.

Davidson, Richard. *Flame of Yahweh: Sexuality in the Old Testament*. Peabody, Mass.: Hendrickson, 2007.

Foucault, Michel. *The History of Sexuality*. 3 vols. New York: Vintage, 1980–1986.

Fox, Michael V. *The Song of Songs and the Ancient Egyptian Love Songs*. Madison: University of Wisconsin Press, 1985.

Levinas, Emmanuel. *Totality and Infinity: An Essay on Exteriority*. Translated by Alphonso Lingis. Pittsburgh: Duquesne University Press, 1969.

Rad, Gerhard von. *Genesis: A Commentary*. Translated by John H. Marks. OTL. Philadelphia: Westminster, 1961.

Ricoeur, Paul. "La maravilla, lo errático, el enigma." Pages 9–21 in *La Sexualidad*. Barcelona: Fonanella, 1979.

Tournay, Raymond J. *Quand Dieu parle aux hommes le langage de l'amour*. Paris: Gabalda, 1982.

Trible, Phyllis. *God and the Rhetoric of Sexuality*. OBT 2. Philadelphia: Fortress, 1978

Walsh, Carey Ellen. *Exquisite Desire: Religion, the Erotic, and the Song of Songs*. Minneapolis: Fortress, 2000.

Weems, Renita. "Song of Songs." Pages 156–60 in *The Woman's Bible Commentary*. Edited by Carol Newsom and Sharon Ringe. Louisville: Westminster, 1995.

GOD'S *ANTHROPOS* PROJECT

James Luther Mays

This essay is offered as an illustration of a theological approach to the interpretation of biblical texts.[1] Interpretation as theological inquiry is not isolated from other disciplines of construal that deal with language, literary character and context, and historical and social setting of biblical texts, that is, the objective questions that the text itself sets for the understanding. A theological approach, however, practices the disciplines of understanding with a set of assumptions derived from the identity and use of the biblical texts as *Scripture*. It assumes, among other things, that the thematic subject of the texts is God and God's way with the world, that coherence informs the diversity of the writings, and that some texts may illumine others.

The illustration takes theological anthropology as a focus and seeks to show how interpretation under such assumptions might contribute to the construal of this topic by a reading of one set of interconnected texts. It begins with a cluster of texts that contain self-descriptions by endangered persons, the prayers for help in the book of the Psalms. The prayers are chosen as a pivotal and organizing group of texts because occupation with the misery and majesty of the human condition is an essential feature of their composition. Questions and clues emerging from the self-descriptions in the prayers then lead to a hymn intercollated in the prayers, Ps 8.

---

1. This essay is a longer, revised, and retitled version of "The Self in the Psalms and the Image of God," originally published in *God and Human Dignity* (ed. R. Kendall Soulen and Linda Woodhead; Grand Rapids: Eerdmans, 2006), 27–43, and subsequently in James L. Mays, *Preaching and Teaching the Psalms* (ed. Patrick D. Miller Jr. and Gene M. Tucker; Louisville: Westminster John Knox, 2006), 51–68. Reprinted by permission of Wm. B. Eerdmans Publishing Company, all rights reserved.

The hymn, with its description of the glory and role of the human being in creation, calls for a consideration of Gen 1–3 as the prolegomena necessary to reading the Psalms. Finally, the connection between the psalmic prayers and the crucial metaphor of the image of God, on the one hand, and the portrayal of the identity and role of Jesus Christ, on the other, leads to texts in the Epistles and Gospels.

The Prayers of the Book of Psalms

The Prayers for Help as Witness to the Human Condition

In Ps 22 there is an arresting disavowal. In the course of describing his affliction, the psalmist says, "But I am a worm, and not human" (v. 6a).[2] This painful negation in its sharp brevity assumes a conviction about what it means to be a human being. The very experience of deprivation evokes a consciousness of what has been lost that is epitomized in the mournful cry, "not human." The description of trouble that forms the context of this negation identifies what it is that diminishes the psalmist's hold on personal identity as *human* and as well what its recovery requires. *Human*, in the psalmist's vocabulary, is not a biological classification. It is instead an existential identity that is realized and enacted in living. It is an awareness of what one is that can be lost and can be restored.

This exclamation about one's identity as *human* and its loss is a witness to what is going on in the prayers for help that compose the stock of the book of Psalms. By far the majority of psalms within the Psalter are, to use the genre customary in form criticism, laments of an individual.[3] They are prayers for help by a beleaguered and beset person. They record the voice of a person addressing God, describing the woes that afflict existence, pleading for deliverance, and anticipating restoration. There is also a smaller subset of prayers of thanksgiving by a person who has been delivered from trouble and a few prayers of trust in the face of danger. Along with the individual laments there is a much smaller group of similar corporate prayers. All of these genres share formal features, motifs, and purposes. The others are all internally related to the

---

2. Quotations of the Bible are from the NRSV unless otherwise noted.

3. For a survey of the laments of an individual and companion genres, see among others, Claus Westermann, *Praise and Lament in the Psalms* (trans. Keith R. Crim and Richard N. Soulen; Atlanta: John Knox, 1981).

individual prayers for help as their center of gravity. Even the hymns in the Psalter have an inner relation to the prayers in a way that holds the whole together in a rhetorical and theological coherence.

The psalmic prayers for help are a virtually unique access to the self-understanding of a human being in the biblical world. Nowhere else in Scripture is the first-person voice heard in such frequency and continuity as here. In the course of pleading for help, an "I" speaks to a "you" about "them" and "me" and "you." If the notion of "self" can be said to represent a consciousness that can employ personal pronouns, then these prayers are poignant disclosures of "self."[4] Though the prayers employ the vocabulary and categories and relationship of their culture and its traditions, they nonetheless reveal contours of a self that transcends a particular era. They are an eloquent testimony to a view of humankind, its conditions and necessities and potentials.

It is not only their character and content that make the prayers for help important tests for theological consideration of the human condition. The psalmic prayers have a double role in Jewish and Christian practice. They are Scripture and are used for instruction about God and God's way with the world and human beings. The prayers are also liturgy, prayers and praise that are said and sung in worship and rehearsed in the exercises of contemplation. When used for liturgy and devotion, the self in the psalmic prayers speaks through the mind and voice of believers.[5] The "I" of the prayer finds voice through the believer and in the process involves the user in the constitutive neediness and aspiration of the self in the prayers. The self whose voice is there in the psalm is always potentially a conditioning reality for the self-understanding of those who hear and say them. One has only to think of the role of the Psalms in Augustine's *Confessions* or Bonhoeffer's meditations to find witness to this interface of the psalmic and personal self. So the way in which the Psalms disclose the human condition continues through their use as

---

4. The use of the term "self" in this way is not intended to introduce the complex discussion in psychology and philosophy about the nature and relationship of self, ego, person, etc. See, e.g., chs. 4–6 in Wolfhart Pannenberg, *Anthropology in Theological Perspective* (trans. Matthew J. O'Connell; Philadelphia: Westminster, 1985).

5. On the identification of the user with the self in the psalms, see James L. Mays, *The Lord Reigns: A Theological Handbook to the Psalms* (Louisville: Westminster John Knox, 1994), 117–46.

Scripture and liturgy to inform and guide believers to self-discovery and expression.

In turning to the psalmic prayers as a resource for thinking about and living the human identity, it is important to read them for what they are. The psalms are largely cultic texts that were originally designed for a specific liturgical usage. The prayers were composed for professionals steeped and gifted in the oral and literary genres of worship. Little is known about the precise character of the ceremonies in which the prayers were used. So these prayers, of course, are not informed by an anthropology in any scientific sense. Their idiom is poetry, their language allusive and multivalent in reference. Their topic is the one who prays and praises. In their portrayals of need and hope for help, the psalms do record in a language shaped by tradition what it is like to be a human being. Their utterance expresses assumptions and convictions that answer questions about the nature and identity of a self. A knowledge of "who and what I am" informs their speech.

It is also important, as will be attempted in this study, to think about the psalmic prayers in their literary and canonical contexts. What is said about the self who speaks in them both assumes and is to be interpreted by what is said in the other psalms that compose their semantic environment and by the connections that inhere in them with other parts of Scripture. The inscripturalization of psalms in the formation of the book of Psalms and in the formation of the Jewish and Christian canons of Scripture provides the thought-world in which they have been and are to be read.

The Typology of the Self of the Prayers

The individual whose voice is heard in the first-person singular psalms is not a particular person. The distinct specific experience of those for whom the prayers were composed is interpreted and described through the conventions of a mode of prayer that had been nurtured in Israel's long history with its God. Because the vocabulary employed to describe the experience of trouble is conventional and formulaic, it is difficult to determine just what trouble occasions the prayer. The language can imply illness or alienation from the community through false accusation or the threatening hostility of others of personal failure and guilty conscience or combinations of such troubles.

The self speaks through a combination of vocabulary and literary elements that belong to the genre of individual prayers for help.[6] The selection of language and the arrangement of literary elements vary from prayer to prayer. It is this creative variation of common features that produces the particular prayers in their distinctness, but the function and language of the elements are so typical as to form a kind of template through which the self of those using the prayers is presented. The one who prays is given a self through which to be present to God.

Through all the variety in the prayers there is a sense in which the self who speaks is the same self. It is the presence of the paradigmatic self in all the prayers that makes it possible to draw general observations about the representation of the self in all of them.

The typical elements of the individual prayer for help are these. The prayers usually begin with a *vocative* that names the one to whom the prayer is addressed. In a *description of trouble*, the one praying speaks of self in terms of a neediness that is the reason for the prayer. The description typically refers to a neediness in relationship to God and self and others and follows a pattern of the three personal pronouns, "you/I/they." A *petition* forms the central organizing element. The petition is usually twofold, a plea to be heard and to be helped. A *motive* stating reasons why the prayer should be heard is frequently attached to the petition. An *affirmation of trust* confesses the confidence in God and God's help. Usually, the prayer concludes with *praise* of God, either expressed or promised or anticipated.

Psalm 13 has long been recognized as an almost formulaic illustration of these typical elements and their use.[7]

Formulaic Elements	Psalm 13
Vocative	O Lord (vv. 1aβ, 3aβ)
Description of trouble	
Second person/you/God	Will you forget me forever? How long will you hide your face from me? (v. 1)

---

6. For an extensive account of the typical elements that compose prayers for help, see ch. 3 of Patrick D. Miller Jr., *They Cried to the Lord: The Form and Theology of Biblical Prayer* (Minneapolis: Fortress, 1994).

7. See the exposition of Ps 13 in Mays, *The Lord Reigns*, 55–58.

First person/I/self	How long must I bear pain in my soul, and have sorrow in my heart all day long? (v. 2a–b)
Third person/they/others	How long shall my enemy be exalted over me? (v. 2c)
Petition	
To be heard	Consider and answer me, O LORD my God! (v. 13a)
To be helped	Give light to my eyes (v. 3b)
Motive	or I will sleep the sleep of death, and my enemy will say, "I have prevailed"; my foes will rejoice because I am shaken. (vv. 3c–4)
Affirmation of trust	But I trust in your steadfast love; my heart will rejoice in your salvation. (v. 5)
Praise	I will sing to the LORD, because he has dealt bountifully with me. (v. 6)

Because these literary elements are so consistently used in the composition of the prayers and their related genres, they imply a set of attributes of the human self that is expressed in them. The profile of the self that is sketched by the prayers is, of course, conditioned by the use for which they were composed. They belong to situations in which the self is endangered or at least conscious of endangerment, but perhaps it is in times of such awareness that the contours of the self come into clearest expression. Because of this, their articulation of an instance of human affliction is based on the actuality of the human and a view of its condition.[8] Five attributes are expressed.

(1) The prayers are the artifacts of a creature that can translate consciousness into communication. Of course, any writing or speech or conversation is an example of the linguisticality of the human animal. But the prayers are particularly evident instances of the capacity to move

---

8. Compare to John Polkinghorne, "Anthropology in an Evolutionary Context," in Soulen and Woodhead, *God and Human Dignity*, 89–103.

what the self experiences beyond the experience itself, so that self-consciousness transcends the self. When language becomes the form that the experience of endangerment takes, something essential is disclosed about this creature. It can move physical and mental pain from the sensory and psychic sphere to the sphere of language. What is felt is brought into reach of will and thought, of memory and anticipation. Through the language the self knows that it is more than the naked experience of affliction. There is a self that can set it forth, establish even a little distance, view it, and speak about it.

(2) The prayers exhibit the self as a relational reality. The consciousness of the self in them comes to expression with the use of the personal pronouns. The style is mostly direct address: an "I" speaks to a "you" about the you and I and a "they." The prayers disclose a self whose consciousness as an I is congruent with a consciousness of others. Even when the one who prays speaks specifically of himself, the speaking is said to another. These prayers support an understanding of the human self as constituted by its relationships to other persons.

(3) The prayers portray a self that exists in three spheres: physical, social, and theological. The threefold pattern of descriptions of trouble is based on the three spheres. The agenda of the descriptions is typically physical and mental affliction, the harmful effect of others, and the absence or wrath of God. The self is an embodied self that feels and thinks. It is a social self whose individual personhood is inextricably involved in a community of others. It is also a religious self that by individual intuition and given traditions needs and depends on a power transcendent of the human realm. In the way the prayers speak in these three constitutive contexts of the self, it is clear that they are interdependent, each conditioning the others. God, others, and the body are the skeins of which the fabric of the praying consciousness is woven.

(4) The prayers are the expression of an inherent neediness of the self. The petitions as the formal expression of the neediness are pleas to be heard and helped. A variety of imperatives are used, such as "heal me" (6:2; 41:4), "deliver me" (e.g., 3:7; 6:4; 7:1), "be gracious to me" (e.g., 4:1; 6:2; 9:13). The petitions seek relief from the troubles that are the occasions for the prayer: restoration of physical well-being, protection, and freedom will be cause to rejoice in praise. All these various needs are indications that the relational self is a dependent self. With dependence comes vulnerability. From time to time the psalmist offers a simple description of the self: "I am poor and needy" (40:17; 70:5; 86:1; 109:22). The assertion does

not refer to economic deprivation. It is rather a confession that existence is structured by finitude and fallibility. Even where physical and social dangers are relieved, the psalmist will say of himself, "I am poor and needy."

(5) The prayers argue that the essential neediness of the human self is for the person and presence of God. The self of the Psalms is inextricably religious in a way that includes and transcends the physical and social dimensions of its existence. The prayers are addressed to the divine "You" as the one who can maintain the self. They are the expression of a consciousness that includes in its nature an expectation of a transcendent being heard. The way in which needs of the physical, psychological, and social spheres are presented shows that they involve the religious need. The pain of the various tangible problems is ultimately their effect on the consciousness of God. The urgency of the resolutions requested is their power to renew the personal knowledge of the divine. In all the prayers, what the human "I" seeks is the divine "You." That God in and through and beyond all else is the need is always assumed and at times poignantly said in such confessions as Ps 73:25:

> Whom have I in heaven but you?
> And there is nothing on earth that I desire other than you.

The Prayers as Witnesses to Human Identity and Worth

There are problems to be recognized in using the psalmic prayers as a resource in a contemporary discussion of anthropology. The prayers are the product of a specific historical culture that qualifies and limits the notions that their composers employed. In their present form, they are attributed to a particular individual and related in some cases to episodes in his life. *Human* as adjective and noun in a taxonomic or moral sense is not part of their vocabulary. Nor is the worth of the individual self grounded in a natural or political status belonging to the individual as such.

In reading the prayers as documents of the self, however, it is important to remember that as a genre of human speech they are part of a larger general literature. The lament prayer was not unique to Israel but was composed and used across the religious cultures of the time and region of which Israel's history was a part.[9] Many of the conventions and much

---

9. See *ANET* for examples of lament prayers from the ancient Near East. On the use of lament in modern and ancient settings, see the essays in Nancy C. Lee and

of the vocabulary used to describe the troubles of the self in the Psalms appear to have been part of this ecumenical genre. This broader setting for the genre and its typical features is evidence that the self-descriptions in the Psalms participate in an "anthropology" that represents the experience of a wide and inclusive population. The self who speaks in the prayers is, of course, an Israelite self whose religious and moral consciousness is shaped by Israel's history with the God it came to know through that history. The psalmists pray as members of a selected people, and their prayers are informed by a particular knowledge and obligation that belongs to that special identity, but their prayers are a version of a general genre and a way of their liturgical participation in a larger humanity that is represented by the self described in the psalms.

Another factor in the paradigmatic character of the self in the prayers is the complexity of its identity.[10] Most of the prayers are introduced as the words of David, the prototypical messianic king whose story is told in the books of Samuel. It is evident from the redaction of the psalms and the formation of the book that the postexilic community used the prayers as expressions of its corporate identity. It is reasonably certain the prayers were as a type originally composed and used by particular hurting Israelites. After the final formation of the book, the psalms composed in first person were read and used by individuals in the community. It is a continuation of this flexible construal that in the Christian tradition the self in the prayers has been understood as a Christian worshiper or as the corporate church or as Christ.

The prayers do reflect a clear strong sense of self worth that is wounded and weakened by the trouble described. The lament in Ps 4:2 is almost thematic: "How long, you people, shall my honor [*kabod*] suffer shame." References to "shame/be ashamed" and "humiliate/be humiliated" as ways of speaking about injury to self worth are scattered through the Psalms (25:3; 31:2; 35:4; 37:19; 40:15–16; 44:16; 69:7–8, 20, 21; 70:3–4; 71:1, 13, 21, 25). "Honor/glory" (*kabod*) is used for the sense and status of worth that the self claims and cherishes in the few cases in which it is spoken of specifically (4:2; 7:5; 16:9; 62:7; 84:11). In these instances it is made clear that the honor claimed by the praying self derives from, is

---

Carleen Mandolfo, eds., *Lamentations in Ancient and Contemporary Cultural Contexts* (SBLSymS 43; Atlanta: Society of Biblical Literature, 2008).

10. The complexity of the self in the prayers is discussed in Mays, *The Lord Reigns*, 40–45.

dependent on, and can be restored by God. Shame is experienced by the self in its social setting, but honor is restored by the deliverance of God. The psalmist can even say, "But you, O LORD, are a shield around me, my glory, and the one who lifts up my head." (3:3).

THE CANONICAL CONTEXT OF THE PRAYERS

PSALM 8 AND THE PRAYERS

How these Israelite psalmists came to claim that God and a relation to God are the reality of their sense of self-worth, the prayers do not explain, but there is a hymn, Ps 8, that does.[11] Typical of the hymns in the Psalter, Ps 8 has as its subject what God is like and does. It is woven into the collection of prayers that compose books 1 and 2 of the Psalter, as if its place there were necessary. The theme stated at its beginning and end is the majesty of the name of the Lord. The theme echoes the close of Ps 7 and opening of Pss 9–10 in a way that shows that they are combined into a larger literary unit. This larger whole has been edited into an interrelated context for reading.

Psalm 8 declares what the prayers assume. The glory and honor of morals is the endowment of God. What the hymn says about the endowment, however, is not coherent with the identity of the self and the condition of humanity as described in the prayers.

The hymn praises God for the creation of humankind and speaks of the human being as the work of God. Humanity is described as God made it to be. The description of God's action in making the human species is composed with the use of a metaphor. God's creative act is portrayed as the inauguration of an official in a royal administration. The Lord appears as sovereign of the universe whose majesty pervades all the earth. The making of humanity consists of appointment to a rank, bestowal of recognition, and assignment of a role. Humankind is installed at a level just below the *'elohim*, the divine members of God's court and administration.[12] The dignity and importance of the human being is marked by the

---

11. On the "anthropology" of Ps 8, see James L. Mays, "What Is a Human Being? Reflections on Psalm 8," *ThTo* 50 (1994): 511–20.

12. See additional below and the investigations in E. Theodore Mullen, *The Divine Council in Canaanite and Early Hebrew Literature* (HSM 24; Cambridge: Harvard University Press, 1980).

bestowal of glory and honor, attributes of divine and human royalty. The assigned role is responsibility for one sector of God's creation, all other living creatures.

So the construing context for the significance and worth of humankind is the kingdom of God. The human, corporately and individually, bears and wears the glory and honor of God in the created world. The species is portrayed as a vassal of the divine rule. What it is and does is a representation of God's reign. Its dominion is intended to correspond to the divine sovereignty and is ordained to conform to God's will and way. Thus, humankind derives its identity and destiny from its relation to God. The relationship is not formal and external. It is constitutive of what the human creature is. Apart from that relation, the human creature has no ultimate meaning different from other living creatures.

In his reflective praise the psalmist wonders, "What are human beings that you are mindful of them, mortals that you care for them?" (8:4). The psalmist's assertion that humankind is created for the kingdom of God in the world is the answer to the question. It is by and through humankind that the reign of God is honored and glorified in the world. The human species, corporately and individually, is the project of God's kingdom. That is the unstated authorizing foundation of the prayers for help. God's endowment and purpose are at issue where the glory and honor of human beings are ignored and obscured.

Psalm 8 speaks about the entire human species, about "man" (MT *'enosh*; NRSV "human beings") and the "son of man" (MT *ben 'adam*; NRSV "mortals") as everyone. The individual of the prayers speaks very much as one of these human beings, but not just as any one being. The self of the prayers is a person whose sense of self is shaped by the memory of a particular people and its traditions. The "I" has a special personal relationship to God who is called "YHWH," the name of Israel's covenant deity, and is addressed as "My God" (e.g., 3:7; 5:2; 22:1–2). The supplicant identifies himself to God as "your servant" as a way of claiming a right to be heard (e.g., 27:9; 31:16; 34:22; 35:27).

Moreover, the picture of humanity reflected in the prayers is that of a fractured and flawed race. The corporate humanity crowned with glory and honor and ordained to dominion over other creatures is distorted. The destiny of corporate dominion is being realized in the domination of some human beings by others. In the prayers framing Ps 8, hostility, affliction, and oppression mark the human scene. Human conduct features arrogance, ruthlessness, and cunning. The predominant human corporate identities are self-seeking autonomous nations. We read of those whose actions deny the reality of God (10:3–11), of terrifying aggressors (10:18), and of petitions that they not succeed in domination (9:19–20).

The dissonance between the hymn's portrayal of created humankind and the hymn's contexting prayers' testimony to historical humankind is deafening. There is a tragic incongruence between what God has created and what the human being has wrought. The royalty conferred on the human being by God has become the kingdoms of this world in which it is forgotten "that they are only human" (9:20). Mortals turn the need for God into greed (10:3) and the glory given by God into pride (10:4). Reading the Ps 8 in the midst of the prayers evokes its eschatological tension. In its present place in the midst of the prayers, it locates the human as it is created to be in the midst of humanity as it is. The human in history is between creation and realization, living an unfulfilled destiny in a flawed and perverted way.

The protological account of this dissonance is, of course, recorded in the sequence of Gen 1 and 2–3. Psalm 8 is a poetic version of Gen 1:26–28. The story of a humanity that leaves Eden (Gen 2–4) to live the curse instead of the blessing, to murder the brother, and to fashion culture as a temple of self-assertion instead of as room for the Presence is the necessary canonical preface to the enigmatic humanity portrayed in the prayers.

The Image and Likeness of God

In Gen 1:26–27 the nature and worth given to human beings by divine creation is designated by the term "image of God." The notion has always been the central theme of theological anthropology.[13] From the patristic to the modern period, Christian theology has connected the dignity of human nature with the theme of the image of God. The inclination has been to define the concept in terms of capacities and attributes such as reason, will, knowledge, righteousness, and happiness that could be reasonably inferred from the term and other texts of Scripture. But there is broad agreement currently that the biblical text does not elaborate

---

13. On "image of God" and its importance in theological anthropology, see Christoph Schwoebel, "Recovering Human Dignity," and Hans S. Reinders, "Human Dignity in the Absence of Agency," in Soulen and Woodhead, *God and Human Dignity*, 44–58 and 121–42.

the term in such a way.[14] Verses 26–27 simply use the words "image" and "likeness" to designate a relation of the human being to God in the human's created nature. The designations apply to both genders of the species and assign dominion over the other creatures as the role of the created human being.

When the usage of these defining words is examined in other texts, their meaning is clear enough, and it is a reasonable assumption that Gen 1:26–27 would be read in a way consistent with these other uses.[15] "Image" (*ṣelem*) is used for representations of a deity (Num 33:52; 2 Kgs 11:18; 2 Chr 23:17; Amos 5:26; Ezek 7:20; 16:17), for a likeness of mice and tumors (1 Sam 6:5–11), and for a likeness to men (Ezek 23:14), all in reference to cultic settings, and once for shadows as fleeting reflections of people (Ps 37:9). In its twenty-five occurrences, "likeness" (*demut*) consistently means "similar to but not the same as." In what the similarity consists depends on context (e.g., Ezek 1:5; Dan 10:16; 2 Kgs 16:10; Isa 40:18). In the repetition of Gen 1:26 in 5:1–2, "likeness" replaces "image," and in 5:3 the order of the two terms is reversed so as to imply that the two are regarded by the writer as virtual synonyms. Here the terms are also used to describe the relation of Seth to his father, Adam. The meaning is not, however, that Seth looked like Adam but that what in Adam made him an image or likeness of God is passed on in the generational process. It is specific to the species, not alone to the individual first man.

The last use of "image of God" as identification of the created nature of man occurs in the context of God's instruction of Noah after the flood (Gen 9:6). The fact that man is made in the image of God is said to be the reason why the life of each person requires ultimate respect from other men. The attribute "image of God" belongs to an individual of the species as well as to the species as a whole. It is what gives each person worth.[16]

---

14. See the discussion in Claus Westermann, *Genesis 1–11: A Commentary* (trans. John J. Scullion; CC; Minneapolis: Augsburg, 1984), 142–61.

15. On *ṣelem* and *demut* in the Old Testament, see Hans Wildberger, "צלם, *ṣelem*, image," *TLOT* 3:1080–85.

16. The human identity and destiny are given to every human irrespective of their condition and capacity. As Hans S. Reinders argues, "[O]ur humanity is a gift from the beginning to the end.... divine agency—not human agency—is the primary concept of theological anthropology" ("Human Dignity in the Absence of Agency," 139).

The postdiluvian setting of this text also shows that the image of God belongs to the human being beyond and through all the drastic failures of mortals recorded in Gen 3–9.

When read in the light of Ps 8, Gen 1:26–28 appears to be based on the same rank and role pattern of identification featured in the hymn's use of a metaphor of royal ordination and installation. The rank in the psalm is "little less than 'elohim [the divine beings?]" and in Genesis it is "image of 'elohim." The role in both is dominion over the creatures. The plural style of the self-exhortation, "let us" and "our image," almost certainly indicates that the notion of the divine royal court staffed by the 'elohim in which God exercises his sovereignty in relation with the human world is assumed by the text.[17] The specification of male and female and the use of the plural "them" to refer to "man" is a way of including both genders in the image-identity rather than an indication of what the image-identity is. The identification of the human being as the image of God belongs to the deep and rich tradition of thinking about God's relation to the universe as a divine sovereignty that is thematic for the breadth of Scripture. The human rank and role in the world corresponds to that of God over the world. Psalm 115:16 remarks that "the heavens are the LORD's heavens, but the earth he has given to human beings," yet another specification of spheres of authority and responsibility as constitutive of the human.

What the "image of God" texts in Genesis and those related to them claim is that the relation of representation and resemblance to God is constitutive of human created nature. It is not separable but part of human nature. It holds for the species and individuals in it. It is central and foundational to the biblical view of God's way with the world as anthropocentric.

THE OTHER LIKENESS

The texts concerning man as image of God all appear in Gen 1–11, a narrative complex that has the protological formation of humankind as its subject. The complex contains a second account of creation in chapters 2–3, which with chapter 1 form a double introduction to the complex.

---

17. The *Sitz im Leben* in the plural style is identified in Patrick D. Miller Jr., *Genesis 1–11: Studies in Structure and Theme* (JSOTSup 8; Sheffield: University of Sheffield, 1978), 9–26.

The second account features another likeness of human beings to the *'elohim* (3:5, 22). This likeness is not a representing and resembling God in the matter of God's sovereignty but rather the opposite. It stands in tension with the created likeness. This likeness consists of "knowing good and evil."

In the story told in Gen 2–3, the knowledge of good and evil is the fruit of the forbidden tree that stands in the center of the garden (2:9, 17), so it is a divinely prohibited possibility for human beings. It is a consummation promised and realized by the contradiction of God (3:1, 4). It is the autonomous prerogative to decide what is nourishing and beautiful and best for living life (3:6). The acquisition of the knowing evokes a self that is self-conscious before others and afraid of God (3:7, 10). It results in an experience of life where blessing is distorted by curse (3:14–19).

"Like *'elohim*, knowing good and evil," means assuming divine autonomy in discerning and deciding what is beneficial to life and what is detrimental.[18] The expression does not refer to the capacity of reason and its use but to a misuse of reason that is centered radically in the self. When the Lord God says, using the plural style of self-reference again, "See, the man has become like one of us, knowing good and evil," the sovereignty of God and its mythic setting in the divine court is again alluded to (3:22; see 1:26). God is sovereign over life and living. The issue of human life and death is thematic in the story of Eden. God is source, support, and limit of human life (2:7, 9; 3:4, 14, 17, 22). That the human being should claim independent sovereignty over life puts the human in conflict with the divine (3:22). To seek in the created world apart from the Creator the source that supports and enriches and directs life is the essential impulse to idolatry (Rom 1:18–25).

After its twofold introduction, the narrative complex of Gen 1–11 unfolds its account of the formation of humankind. The human as protagonist of history is portrayed in stories and genealogies. The themes are relationships and alienations: between genders, siblings, occupations, parents and children, kindred, languages, nations, and throughout the narrative sequence between the human being and God. The stories are all a sequel to 3:22. They concern a corporate and individual self that has become its own center and reference in the matter of life and death. Twice in the narrative sequence there are reminders that this self is a

---

18. On the phrase "knowledge of good and evil," see *TLOT* 2:512–14.

God-imaged creature (5:1–2; 9:6), but nothing in the telling reconciles the contradiction between the two likenesses of God and man. The creation of the human being to represent and resemble God's sovereignty in the world seems to be a given of human identity, but a given of an essential destiny that has to be realized. The self-centered enterprise to take possession of life is a radical disconnection with the original likeness. The two identify the human creature in their contradiction, and the contrast between the two is the analogue and theological preface to the disparity between the prayers for help and their explanatory hymn. If one begins with Gen 1–11 to learn about the human condition, the disparity between Ps 8 and its companion prayers for help is no surprise.

Representation and Likeness as Call and Promise

It is an apparent anomaly that "image of God" does not recur in the rest of the Old Testament. As crucial as it is in the account of the beginnings, the phrase as identification of the human being disappears, leaving its one poetic echo in Ps 8. In Gen 12:1–3 a further identification of human beings beyond creation is inaugurated by God. It is a particular identity constituted by a command and a promise. The command is a call to a future that God will provide; the promise is a history of greatness in which God offers to all humankind the lost blessing purposed at creation. From Gen 12 forward the biblical story will focus on particular identities of human beings created by command and promise. These further identities become the surrogate enactors of the values and significance of human beings. Corporately and individually these further identities are people of God, covenant people, servant of God. In the biblical story the rest of humanity, social groups and nations and individuals, are viewed in relation to these identities created by the command and promise of God.

While "image of God" is no longer used for the human being in the biblical story, its actuality is a structural theme of the biblical account of God and humankind. The actuality continues in the calling and destiny of human beings to represent and resemble God in the world. When this calling and destiny is given to some, it assumes and continues the purpose and possibility vested in the creation of humankind. The pivotal defining text is Exod 19:3–6, God's inaugural words to Israel as a covenant people. Israel is given a role and destiny to represent and resemble God among the peoples of the world. Though an existence defined by the demands and promise of the covenant, Israel will have a particular and special relation to the Lord as God's priestly kingdom and holy nation who represent God's sovereignty over all the earth. The corporate people are even referred to as "Son of God" (Exod 4:22; Hos 11:1). Their corporate and individual life is to resemble the God whose they are. The primary divine attributes of holiness, righteousness, justice, and lovingkindness are the ethical responsibility of the people, a responsibility urged by exhortations such as, "You shall be holy to me, for I the LORD am holy" (Lev 20:26). Within the people of God the Davidic messianic king especially is given the role of representing and resembling God, first of all to his subjects but also to the nations. He is called "Son of God." He is to exemplify the attributes and do the work of the Lord. Dominion is his vocation; righteousness, justice, and peace are his tasks. All humankind in their historical identity as the "nations" is his domain (see, e.g., Pss 2; 18; 20; 21; 72).[19]

The story of Israel as told in the Old Testaments is broadly a sequel to Gen 1–11. Israel is a part of the humanity described there, and its career concerns all humankind. Their identity and destiny as the people of the Lord is a movement toward the realization of humanity's identity and destiny as image of God.

THE PRAYERS IN CONTEXT

The psalmic prayers need to be read in light of this deep background and in the context of the biblical story. They are the prayers of a creature created to be the image and likeness of God, a self that seeks life by knowing good and evil, an individual in community chosen and called to be the servant of God.

As creatures whose destiny and identity is to represent and resemble God in the matter of God's sovereignty, the psalmists bear an indissoluble relation to God. The prayers are the expression of an intimation of dependence that informs all human beings, whether denied or confessed, a longing that cannot be satisfied within and by the self alone. The prayers arise out of an inherent need for meaningfulness for existence, a compulsion of the self to find its own meaning in mastery of the world and its creatures. The psalmists pray out of an ineradicable instinct of human sig-

---

19. See "'In a Vision': The Portrayal of the Messiah in the Psalms" in Mays, *The Lord Reigns*, 99–107.

nificance in the world. In them a self pleads for the attention that is due the one to whom the central place within creation belongs.

As the "living beings" of Gen 2:7, the psalmists want to live. The prayers come from a self whose deepest essential hunger is for life. They put in words an awareness that life is more than being alive. As a self that decides for itself what it wants and needs for life, the psalmist prays for what it wants and needs for life as a physical, social, and religious being. In the anxiety that arises in a self over its life, the psalmists see body and others and God in terms of the struggle to possess and control life. In their frequent defense and justification of the self who prays, in the absolute categorization of others in terms of the needs of the self, and in their appeal to self-concern as a motivation for God's help, the prayers are the voice of that struggle to own and possess life.

The specific identity and destiny of the psalmists as they pray is "servant of the LORD," the human beings made able by the electing formation of their history to say "my God" to the power and mystery of the universe. They are selves formed by this further creative knowing. At their deepest level the prayers are a giving way of one person to the other. In the prayers God is not just and only the transcendent counterpart to human finitude and fallibility, a power called on to save and serve the miseries of life. The God of the prayers has a name, a person to person identity. The Lord is a divine self with characteristics of person and work. In the biblical vocabulary, "servant" designates one whose identity and doing are determined by belonging to another. The servant is a person whose self is that of another. The praying self is itself in the relation of belonging, depending, and trusting. That is a relationship in which the autonomous knowledge of good and evil is drawn toward the knowledge of the Lord.

So the psalmic prayers are fraught with an eschatological tension. The help the psalmists seek from God is more than relief and rescue from current plights. Their petitions are the voice of an identity not yet complete and a destiny to be fulfilled. The prayers are a litany of a longing to be what the psalmists are: the creatures created in the image of God.

Jesus as Call and Promise of Representation and Likeness

In the New Testament, Ps 8 is cited, the term "image of God" reappears, and descriptions of trouble from the psalmic prayers are used to tell the story of one man's tribulation—all this concerning Jesus of Nazareth. In concert these resumptions from the Old Testament set his person in connection with the promise and predicament of the human recounted there and claim him as the realization of the identity and destiny for which humankind was created. The author of Hebrews, after quoting Ps 8, says that the realization of humankind's destiny to represent and resemble the sovereignty of God in the world is not visible in the world, then adds, "but we do see Jesus" (Heb 2:9a), and he means the crucified and risen Jesus. In his suffering and death, Jesus is one with humankind. Through the power of his resurrection he incorporates humankind in his realization of the identity and destiny for which they are created.

In the Gospels the accounts of the suffering and death of Jesus use elements from three of the prayers for help, Pss 22, 31, and 69.[20] The words and experiences of the psalmists are woven into the fabric of the passion narratives. What the self in the prayers said and suffered become the words and tribulations of Jesus. In this way the accounts draw a connection not only between the prayers of Jesus and the Psalms but also between the person of Jesus and the person portrayed in the self-description of the psalm. The result is a mutual twofold identification. Jesus identifies himself as one of "the poor and needy," joins himself to the company of the afflicted, and asserts a solidarity with them. The psalmic prayers, on the other hand, identify Jesus as a self like the psalmists, a mortal, vulnerable in physical, social, and religious being, who cries out for life and asks in prayer that God's will should serve his life. "In the days of his flesh, Jesus offered up prayers and supplications, with loud cries and tears, to the one who was able to save him from death," observes the author of Hebrews (5:7).

He is one like the psalmists, but unlike in one radical way that is disclosed in his Gethsemene prayer: "Abba, Father, for you all things are possible; remove this cup from me; yet, not what I want, but what you want" (Mark 14:36).[21] In the matter of life, Jesus' reference to his own will is a link to the psalmic identification, but the phrase "not what I want" is not heard in the prayers in the Psalms, an unqualified offering of the self

---

20. On the prayers for help as used in the passion narrative of the Gospels, see James L. Mays, "Prayer and Christology: Psalm 22 as Perspective on the Passion," *ThTo* 42 (1985): 322–31.

21. On the importance of this saying for Christology, see James L. Mays, "'Now I Know': An Exposition of Genesis 22:1–19 and Matthew 26:36–46," *ThTo* 58 (2004): 519–25.

of a human to the You of God. "Although he was a Son, he learned obedience through what he suffered; and having been made perfect, he became the source of eternal salvation for all who obey him" (Heb 5:8–9). This crucified, risen Jesus is a perfected human self whose person opens up a possibility for other humans that the Pauline letters will call "the image of God."

In the letters attributed to Paul, the concept of "image" reappears to be used to speak of the relationship between God and humankind.[22] It is used first of all to speak about who and what Jesus Christ is. Christ is "the image of the invisible God, the firstborn of all creation" (Col 1:15). He renders the invisible God visible in the created world. He as image preceded the existence of all that was created, so that from the beginning he was the destiny given humankind in its creation as image of God. The gospel brings to light the glory of Christ as "image of God" as it reveals him as the manifestation and likeness of God (2 Cor 4:4).

The second way "image" is used is to speak of the relationship between Christ and those who are being incorporated in him through faith. Christ Jesus so absolutely preempts the role of image of God that the vocation and destiny of human beings can be realized only through a transformation of their existence by his spirit (2 Cor 3:1–8). Once in a case of misguided interpretation, Paul does call the male "the image and glory of God" (1 Cor 11:7), so Paul thinks of humankind as image of God in their created identity. It is, however, an identity that in human historical life has not been actualized. It is by the transformative power of the gospel that human beings are progressively conformed and transformed to the self they are created to become (Rom 8:29; 1 Cor 15:49–51; 2 Cor 3:18), a transformation that is consummated eschatologically. This transformation that is being conformed to Christ is discussed in terms besides "image," such as old and new man (Col 3:9; Eph 4:22–24), old and new creation (2 Cor 5:17; Gal 6:15).

The paradigmatic action that originates the transformation is the crucifixion and resurrection of Jesus (e.g., Rom 6:11–14). Paul can say of his own self, "I have been crucified with Christ; and it is no longer I who live, but it is Christ who lives in me. And the life I now live in the flesh I

---

22. On "image of God" in Pauline letters, see Udo Schnelle, *The Human Condition: Anthropology in the Teachings of Jesus, Paul and John* (Minneapolis: Fortress, 1996), 98–102.

live by faith in the Son of God, who loved me and gave himself for me" (Gal 2:20). Through faith, the love and self-giving of the representative and likeness of God begins to reconfigure the self of others in his own image.

In the Gospels, when Jesus appears proclaiming "The kingdom of God is at hand" and calling his hearers to repentance, it is because the reign of God is present in his person and worth. His presence brings the possibility for people to undergo the transformation that relocates them in the coming kingdom of God and so to realize their identity and destiny for which they are created. The parallel in the Gospels to Christ's taking over the self of the believer is found in Jesus' way with the disciples. He interrupts their lives with an unconditional call to follow him. His way is to be their way. Following was a giving up of self to Christ that was a form of crucifixion. They were to learn through Jesus that the effort to be the humankind of Gen 3:2 and so to save their existence as selves is a way of losing the self (Matt 16:24–28; Mark 8:34–38; Luke 9:23–27). Along with the entire New Testament, the Gospels teach that encountering the crucified, risen Jesus inaugurates the transforming of the believer's self.

God's *Anthropos* Project

This essay illustrates a theological approach to the interpretation of a set of texts from the Protestant canon—the use of biblical texts as Scripture—and the approach yields theological conclusions. The approach assumes that the texts speak about God and God's way with the world and that the texts cohere and contribute meaning to each other intertextually.

The psalmic prayers read in the context of the related texts that form their canonical environment support a vision of the meaning and worth of the human being. The self whose voice is heard in the prayers confesses a vulnerability and fallibility of life that belong to every mortal. That the afflictions of finitude and failure are held up to God in prayers is a disclosure of the essential neediness of the human condition. To be human is to be a creature whose nature and destiny in life is incomplete apart from God.

The presupposition and past behind the prayers is creation and covenant. Those who pray are first of all "living beings" created to glorify their creator in lives that represent and resemble God, but "all have sinned and fall short of the glory of God" (Rom 3:23). They are also those sinners to whom God has irrevocably committed himself in order that by call and commandments they may be drawn to a fulfillment of their created destiny in ministry to all human beings.

The prospect and promise before the prayers is Christ and consummation. Among the company of the called and commanded, one appears who bears the afflictions of mortal living in a life that perfectly represents and resembles the Creator. The Spirit of his offered and resurrected life is power to transform all and each in the whole human race into fulfillment of the destiny for which *anthropos* was created.

The human race and every individual in it are given their meaning and worth by their location within this plan, this economy of God that runs from creation to consummation.[23] The "mystery" of God and God's way with the world is disclosed in it. The story of the world is the story of God's *anthropos* project. God's *anthropos* project is the divine economy through which God is glorified. As one summary of the Christian faith says as introduction, "The chief end of man is to glorify God and enjoy him forever" (Westminster Shorter Catechism, question 1). As Irenaeus of Lyon declares, "The glory of God is a living man and the life of man is the vision of God" (*Haer.* 4.20.7).

Bibliography

Lee, Nancy C., and Carleen Mandolfo, eds. *Lamentations in Ancient and Contemporary Cultural Contexts*. SBLSymS 43. Atlanta: Society of Biblical Literature, 2008.

Mays, James L. *The Lord Reigns: A Theological Handbook to the Psalms*. Louisville: Westminster John Knox, 1994.

———. " 'Now I Know': An Exposition of Genesis 22:1–19 and Matthew 26:36–46." *ThTo* 58 (2004): 519–25.

———. "Prayer and Christology: Psalm 22 as Perspective on the Passion." *ThTo* 42 (1985): 322–31.

———. "The Self in the Psalms and the Image of God." Pages 27–43 in *God and Human Dignity*. Edited by R. Kendall Soulen and Linda Woodhead. Grand Rapids: Eerdmans, 2006.

———. "What Is a Human Being? Reflections on Psalm 8" *ThTo* 50 (1994): 511–20.

---

23. See the elaboration of M. Douglas Meeks, "The Economy of Grace," in Soulen and Woodhead, *God and Human Dignity*, 196–214.

Meeks, M. Douglas. "The Economy of Grace." Pages 196–214 in *God and Human Dignity*. Edited by R. Kendall Soulen and Linda Woodhead. Grand Rapids: Eerdmans, 2006.

Miller, Patrick D., Jr. *Genesis 1–11: Studies in Structure and Theme*. JSOTSup 8. Sheffield: University of Sheffield, 1978.

———. *They Cried to the Lord: The Form and Theology of Biblical Prayer*. Minneapolis: Fortress, 1994.

Mullen, E. Theodore. *The Divine Council in Canaanite and Early Hebrew Literature*. HSM 24. Cambridge: Harvard University Press, 1980.

Pannenberg, Wolfhart. *Anthropology in Theological Perspective*. Translated by Matthew J. O'Connell. Philadelphia: Westminster, 1985.

Polkinghorne, John. "Anthropology in an Evolutionary Context." Pages 89–103 in *God and Human Dignity*. Edited by R. Kendall Soulen and Linda Woodhead. Grand Rapids: Eerdmans, 2006.

Reinders, Hans S. "Human Dignity in the Absence of Agency." Pages 121–42 in *God and Human Dignity*. Edited by R. Kendall Soulen and Linda Woodhead. Grand Rapids: Eerdmans, 2006.

Schnelle, Udo. *The Human Condition: Anthropology in the Teachings of Jesus, Paul and John*. Minneapolis: Fortress, 1996.

Schwoebel, Christoph. "Recovering Human Dignity." Pages 44–58 in *God and Human Dignity*. Edited by R. Kendall Soulen and Linda Woodhead. Grand Rapids: Eerdmans, 2006.

Westermann, Claus. *Genesis 1–11: A Commentary*. Translated by John J. Scullion. CC. Minneapolis: Augsburg, 1984.

———. *Praise and Lament in the Psalms*. Translated by Keith R. Crim and Richard N. Soulen. Atlanta: John Knox, 1981.

Liberating Readings of the Bible: Contexts and Conditions

Erhard S. Gerstenberger

Probing into the Matter

One of the central questions of the ongoing debate about liberation theology is, What makes the Holy Scriptures of Jewish-Christian tradition such a revolutionary, antiestablishment force?[1] Dogmatic answers assert that it is the will of God revealed in the Scriptures, which should simply be obeyed. Ironically, however, those who cling to dogmatic affirmations about the Bible rarely discover the Word that liberates from oppression, hunger, and need. Many opt for traditional values and existing structures to avoid political, social, or economic turmoil. The dogmatic stance ranges from conservative to reactionary in its attitudes. In any case, an answer that relies on an absolute presupposition will prove inadequate in scholarly discourse (and in the rationality of faith; see 1 Pet 3:15). Why, then, should the Bible contain powerful criticism and outright rejection of divine powers and monarchic governments that ancient Near Eastern and modern societies believe essential for human life and social organization?[2]

Looking at the Old Testament in particular, we may find a satisfying answer to our query. In my estimation, the major part of the Hebrew

---

1. John F. A. Sawyer writes, "The multi-faceted nature of the Bible ... seem[s] to have provided its readers with all the inspiration and authority they need, whether to justify a theological doctrine or to create a work of art or to rebel against an oppressive regime" ("Introduction," in *The Blackwell Companion to the Bible and Culture* [ed. John F. A. Sawyer; Oxford: Blackwell, 2006], 2).

2. Israel certainly took part in a basically positive appreciation of divine kingship as a mediator of God's will and as a blessing to the people. See 2 Sam 7; Pss 2, 45, 89, 110, and many other passages.

Scriptures does not report many experiences of glorious reigns, political power, and economic wealth of the people of Israel. There certainly are extant some echoes of such high points of national life—more plausibly expressed in chance lamenting remarks such as "In those days there was no king in Israel" (Judg 21:25) than in fictitious, exaggerating episodes such as 1 Kgs 10—but the overwhelming witness of the Bible (and we may well include the New Testament writings at this point) comes out of low and precarious conditions of life or is ventilating such experiences of danger, insecurity, powerlessness, and minority status that over centuries did engulf families, clans, and that group that came to nominate itself "Israel," claiming to be the sole people of God. Judah's history of suffering and of being dominated in its homeland came to a culmination in its defeat by the Babylonians (597–587 B.C.E.), the great deportations, and the reorganization of the people on the basis of exclusive Yahweh-faith during the sixth and fifth centuries B.C.E.[3]

The difference between human groups exercising a dominant role and those leading their lives in subjugated, marginalized, and minority positions does heavily influence the way that God is conceptualized and human affairs are regulated. Theology and ethics, at least to a large extent, are shaped by the experiences of social life. Large accumulations of political and economic power cannot but produce a dominant, even hegemonic, theology, namely, a state-preserving religious ideology. The Byzantine and Roman Empires of the Christian era are good examples, but also the medieval super-states in the wake of ancient Rome, with the Vatican as center or opponent. Many thinkers throughout the centuries have commented on the characteristics of imperial thinking, claims, and excesses. In modern times, it was philosophers such as Karl Marx, Max Weber, and Ernst Bloch who analyzed the aspirations of big government, and it was, for example, William Fulbright who sharply denounced as "arrogant" the ambitions of world powers to dominate the world (cf.

---

3. I personally hold the exilic and postexilic periods to be the real cradle of Yahweh-faith (monotheism), Scripture (Torah), ecclesiastical organization, religious feasts and customs, synagogue service, etc. See Erhard S. Gerstenberger, *Theologies in the Old Testament* (trans. John Bowden. Minneapolis: Fortress; London: T&T Clark, 2002), 207–81; and idem, *Israel in der Perserzeit: 5. und 4. Jahrhundert v. Chr.* (Biblische Enzyklopädie 8; Stuttgart: Kohlhammer, 2005), trans. as *Israel in the Persian Period: The Fifth and Fourth Centuries B.C.E.* (trans. Siegfried Schatzmann; Atlanta: Society of Biblical Literature, forthcoming).

Gen 11:1–9). All the empire-like associations we experience need to produce, in order to undergird their status and ambitions, an empire-like and "arrogant" theology, glorifying and guarding their own powers.[4]

Not so those groups that gave birth to the canon of Hebrew Scriptures and, later, the Christian Scriptures. They, for the most part, emerge from precarious conditions of life, their authors and transmitters living in lower stratums of the social pyramid, often in precarious conditions. Their God is a familial-type of deity with great concerns for the lowly and suffering, a God who seeks to liberate people and who, taking the side of underdogs in history and society, is opposed to oppressors. Of course, the result is a partisan theology in favor of lower-class and minority groups.

Personal Experiences

Personal socialization and outlook, no doubt, play a large part in the formation of theological concepts. Therefore, I recount briefly my own experiences that brought me close to liberation theology. Born into a miner's family of the industrial Ruhr area, I inherited a good amount of lower-class feelings. This potential for social critique was strengthened by postwar opposition against German rearmament, to which I was drawn through the influence of Hans-Walter Wolff at Wuppertal church seminary (later at Heidelberg University) and by politicians such as Gustav Heinemann and Johannes Rau. With the predisposition to question all kinds of haughtiness and chauvinism, I came to the United States and learned much about grass-roots-level participation through the Centre for the Study of Democratic Institutions, as well as through many conversations, lectures, and conferences while studying and teaching at Yale Divinity School. From there I came back to a lower-class German parish at Essen, Ruhr area, and went out again to teach in Brazil. My sojourn there, in the southern region of that Portuguese-speaking commonwealth, probably was the decisive step toward identifying (although not uncritically) with liberating exegesis, principally in my field of Old Testament studies. To be so close to unmitigated exploitation and utter human despair—behind our house, dozens of families were living from the waste dumps—to be involved in warm-hearted basic movements striving for human dignity and peace (against repressive military govern-

---

4. See Jörg Rieger, *Christus und das Imperium* (Münster: LIT-Verlag, 2009).

ments), and to discuss fervently the matters of injustice and oppression at the Faculdade de Teologia of São Leopoldo, as well as in Roman Catholic institutions and parishes—all this convinced me to take the side of people who cry for liberation from their wretched living conditions (see Exod 2:23).[5]

Latin American Conditions and Connotations

Brazil, that huge country covering about a third of Latin America, suffered tremendous economic and political ills in the 1970s. The military junta tried to cling to power by torture, censure, and all the other measures of dictatorial regimes. Their economic programs had failed, inflation went up to dazzling heights, foreign investors plundered national resources, and internal corruption of the ruling class ate up the rest. In consequence, more than half of the population was sinking into poverty. As it may be expected, but still remains a miracle in my eyes, within the traditional churches—Roman Catholicism counted for 95 percent of the populace—a strong minority of Christians became alerted to the inhuman conditions of the marginalized majority. Seas of *favelas* (slums) in and around the big cities testified to the dire lack of rights, jobs, medical care, and education for the masses. Only extremely diehard conservatives would shut their eyes to the problems at hand, like the lady who told us, on stepping ashore in Rio de Janeiro, on 9 March 1975, that there was no poverty in Brazil. She said, "The beggars that you may encounter, deserve their fate. They do not want to work, that's all." Right-wing Christians would typically agree. But the miracle of (small-scale, it is true) liberation movements, within and without the churches, was overwhelming.

The Bible clearly was one, if not the decisive, motif and spiritual fountain for a large segment of these liberating movements. The Bible, it seemed to me, was present everywhere when Christians came together to discuss the social abyss of the time. Study groups sprang up, already in the early 1960s, in many "basic communities" (*Comunidades de Base*). The larger public, in a way, was caught by the enthusiasm around the Bible. There were Bible monuments, Bible festivals, and Bible readings all

---

5. See my autobiographical sketch in Sebastian Grätz and Bernd U. Schipper, eds., *Alttestamentliche Wissenschaft in Selbstdarstellungen* (Göttingen: Vandenhoeck & Ruprecht, 2007), 140–52.

over the country. People reading a Bible on long bus rides or in parks and public places was a common sight. One significant example of the liberating force developed through biblical interpretation was (and still is) the Centro Biblico established by Carlos Mesters and others.[6] The school uses modern methods of biblical exegesis in courses and a host of publications in order to enable lay people to lead study groups in their communities nationwide. Innumerable local and regional enterprises of this kind have sprung up over the time. They all demonstrate one thing, that the Scriptures in themselves carry liberating messages through the ages down to our own times. What is more important, it seems to me, is that this old message, in order to be activated again, needs to meet social conditions that are similar to those prevalent in biblical times.

We need to reflect about this hermeneutical condition for letting old traditional voices speak out again, because there certainly are risks involved in this procedure. If present-day situations are considered relevant to the interpretation of the biblical contents, then what happens to the old Protestant principle of "letting the Bible speak for itself" (one of the strong statements of Gerhard von Rad!)? Do we concede it as an improper, if not warranted, influence on exegesis to employ modern life-conditions? I do not think so. On the contrary, in my opinion we must interpret Scripture always within the tense relationship of ancient and present-day conditions and viewpoints. Using the famous threefold approach to the Bible spelled out by Carlos Mesters (starting from our own lives, going back to the Bible, and coming again to our situation), we may recognize a continuous back and forth between present and past in the process of exegesis. It is the past witness of the Scriptures that can open minds to the inhuman sufferings of contemporaries. Realizing this life-situation today, and believing that God does not accept such a state of affairs caused by the human mismanagement of resources and labor, one may discuss the measures to be taken today in full responsibility over against the living God. The other problem that immediately comes to the fore when admitting any necessary affinity between ancient and modern social conditions to facilitate interpretation is this: If the experiences of

---

6. Two recent German studies give an excellent overview of the work done: Wolfgang Schürger, *Theologie auf dem Weg der Befreiung* (Erlanger Monographien 24; Erlangen: Verlag für Mission und Ökumene, 1995); and Susann Schüepp, *Bibellektüre und Befreiungsprozesse: Eine empirisch-theologische Untersuchung mit Frauen in Brasilien* (Exegese in unserer Zeit 16; Münster: LIT-Verlag, 2006).

oppression and misery need to coincide in order to make biblical cries for liberation audible again, what about present-day interpreters, who in the vast majority are reasonably secure, well-to-do, and middle-class and who claim to be spokespersons for biblical concerns? Are we not more likely to be a part of oppressive systems that, in reality, cause the split of the global population into huge blocks of have-nots and possessors of goods? Should we really be entitled to speak up for the excluded masses while we are, as members of the consuming class, actively contributing to their exclusion from a dignified human existence? Another irritating question is linked to this very state of affairs: Does a theology of liberation, leaning too much to the side of the dispossessed, in effect, ostracize the wealthy, the shareholders, those who take part, regardless of how little it may be, in the governance of the world? We will address both of these queries in the concluding section.

African and Asian Revolts

I cannot speak about Africa and Asia from much personal knowledge, considering the short and limited visits I have paid to both continents. But we all realize that in enormous regions of the earth billions of people were reduced to similar conditions as in Latin America, although the details of dominion and oppression vary from place to place. Africa, to mention a few items, was kept under West European colonial rule more than a century longer than Latin America. This fact alone may account for special developments on that continent. Colonialism not only exploits the subjugated people but willfully destroys cultures and social organizations in order to implant mores and institutions that accord with Western taste and fashion. Asia, for its part, comprises a number of quite distinct and ancient cultures and religions. It did experience Western imperialism, as well as some home-made colonialism, while at the same time struggling with modern industrialization. The misery of the masses of people is equal to that found in Africa and Latin America, due to a common system of globalizing liberal markets. In our time a few nations of Asia, as in Latin America, are rallying their forces to catch up economically with the states of the northern hemisphere, with all the consequences of rapid industrialization under capitalistic auspices. The social improvements for the marginalized, however, are still relatively small.

Small wonder, then, that there are traces of a biblical conscientization here and there also in these parts of the world. We have, of course, to consider the particular conditions of Christianity in both areas. To begin with Asia,[7] a great majority resisted the Christian missionary efforts because of strong traditional cultures standing behind the people. In most states and regions, the churches hold a minority position, with less than 10 percent of the inhabitants adhering to Christian confessions. After a period of strong influence from the European mission societies, Asian Christians slowly discovered the cultural differences between Western patterns of thinking and their own native heritage. Thus, some southern Indian Protestant churches deemed obsolete the confessional divisions and creedal statements brought to them by European missionaries and merged into the Church of South India as early as 1947. In later decades and in many places, Christians of diverse Asian cultures and countries became ever more aware of how dependent their Bible translations and interpretations were on European dogmatic prejudices. They began to question the doctrines drawn from biblical texts, searching for the Bible's meaning in its original Palestinian context, which appeared more Asian than European. From an Asian perspective, the doctrinal interpretations of missionaries now seemed to be like straightjackets put on the biblical witness. Therefore, Bible reading had to be liberated from European compulsory mechanisms and placed into the context of relevant Asian cultures. One is reminded of Paul's affirmation: "a Jew to the Jews, a non-Jew to the non-Jews" (see 1 Cor 9:19–23). Of course, this introduces a new cultural tinge to interpretation, but it is appropriate under extant cultural conditions. Liberation of the Bible from foreign coercion, then, was the first step in Asian exegesis, followed in some parts of the continent by a reappraisal of social conditions. The fate of the Dalit, the "untouchables," of India, for example, had always drawn the attention of Christians. Most Indian Christians come out of this lowest of castes. Still, the structure of the churches resembled elite organizations until, in the 1980s, voices spoke out for an equal standing of the miserable, pointing to Jesus and the suffering servant of Isa 53, who themselves had been Dalits of their time and culture.[8] Another well-known example

---

7. Choan-Seng Song, "Asia," in Sawyer, *Blackwell Companion to the Bible and Culture*, 158–75.

8. Vedanayagam Devasahayam, ed., *Frontiers of Dalit Theology* (Gurukul: ISPCK, 1997); and Peniel Rajkumar, *Dalit Theology and Dalit Liberation: Problems, Paradigms, and Possibilities* (Farnham: Ashgate, 2010).

is the Minjung theology of South Korea.[9] Here the workers, in fast-growing South Korean industry, suffered from exploitation and oppression, which occurs in many similar situations around the world. In the Christian tradition, these sufferings contradict the will of God and the express intentions of Jesus, who suffered himself in order to give life to humankind. Minjung means "wretched, despised people," so their theology is a practice of Christian love and acceptance of Christian suffering in order to promote the good world of God against political and economic arbitrariness and degradation.

African experiences with the liberating Word are of a similar kind, albeit in the context of somewhat different social and cultural conditions.[10] The continent is much smaller than the Asian land mass, yet it still shows a similar diversity of cultures, ethnic groups, and histories. The northern and eastern regions of Africa, as well as the central and southernmost regions, have their specific and multilayered, ramified characteristics. As a rule, if trying at all, observers attempt to generalize about the "sub-Sahara" part of Africa. Draper points out a few "commonalities," the basic assumptions shared by people living in this lower half of the continent. They all are tied together by their high estimation of community, including strong family ties with continued union between the living and the dead and offerings to the ancestors.[11] These central pieces of the African worldview were denounced by missionaries as irreconcilable with Christian faith. The converts from native religions, however, would not abandon their traditional views. Bible translations into the vernacular idioms transported much of old African beliefs right into Christian Scriptures. Independent Bible readings by Africans led them to appreciate many features of ancient life as being perfectly congenial to their own mores, beliefs, and institutions. Examples include polygamy of the principal fathers, veneration of the creator god, belief in dream communication with the deity, and staying in contact with ancestral spirits.[12] Independent African churches and religious leaders often have appropriated the Chris-

---

9. One of the founders was Byung-Mu Ahn (1922–1996). See his *Draußen vor dem Tor: Kirche und Minjung in Korea, theologische Beiträge und Reflexionen* (Theologie der Ökumene 20; Göttingen: Vandenhoeck & Ruprecht, 1986).

10. See Jonathan A. Draper, "Africa," in Sawyer, *Blackwell Companion to the Bible and Culture*, 176–97.

11. Ibid., 176–77.

12. Ibid., 183–91. Jesus may even become an ancestral figure himself (186).

tian Bible and freely combined it with their own religious traditions.[13] The past decades saw increasing efforts by Christian theologians and places of higher education to bring African traditions and the biblical witness, freed from superimposed Western ideas, into contact and harmony, ever since John Mbiti paved the way for this new evaluation of the formerly demonized tradition.[14] Christian theologians today, however, still cannot easily follow this kind of Africanization of Christian faith.[15] We may take it, along with many African colleagues, as a positive effect of the Bible itself that liberates all nations in order to find and adhere to the unique and universal God. Beyond this spiritual liberation, the biblical witness in Africa here and there also opens eyes to see and to counteract dehumanization through enforced economic depravation of enormous parts of society.

Redesigning Gender Roles

Poverty and marginalization are not the only symptoms of decadence and unbearable living conditions that Bible-reading Christians come across when living with the biblical messages. The systems of oppression turned out quite variable and multilayered at that. Women in the United States, the Netherlands, but also in Latin America, Africa, and Asia often joined in protests against oppression. In the course even of guerrilla campaigns in which women took part, they realized that there was another system of domination inherent in most European and American societies: the traditional patriarchal structure of social organizations. Very probably male dominance dates back tens of thousands of years in the

---

13. See Katesa Schlosser, ed., *Die Bantubibel des Blitzzauberers Laduma Madela: Schöpfungsgeschichte der Zulu* (Kiel: Schmidt & Klaunig, 1977).

14. John Mbiti, *African Religions and Philosophy* (2nd ed.; King's Lynn: Biddles, 1990).

15. A very sensitive analysis of ancestral beliefs was written by South-African Klaus Nürnberger, *The Living Dead and the Living God* (Pretoria: C B Powell Bible Centre, 2007). Throughout the varying demands of relevant ancient and modern systems of theological thinking, the author maintains the sole prerogative of the first commandment, which excludes veneration of anyone and anything besides God. This is very much in line with the Western doctrine of "God alone, and nothing but God," also very much present in Islamic theology. But what happens if, in another kind of African Christian conceptualization of God, ancestor worship would simply merge, without conflict, into God veneration?

history of humankind. Sober sociological scrutiny of the history of social development suggests that early division of labor into home-centered and out-of-house activities was neatly differentiated. Because of her inestimable value as child-bearer and child-rearer, the female would be held responsible for all domestic chores, while males had to take care of herds, hunting, defense, and outside relations. Some areas of common interest were worked on by both parents (nucleus of family group; cf. education in Prov 1–9), or they were entrusted to children (e.g., herding sheep). Settled life with a strong commitment to agriculture and husbandry lends itself to such a division of labor, and there are scholars who claim that old peasantry was content with this order of production, procreation, and maintenance.[16]

The Bible and even more so the Christian tradition of Bible interpretation seem to take on quite a different role from the liberating one we discussed before. There was a suspicion in the air, especially in the early feminist movement, that Holy Scriptures enslaved and did not liberate women, and this suspicion is not completely unjustified. In spite of efforts of later feminist exegetes to blame views discriminating against women on later Judaic writings and on the early church fathers alone,[17] there remains a pervasive attitude within the Hebrew Scriptures that considers males the first and foremost human beings and females as being subservient to them. Phyllis Trible quite rightly has labeled extreme expressions of such a belief of male dominance as "texts of terror."[18] Here we get down to the limitations of biblical writings: they are all deeply embedded in their times of origin. Visionary outlooks into a distant future in which "democracy" reigns and equal rights are the firm foundation of political life are not to be expected of ancient prophets. The experience of Israel, from our perspective today, remains ambivalent in certain regards, especially as to gender roles and societal constitution (e.g., monarchy versus tribal freedom).

---

16. Carol L. Meyers makes a strong point for a gendered but balanced society in ancient Israel in *Discovering Eve: Ancient Israelite Women in Context* (Oxford: Oxford University Press, 1988). See also her sociological model in "Procreation, Production, and Protection: Male-Female Balance in Early Israel," *JAAR* 51 (1983): 569–93.

17. See, e.g., Helen Schüngel-Strauman, *Die Frau am Anfang: Eva und die Folgen* (2nd ed.; ExuZ 6; Münster: LIT-Verlag, 1997).

18. Phyllis Trible, *Texts of Terror: Literary-Feminist Readings of Biblical Narratives* (OBT; Philadelphia: Fortress, 1984).

Hermeneutical considerations, however, in spite of all difficulties, may lead us to discover the liberating impulses in the area of gender constructions. First, we must take the biblical evidence as it is, tied to its contemporary values and institutions. Next, we must take seriously our own times and mores, in regard to personal freedom and equal rights, as our basic orientation. The third step is to engage in a theological discussion with our spiritual ancestors of old. How would they decide gender issues if they were conscious of our modern values and customs, institutions, and ways of life? What would they declare to be the will of God under present-day living conditions? No doubt, there would be some necessary critique from their side in regard to modern excesses of individualistic thinking and the lack of solidarity with millions of discriminated, segregated, abused, and starving human beings on this globe. We might be confronted with charges of scientific arrogance, suicidal management of global resources, vile destruction of living species, haughty interventions with the microcosm of life, and many more modern nightmares. When we get down to arguing about gender equality, however, our ancient partners in dialogue might acknowledge our reasoning in the light of the Old Testament estimation of the "other person," the "neighbor." Living conditions have changed over the centuries to such an extent as to make old-time patriarchy and paternalism obsolete. Equal chances for males and females in education, professional careers, legal procedures, social standing, and public life are indispensable if we want to continue pursuing Western ideals of liberty and justice. Theologically speaking, one may voice the conviction that, among other rules of social behavior seemingly deviating from biblical norms, God decreed for the twenty-first century C.E. full equal rights for females and for males (and, naturally, for persons of all sexual orientations, for all races and creeds, for all minorities, and for all classes). All this may be affirmed on the basis of ancient Hebrew conceptions of human dignity, solidarity, and frailty, as well as in due consideration of the present-day ethos, human rights standards, and democratic responsibility.

European Antecedents?

Liberation hermeneutics, in biblical interpretation, is by no means restricted to "underdeveloped countries." It may be discovered in traditional-minded societies as well. The subversive potential of the biblical witness is right there, around the world, in the Holy Book, waiting to be retrieved by sensitive people who have been suffering from oppression and degradation administered by unjust institutions and governance. To take Old Europe as an example: Are there traces of a liberating force emanating from Bible reading?[19] Musing over the spiritual history of traditional-minded Germany (at times even reactionary and chauvinistic to the extreme), the careful observer will note periods during which the Bible sparked social movements or upheavals, even within solidly conservative societies. The Franciscan monks, as serious followers of Jesus Christ, turned to the poor; the Hussite, Waldensian, Lutheran, Zwinglian, and Calvinistic Reformations surely were ignited by biblical ideas of freedom from ecclesiastical arbitrariness; Protestant social engagement in the early phase of industrialization, albeit small, was propelled by a biblical consciousness of justice; opposition against Hitler and later against Stalinist dictatorship, in some circles, was fostered by Bible reading and Bible homilies. In short, the history of Christianity is unimaginable without the grain of salt, the ferment[20] of social organization implicit in the biblical messages of justice, human dignity, the kingdom of God, and, for that matter, the liberation of captives of all times. The message is there. All depends on the receptiveness of readers and listeners, and this receptiveness is closely tied to the reality of suffering that comes from the ills of human organization, as well as to the ability to recognize living conditions as unjust.

Another concomitant observation is in order. European Christian history, like other historical developments, calls to mind that there is a great amount of biblical critique in regard to social injustice and the oppression of the poor. But there are few efforts of biblical writers and transmitters to spell out in detail the new and just society for which they are campaigning. Models of "liberated Israel" (Norman Gottwald) may be found in pentateuchal legal norms. Their forms and content, however, are not so new and unheard of as we might wish.[21] The rules of social behavior extant in

---

19. See further Erhard S. Gerstenberger, "Liberation Hermeneutics in Old Europe, Especially Germany," in *The Bible and the Hermeneutics of Liberation* (ed. Alejandro F. Botta and Pablo R. Andiñach; SemeiaSt 59; Atlanta: Society of Biblical Literature, 2009), 61–84.

20. See Erhard S. Gerstenberger, "A Bíblia-fermento da sociedade humana: Reflexões de uma perspectiva européia," in *Profecia e esperança: Um tributo a Milton Schwantes* (ed. Carlos Dreher et al.; São Leopoldo: Oikos, 2006), 68–80.

21. See Erhard S. Gerstenberger, *Wesen und Herkunft des "apodiktischen Rechts"* (WMANT 20; Neukirchen-Vluyn: Neukirchener, 1965; repr., Wipf & Stock, 2009).

the Old Testament codices (from Exod 20 to Deut 25) are largely rooted in ancient Near Eastern neighborhood ethics and are, by no means, innovative. Eschatological visions of a new world, on the other hand (see Isa 11:1–9; 60–62; Zech 8:2–5), are plainly utopian. Other plans of construing a just order, like that of Ezek 40–48, are of partisan priestly extract and are indigestible for our stomachs. What is more serious, furthermore, is the fact that the Hebrew Scriptures lack blueprints for overarching social organizations such as states, economic networks, and financial structures. The pentateuchal ethos is more or less limited to neighborhood or parochial group interests.[22] For this wide field of human life so important for us in a truly globalizing age, the Hebrew Scriptures offer few suggestions. That is to say, we are left with our own judgment in regard to the right ways of interaction and to the construction of a just society at large. To the degree that the message of liberation sounded by biblical witnesses of old does call for a renovation or at least reform of existing social institutions because existing organizations have proven wrong in the sight of God, we gladly accept the sound of the ancient trumpets and foment.

Liberating Readings of the Bible?

In conclusion, we must raise the decisive question: Is it legitimate to jump on that train called "liberation theology" and "liberating interpretation of the Bible"? Are we not entering a very biased and partisan enterprise when doing so? How can we dare, in the face of Jesus Christ coming to save the whole world, to speak or think of God's preferential option for the poor?

To begin with, the pluriform and many-layered testimonies of ancient Israel—which cannot be squeezed into a one-dimensional doctrine and, therefore, must not be misunderstood as a dogmatic handbook for our faith—tell us about changing times, societies, and social organizations.[23] Each particular period and historical and cultural circumstance provokes

---

22. All the extant studies on Old Testament ethics are not able to overcome this deficit of a narrowed horizon. Few scholars try to bring light into this matter and expand the biblical witness to large-scale modern societies. See Franz Segbers, *Die Hausordnung der Tora: Biblische Impulse für eine theologische Wirtschaftsethik* (Luzern: Edition Exodus, 1999). See also Gerstenberger, *Theologies in the Old Testament*, which investigates the reason for the limited biblical outlook.

23. See Gerstenberger, *Theologies in the Old Testament*.

different responses from believers. Conceptions of God change according to life situations and human religious experiences. The will of the Supreme always has to be sought and established by looking into the past for orientation (What does Torah say?) and, at the same time, by searching present-day situations for signs of the living God (see, e.g., Num 15:32–36, where the Sabbath violator was "put in custody because it was not clear what should be done to him" [15:34]; see also Lev 24:10–16). Only a fresh oracle can give the necessary instruction. Torah up to that point is incomplete, and it remains incomplete. Therefore a never-ending debate about the actual significance of divine norms must take place.

Thus we are condemned to interpret Scriptures, and that interpretation is feasible only with proper attention to present-day calamities and hopes, values, and institutions. All these criteria of our theological work and modern existence need to be applied whenever we do exegesis or talk about God. That means we must analyze our world and find out the theologically significant parameters, which then will play a role in interpretation. As Hugo Assmann and other Latin American liberationists put it, we are guided by the *relevant* facts and developments today when seeking the will of God in the Scriptures. To ensure that this seeking and finding is indeed a dialogical process with witnesses of old, I do add the affirmation that, of course, the biblical witness is highly significant in determining which issues are theologically relevant for our work.

Taking or not taking a theological stance in favor of the poor, consequently, depends on the analysis of our own time and living situations. The analysis, for its part, is connected to the evaluation of the biblical witness, which, to my mind, places great emphasis on the living conditions of the lowly, practically giving Christians a mandate for inquiring, every time anew, about their fate and destiny. Are they doing well? Do they encounter humane conditions of life? Looking, therefore, at the global situation of humanity and recognizing the dire misery of at least a third of the world's population, the negative trends of worsening situations, and a very thin layer of global financial players reaping in ever-higher percentages of world income (with concomitant devastations of nature, destructions of living species), I cannot help but feel that injustice, fraud, and cynicism are growing at a fast pace and distorting any original good intentions for the divine creation. I fully realize that there are Christian and semi-Christian theological affirmations to the opposite effect, arguing to maintain and to promote the current systems of economy and politics. A confession of faith is called for at this point. I decidedly take the side of liberationist theologians and congregations. My own analysis of our time and my understanding of Scripture tell me that God is still opting for the enslaved and oppressed, for the violated creation, for the discriminated individuals and groups, for persecuted minorities, and, not to forget, for equal rights for women all over the world. They have borne the brunt of all kinds of labor over the millennia, guaranteeing the survival of humankind. To my mind, a lopsided theology and exegesis in favor of all the underprivileged is fully justified. Perhaps in the twenty-second century, after all the social and environmental problems have been solved, we may switch again to other kinds of theology—theologies of beauty, glory, contentment, harmony, joy, or what have you. For the present time, and into the future, I believe it is imperative for Christians to engage in liberating readings of the Bible.

Bibliography

Ahn, Byung-Mu. *Draußen vor dem Tor: Kirche und Minjung in Korea, theologische Beiträge und Reflexionen.* Theologie der Ökumene 20. Göttingen: Vandenhoeck & Ruprecht, 1986.

Devasahayam, Vedanayagam, ed. *Frontiers of Dalit Theology.* Gurukul: ISPCK, 1997.

Draper, Jonathan A. "Africa." Pages 176–97 in *The Blackwell Companion to the Bible and Culture.* Edited by John F. A. Sawyer. Oxford: Blackwell, 2006.

Gerstenberger, Erhard S. "A Bíblia-fermento da sociedade humana: Reflexões de uma perspectiva européia." Pages 68–80 in *Profecia e esperança: Um tributo a Milton Schwantes.* Edited by Carlos Dreher et al. São Leopoldo: Oikos, 2006.

———. *Israel in der Perserzeit: 5. und 4. Jahrhundert v. Chr.* Biblische Enzyklopädie 8. Stuttgart: Kohlhammer, 2005. English: *Israel in the Persian Period: The Fifth and Fourth Centuries B.C.E.* Translated by Siegfried Schatzmann. Atlanta: Society of Biblical Literature, forthcoming.

———. "Liberation Hermeneutics in Old Europe, Especially Germany." Pages 61–84 in *The Bible and the Hermeneutics of Liberation.* Edited by Alejandro F. Botta and Pablo R. Andiñach. SemeiaSt 59. Atlanta: Society of Biblical Literature, 2009.

———. *Theologies in the Old Testament.* Translated by John Bowden. Minneapolis: Fortress; London: T&T Clark, 2002.

———. *Wesen und Herkunft des "apodiktischen Rechts."* WMANT 20. Neukirchen-Vluyn: Neukirchener, 1965. Repr., Wipf & Stock, 2009.

Grätz, Sebastian, and Bernd Schipper, eds. *Alttestamentliche Wissenschaft in Selbstdarstellungen.* Göttingen: Vandenhoeck & Ruprecht, 2007.

Mbiti, John. *African Religions and Philosophy.* 2nd ed. King's Lynn: Biddles, 1990.

Meyers, Carol L. *Discovering Eve: Ancient Israelite Women in Context.* Oxford: Oxford University Press, 1988.

———. "Procreation, Production, and Protection: Male-Female Balance in Early Israel," *JAAR* 51 (1983): 569–93.

Nürnberger, Klaus. *The Living Dead and the Living God: Christ and the Ancestors in a Changing Africa.* Pretoria: C B Powell Bible Centre, 2007.

Rajkumar, Peniel. *Dalit Theology and Dalit Liberation: Problems, Paradigms, and Possibilities.* Farnham: Ashgate, 2010.

Rieger, Jörg. *Christus und das Imperium.* Münster: LIT-Verlag, 2009.

Sawyer, John F. A., "Introduction." Pages 1–8 in *The Blackwell Companion to the Bible and Culture.* Edited by John F. A. Sawyer. Oxford: Blackwell, 2006.

Schlosser, Katesa, ed. *Die Bantubibel des Blitzzauberers Laduma Madela: Schöpfungsgeschichte der Zulu.* Kiel: Schmidt & Klaunig, 1977.

Schüepp, Susann. *Bibellektüre und Befreiungsprozesse: Eine empirisch-theologische Untersuchung mit Frauen in Brasilien.* Exegese in unserer Zeit 16. Münster: LIT-Verlag, 2006.

Schüngel-Straumann, Helen. *Die Frau am Anfang: Eva und die Folgen.* 2nd ed. Exegese in unserer Zeit 6. Münster: LIT-Verlag, 1997.

Schürger, Wolfgang. *Theologie auf dem Weg der Befreiung.* Erlanger Monographien 24. Erlangen: Verlag für Mission und Ökumene, 1995.

Segbers, Franz. *Die Hausordnung der Tora: Biblische Impulse für eine theologische Wirtschaftsethik.* Luzern: Edition Exodus, 1999.

Song, Choan-Seng. "Asia." Pages 158–75 in *The Blackwell Companion to the Bible and Culture.* Edited by John F. A. Sawyer. Oxford: Blackwell, 2006.

Trible, Phyllis. *Texts of Terror: Literary-Feminist Readings of Biblical Narratives.* OBT. Minneapolis: Fortress, 1984.

Contributors

Paul J. Achtemeier, Herbert Worth and Anne H. Jackson Professor of Biblical Literature Emeritus at Union Theological Seminary in Virginia, is general editor of *The HarperCollins Bible Dictionary* (HarperCollins, 1996); author of *1 Peter* (Augsburg Fortress, 1996), *Inspiration and Authority: Nature and Function of Christian Scripture* (Hendrickson, 1999), *Mark* (Wipf & Stock, 2004), *Jesus and the Miracle Tradition* (Cascade, 2008), and *Romans* (Westminster John Knox, 2010); and co-author of *The Old Testament Roots of Our Faith* (Abingdon, 1962), *Introducing the New Testament: Its Literature and Theology* (Eerdmans, 2001), and *The Forgotten God: Perspectives in Biblical Theology* (Westminster John Knox, 2002). He is also the first non-Catholic to have served as President of the Catholic Biblical Association and is former Executive Secretary of the Society of Biblical Literature, as well as a past President (1989).

Frank Ritchel Ames is Professor of Medical Informatics and Director of Library Services at Rocky Vista University, Colorado's new medical college, where he also teaches clinical ethics. He is co-editor of *Writing and Reading War: Rhetoric, Gender, and Ethics in Biblical and Modern Contexts* (Society of Biblical Literature, 2008) and a companion volume in preparation, *Interpreting Exile: Interdisciplinary Studies of Displacement and Deportation in Biblical and Modern Contexts*. In 2003, he served as the Society of Biblical Literature's Director of Programs and Initiatives.

Pablo R. Andiñach is President and Old Testament Professor of the Instituto Universitario ISEDET, Buenos Aires, and has been Visiting Professor at the Perkins School of Theology. Among others, his publications include *El libro del Éxodo* (Spanish: Salamanca, Sígueme, 2006; Portuguese: Sinodal, 2010), *El fuego y la ternura: Comentario al Cantar de los Cantares* (Spanish: Lumen, 1997; Portuguese: Vozes, 1998), and *Ser Iglesia: Eclesiología en perspectiva evangélica* (Lumen, 2007). He is co-editor of *The*

Bible and the Hermeneutics of Liberation (Society of Biblical Literature, 2009) and director of the journal *Cuadernos de Teología*.

Harold W. Attridge is Reverend Henry L. Slack Dean and Lillian Claus Professor of New Testament at Yale Divinity School. His publications include *The Interpretation of Biblical History in the* Antiquitates Judaicae *of Flavius Josephus* (Scholars Press, 1976), *First-Century Cynicism in the Epistles of Heraclitus* (Scholars Press, 1976), *Nag Hammadi Codex I: The Jung Codex* (Brill, 1985), and *Hebrews: A Commentary on the Epistle to the Hebrews* (Augsburg Fortress, 1989), as well as numerous essays and articles. He has edited or co-edited eleven books and has been an editorial board member of *Catholic Biblical Quarterly*, *Harvard Theological Review*, *Journal of Biblical Literature*, and the Hermeneia commentary series. He served as President of the Society of Biblical Literature in 2001.

Athalya Brenner is Professor in Biblical Studies, Department of Hebrew Culture, Tel Aviv University, and Professor Emeritus and Research Fellow, University of Amsterdam. She is co-editor of *Genesis: Texts @ Contexts* (Fortress, 2010), chief editor of the Texts @ Contexts Series, Hebrew Bible section (forthcoming), co-editor of *Bible Translation on the Threshold of the Twenty-First Century* (Sheffield, 2002), and co-author of *On Gendering Texts: Female and Male Voices in the Hebrew Bible* (Brill, 1993). Her monographs include *I Am: Biblical Women Tell Their Own Stories* (Fortress, 2004), *The Intercourse of Knowledge: On Gendering Desire and "Sexuality" in the Hebrew Bible* (Brill, 1997), *The Song of Songs* (Sheffield Academic Press, 1989), *The Israelite Woman: Social Role and Literary Type in Biblical Narrative* (JSOT Press, 1985), and *Colour Terms in the Old Testament* (Almond Press, 1982). Brenner founded and edited the Feminist Companion to the Bible First and Second series (19 volumes, 1993–2001) and has served on the editorial boards of the *Journal of Biblical Literature* and *Semeia*, among others.

David J. A. Clines is Professor Emeritus of Biblical Studies, University of Sheffield, and Director of Sheffield Phoenix Press. He is editor of the *Dictionary of Classical Hebrew* (Sheffield Phoenix, 1993–) and author of the Word Biblical Commentary on Job (3 vols., Thomas Nelson, 1989–2011), *Interested Parties: The Ideology of Writers and Readers of the Hebrew Bible* (Sheffield Phoenix, 2009), *On the Way to the Postmodern: Old Testament Essays, 1967–1998* (Sheffield Academic Press, 1998), and *The Theme of the*

Pentateuch (2nd ed., Sheffield Academic Press, 1997), among others. He has been President of the Society for Old Testament Study (1996) and of the Society of Biblical Literature (2009).

John J. Collins, Holmes Professor of Old Testament Criticism and Interpretation at Yale University, previously taught at the University of Chicago and at Notre Dame. His books include *Introduction to the Hebrew Bible* (Fortress, 2004), *Does the Bible Justify Violence?* (Fortress, 2004), *Jewish Cult and Hellenistic Culture* (Brill, 2005), *Encounters with Biblical Theology* (Fortress, 2005), *The Bible after Babel: Historical Criticism in a Postmodern Age* (Eerdmans, 2005), *King and Messiah as Son of God* (Eerdmans, 2008, co-author), and *Beyond the Qumran Community: Sectarian Communities in the Dead Sea Scrolls* (Eerdmans, 2009). He is co-editor of *The Encyclopedia of Apocalypticism* (Continuum, 1998), *Dictionary of Early Judaism* (Eerdmans, 2010), and the *Oxford Handbook of the Dead Sea Scrolls* (Oxford, 2010). He has served as editor of the *Journal of Biblical Literature* and has been a president of the Catholic Biblical Association (1997) and the Society of Biblical Literature (2002).

Tamara Cohn Eskenazi is Professor of Bible, Hebrew Union College-Jewish Institute of Religion, Los Angeles Campus. Eskenazi is author of *In an Age of Prose: A Literary Approach to Ezra-Nehemiah* (Scholars Press, 1988), co-editor with Kent Harold Richards of *Second Temple Studies 2: Temple and Community in the Persian Period* (Sheffield Academic Press, 1994), and chief editor of *The Torah: A Women's Commentary* (URJ Press and Women of Reform Judaism, 2007), which won the National Jewish Book of the Year Award in 2008.

J. Cheryl Exum is Professor Emerita of Biblical Studies at the University of Sheffield and a Director of Sheffield Phoenix Press. Her publications include, among others, *Between the Text and the Canvas: The Bible and Art in Dialogue* (Sheffield Phoenix, 2007), *Retellings: The Bible in Literature, Music, Art and Film* (Brill, 2007), *Song of Songs: A Commentary* (Westminster John Knox, 2005), *Plotted, Shot, and Painted: Cultural Representations of Biblical Women* (Sheffield Academic Press, 1996), *Fragmented Women: Feminist (Sub)versions of Biblical Narratives* (Trinity Press International, 1993), and *Tragedy and Biblical Narrative: Arrows of the Almighty* (Cambridge University Press, 1992). She is currently writing a book on the Bible and the arts.

Erhard S. Gerstenberger, Professor of Old Testament at Philipps-Universität Marburg, has taught at EST São Leopoldo and Gießen University and has served as a parish minister in Essen, Germany. His publications include *Israel in der Perserzeit* (Kohlhammer, 2005), *Theologies in the Old Testament* (Fortress, 2002), *Psalms* (Eerdmans, 1998, 2001), *Leviticus: A Commentary* (Westminster John Knox, 1996), *Yahweh the Patriarch: Ancient Images of God and Feminist Theology* (Augsburg Fortress, 1996), and *Woman and Man* (Abingdon, 1981).

Norman C. Habel is Professorial Fellow in Biblical Studies at Flinders University in South Australia. His publications include the multivolume *Earth Bible* (Sheffield Academic Press, 2000–2002), *Seven Songs of Creation* (Pilgrim, 2004), *Exploring Ecological Hermeneutics* (Society of Biblical Literature, 2008), *An Inconvenient Text* (ATF, 2009), *The Book of Job* (Westminster John Knox, 1985), and *The Land Is Mine* (Fortress, 1993), among other volumes. He has long been involved in issues of biblical interpretation relating to social justice and eco-justice.

Douglas A. Knight is Drucilla Moore Buffington Professor of Hebrew Bible and Professor of Jewish Studies at Vanderbilt University, where he has also served as Director and Senior Fellow of the Center for the Study of Religion and Culture. His editorial activities have included the Society of Biblical Literature's Dissertation Series, Centennial Publications Series, and *Journal of Biblical Literature*, and he now serves as General Editor for The Library of Ancient Israel series (Westminster John Knox). Works published by the Society of Biblical Literature include *Rediscovering the Traditions of Israel* (1973; repr. 2006), *Tradition and Theology in the Old Testament* (1977; repr. 2007), *Humanizing America's Iconic Book* (1982), *Julius Wellhausen and His Prolegomena to the History of Israel* (1983), *The Hebrew Bible and Its Modern Interpreters* (1985), *Justice and the Holy* (1989), and *Ethics and Politics in the Hebrew Bible* (1995).

Elizabeth Struthers Malbon, Professor in the Department of Religion and Culture at Virginia Polytechnic Institute and State University (Virginia Tech), is author of *Mark's Jesus: Characterization as Narrative* Christology (Baylor University Press, 2009), *Hearing Mark: A Listener's Guide* (Trinity Press International, 2002), *In the Company of Jesus* (Westminster John Knox, 2000), *Narrative Space and Mythic Meaning in Mark* (Harper San Francisco, 1986), and *The Iconography of the Sarcophagus of Junius Bassus*

(Princeton University Press, 1990). She has also edited or co-edited four volumes. She is an elected member of the international Studiorum Novi Testamenti Societas and has been active in the Society of Biblical Literature as a regional president and chair of several program units.

James Luther Mays is Cyrus McCormick Professor Emeritus of Hebrew and Old Testament, Union Theological Seminary, Virginia. He served as editor of *Harper's Bible Commentary* (Harper & Row, 1988) and for The Old Testament Library and Interpretation commentaries and is the author of the Westminster John Knox publications *Preaching and Teaching the Psalms* (2006), *Psalms* (1994), *The Lord Reigns: A Theological Handbook to the Psalms* (1994), *Micah* (1976), *Amos* (1969), and *Hosea* (1969), among other authored and edited works. Mays was President of the Society of Biblical Literature in 1986.

Charles William Miller is Associate Professor of Religion at the University of North Dakota and previously taught at Pacific Theological College in Suva, Fiji. His research interests are primarily on the significance of social location for biblical interpretation. He has published in a range of journals, including *Biblical Interpretation*, *Hawaiian Journal of History*, and *Journal of Religion and Society*.

Gail R. O'Day is Dean and Professor of New Testament and Preaching at the Wake Forest University School of Divinity. She has written the commentary on the Gospel of John in *The New Interpreter's Bible* (Abingdon, 1996) and is editor or co-editor of several volumes, including the *Oxford Access Bible* (Oxford University Press, 1999) and the *Theological Bible Commentary* (Westminster John Knox Press, 2009). She was editor of *Journal of Biblical Literature* from 1999 to 2006 and is currently General Editor of the Society of Biblical Literature Early Christianity and Its Literature book series.

David L. Petersen, Associate Dean of Faculty and Academic Affairs and Franklin N. Parker Professor of Old Testament at Candler School of Theology, Emory University, is the author of *The Prophetic Literature: An Introduction* (Westminster John Knox, 2002), *Prophecy in Ancient Israel* (Fortress, 1987), and *Late Israelite Prophecy* (Society of Biblical Literature, 1977). He is co-author of *A Theological Introduction to the Old Testament* (Abingdon, 2005) and, with Kent Harold Richards, *Interpreting Hebrew*

Poetry (Augsburg Fortress, 1992), among other monographs and edited volumes. He was President of the Society of Biblical Literature in 2004.

Elisabeth Schüssler Fiorenza, Krister Stendahl Professor, Harvard University, The Divinity School, is the author of, among other works, *Democratizing Biblical Studies: Toward an Emancipatory Educational Space* (Westminster John Knox, 2009), *The Power of the Word: Scripture and the Rhetoric of Empire* (Fortress, 2007), *Jesus and the Politics of Interpretation* (Continuum, 2000), *Rhetoric and Ethic: The Politics of Biblical Studies* (Fortress, 1999), *But She Said: Feminist Practices of Biblical Interpretation* (Beacon, 1992), *Bread Not Stone: The Challenge of Feminist Biblical Interpretation* (Fortress, 1985), and *In Memory of Her: A Feminist Theological Reconstruction of Christian Origins* (Crossroads, 1983). Schüssler Fiorenza is also co-founder and co-editor of the *Journal of Feminist Studies in Religion* and is past President of the Society of Biblical Literature (1987).

Gene M. Tucker is Professor of Old Testament, Emeritus, Candler School of Theology, Emory University. His publications include *Form Criticism of the Old Testament* (Fortress, 1971), *The Book of Joshua* (Cambridge University Press, 1974), *Humanizing America's Iconic Book* (1982), *The Hebrew Bible and Its Modern Interpreters* (1985), *Canon, Theology, and Old Testament Interpretation* (Fortress, 1988), *Preaching through the Christian Year* (1994), and *The Minor Prophets* (Abingdon, 1997), among others. He served on the New Revised Standard Version Translation Committee, as an editor of the Forms of the Old Testament Literature and Guides to Biblical Scholarship series, and as President of the Society of Biblical Literature (1996).

Vincent L. Wimbush is Professor of Religion and Founding Director of the Institute for Signifying Scriptures, Claremont Graduate University, where his research interests are comparative phenomenology and cultural-critical study of scriptures. Among his most recent publications are *Theorizing Scriptures: New Critical Orientations to a Cultural Phenomenon* (Rutgers University Press, 2008), *The Bible and African Americans: A Brief History* (Fortress, 2003), and *African Americans and the Bible: Sacred Texts and Social Textures* (Continuum, 2000). He has served in many different capacities within the Society of Biblical Literature and is the current President of the Society (2010).